THE FRACTURE OF MEANING

THE FRACTURE
OF MEANING

Japan's Synthesis of China from the Eighth through the Eighteenth Centuries

DAVID POLLACK

PRINCETON UNIVERSITY PRESS

Library of Congress Cataloging in Publication Data will be found on the last printed page of
this book

ISBN 0-691-06678-7

Publication of this book has been aided by a grant from the Louis A. Robb Fund of Princeton
University Press

This book has been composed in Bembo by Asco Trade Typesetting Ltd., Hong Kong

Clothbound editions of Princeton University Press books are printed on acid-free paper, and
binding materials are chosen for strength and durability
Printed in the United States of America by Princeton University Press, Princeton, New Jersey

CONTENTS

LIST OF ILLUSTRATIONS

ABBREVIATIONS

GBSS	Tamamura Takeji, comp., *Gozan Bungaku Shinshū*
GBZS	Uemura Kankō, comp., *Gozan Bungaku Zenshū*
MNZ	Ono Susumu, ed., *Motoori Norinaga Zenshū*
NKBT	*Nihon Koten Bungaku Taikei*, Iwanami Shoten
NKBZ	*Nihon Koten Bungaku Zenshū*, Shogakkan
NST	*Nihon Shisō Taikei*, Iwanami Shoten
T	Takakusu and Watanabe, eds., *Taishō Shinshū Daizōkyō*
WWW	Donald Keene, *World Within Walls*

PREFACE

Books on such exotic subjects as Japanese culture customarily require preliminary discussion of their machinery; these odd chronologies and unpronounceable names fairly cry out for explanation. I find this in itself to be a fascinating example of the tendency, observed of Japan in this study, of the signifier toward opacity, drawing attention to itself rather than to what it is supposed to signify—but in the interests of brevity, I shall refrain here from discoursing on the potholes in favor of getting on down the road.

Dates are generally of two sorts. Precise dates given in old texts are in a form that refers to the month and day of the reign-period of an emperor (who may have had several); thus, third month, twenty-third day of the third year of the Genroku era. Since such dates are in reference to a lunar calendar they are not precise equivalents to our March 23, 1690, and to avoid giving a false impression of accuracy such dates have been left as they are. The other sorts of dates are those generally accepted for periodization, birth and death dates, and the like. Scholars are sometimes in agreement on them, sometimes not, with different sources providing different numbers. Mine may therefore be somewhat different from someone else's.

Reference to Japanese names follows the convention of using the given name for people who lived before 1868 (Teika and Razan, not Fujiwara and Hayashi), and family names for those who lived after 1868 (Mishima and Maruyama, not Yukio and Masao). I have tried to use one name for each person, although he may have been called by several, including ranks, titles, and pen-names. The reader will already have noticed that I use the customary masculine pronoun to represent the indeterminate gender.

The names of periods are customary ones, with the caveat that different sources give slightly different dates for some of them. It is when one uses a term to characterize them that things get cloudy; thus, "early modern" usually means the Tokugawa period (1603–1867 by most accounts), while "medieval" means some less easily defined stretch of time—I use it to indicate the period roughly between 1200 and 1500, give or take a few decades, and think of it as divided (neatly but no doubt misleadingly) into "early," "middle," and "late" centuries for reasons that become apparent in the text. The problem of how to characterize the sixteenth century—postmedieval? pre-early modern?—has been mooted by the simple fact that I do not discuss it. Some periods have alternative names depending on whether one is talking about them as political units designated by the name of the ruling clan (Fujiwara, Ashikaga, Tokugawa), or as cultural units designated by cultural and political centers (Heian, Muromachi, Edo). Thus one usually talks about Tokugawa government (*bakufu*) but Edo art, even though this is somewhat misleading since the city of Edo did not really become the cultural capital of Japan until after 1750.

Transliteration of Japanese follows the standard modified Hepburn system, with italics, macrons, and definitions eliminated for words that appear in English dictionaries: Tokyo, Kyoto, koan, shogun. Hypothetical reconstructions of the ancient Japanese and Chinese languages are preceded by an asterisk: *nö*. I have provided the customary transliterations of Japanese poems because they are comprehensible as they stand, but not of Chinese poems because they are of little use without the characters. For rendering Chinese I obstinately persist in using a slightly modified Wade-Giles transliteration; the day I find the layman who can pronounce the name of Ts'ao Hsüeh-ch'in, the author of the Ch'ing dynasty Chinese novel *Dream of the Red Chamber*, more accurately from its Pinyin rendering of Cao Xueqin, I shall change to Pinyin. I have provided characters only when I felt it would be helpful to the reader's understanding of an idea. Common sense tells me that the specialist will not need all the characters because he already knows what I am talking about or can find them readily enough, while the general reader will neither care nor be helped by their inclusion. Besides, I am told they are expensive to set and frightening to the uninititated, and clutter up the page.

This book covers more than a thousand years and almost every conceivable area of scholarly endeavor. I could not possibly be an expert in all these periods and fields, and there have been and will no doubt continue to be specialists able to remind me of it. I can only apologize for my shortcomings, and for the impression I may occasionally give of riding roughshod over terrain that others more knowledgeable than myself have been carefully cultivating for a lifetime. I continue to learn, unfortunately sometimes by my mistakes.

I would like to acknowledge two important debts. The first is to Professor Masao Miyoshi, who, in the course of an NEH Institute that he and Earl Miner led at Princeton in 1979 on "Curricular Models in Japanese Literature," asked why I didn't try to get underneath my ideas more. Thus was instigated a journey below the surface of things out of which was to develop the spirit underlying the methodology of this book (I should also take this opportunity to thank the National Endowment for the Humanities for allowing me to participate in the Institute). His advice was usefully supplemented by that of another friend, Ellis Krauss, who, happening to find me one day wallowing in a slough of despond, told me to keep my head down and get back to work—always sound advice under any circumstances.

The second debt is to my colleagues in the Department of Foreign Languages, Literatures, and Linguistics at the University of Rochester. If I had been in a more narrowly specialized department I doubt that I would have had the freedom to do this kind of work, or colleagues like Alice Benston, Philip Berk, and Gerald Bond to make me think about the place of East Asian literature in the world beyond its own rather recondite concerns. Nothing makes one think more about what one is doing than having to explain oneself to intelligent, curious, and well-read colleagues.

I would like to thank those who saw various parts of this book in earlier stages and offered helpful comments. Martin Collcutt of Princeton University properly insisted that I shelve some lesser material in favor of what turned out to be chapter seven. Harry Harootunian of the University of Chicago has rather pioneered the deconstructionist and postdeconstructionist approach to Japanese intellectual history in this country, and offered critical observations on chapter one and a model of intellectual endeavor for chapter seven. And although I have already mentioned him once, I remain grateful to Masao Miyoshi of the University of California at Berkeley, not only for his generosity in encouraging others, but also for his willingness to engage them in lively debate and shoot down any argument, at any time, in any place.

Finally, I would like to acknowledge the kind permission of *Monumenta Nipponica*, *The Journal of the International Association of Buddhist Studies*, and *The Harvard Journal of Asiatic Studies* to reproduce here material first published in those journals.

THE FRACTURE OF MEANING

Introduction

Until modern times the Chinese rarely troubled themselves about Japan; the Japanese, however, were preoccupied with China from the beginning of their recorded history until the opening to the West in the last century. As one scholar has put it, "The central factor of Japanese literature—if not the entire traditional culture—was the love for and the rejection of Chinese influence."[1] In the chapters that follow, I have attempted to examine particular facets of that love-hate relationship. I cannot pretend to have done complete justice to a subject that ranges over a thousand years and nearly every conceivable subject. Instead, I have chosen to focus on what seem to me to be particularly crucial periods and issues in as close detail as possible.

For the Japanese, what was "Japanese" had always to be considered in relation to what was thought to be "Chinese"—and I must stress from the outset that I am not dealing here so much with the "objective" facts of cultural influence so much as with the history of its interpretation, with what was "thought" to be. In other words, this study falls within the field of critical inquiry that modern theory calls hermeneutics, the study of the history of interpretation, of the ways in which men have represented their cultures to themselves. If I say that the notion of Japaneseness was meaningful only as it was considered against the background of the otherness of China, then, it is clear that I am no longer speaking of "China" and "Japan" in the usual senses of those words. Rather, I am considering them only as they existed in relation to each other as the antithetical terms of a uniquely Japanese dialectic to which the Japanese gave the name *wakan*, "Japanese/Chinese."

Even though I am considering China only as one of the terms of this dialectic of wakan, I shall inevitably have to discuss a wide spectrum of the concrete elements of Chinese culture. Thus I touch, for example, on aspects of the Chinese language and script in chapter one; on T'ang and Sung poetry and poetic theory in later chapters; on religious and philosophical thought throughout; and in general on the Chinese arts and artifacts that were of perennial interest to the Japanese in the period under consideration.

But it is the view from the islands that will limit our view of the continent here. I am concerned with the Japanese interpretations of what they saw as

---

[1] Donald Keene, "Literature," in Arthur E. Tiedemann, ed., *An Introduction to Japanese Civilization* (New York: Columbia University Press, 1974), 383. Keene develops this thesis to a considerable degree.

essentially "Chinese," rather than our own interpretations or those of the Chinese themselves. The difference is considerable, for the Japanese invariably seemed to find the most profound significance of Chinese culture far from where the Chinese themselves would ever have thought to seek it. It would no more have occurred to the Chinese, for example, than it would to us to find a "problem" in the adequacy of their own script to represent their thoughts. And yet our investigation begins precisely with the problem of the adoption of Chinese script in Japan's "first" text, a problem that will become paradigmatic for all that follows. Again, the Chinese would have been appalled at the Heian Japanese deification of a single T'ang poet, Po Chü-i (772–846), to the almost complete exclusion of poets the Chinese have always regarded as superior. The same is true of the later Japanese infatuation with certain Sung dynasty styles in art and ceramics, or with certain directions in Neo-Confucian thought, that the Chinese themselves have usually tended to regard as extreme or eccentric tendencies and not at all representative of what they feel to be properly "Chinese."

The Japanese viewpoint that I am proposing here can be likened to that of a frog from the bottom of its well, who would define its world almost exclusively in terms of its walls: the sky and world outside the well, the shape of the water in which it lived, its notions of security and danger, the proper dimensions and proportions of things, would all be most meaningfully expressed in terms of "walls." For that frog, indeed, the fundamental meaning of life itself could be expressed only in terms of walls, for nothing else could hold as much significance for its world. China was Japan's walls, the very terms by which Japan defined its own existence.[2]

How did this happen? One can only hypothesize about such matters, of course, but I can begin with the simple and very modern sounding premise that culture and language reflect and are informed by the same structures. Therefore I have chosen to begin my study with the broad cultural problem that is posed by the relationship between the spoken and written languages in Japan, which is in even more general terms the particularly problematic nature of the transition from orality to literacy in that country. Again with the proviso that I am considering China and Japan only in the context of their relationship to each other and not as separable entities, I propose an "origin" of the wakan dialectic in terms of the early and even traumatic fracture in Japan between oral and literate representation.

The Chinese and Japanese languages and the sorts of intellectual, social, and cultural structures they shape and reflect can be said to be in fundamental ways

---

[2] Should an analogy to a frog seem offensive, the reader is asked to recall the sympathetic identification all Japanese seem to feel with Issa's "skinny frog," as well as the national tradition of *hōganbiiki* (explored in Ivan Morris's *The Nobility of Failure: Tragic Heroes in the History of Japan* [New York: Meridian, 1975]), or rooting for the underfrog.

almost entirely antithetical—a breathtakingly sweeping statement that is ampli-
fied considerably in chapter one, if not perhaps made any the less breathtaking.
The same might be postulated perhaps of many languages and cultures. What
is unique about the Chinese-Japanese polarity, however, must be sought in
the geographical relationship between the two countries, as we might have
gathered from the homely analogy of the frog in its well. The insular Japanese
were near enough to China to have been within the inexorable reach of the
powerfully attractive Chinese cultural sphere; yet they were also far enough
away from China and securely enough isolated from it that its influence seemed
considerably less inexorable than it did to most of China's neighbors. The
Japanese were more able than other peoples at the edge of the Chinese *oikoumenē*
to exist in a dialectical relationship with the larger country, rather than in the
subordinate relationship, if often only nominal, customarily insisted upon by
China in her dealings with her neighbors. The other cultures of the Altaic
language group were all at some point in direct contact with China. The early
Korean states, for example, were as far as the Japanese were concerned much the
same as China itself, and posed a particularly thorny problem in that Japan was
early populated and acculturated by successive waves of Korean immigrants
(Japan's racial intolerance of Koreans today seems a continuing reflection of the
truth that we often despise most intensely those from whom it is most difficult
to distinguish ourselves). Other Altaic peoples, such as the Mongols who
conquered China to establish the Yüan dynasty (but failed, significantly, to
conquer Japan) and the Manchus who established the Ch'ing dynasty, ended by
giving up their own cultural identities to some degree to the amenities of
Chinese culture to become "Chinese" themselves. Or rather, the accommodation can be understood as another sort of dialectic in which formerly non-
Chinese "barbarians" became more Sinicized than the Chinese themselves
became barbarianized.[3]

---

[3] Since I am dealing here with China only insofar as it affects Japan, we must bear in mind that it is
a China that is already highly developed and politically centralized. The early growth of Chinese
civilization is held by Owen Lattimore in *Inner-Asian Frontiers of China* (Boston: Beacon Press,
1962), 409–10, to have been itself the product of a strongly dialectical relationship between cultures
that were increasingly differentiated by primarily geographic factors. By the time the present study
begins, however, we find ourselves well beyond the point where to be Chinese, as Lattimore puts it,
meant exclusively to participate in China's characteristic type of intensive agriculture rather than in
some form of nomadic culture (381). This had in fact ceased to entirely define Chineseness by the
third century B.C. (418). My own view of China may be encapsulated in Lattimore's vision of China
during this period as "gravitating toward the center" (417). Indeed, Lattimore's "marginal fron-
tier" model breaks down critically at the point where he must fall back on this sort of appeal to what
he calls "the overarching trend of history" (431) to explain why, at certain crucial times in history,
non-Chinese peoples on China's borders became Chinese and the Chinese became even "more
Chinese" than before, rather than the other way around. In the long run the effects of this obvious
"centripetal" quality may prove more important in defining Chineseness than geographical
determinism. Its basic unit may still very well be Lattimore's "cell" of Chinese civilization

Differences of Han as opposed to non-Han peoples aside, the final test of whether or not a people can be considered "Chinese" might be thought to lie more in their use of the hard, unyielding touchstone of the Chinese script and its orthodox texts to the exclusion of any other than in any particular racial or linguistic affinities. Certainly that script is based upon a particular ancient spoken Chinese language, but its historical presence and evolution often seem curiously divorced from Chinese as a spoken language. It has in fact come to bear far more weight in defining Chineseness than any one of the spoken Sinitic tongues, for what we call Chinese is actually a group of mutually unintelligible languages—not merely "dialects" as we think of that term—as similar to one another as Dutch and German or French and Italian, or as different from one another as Dutch and English. On this enormous cultural significance of the Chinese script, one of our most popular college texts on East Asia notes that "Chinese characters seem to carry with them richer substance and subtler overtones than the oral words they were designed to represent,"[4] and the historian Arthur F. Wright has commented upon "that elusive but important chracteristic of the individual symbol which one can only call its 'weight.' It was a far more esteemed and significant symbol than any syllable of Indo-European languages."[5] Or of any spoken Chinese language as well, we might add. Suffice it to say that the Japanese felt the full weight of that script and the culture it represented and yet managed never to become entirely subordinated to it. In fact, the very history of the evolution of the Japanese script itself demonstrates the extraordinary complexity and persistence of the dialectical relationship between the two cultures as that dialectic developed in Japan.

I have already mentioned that the problem of the origin of writing in Japan asserts itself as a natural paradigm of the wakan dialectic, and so it is with this problem as it is first encountered in the *Kojiki* (Records of Ancient Matters, 712) that I begin in chapter one. The very way that meaning would be structured in Japan was determined from the outset by the primacy of the dialectical relationship between the antitheses of alien form and native content. It is here that I

consisting of a walled city and its supporting land, and its internal dynamics those of the "hydraulic society" as described by Karl Wittfogel in his study on *Oriental Despotism* (New Haven: Yale University Press, 1957). These, however, depended in the end upon the existence of an informing and supporting script for bureaucratic and ideological cohesion. Thus, I have found it most profitable ultimately to locate my initial paradigm of the wakan dialectic in the Japanese adoption of the Chinese script.

[4] John K. Fairbanks, Edwin O. Reischauer, and Albert O. Craig, *East Asia* (New York: Houghton-Mifflin, 1973), 26.

[5] Arthur F. Wright, "The Chinese Language and Foreign Ideas," in Wright, ed., *Studies in Chinese Thought* (Chicago: University of Chicago Press, 1967), 287. See also Joseph Needham's observation of "the extraordinary integrative and absorptive power of Chinese civilization" based on mastery of the written language in *Science and Civilization in China* (Cambridge: Cambridge University Press, 1954), vol. 1, 119.

locate the beginning of the "fracture of meaning" that forms the title of this study. This is not to say that this problem is itself the origin of the fracture, but rather that the problem is first revealed in and pervades this earliest of Japanese texts.

In chapter two I turn to a consideration of the later development of this dialectical structure of signification as it informs the great Heian masterpiece of fiction *Genji Monogatari* (The Tale of Genji), composed in the first decade of the eleventh century. In the course of the three hundred years that had lapsed between the writing of the *Kojiki* and *The Tale of Genji*, the matter of writing per se ceased to represent a "problem" as the script gradually evolved into an entirely Japanese medium of great complexity and expressive power. But the tensions of the cultural antitheses that had been mediated in its creation continued to exert a powerful pressure on every act of culture, fracturing signification along the same line that had resulted in the creation of the *Kojiki*: content, felt to be quintessentially Japanese, was unformed and ineffable, while that which gave form—the informing or formal aspects of meaning—remained in some sense "alien," at once powerfully attractive and fundamentally disquieting.[6]

This paradox of the nature of meaning can serve to characterize the image of China as it is developed in *The Tale of Genji*. I have attempted to show in chapter two that if we look beneath the surface-level flow of the narrative in *Genji*, we find that the story of these delicate, intensely Japanese men and women is everywhere underlaid by a structure of Chinese archetype. To be sure, *Genji* is an entirely Japanese creation, and as such it does not incorporate China so much as play against it. We are scarcely aware of its presence beyond the occasional obvious allusion or direct reference, because *Genji* is written and read at the level of the conscious act, so to speak, while China exists at the unconscious level—dark, powerful, archetypal. For the most part too intensely alien to be capable of entering into the realm of consciousness, China functions rather to give a sense of depth to an otherwise planar surface, and intensifies the ubiquitous polarity in the novel between the small but brilliant point of light that is the Japanese court and the surrounding darkness that threatens to engulf it. Even more than the sadness of the Buddhist view of this world, the dark workings of the human spirit, or the gloominess of Uji, China can be seen as the darkest ground against which the Shining Genji attains his greatest definition.

While the use of script in the Genji period represents an entirely native creation, we can see a parallel between the way script is used in *The Tale of Genji*

---

[6] Such a thesis leads inevitably to the sort of emphasis on the near reverence of "silence" and the extreme antipathy toward utterance as a betrayal that seems so paradoxical in so loquacious a people, as postulated by Masao Miyoshi in his trenchant study *Accomplices of Silence: The Modern Japanese Novel* (Berkeley: University of California Press, 1975). See my concluding remarks below, pp. 229–230.

Scroll (Genji Monogatari Emaki) of the mid-twelfth century and the way China appears in the story itself. First of all, both the written script and the artistic techniques used in the scroll, as well as the narrative techniques used in the novel itself, are entirely Japanese. The occasional appearance of a more complex Chinese character in the smooth flow of cursive Japanese script lends texture and rhythm to the writing, providing contrast and setting off the pleasant and graceful linearity of the script on the page. We might even see in the frequent use of alternative shapes for the Japanese *kana* syllabary (what are called *hentaigana* in Japanese, and perfectly normal calligraphic custom still today) a parallel to the way that characters in the novel and the scroll-paintings often seem little more than variations on a type. We can also note here the simple fact of this separation into complementary modes of representation. *Genji* and similar Heian tales were not meant to be read silently but rather to be simultaneously viewed and heard, an audience of court ladies looking at the paintings while someone read the story aloud, as we can see from a scene depicted in the *Genji Scroll* (fig. 1).

The important changes in aesthetic vision that were taking place around 1200 can be understood in terms of the Japanese response to changes in the nature of the Chinese "archetype" itself. The deep debt that Heian sensibility owed to a single T'ang poet, Po Chü-i, and the extent to which the subsequent history of Japanese poetics is the history of his continuing reinterpretation are well known. What I propose in chapter three is very simple but requires a certain amount of revision of our usual historical understanding of the literary contexts of this period. The search for a new "depth" in poetry that marks the transition from the *Kokinshū* (905) to the *Shinkokinshū* (1206) imperial poetry collections can best be understood in the light of the changing interpretation of Po Chü-i in the Heian period, as he was read against the background of Six Dynasties and Early T'ang poetics, to that of the Kamakura period, as he was read against the background of the radically new Sung dynasty poetics. Received history tells us that Sung culture does not begin to figure in the formation of Japanese aesthetics until after the middle of the thirteenth century at the earliest. But this view is based almost entirely upon the fact that the officially established medieval Japanese Zen organization (the Gozan, or Five Mountains, to use its Japanese name), the most obvious route by which much Sung culture arrived in Japan, did not begin to function as an institution until that time. The new Chinese influences have long been naively viewed as coterminous with the arrival of Chinese Ch'an monks in Japan from about the middle of the thirteenth century.

I show, to the contrary, that a great deal of the new Sung style must have been making itself felt in Japan by 1200, that Japanese poetic theory and practice were already being redefined against their changing Chinese background, and that the new poetic vision of the poets of the Shinkokin period can be understood as continuing the reinterpretation of Po Chü-i in the context of the Sung

1. *Genji Monogatari Emaki*, "Azumaya I" (Tokugawa Reimeikan, Nagoya). Ukifune and her women are shown looking at illustrated tales in book and scroll form. "The Princess took out illustrations to old romances, which they examined while Ukon read from the texts" (Seidensticker, *Genji*, 958). Her sister Ukifune listens; both are deep in thought about other matters. From Ivan Morris, *The Tale of Genji Scroll* (Tokyo and New York, 1971), pl. 13.

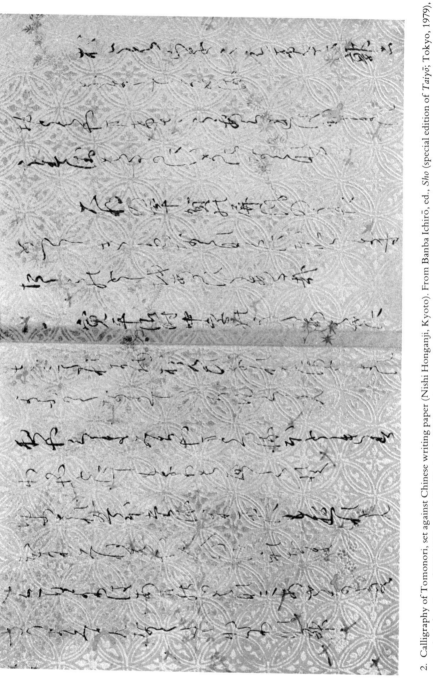

2. Calligraphy of Tomonori, set against Chinese writing paper (Nishi Honganji, Kyoto). From Banba Ichirō, ed., *Sho* (special edition of *Taiyō*, Tokyo, 1979), unpaginated section of "Nishi Honganji Sanjurokuninshū," no. 6.

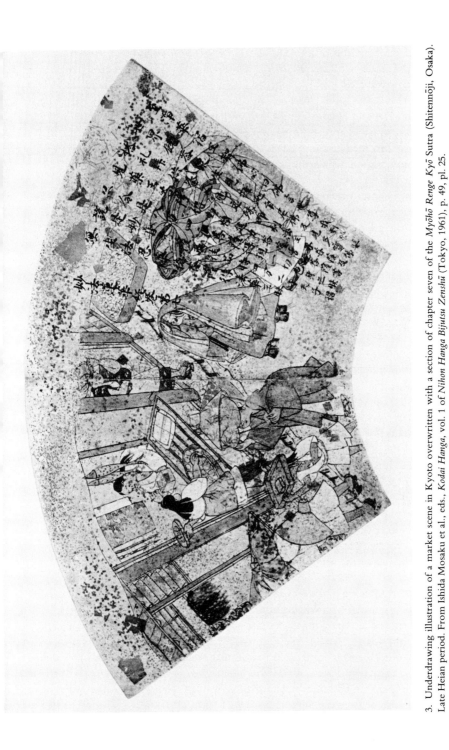

3. Underdrawing illustration of a market scene in Kyoto overwritten with a section of chapter seven of the *Myōhō Renge Kyō* Sutra (Shitennōji, Osaka). Late Heian period. From Ishida Mosaku et al., eds., *Kodai Hanga*, vol. 1 of *Nihon Hanga Bijutsu Zenshū* (Tokyo, 1961), p. 49, pl. 25.

Chinese poets' vision of him. Po no longer represented in this period the Six Dynasties and Heian ideals of fluent ease and courtly elegance. Teika's age was suddenly aware, as earlier generations were not, of a new "depth" in Po's poetry that corresponds closely to the Sung reinterpretation of Po by poets like Su Tung-P'o and Huang T'ing-chien. Where Po was merely "sitting" in the Heian view, for example, Kamakura poets became aware that Po was usually sitting in Zen meditation. Indeed, Po's strongly Buddhist and predominantly Ch'an orientation seems the starting point for much of medieval Japanese writing about poetry.

In the chapter on *Genji* I have used the visual analogy, made in the novel itself, of the lyrically graceful, feminine effect of the Japanese script set off against the geometric, masculine regularity of Chinese writing paper (fig. 2). The significance of the work of the Gozan monks Kokan Shiren and Musō Soseki to the Japanese culture in which they lived, which is the subject of chapter four, by contrast is suggested by contemporary Buddhist manuscripts in which Chinese characters appear in a neat, bold, clear, and impressive Chinese hand against a delicate, lyrically graceful background of Japanese design (fig. 3). While the two elements are reversed, it is their contrast that is important. As in these new manuscripts, the "Chineseness" of these monks that assumes the foreground serves to bring out the increasing sense of the "Japaneseness" of the context of their lives and work. It is their role in assimilating Chinese culture to the mainstream of native Japanese, rather than the degree to which they may be thought of as "Chinese," that is the Gozan monks' most important contribution to the development of Japanese cultural history.

At the same time, I show in the striking difference between these two medieval Zen figures that the Gozan was far from being the homogeneous monolith it is usually thought to be. Rather, the Gozan admitted a wide range of more "Chinese" and more "Japanese" elements, all of which were important in the development of a uniquely Japanese medieval aesthetics. One notable background element in this development and the concomitant changes in the perception of the relation of Japan to China was the fall of the Southern Sung dynasty to the Mongols in 1279, a calamity the Japanese placed in the context of the failure of the attempted Mongol invasions of Japan in 1274 and 1281. These events emphasized to the Japanese a China that was still alien and could be quite frightening in the sense that I explore in the chapter on *Genji*. But even more important, China was beginning to be seen as frankly inferior to Japan as well as entirely unsuited to Japanese sensibilities. This view built slowly through the centuries with fluctuations, culminating in the extreme anti-Chinese views of Motoori Norinaga in the Edo period that are explored first in chapter one and later in chapter seven.

Having examined in chapter four the complex relations of Musō with the warrior and aristocratic elite of his day, I turn in chapter five to a detailed consideration of the relationship of Musō's most famous disciple, Gidō Shūshin, with Nijō Yoshimoto, the most noted renga theorist of his time. Yoshimoto's renga theory, involving as it did the practice and theory of wakan in linked-verse poetry, revolves around a new perception in the fourteenth century of wakan in the *Genji* age, when what was Japanese was the particularity of pattern and design that lay upon the surface, while what was Chinese was the archetypal ground that underlay it. Yoshimoto similarly understood China as capable of lending new depth and dimension to Japan, otherwise petty and trivial Japanese detail attaining against it the status of meaningful design.

These concerns can be seen in Yoshimoto's renga theory in two crucial areas. The first is the emphasis on the distinction he stressed between linking by "heart" and linking by "words"; and the second the equally important distinction between "ground" and "pattern." In both cases, the central quality of meaning extends outward from the principle of wakan to create a new sense of dimensionality. At the most superficial level, influence from China, whether more or less direct, would continue to be significant in Japanese culture for many centuries. But at least as important are the manifold ramifications of the ancient wakan dialectic as it operated to structure meaning itself in these antithetical terms of surface and depth, pattern and ground. The results of this reaffirmation of the synthetic nature of meaning are further explored in chapter six in the important aesthetic theories of Zeami, Shōtetsu, Shinkei, and Sōgi.

As I show at the start of chapter seven, there was little difference between the sorts of lives led by late Muromachi Zen monks and early Edo Neo-Confucian thinkers. What had changed, and what permits historians to draw the distinction between late medieval on the one hand and early modern on the other, is the context of the social and political parameters within which those lives were conducted. Perhaps the most significant difference is the apparent secularization of thought in the Edo period. I say apparent, for the primacy of the Buddhist metaphor continued unabated in every realm of aesthetics. The power of the Buddhist world-view to inform meaning for more than a millennium was not likely to disappear with the turn of a new century. Rather, it was subsumed within a new context, as Buddhism had been subsumed within a new Neo-Confucian synthesis in China centuries before. What is important, as always, are the particular directions taken by Japanese thought in the synthesis of this new "Chinese" relationship.

I have chosen to explore in chapter seven one of the new relationships that emerged between Neo-Confucian philosophy and aesthetics during the crucial Genroku period circa 1700. The examination of the centrality of a new opposition of "restraint" to "emotion" (*giri-ninjō*) to both areas leads inevitably to the question of the developing understanding of the relationship between China and Japan in this period. If early Edo philosophy seems to be lost in scrutinizing an enormously complex mural of China, by 1800 philosophical inquiry seems to have found itself staring into a mirror in which men like Kada no Azumamaro, Kamo no Mabuchi, and Motoori Norinaga saw not China but Japan instead.

And keeping in mind this complex image of Japan reflected in a Chinese mirror, let us turn now to a more detailed examination of the question of Japan's synthesis of China from the eighth to the eighteenth centuries.

CHAPTER ONE

Script and Scripture: The *Kojiki* and the Problem of Writing

Fumiwake yo	Walk your own path!
Yamato ni wa aranu	To follow only in the tracks
Kara tori no	Made by Chinese birds
Ato o miru nomi	Not found here in Japan—
Hito no michi ka wa	Is that a man's Way?
(Kada no Azumamaro, 1669–1736)	

This study begins and ends with the writing of a text, taking as its starting point the creation of Japan's first extant text, the *Kojiki* (Records of Ancient Matters, A.D. 712), and ending with the important re-"writing" of the same text at the end of the eighteenth century by the nativist scholar Motoori Norinaga (1730–1801).[1] These two acts of writing can be thought of as having defined between them over more than a millennium much of the course of Japanese semiotics, that is, the manipulation of signs to form the symbolic systems by which men create meaning.

The *Kojiki* begins with the origins of the cosmos, the birth of the gods, and their creation of Japan, and is a primary locus of Japanese myth. Because at the time it was written the Japanese had developed no script of their own, however, they were constrained to record these primal matters in the script of an alien culture, China. The dissonances that resulted from the harnessing together of two forces as powerfully antagonistic to each other as we shall see Japanese matter and Chinese script to be created a primitive and almost geological strain that permanently fractured the surface of the entire semiotic field of culture. This important semiotic fracture continued thereafter to spread itself over a thousand years and more of Japanese cultural history.

The term "fracture" is associated with the semiotic investigations of Roland Barthes and Jacques Derrida, who see in it the visible sign of cultural *aporia*, or apparently unresolvable paradox. Derrida, based on Saussure, further understands that fracture to be only the most visible sign of a generative complex he

---

[1] References to the *Kojiki* in Japanese are to Kurano Kenji, ed., *Kojiki*, vol. 1 of *Nihon Koten Bungaku Taikei* (hereafter cited as *NKBT*, 1; Tokyo: Iwanami Shoten, 1962).

terms *différence/différance* (difference/deferal), which is to say that meaning is the result of a process of differentiation, in the course of which arrival at an ultimate Meaning is endlessly deferred. Meaning thus arises from the polarity of ego and alter, self and other, and its creation involves a dialectical force of such magnitude as to be called violent. A force of the magnitude required to create being he calls "ontological violence" ("Violence et Metaphysique," 1964). In Derrida's thought, then, the fracture that reveals that violence can be understood as a sign of the creation of meaning itself. Some idea of the magnitude of the violence that Derrida finds in the relationship between speech and writing is suggested by his view of writing as exerting a "permanent and obsessive pressure from the place where it remains held in check."[2] This phrase indicates the forces, inherent in the strain of harnessing together meaning (or ego) and sign (or alter), that are unleashed by the shock waves of semiotic dissonance as writing expands through the manifold cultural contexts in which it is embedded.

I use the term "writing" here in two senses at once, both in the narrow sense to connote what is usually meant by the act of writing and in the larger to connote everything that is the subject matter of that aspect of semiotics Derrida calls "grammatology." Clearly, the notion of a "fracture of the semiotic field of culture" is not unique to Japan; nor is modern semiotics, after all, a subject particularly associated with Japan. In dealing here specifically with the implications of this general problem for our immediate concerns, therefore, I shall need to relate particular Japanese instance to general theory. Much scholarship has been devoted to exploring the significance of literacy for culture, but it still remains to be seen how well the European study of semiotics can be made to deal with non-Western materials. Since the study of semiotics arose out of French structuralism and owes much of its methodology to modern Marxist thought stemming from Hegelian philosophy, we may well wonder about any claim to a general "universality." Yet we might recall that China had long been a subject of great fascination for Europe, and its writing system a matter of intense curiosity there. The impact of the visual arts of China and Japan especially, with their lavish use of calligraphic inscription on paintings that emphasized some peculiarly nonreferential quality in the characters, buttressed by the age-old Chinese insistence on the inseparability of writing and painting, is clearly one important element in the creation in Europe of an environment that jolted thinkers into a consideration of the sign as something possessing a life of its own independent of referential meaning. Roland Barthes is just one in a long line of men that the Chinese writing system, as one of many systems

---

[2] *Of Grammatology* (*De la Grammatologie*, 1967), trans. Gayatri Chakravorty Spivak (Baltimore: Johns Hopkins University Press, 1976), 270. I should emphasize that I am not attempting here to apply Derrida's or Barthes' theories in any systematic way, but rather find in their analysis and terminology an often provocative and illuminating (if as often an exasperating and confusing) way of thinking about the problem of writing.

uncovered by European archeology, in all its unbridled difference, forced to rethink the relationships between nature, culture, and language.

For all that he is a naive observer of Japan and so often requires a certain amount of corrective commentary, Barthes is, perhaps in part for that naiveté, all the more perceptive an observer of the telling cultural *différence*, which usually seems so trivial that it is taken for granted or ignored by the "expert." Barthes has noted this fracture of the Japanese semiotic field in the following remarkable observation in *L'Empire des Signes* (1970):

> One might say that an age-old technique permits the landscape or the spectacle to produce itself, to occur in pure significance, abrupt, empty, like a fracture. Empire of Signs? Yes, if it is understood that these signs are empty and that the ritual is without a god. Look at the cabinet of Signs (which was the Mallarmean habitat), i.e., in that country, any view, urban, domestic, rural, and the better to see how it is made, take for example the Shikidai gallery; tapestried with openings, framed with emptiness and framing nothing, decorated no doubt, but so that the figuration (flowers, birds, trees, animals) is removed, sublimated, displaced far from the foreground of the view, there is in it place for furniture (a paradoxical word in French—*meuble*—since it generally designates a property anything but mobile, concerning which one does everything so that it will endure: with us, furniture has an immobilizing vocation, whereas in Japan the house, often deconstructed, is scarcely more than a furnishing—mobile—element); in the Shikidai gallery, as in the ideal Japanese house, stripped of furniture (or scantily furnished), there is no site which designates the slightest propriety [*propriété*] in the strict sense of the word— ownership: neither seat nor bed nor table out of which the body might constitute itself as the subject (or master) of space: the center is rejected (painful frustration for Western man, everywhere "furnished" with his armchair, his bed, proprietor of a domestic location). Uncentered space is also reversible: you can turn the Shikidai gallery upside down and nothing would happen except for an inconsequential inversion of top and bottom, of right and left: the content is irretrievably dismissed: whether we pass by, cross it, or sit down on the floor (or the ceiling, if you reverse the image), there is nothing to *grasp*.[3]

By "Shikidai gallery" Barthes refers specifically to the medieval architectural style of the upper samurai class that is known as "study-alcove style" (*shoin-zukuri*), perhaps best known to the West as it is embodied in the architecture of the seventeenth-century Katsura Detached Palace in the southwestern suburbs of Kyoto. Certainly Barthes, who had traveled throughout Japan, could not have believed that this is the way the modern Japanese live. But any foreigner brought up on the mythologies of samurai movies or, more aesthetically,

---

[3] *The Empire of Signs* (*L'Empire des Signes*, 1970), trans. Richard Howard (New York: Hill and Wang, 1982), 108–109.

photographs of lovely ancient temple gardens will have to be prepared for something of a shock when this "ideal" of the fifteenth-century ruling classes encounters the reality of the typical modern Japanese dwelling, claustrophobically small and above all stuffed almost to the point of impossibility with "furniture" that can include heavy chandeliers, thick carpeting and draperies, and reproductions of the Mona Lisa, not to mention the expected array of electronic equipment.

Barthes' observations are in fact true only in the extreme theoretical instance, and especially only as one term of the attempt to synthesize the *différence* between Japanese and French perceptions of reality. One cannot literally invert this "Shikidai gallery" (or corridor, room, hall, veranda, or whatever name one might apply to it in English) if one happens to be Japanese—there are among other obstacles tatami mats on the floor, porches beyond the sliding doors and filigreed transoms above them, alcoves with built-in writing surfaces—any more than one can invert a page of Japanese script (which would also matter little to anyone who was unable to "decode," i.e., read, Japanese) and still expect it to contain meaning. What is considered movable (*meuble*) or incidental and what structural depends, after all, entirely upon one's cultural orientation.

Still, when Barthes, the observant "deconstructor" of Western codes of dress, food, furnishings, and manners, analyzes a Japanese room to discover its informing codes, we would expect to learn something. I would like to emphasize especially his observation that, as his analogy of the room is intended to demonstrate, the space is "empty" only in the sense that there is nothing within that would appear to extrinsically define the form of the room; rather, it is the form of the architecture itself that defines the meaning of the space. The *shikidai*, literally a ceremonial dais, is a structure whose function is to demarcate a locus of ritual activity. It is "empty," as I shall further elaborate, in exactly the same sense as a Shinto shrine: "empty," that is, of anything that, "furniture"-like, defines the space, but "full" of meaning—or as Barthes puts it, the "signs are empty and the ritual is without a god." The fracture that Barthes perceives is precisely the fundamental disjunction between form and meaning that hinges upon the fact that meaning is felt in Japan to be central and formless, and form peripheral and meaningless. With the *Kojiki* as our central text, we shall see how meaning is consistently understood to be Japanese, and form to be alien, which for premodern Japan is to say "Chinese." From its inception, poetic discourse in Japan was always aware of the centrality of the paradox that meaning (*kokoro*, heart), which is profound and structural, must be expressed by form (*kotoba*, words), which is extrinsic and superficial.

From what can be considered the first act of writing in Japan was born a dialectic, in the ongoing synthesis of whose terms—the fullness, implicitness, and ineffability of native Japanese content on the one hand, the emptiness, explicitness, and power to signify of alien Chinese form on the other—can be "read" the history of Japanese literature in the broadest sense, and indeed of Japan itself. Once we have established the significance of this primal and generative fracture, we find little problem in tracing its course from the *Kojiki* as it underlies and informs a wide variety of subject matter, for there is little in premodern, and even still in modern, Japan that is not reached by at least a small craze of this primitive fracture of the semiotic field of culture.[4]

Assuming in its intensity and enormous power of ramification the paradigmatic status of the problem of writing, we can now proceed to examine in more detail the particular Japanese case. Any problem that modern theory is able to identify with regard to the relationship between speech and writing, and the role of the development of writing in the all-important transition from orality to literacy, is made much more complex in the case of Japan by at least two factors.

The first of these factors is that Japan and China are not merely two different countries and cultures. Their languages belong to two groups that are not only entirely unrelated but appear almost exactly antithetical in their phonological, morphological, and syntactic systems, which is to say in their deepest linguistic structures. In terms of their contrast only (and I must always emphasize this limitation), Chinese and Japanese can be, and often have been, characterized as, respectively, monosyllabic as opposed to polysyllabic, isolating as opposed to agglutinating, and uninflected as opposed to highly inflected. In Chinese, to borrow the vocabulary of astronomy, we might see an instance of language as "black hole," a dense core creating a gravity so powerful that meaning collapses inward upon itself centripetally, with the result that little escapes outward. In this state of language, meaning is highly paradigmatic or relational, established through codes which govern the association of similar units; in other words, meaning in Chinese is located primarily in the creation of formal structures.[5] Japanese, on the other hand, seems by contrast to represent language as "supernova," a central core radiating meaning outward with such energy that it can scarcely be contained. Meaning in the case of Japanese is created of extreme polysemy by syntagmatic codes of linking that, by limiting the direction of radiation, serve to polarize and give coherence.

[4] The punning meanings of "craze" fortuitously reflect something of Derrida's view of the role of language in establishing a *différence* between meaning and nonmeaning or madness; see "Cogito and the History of Madness" ("Cogito et l'histoire de la folie," 1964), in Derrida, *Writing and Difference* (*L'Ecriture et la Différence*, 1967), trans. Alan Bass (Chicago: University of Chicago Press, 1978), 31–63: "It is through this relationship to the other as an other self that meaning reassures itself against madness and nonmeaning" (59).

[5] Yu-kuang Chu, "The Chinese Language," in John Meskill, ed., *An Introduction to Chinese Civilization* (New York: Columbia University Press, 1973), 599–664, makes much the same point in his section on "word relations and relational thinking." Chu notes that meaning in Chinese is essentially relational in nature, established that is through relationships and patterns. He also notes that this is best seen in the extreme antithetical parallelism exhibited by Chinese poetic structures.

We find these admittedly suspect analogies to cosmic forces operating most credibly and concretely in the structures of poetry. One of the most powerful determinants of meaning in Chinese poetry is end-rhyme, a device that functions to establish a highly formal heuristic matrix. In Japanese poetry, which lacks rhyme, one of the most powerful formal structures is the "pivot-word" (*kakekotoba*), a linking device (sometimes erroneously assumed to illustrate the "nonlinearity" of the language) that allows a certain linear coherence of meaning while simultaneously permitting, by its creation of two-way polarity, the fundamental underlying multivalence of meaning in Japanese.[6] Another structure of Japanese poetry that permits this play of multivalent meaning while simultaneously ordering it is the extreme degree of syntactical hypotaxis or subordination. Again often mistaken as an indication of "linearity," it is instead a device that, while ordering meaning, allows for interlocking structures of complex modification. It is in fact a primary logical structure that, much like the pivot-word, allows a measure of linear coherence while permitting multivalence of meaning. This can be contrasted with the equally extreme syntactical parataxis or parallelism of Chinese poetry, which results in the creation of structures so highly antithetical that meaning seems substantially dependent upon the operation of antithesis itself, at least at the surface levels of language.

The comparison of Chinese and Japanese poetic and linguistic structures quite neatly illustrates Roman Jakobson's well-known division of language into polar "metaphoric" and "metonymic" types, another way of speaking of language in its synchronic and diachronic aspects. Chinese operates in a dominantly synchronic mode, relying almost entirely upon parallelism and rhyme, its logic governed by the association of like categories; Japanese, to the contrary, is a diachronic language governed by hypotactic subordination, its logic predominantly that of the combination of dissimilar categories.

Terence Hawkes has summarized the importance of the distinction between these two types of language, and so indirectly between the two languages under discussion: "Jakobson's 'polarities' thus seem to take us to the heart of the act of signification itself and in so doing to suggest very important ways in which modes of signification may be distinguished from each other."[7] In terms of Jakobson's analysis, Chinese is a "vertical" language while Japanese is a "hori-

---

[6] Noël Burch, *To the Distant Observer: Form and Meaning in the Japanese Cinema* (London: Scholar Press, 1979), while as naive as Barthes and heavily indebted to him, offers some equally provocative insights in his general introductory chapters, especially "A System of Signs" (35–41). Because of his deeper involvement with literary materials beyond his competence, however, Burch's statements often require even more corrective than Barthes'. His comment on the "pivot-word" as "rejecting linearity" (47) is one instance in which he is provocative, but only partially correct.

[7] Terence Hawkes, *Structuralism and Semiotics* (Berkeley: University of California Press, 1977), 76ff. See also Todō Akiyasu, "Nihongo to Kango," in Bitō Masahide, ed., *Nihon Bunka to Chūgoku*, vol. 10 of *Chūgoku Bunka Sōsho* (Tokyo: Taishūkan, 1968), 80.

zontal" one (a dimensional sense of language adopted by the Japanese as well). This extension of the spatial metaphor makes it clear that the two languages, ninety degrees out of phase, necessarily operate at linguistic cross-purposes. These profound differences in the deepest structures of the languages themselves lie at the bottom of any attempt to account for the extreme magnitude of the forces unleashed in the dialectical synthesis of Japanese meaning expressed by means of the formal logic of Chinese.

We must of course be careful to separate the spoken from the written language. The Chinese writing system was already several thousand years old by the time the Japanese first began to use it sometime between the third and the fifth centuries A.D. Like any other highly evolved script, the writing system is inseparable from its texts, and Chinese was by then the graphic medium of a large body of texts that included poetry, philosophy, history, ritual, metaphysics, and political and religious thought. When the Japanese first encountered writing, they were confronted not simply with a script but with all the prestige and power of an ancient civilization that had come to regard its own written texts as icons of that prestige and as the vectors of its geopolitical influence in the peripheral world.

Traditional Chinese historiography, whether justified or not, tended to portray those at the edges of the Chinese world-order as benighted barbarians to whom China nobly extended the benefits of its superior culture, and who in turn were expected to assume the respectful if nominal status of tributary states whose existence the Chinese held to be meaningful only by authority of the power that radiated outward from the Central Kingdom. The closer and more accessible to China's culture and armies, the less room there was for compromise with this philosophy; peoples living on China's inner-Asian frontiers, if not nomadic and able to flee, eventually tended to become Chinese, or at least to assume the outward trappings of Chineseness more often than their Chinese neighbors assumed those of "barbarism."

The Japanese have long understood their unique geographical relationship to China to be one of the most important conditions governing the relationship between the two countries. An island close enough to the continent and with easy enough access to make the benefits of Chinese civilization available, yet distant and isolated enough to prevent physical invasion and so allow them to retain their cultural identity, Japan has enjoyed a situation unique among China's neighbors. Many other peoples, Altaic or otherwise, never had the breathing-space necessary to permit the establishment of a dialectic between the native and the alien. Rather, they were subjected to wholesale cultural absorption, still attested to today by the existence within the land of the Hans of some fifty-five officially recognized "minority peoples," among them such members of the Altaic language group as Mongols, Koreans, Turks, and Manchus, each with its different and distinct language, religion, and culture.

While scholars today still do not entirely agree on the linguistic affiliation of the Japanese language, the general consensus is that Japanese is related to the Altaic languages, which can be traced backward in a migration across northern Asia through Korean, Manchu, Mongolian, and Turkic.[8] To the Japanese—the only of these peoples not represented among China's national minorities—the case of Korea has been particularly instructive. Often the route by which mainland cultural influences reached Japan, Korea was largely a cultural dependent of the greater civilization, and a political client state as well when it was not being invaded or colonized by the Japanese themselves. Today, many aspects of Korean culture may well be most easily identifiable to the untrained eye as *like* Chinese or Japanese while not obviously either. The Koreans of the ancient states of Koguryŏ, Paekche, and Silla, as immigrants to Japan between the fourth and eighth centuries, were especially instrumental in bringing the culture of the mainland with them to their new home.

The second factor that complicates the problem of Japan's adoption of Chinese script is that Chinese writing is not, like letters or syllabaries, entirely phonetic. This qualification may come as some surprise, for until quite recently even learned and well-documented treatises on the relationship between writing and culture in the West have assumed Chinese to be entirely "ideographic" as well as nonphonetic. In fact, Chinese characters range from the entirely phonetic, representing sound and bearing no semantic burden at all, to the entirely logographic (that is, representing *words*, not ideas), conveying meaning with no obvious graphic indication of sound. Most characters fall into a broad middle category that is to some degree both phonetic and logographic, but not reliably or even obviously either. Whatever phonetic coherence remained embedded within the Chinese script by the time it came to be used in Japan between the third and fifth centuries A.D. was already problematic even in China, for the script's phonetic basis in the phonology of ancient Chinese no longer reflected with any degree of accuracy what was being spoken by Chinese in various parts of the expansive territory that was China in the fifth century A.D.

The difficulties inherent in adapting the Chinese phonological system to Japanese needs were alleviated somewhat by the fact that the Japanese phonological system was, and remains, far simpler than the Chinese. Besides not having to bother with considerations of tonality, Japanese in the early eighth century (the earliest period for which linguistic evidence exists) is known to have consisted of eight vowels and thirteen consonants used to represent a total of only eighty–eight sounds, without any of the dipthongs, glides, consonantal clusters, or finals characteristic of Chinese as it has been reconstructed for that period. The adoption of Chinese characters solely on a phonetic basis to represent each of the eighty–eight sounds as syllables was to obscure the true

[8] Roy Andrew Miller, *The Japanese Language* (Chicago: University of Chicago Press, 1967), 95 and 112.

nature of Japanese morphology, and so some obvious links to the Altaic language group.[9] Matters of phonology and morphology aside, the extreme difference already noted—almost an exact polarity, really—between the deepest structures of the Japanese and Chinese languages seems a poor recommendation for the adoption of the Chinese script by the Japanese had it not been for the proximity of Japan to the alluring flame of advanced Chinese culture (the metaphor begs the question of the danger of that flame, to which I shall return in due course).

These difficulties represent only the starting point for a discussion of the profound dissonances created when Chinese forms were used to express Japanese meaning. Surfacing in the superficial phenomena of language, those dissonances can be traced into the deepest structures of language, and so inevitably into the manifold ways that language and culture shape each other. Before we can proceed to discuss these more complex considerations, it may be helpful to provide some further idea of the ways in which Chinese script was adapted for use in Japan before the writing of the *Kojiki*. This is possible only from scant epigraphic materials; still, on the basis of these materials, it may be possible to make some distinctions that will be useful in later discussion. While the *Kojiki* is indeed considered to be Japan's "first text," it was clearly written within the context of already considerably sophisticated adaptations revealed in a variety of short inscriptions on objects.[10]

The earliest archeological evidence to date attesting to the presence of Chinese writing in Japan is a Chinese coin inscribed with two characters, dating from the period of the brief interregnum of Wang Mang's (r. A.D. 9–22) Hsin Dynasty between the Former and Later Han, excavated from a Yayoi site dated to circa A.D. 100. The coin tells us nothing at all about the Japanese, of course; it is evidence only of the presence, welcome or otherwise, of Chinese cultural artifacts in Japan by a certain date. The coin is, however, an apt symbol of the expansion of the Chinese *oikoumenē* into the lands around it, the power of its prestigious politicoeconomic system superinscribed and preceded by that of its equally prestigious writing.

The first use of Chinese script by Japanese does not appear until much later. Until recently, scholars generally dated this event from an inscription on a sword excavated from a tumulus in modern Saitama Prefecture.[11] From later

---

[9] Roy Andrew Miller, *Japanese and the Other Altaic Languages* (Chicago: University of Chicago Press, 1971).

[10] The following discussion is based on Ōno Susumu, *Nihongo no Seiritsu*, vol. 1 of *Nihongo no Sekai* (Tokyo: Chūō Kōronsha, 1980); Shimonaka Kunihiko, *Moji no Meguriai*, vol. 2 of *Nihongo no Rekishi* (Tokyo: Heibonsha, 1965); and Nakada Norio, *Nihon no Kanji*, vol. 4 of *Nihongo no Sekai* (Tokyo: Chūō Kōronsha, 1982).

[11] See Murayama Shichirō and Roy Andrew Miller, "The Inariyama Tumulus Sword Inscription," *Journal of Japanese Studies* 5:12 (Summer 1979), 405–38.

evidence brought to light concerning the likelihood of characters that once
were inscribed but are now no longer visible, it has become clear that the
inscription on this sword consists entirely of Chinese used *as* Chinese. Although
the writing does include characters used only for the purpose of representing
Japanese proper nouns phonetically, the Chinese themselves had long used
characters in exactly the same way to represent proper nouns in languages with
which they had come into contact—including Japanese—so this cannot be said
to represent anything more than an entirely Chinese use of script.

It is of course difficult to accept seriously any report of the "first" introduction of writing into a culture, but one passage in the *Kojiki* provides, with
dubious precision, at least an indication of about when the Japanese began to be
self–conscious about the use of Chinese writing. This passage, which details the
importation of continental culture as part of the phenomenon of a tide of
Korean immigration to Japan during the reign of Emperor Ōjin (ca. 362–394?),
states that one Wani, ancestor of a clan of scribes in Japan, introduced two
fundamental Chinese texts, *The Confucian Analects* (*Lun Yü*) and *The Thousand–
Character Classic* (*Ch'ien–tzu Ching*), into Japan in A.D. 369.[12] A parallel text in
the *Nihongi* (Chronicles of Japan, 720, which I will discuss later) records this
event as having taken place in A.D. 285, and states that the royal heir–apparent
"took [Wani] as teacher and learned various books from him. There was none
which he did not thoroughly understand. Therefore, the man called Wang-in
[Wani] was the first ancestor of the chiefs of writing [*fumi no obito*]." [13] Scholars
have revised the date of Wani's arrival in Japan, given in the characters of the
traditional sixty–year Chinese calendrical cycle, to two cycles or 120 years later
and established the more likely date of 405, which follows by only thirty years
what is recorded in other sources as the "first" introduction of Chinese writing
into Korea.

Two facts about this event seem important. First, the script was introduced
within the larger context of the fundamental texts of Chinese culture, rather
than the more limited context of merchants' records and the like. Second, these
texts were accompanied by a teacher—that is, someone who was authorized in
their legitimate, orthodox interpretation—and this person founded a clan of
hereditary scribes. While it may well be that Wani was thoroughly versed in
these particular texts, and even possible that indeed "there was none which he
did not thoroughly understand," we cannot interpret this to mean that the
study of Chinese writing necessarily made continuous and incremental progress

[12] *Kojiki*, *NKBT*, 1:294; Donald L. Philippi, trans. and ann., *Kojiki* (Princeton: Princeton
University Press, 1969), 285. Philippi also points out in n. 7, *ibid.*, that this could not have been the
same "Thousand-Character Classic" known to history.
[13] Tsukamoto Tarō et al., *Nihon Shoki* (Tokyo: Iwanami Shoten, 1974), *NKBT*, 67:373. See
W. G. Aston, trans. *Nihongi: Chronicles of Japan from Earliest Times to 697*, 2 vols. (London: Allen
and Unwin, 1956), vol. 1, 262–63.

following its introduction. In fact, to judge from the following anecdote about the hereditary scribes who were in imperial service in 596, nearly two centuries after this "first" introduction of Chinese script into Japan , they had apparently still not made entirely satisfactory progress in the written language:

> The Empress [Suiko] passed the Chronicles of Korea [written in Chinese] to the Minister [Soga no Umako], who ordered his scribes to interpret them. After three days, however, none of the scribes could interpret them. There was one Wang Chen-erh [usually transliterated into modern Japanese as Ōjinni, but might have represented something like Wajini] of boat–scribe [i.e., Korean immigrant] ancestry who was able to interpret the documents. The Empress and all her ministers praised him, saying, "Wonderful! Good work, Chen-erh! If it were not for your love of Chinese studies, who would ever have been able to interpret these?" From that time on Wang was employed within the Palace. The Empress summoned all the scribes of the East and West and said, "Why is it that, for all your study, you were not able to interpret the documents? The whole lot of you can't compare to Wang Chen-erh!" [14]

The earliest extant example of Chinese script actually used to represent the Japanese language rather than to represent Chinese is now thought to be found in an inscription dated A.D. 607 on the back of the aureole of a statue of Yaku-shi Buddha at Hōryūji Temple in Nara. There are two reasons for believing that the language of this inscription was in fact intended to convey Japanese rather than Chinese. First, the syntax follows sometimes Japanese word order (object–verb), sometimes Chinese (verb–object), which suggests a scribe whose native language was not Chinese. This fact alone, however, is of course inconclusive since even a Korean immigrant familiar with Chinese and Japanese might make this sort of error. More compelling is the use of several Chinese characters clearly intended to express Japanese honorifics. Written classical Chinese could itself be elaborately honorific when used for memorials to the throne and the like, but the words used as honorifics in this inscription were never used for that purpose in Chinese to mean what they obviously mean here in Japanese.

The occasional inversions of normal Chinese word order in this inscription present an interesting problem to the interpreter of cultural signs: Are we to read such lapses as an indication of the inadequacy of Japanese understanding of Chinese culture? The Empress Suiko's impatience with her scribes' failure to interpret documents written in Chinese suggests that there is little reason to believe that scribes were encouraged to write anything but standard literary Chinese. Signs of an innate pattern of adaptation of Chinese forms to native

---

[14] *Kokushi Taikei*, vol. 2, 102; cited in Kamei Takashi, "*Kojiki* wa Yomeru ka," in Takeda Yūkichi, ed., *Kojiki Taisei* (Tokyo: Heibonsha, 1957), vol. 1, 133.

needs, however, must be read through the distortions created by the powerfully ethnocentric forms. When one learns to read and write for the first time from the texts of acculturation themselves, not only the script but an entire way of thinking is superimposed over native modes of expression. These latter modes, which represent all that we can know of the ways of thinking of preliterate Japan, are perceived only as slight dissonances or disturbances not normally perceived within the culturally homogeneous Chinese forms. During the course of our explorations we shall find over and over that what we, with our inherited Sinocentric sympathies, have perceived as persistent Japanese failures to conform adequately to standard Chinese forms and their cultural interpretations can more meaningfully be considered as signs of the persistence of native patterns revealing themselves through an alien mode of representation.

When we turn to Chinese historical accounts of the early seventh century, we find the arrival of writing in Japan reported, as we might expect, from a very different point of view. According to *The History of the Sui Dynasty* (*Sui Shu*, compiled 636), at about the time that the Hōryūji inscription was being written, the Japanese had "no written language and understand only the use of notched sticks and knotted ropes. They revere Buddha and have obtained Buddhist scriptures from Paekche, which was their first contact with characters." [15] The writing of the civilizing texts of culture was thus also embedded within the religious matrix of Buddhism, a context very different from the sociopolitical matrix of Confucianism. Both Confucianism and Buddhism can be seen to have undergone considerable remolding in Japan that reveals the contours of a Japanese landscape beneath.

The *Sui Shu*'s account continues with a message addressed from the Japanese court to the Chinese emperor. Though the message is only paraphrased, we can assume that it was probably written in decent Chinese (not that the dynastic histories would ever have reported pidgin Chinese verbatim!), for numerous Chinese immigrants already lived in Japan by this time. In fact, the same report tells us that native Chinese and their descendents were so numerous in Japan that "it seems rather strange to call this land a country of barbarians [i.e., non-Chinese] at all." While the message itself seems courteous enough, expressing a hope that the Chinese emperor is healthy, it is addressed "from the Son of Heaven in the land where the sun rises to the Son of Heaven in the land where the sun sets." From the point of view of the Chinese Son of Heaven, who considered himself the only one to be addressed by that title, the sun rose and set on China alone. The emperor was so displeased by the presumption of this rude communication, we are told, that he ordered it never to be brought to his notice again.

[15] T'ang Wei-ch'eng et al., comps., *Sui Shu*, 6 vols. (Peking: Chung-hua Shu-chü, 1973), vol. 6, 1825–59, esp. 1827. Translated in Ryusaku Tsunoda and L. Carrington Goodrich, *Japan in the Chinese Dynastic Histories* (Pasadena: Perkins Asiatic Monograph Series, 1951), 31.

We may also wonder exactly what construction the Japanese themselves may have placed on the simple geographical fact that, following the course of the sun, Japan lay to the east of China? The implications of the sun rising over the one land and setting over the other were undoubtedly as aggressive in their political overtones as they seem to us today. Surely, whoever wrote out this message had to have been aware that one did not think this way in Chinese but rather followed a form in which the Chinese Son of Heaven was addressed in the most servile of language by a barbarian visible to the Chinese only in his role of tribute-bearer.

This message would seem to indicate that from the moment they found a voice that could carry all the way back to the realm where writing originated, the Japanese, not surprisingly, showed little sign of thinking in Chinese at all. To the contrary, when they began for the first time to use the Chinese script, the Japanese were already emptying these handy semiotic markers of their culture–bound Chinese content, even though the script had been brought to them quite full. This is not of course to deny that the Japanese adapted Chinese Confucianism and Buddhism to their own ends, but rather to suggest that just as they were eventually able to empty the Chinese writing system of its burden of content, so they seem similarly to have managed to separate the formal aspects of these philosophical systems from their alien significance and infuse them with entirely Japanese meaning.

It is interesting, although perhaps ultimately futile, to speculate about the source of this unique Japanese response to Chinese cultural forms. The Japanese themselves propose two complementary reasons. The first, as I have mentioned, is their felicitous geographical position vis-a-vis China, neither too far nor too close. The Japanese also stress something innate in the "Japanese spirit" that permitted contact with China and adoption of its cultural forms without danger of the larger culture simply engulfing the smaller. We shall see that from its earliest mention the word "Japanese spirit" was always used in contrast to what was felt to be "Chinese"—form, *technē*, learning—and existed as a concept only as one of the paired terms of an antithesis.[16]

It is not only in their deepest linguistic structures that Chinese and Japanese show extreme opposition: since language is central to all cultural phenomena, it is inevitable that these differences should be reflected in similar differences in cultural, social, and political forms as well. Again in terms of their contrast only, China has often been perceived as the more inflexible, monolithic, centripetal, a center that functioned historically to define anything alien on its periphery by absorption;[17] and Japan as the more flexible, with a set of linguistic and semiotic

---

[16] See chapter two; also Roy Andrew Miller's provocative essay "The 'Spirit' of the Japanese Language," *Journal of Japanese Studies* 3:2 (Summer 1977), 251–98.

[17] Joseph Needham, *Science and Civilization in China* (Cambridge: Cambridge University Press, 1961), vol. 1, 119.

codes that permitted adaptation and change, a center defined only in the act of differentiating itself from whatever it found to be alien. Barthes remarks especially on what he perceives to be this lack of a "proprietary" center (Derrida uses the same word, *propriété*, to mean the "literalness" or "selfness" of a thing),[18] seeing in Japan an empty center whose existence is defined by its context rather than by its "furniture." From another point of view, however, that apparently "empty" space is full, in the sense that it is the generatrix, itself empty, of as yet unformed meaning.

It is in this sense that we can perceive in the structure of the Shinto shrine, relatively unchanged in its most basic form since the *Kojiki* was written down (as Barthes saw in his "Shikidai gallery" of a millennium later), a primary locus of the set of signs for the deconstruction of the Japanese semiotic field. The Shinto shrine is, after all, entirely a matter of aesthetically (which is to say in Japanese terms, religiously) delineated space, a series of structurally fragile enclosures, reminiscent of the frequently reiterated ancient formulaic word *yaegaki* (eight-fold enclosure), that gradually admit those of proper ritual purity to closer proximity to the center—a center finally discovered ("painful frustration for Western man") to be empty, entirely devoid of icons. Barthes found the center to be "without a god"; and yet it is here in fact that deity dwells, generative and formless, invisible but omnipresent, creating all things. The nativized Buddhist temple, enshrining its multitude of figures and relics amid a panoply of glitter, offers a clear contrast. The light wooden framework of the Shinto shrine, permeable in both directions, marked only by straw ropes, branches of sacred *sakaki* leaves, sand, and wood, simply alludes to the deity within; the massive Buddhist temple architecture seems, to the contrary, an attempt to delay the imminent (and immanent) collapse of the phenomenal world, symbolized by its heavy tile roof, pulled inward by the dense gravity of its central icons.

Something of the degree of intricacy of the dialectic that governed Japan's gradual adaptation of the Chinese writing system to its own needs can be observed in the *Kojiki* itself, which opens with the following passage that I shall simply transcribe into modern orthographic equivalents:

天地初發之時［１］，於高天原［２］成神名，天之御中主神。次高御產巢日神。次神產巢日神。此三柱神者［３］，並獨神［４］成坐而［５］，隱身也［６］。

Ametsuchi hajimete hirakeshi toki [1], takama no hara ni [2] nareru kami no na wa, Ame-no-minaka-nushi-no-kami. Tsugi ni takami-musubi-no-kami. Tsugi ni kami-musubi-no-kami. Kono mihashira no kami wa [3], mina hitorigami [4] to nari-mashite [5], mi o kakushitamaiki [6].

[18] Derrida, *Of Grammatology*, 271.

At the time [1] of the beginning of heaven and earth, there came into existence in [2] Takami-no-hara a deity named Ame-no-minaka-nushi-no-kami; next, Takami-musubi-no-kami; next, Kami-musubi-no-kami. These three deities [3] all came into existence [5] as single deities [4], and their forms were not visible [6].[19]

1. The character text has *no toki*, using the Chinese relational word *chih*, 之, customarily omitted in the Japanese reading gloss and often omitted in the character text as well when Japanese grammar requires (compare p. 56, *hikiage-tamau toki*).

2. The character text has *ni oite*, the use of which is much as in the point above.

3. The character text has 者, and the Japanese reading is given as *wa*; but often the character is not present when the reading *wa* is demanded (compare above, "takami-no-hara ni nareru kami no na *wa*").

4. The word *hitorigami* (single deities), although written with Chinese characters, is not attested in any Chinese text.

5. *Narimashite*, written with the characters 成坐而, represents a verb that makes no sense in Chinese, *nar[u]*, and its Japanese inflectional ending-*mashite*. Continued throughout the text, this is the clearest use to this point of Chinese characters to represent Japanese.

6. The syntax of the character text is verb–object, which is inverted in the Japanese reading gloss, while the object-marker *o* is inserted and the past ending inflection is added. The final character, 也, used in Chinese as a copula, is used to represent the completive aspect inflection-*ki* in the Japanese reading. The text continues:

次國稚如浮脂而 [１], 久羅下那州 [２] 多陀用弊流 [３] 之時, 如葦牙因萌騰之物而成神名, 宇摩志阿斯訶備比古遲神。

Tsugi ni kuni wakaku ukishi abura no gotoku shite [1], kuragenasu [2] tadayoeru [3] toki, ashikabi no gotoku moeagaru mono ni yorite nareru kami no na wa, Umashi-ashi-kabi-hiko-ji-no-kami.

Next, when the land was young, resembling [1] floating oil and drifting [3] like [1] a jellyfish [2], there sprouted forth something like reed-shoots. From these came into existence the deity Umashi-ashi-kabi-hiko-ji-no-kami.

1. The character text begins by using the characters in correct Chinese syntax for the simile "like," but adds the Japanese reading *shite* afterwards by adding the character 而.

2. The Japanese word for "jellyfish," *kuragenasu*, is sounded out phonetically

---

[19] Following the *NKBT* text (1:50); Philippi, *Kojiki*, 47. These readings are not of course necessarily definitive; for a discussion of the problems of the received readings in several of the major contemporary editions of the *Kojiki*, see Kobayashi Yoshinori, "The *Kun* Readings of the *Kojiki*," *Acta Asiatica* 46 (1984), 62–84.

in Chinese characters, most likely because there was no written Chinese word in the classical texts for this vulgar common edible. (The modern Chinese word is *hai-che*, 海蜇, a manufactured compound that seems less directly prompted by familiar experience of the object itself than the Japanese word, reminding us that literary Chinese was primarily an inland language.)

3. Characters are used phonetically to sound out the Japanese verb *tadayoeru* (float), but this seems odd since the Chinese character for this word, 漂, is attested in classical texts and so ought to have been used. (The entire phrase *kuragenasu tadayoeru* is followed by a textual note stating that the characters used to represent these ten syllables are to be sounded out phonetically.) Compare the corresponding passage in the entirely Sinicized *Nihongi* (*NKBT*, 67:77), where the usual Chinese character for "float" is used. This raises the possibility that an awareness of the problem posed by rendering the inflectional ending is what made it necessary to sound the word out rather than to write the character with the same semantic meaning, a point I shall return to shortly.

My final illustration is a passage that contains one of the most interesting uses of Chinese characters to represent Japanese in the entire text:

故，二柱神立［２］天浮橋［１］而，指下其沼矛以畫者［３］，鹽許々袁々呂々［４］邇畫鳴而［５］。

Kare, futahashira no kami, ame no ukihashi ni [1] tatashite [2], sono nuboko o sashioroshite kakitamaeba [3] shio kōrokōro ni [4] kakinashite [5].

Thereupon, the two deities stood [2] on [1] the Heavenly Floating Bridge and, lowering the jeweled spear, stirred [3] with it. They stirred [5] the brine with a churning-churning sound [4].[20]

1. The expected Chinese locative that is present in the first passage (see note 2) is absent here.

2. The character text has the verbal inflection *-shite* immediately following the object as in the second passage (see note 1) above.

3. The character text has the word 者, used above to render the Japanese case particle *wa*, and used here as well and regularly in this sort of transcription of Japanese as it never is in Chinese, to render the Japanese inflectional ending *-eba* (when).

4. The onomatopoeia that Philippi renders "churning-churning sound" is written with Chinese characters used phonetically. Literally it is sounded out as "*ko-ko o-o ro-ro*." This is Japanese onomatopoeia for a rolling or churning sound (compare modern Japanese *korokoro* as well as the many words with the base *koro-*). The same sound is used in *Kojiki*, 364 (*NKBT*, 1:320), but is written as

[20] *NKBT*, 1:52; Philippi, *Kojiki*, 49.

ko-o-ro, i.e., *kōro*. Note also the use of the character 邇 to represent the Japanese adverbial particle *ni*.

5. *Kaki-* (paddle) is written with a character whose Chinese reading is the homophone *kaki-* (divide by a stroke). The inflectional part of the verb *-nashite* (*kakinasu*) is written with a character one of whose readings in Japanese is *nasu* (make sing), obviously used here only for its Japanese reading. The inflection *-te* is represented as usual by 而, and the author's original gloss informs us that "鳴 is to be read *nashi*."

Such passages demonstrate that by the beginning of the eighth century the Japanese were already showing considerable ingenuity in attempting to confront some of the myriad technical problems raised in adapting Chinese script to represent Japanese meaning. It is of course not to be thought that this was literally the first attempt to do so, nor does it represent any more than tentative and provisional solutions to problems some of which were to endure for centuries. We find, for example, that half a century later the use of Chinese script to record Japan's earliest collection of poetry, the *Man'yōshū* (compiled 759), reveals a remarkably cumbersome and even more complex adaptation of Chinese script. In this adaptation, known as *Man'yōgana* or "*Man'yōshū*-style script," Chinese characters are used in at least three different ways, which the linguist Ōno Susumu has illustrated in the following poem (*MYS*, 1:4) describing the scene at a morning hunt in the spring in the fields near Nara (groups within hyphens represent one character):

玉刻春	
Tama-ki-haru	On the field of Uchi
內乃大野爾	
Uchi-*no*-ō-*no*-*ni*	Radiating the power of cut gems
馬數而	
Uma-name-te	The horses are lined up
朝布麻須等六	
Asa-*fu-ma-su*-**ra-mu**	Stamping in the morning
其草深野	
Sono-kusa-buka-no	That grass-deep field.[21]

1. Italicized words represent characters used only for their phonetic values to represent Japanese sounds (about twenty-five percent of the total).

2. Words in bold italics represent the most complex transitional form, Chinese characters used to represent, by the sound of the native Japanese reading that translates their Chinese meaning, a Japanese word with an entirely different meaning. Because one character often represents more than one syllable, this technique results in a saving of space, reducing the number of

---

[21] Ōno, *Nihongo no Seiritsu*, 194ff.

characters necessary to write this thirty-one syllable *tanka* poem to twenty-one (also about twenty-five percent).

3. The rest of the words represent Chinese characters that have the same semantic values as the Japanese words they are used to represent but are read entirely in Japanese (about fifty percent).

This ingenious intermediary transcription system poses questions that no one seems yet to have answered entirely satisfactorily. To begin with the first and simplest case, phonetic transcription, it is clear why the relational particles *no* and *ni* in the second line, possessing no semantic value of themselves, should be written using characters for their Chinese phonetic values alone (as these were heard and reproduced by Japanese of the time). The modern Chinese *nai* (ancient *nəg) thus becomes modern Japanese *no* (*nö), and *erh* (*ńiӗr) becomes *ni*. The case of *fumasu* is more complicated, and I shall discuss it after dealing with the other categories.

Category two is much more complicated than simple phonetic transcription. *Ramu*, for example, is a separate inflectional word added to one base form of verbs to indicate, among other things, supposition or probability. Here it is written, however, with Chinese characters that have no such meaning: the expression of these particular cognitive states reflected in "moods" of the verb were not part of the logic of Chinese and so had no equivalent linguistic structures expressed in characters. This can be contrasted with the inflectional ending -*te* added to the base of the verb *name(ru)* and elsewhere in the *Kojiki* passages cited earlier: the Chinese character used to represent the *meaning* of this verbal state (*erh*, 而) itself means "given an immediately prior stated condition, then another condition follows," and the Japanese meaning of the -*te* inflection indicates the very similar idea "under the condition that one action has been completed, another action then happens." The characters chosen to represent *ramu* are therefore used not for their Chinese but rather for their Japanese phonetic values in the following way: the *meaning* of the Chinese character is first translated into Japanese, which then in turn is used only for its sound. Thus, *ra* is represented by a Chinese character whose Chinese pronunciation, *teng*, is entirely dissimilar; one of the semantic values of this word *teng*, though, is "and others in the same category," which is translated into Japanese by the Japanese suffix -*ra*. Again, the Japanese sound *mu* is represented by the Chinese character *liu* meaning "six," since the native Japanese word for six is *mu* . This complex usage clearly distinguishes between relational particles, easily detachable from the words they govern, and verbal inflections, which present a much more complex problem. We saw a similar solution to this problem in the use of the Chinese character for the word "sing," translated as *nasu* in Japanese and used in the *Kojiki* to represent only the verbal inflection -*nasu* with no reference at all to this meaning.

The second category also includes the word Uchi, a place name, now written phonetically (as many proper nouns are) but with entirely different characters (宇智). There also exists, however, a Japanese word *uchi* denoting what belongs to one's own group and signifying "within." The place name is written here with the Chinese character *nei* that also means "within," and so has the effect of creating a visual pun that matches the sound of the name in Japanese. This provides an opportunity to save space by writing two syllables with one character (though strangely enough, the modern place name Uchi is written with two characters).

The words *tamaki haru* also fall within this very ambiguous category but represent an even more severe problem of interpretation, in response to which any translation can only be tentative and provisional. This phrase is what is called a "pillow-word" (*makurakotoba*), usually a five-syllable phrase that often constitutes the first line of a *tanka* poem and is a highly conventional, archaic epithet that modifies the following word. Hundreds are used in the *Man'yōshū*, and their meanings, as in this case, are more often than not uncertain. One thesis holds, for example, that Uchi, near Nara, was a center where gems (*tama*) were cut (*ki*). This leaves *haru*, written with the Chinese character for "spring," to represent the season of this hunt, but the word is otherwise meaningless here. Another theory is that *tama* is the word that means "the power of a deity" and is followed by *kiharu* (or *kiwaru*, an uncommon alternative form of *kiwamu*, "to be extreme"), so that it modifies as "Uchi, whose deities are extremely powerful." A third possibility would interpret *tamaki* as the "arm-guard" used by archers and *haru* as "wear," so that the phrase would mean "Uchi, where arm-guards are worn." It is even possible that all of these meanings were intended to resonate in the phrase *tamaki haru*. The compiler of the *Man'yōshū* used characters to write the phrase that makes the semantic burden of these sounds the translation I have given. Elsewhere (*MYS*, 897, 4003, 4408) other characters are used to transcribe the same phrase, with equally ambiguous results.

The third category is almost as simple and unambiguous as the first. The two Chinese characters used to represent the Japanese words *ō-no* (large field) mean in Chinese exactly what they do in Japanese. The same is also true of the characters used for "horse" (*uma*, whose ancient pronunciation *muma* makes it one of a group of words thought to have been borrowed directly from Chinese, in this case *ma*), "morning" (*asa*), and so on. Clearly the use of such simple, automatic equivalents represents the most economic use of time and space, even if, as we shall see, there should be some discomfort with the fact that a Japanese horse may not have been felt to be exactly the same as a Chinese horse, or a Japanese morning quite like a Chinese one, in all their native connotations.

The first category also includes the verb *fumasu* ("stamp" or "tread"), which represents a problem because we know that, as with the word *tadayoeru* in the *Kojiki* passage cited above, a Chinese character (e.g., 踏, *t'a*) existed and was available to the Japanese to represent the same meaning. Thus, on the analogy of the verb-stem-plus-inflection *name(te)* we would have expected here a Chinese character for the word "stamp" in the form of the verb-stem-plus-inflection *fu(masu)*. The fact that this logical step was not taken seems to indicate the still transitional nature of this particular stage of adaptation of the Chinese script to Japanese needs.

It is likely that whoever used this orthography—Ōtomo no Yakamochi was the final compiler of the *Man'yōshū*, but the poems in this first book were set down before his time—did not think of the inflectional ending (a causative as it is usually explained [(−mu>ma)+su]) as a quantity that, like *ramu*, could easily or logically be detached from the verb (it is properly analyzed morphologically as [(fum+a) + su]) and so could not write it, either because there was still an awareness that the verb-stem retained the consonant final that was unwritable in the syllabic transcription of Chinese or because it did not seem proper to render part of the very mood of the verb itself with meaningless syllables. The same logic also applies to the transcription in the *Kojiki* of the verb *tadayoeru*, more accurately rendered in the modern conventional transcription **tadayoFeru* to indicate the presence of the ancient consonant that is now lost. For whatever reason, but clearly at a loss as to how to treat the inflected part of the verb, he simply encoded the entire word into phonetic signs that he could be certain his literate readers would automatically decode as *fu-ma-su* (stamping). This may not seem a particularly brilliant solution to the problem; in fact, it strikes me as the cautious solution of a sensible bureaucrat less interested in innovative uses of orthography than in conveying with as little confusion as possible the meaning of the text.

An eventual "final" solution to these baffling sorts of problems would require another few centuries to perfect. The process was both slowed and hastened by the fact that just as the *Man'yōshū* was being set down in its final form by Yakamochi, a new and powerful wave of interest in Chinese was sweeping Japan that was to have the effect of leaving the literate male nobility with little but Chinese to write for a century. History, texts in Confucian philosophy and Buddhist religion, and all official documents at court were written in Chinese.

There was a natural tendency for this masculine bureaucratization of writing in Chinese, and of the consequent trend toward making the use of Chinese script an entirely masculine prerogative, to be paralleled by the development of some form of writing that could be used by women. A significant amount of writing was already a normal part of female life, and literate noblewomen, whose social privileges were often as substantial as those of their male counterparts, were hardly likely to accept a sexual valorization of writing that would result in the loss of a substantial, if not indispensible, cultural benefit. It is generally assumed that this crisis was the motivating factor in the eventual development of a phonetic syllabary derived from the complex *Man'yō* phonetic script adaptation whose proper Chinese forms were further abbreviated, written cursively, or most often both abbreviated *and* made cursive. The eventual result of this process was the *hiragana* or "easy phonetic" script, considered up to modern times especially suitable for use by women. Women seem to have had the last laugh, however, for with this marvelous invention and the judicious use of an occasional Chinese character for aesthetic balance (and women writers often knew Chinese better than men did) were written the early fictional masterpieces of Japanese literature. A man who wanted to write fiction would, for some time to come, have to assume the persona of a woman.

To this more or less standard account of the rise of the *kana* syllabary (which has its male counterpart in the development of *katakana* or "part phonetic" script, probably invented as envious males peeked over women's shoulders and saw them having a good time actually writing in *Japanese*), we might add another dimension of problematic observations. One of the main theoretical problems that can be seen in the Japanese attempt to adapt Chinese script to native uses lay, after all, not so much in trying to use Chinese characters for their phonetic values alone—we have seen that the Chinese had long before done this themselves in transliterating foreign proper nouns—as that the character did not in fact represent from the Chinese point of view what Barthes has called an "empty sign," a symbol devoid of any meaning other than to point to itself. To the contrary, these signs were *full* of meaning when they arrived in Japan as the medium for Confucian and Buddhist ideas that were entirely new in Japan; they were not simply an alphabet, whose sounds could easily be abstracted from the cultural complex they had once represented. Before these signs could be made to represent sound alone, they had first to be emptied of their alien significance by a mental act that attributed only a sound value to each sign and completely ignored its powerful semantic burden.

We have discovered of late that a society cannot easily will itself to forego what appear to be the benefits of a cultural advance, and what is true now of the secrets of the atom and the gene was likely true of the powerful secret of writing: for a Japanese literate in the semantic values of Chinese script, it was clearly impossible to consciously leave characters "empty" of meaning for long, nor could this have seemed a very useful procedure. When one knows what the characters mean, meaning arrives automatically to flood back into them. It may thus have been as much the stick of inevitable discomfort caused by the natural "interference" created by ostensibly empty signs as it was the carrot of the natural tendency to reduce complex characters used only for their sound values to simpler forms that eventually led to the development of the simplified *kana* syllabary. One could use these truly empty signs to write the sound *ka* without having to be reminded each time one did that the graph "meant" the lexical item "increase," for example, when in fact one only wanted it to "mean" the sound *ka* in the word *kami* (deity) or *kawaru* (change).

Thus by the time the *Kojiki* was compiled in the early eight century, and the

Man'yōshū in the mid-eighth century, we find that the Japanese were already making extremely sophisticated use of the Chinese writing system to record their own language. The complexity of this adaptation merely reflects that of the underlying problems. Having discovered the great economy of the semantic values of characters to represent the equivalent semantic values in Japanese, they progressed to using these characters to represent the uninflected root elements of inflected words, and were already beginning to find ways to regularize the ways that characters used only for their phonetic values could be affixed to these roots as the inflected parts of words or serve as particles to represent syntactic markers.

The twin aspects of literacy, reading and writing, involve a number of important ramifications that became significant well before A.D. 600. The clans whose hereditary occupation was the memorization and transmission of politically important material such as myth, legend, genealogies, laws, and so forth (*kataribe*, clan of reciters) would naturally have found their social position and political power challenged by any group that was able to control, or was even privy to, this powerful and convenient replacement for a good memory. It is perhaps in this revolutionary change that we can locate the Japanese notion of a "golden age" of strong memory, existing in a happy preliterate past, that had long ago given way to a "fallen" state of writing. The Japanese version of this nearly universal account of the origin of writing is attested in the opening words of the Heian text *Kogo Shūi* (*Gleanings of Ancient Language*, A.D. 808):

> In ancient times before there was writing, noble and base, young and old alike, transmitted information by word of mouth, and the events of antiquity were not forgotten. But after the development of writing, people came to dislike recounting the events of antiquity. Instead, they competed in using ornate language [i.e., writing in Chinese], and the events of antiquity came to be laughed at [as unsophisticated in their lack of such ornateness].[22]

Implicit in this revealing account is the idea that the use of "ornate" Chinese script was directly responsible for the loss of the much "simpler" ancient native material, an idea I shall treat more explicitly later in this chapter.

The issue that I have discussed so far of the very real differences in the linguistic structures, and so in the mentalities, of the two cultures is further complicated by this idea of a golden age that seems to be a standard part of every literate culture's account of the origins of its language. The idea of a golden age contrasts the present fallen state of man to a mythical, idealized past in which there was as yet no distinction between reality and the words that pointed to it,

---

[22] *Gunsho Ruijū* (1977), vol. 29, 359; cited in Kojima Noriyuki, "*Kojiki* no Bunshō," in Takeda, ed., *Kojiki Taisei*, vol. 3, 216.

between things and the names that stood for them. In this account, the advent of writing is held responsible not only for the destruction of memory, but for the malevolent destruction of "antiquity" itself.

Our own account of the destruction of this innocent age centers on the discovery by Adam and Eve of their "nakedness." In their previous state of innocence, the biblical account tells us, fact and word were as yet still unseparated; because the word "naked" did not exist neither did the fact. The awareness of the name of their previously innocent state followed only as the consequence of eating the forbidden fruit of the knowledge of good and evil. "Who told you that you were 'naked?'" asks God, and their rebellion is punished by expulsion forever from the paradise of unselfconscious reality that existed only prior to the intrusion of names. The word "naked," far from the creative informing Word that wrote the world, is the corrupting word of culture that at once separates man from nature and makes him painfully conscious of the separation, the price he must pay for consciousness.

Language and "reality" are almost universally held to exist in the privileged relationship of metaphor, and the two taken together are in literate cultures usually further placed in opposition to writing, which is just as universally considered to be a secondary cultural characteristic that merely points to the spoken word but lacks any direct relation to "reality." The myth of a golden age or ancient state of innocence was one of the major informing themes of the Romantic movement in Europe, which saw especially in the figure of the child the state of nature as yet uncorrupted by the evil that inevitably attended as the shadow cast by the light of knowledge. The plight of children made to perform adult labor in factories during the industrial age made childhood innocence an increasingly less likely construct, if an increasingly desirable one. The pervasive sway of this image was finally shattered by the publication of Freud's theories of infant sexuality that created in the minds of a scandalized bourgeoisie the image of the child as savage or monster that continues to replace the Romantic myth in our time.

This ontogenic myth of the innocent child, with its phylogenic parallel of a preliterate state of verbal innocence in culture, has come under the attack of such recent theorists as Derrida, who, in his examination of writing in *Of Grammatology* (1967), argues strenuously against the long-established view of writing as a mere "supplement" secondary to speech. Derrida fulminates not only against Rousseau, in whose *Essay on the Origin of Languages* he finds the classic paradigm of the idea of the primacy of speech over writing, but also against such modern structuralist theorists as Saussure, whom he finds guilty of "logocentrism," and Levi-Strauss, whom he holds guilty of behaving in "Orientalist" fashion (to use the word in the sense that Edward Said has) toward the subjects of his anthropological researches. In arguing against the notion of the primacy of speech and the posteriority of writing as a corruption of an earlier innocent state of metaphoric meaning, Derrida comments that the unexamined relationship between the two has gone on long enough. "Either writing was never a simple 'supplement,'" he remarks at the start of his essay, "or it is urgently necessary to construct a new logic of the 'supplement.'"[23] Derrida is concerned here with attacking the long-held Western belief in the privileged nature of speech over writing, the latter held to be secondary, and with a greatly expanded definition of "writing" as the medium of all semiotics in the science he calls "grammatology." While these are not my own concerns, or even our concern here, I have found his analysis of Rousseau helpful in dealing with the complex ideas involved in the notion of writing as a "fallen" language, and so of the primary role of language in the polarization of good and evil.

The familiar logocentrist position presumes the common-sense biological model of the child who learns to speak before he learns to write. "Grammatology" would oppose this model with the assumption that humans can be said to "write" (in a broader sense of the term by no means universally accepted as subsuming the usual narrower usage) independent of the act of speech itself. If we can accept the infant's incoherent babbling as the necessary precursor of speech, after all, then might we not also accept its apparently random arm-wavings as the necessary precursors of "writing" in their development of a potential for symbolic representation? Before a child can say "toe," it has performed countless complex visual/cerebral/manual operations upon that object that can be thought of as an early stage of the inseparable twin components of literacy, reading/writing. The act is as yet simply not polarized into these technically differentiated transitivities. An object acting upon the eye to produce recognition, cognition acting upon the hand to "produce" the object, are simultaneous aspects of the same act that contain the other. For the sake of getting on with everyday discussion, we accept the distinction and contrive to separate these transitivities into distinct acts; but cognition/recognition and reading/writing are in a more profound sense no more separable, or exist independently of each other, than breathing in and breathing out.

Derrida argues that the notion of the primacy of speech over writing is an equally fragile construct. The word and the written symbol are both present in one complex relation; the relationship between verbal utterance and written graph is by no means as simple as anterior and posterior, but is rather a dialectical process whose terms are constantly resumed in an ongoing synthesis. It seems as likely that primitive man's "earliest" communication of anything more complex than incoherent anger, joy, or frustration (the location of a food source, for example, what was there, how far) was in the form of a gesture or a figure of some sort scratched in the dirt as it is that it was some vocalization that the other understood to mean "food over there." The evolution of both verbal and graphic representation would appear to be predicated upon their complementarity. Modern linguistic theory understands their complex interrelation; even if we are unwilling to accept Derrida's radical theoretical insistence that writing subsumes language, any biological, social, or other theoretical model that advocates the genetic primacy of either still remains open to debate. From this point of view, the speech/writing complex in its largest sense is only an often useful construct that, like reading/writing, obscures in the technical polarization of its terms its essential unitary nature.

The record of an increasing consciousness of the technical differentiation of these mediums of representation, which we understand to be the awareness of culture as distinct from nature, is recapitulated in the myth of a golden age in which the latter was as yet "uncorrupted" by the former. The word "uncorrupted" is especially significant as it not only implies polarization and technical differentiation of modalities but further imputes moral qualities to them: the knowledge that results in self-consciousness bears inevitably within it the antitheses of good and evil, and this polarization then proceeds to valorize the entire cosmos. It is in this sense that Derrida refers to "the metaphor of divine or natural writing versus man's fallen, finite writing" (pp. 16–17). Stating that "writing has always been considered by Western tradition as the body and matter external to the spirit, to breath, to speech, and to the logos" (p. 35), Derrida cites among many historical examples the *Phaedrus*, which "denounced writing as the intrusion of an artful technique, a forced entry of a totally original sort, an archetypal violence: eruption of the *outside* within the *inside*, breaching into the interiority of the soul, the living self-presence of the soul within the true logos . . . " (p.34).

Having thus established the historical interpretation of a violent and unnatural usurpation of writing as the cultural equivalent of sexual rape, Derrida goes on to further attack the cynically prudish reaction to "this problem of the soul and body" in which the "original sin of writing" is considered a "clothing" of the nakedness of language. His attack has as its avowed goal the final liberation of the text from the tyranny of the logos, which indeed he holds, quixotically enough, to be the goal of all Western civilization. Much like Derrida, the eighteenth-century Japanese scholar Motoori Norinaga in his classic study of the *Kojiki* also saw the problem of "writing" as central to the problem of good and evil. In his opinion, however, the goal of Japanese civilization was, to the contrary, the final liberation of a pure native logos from the tyranny of corrupt alien text.

The introduction into Japan of the knowledge of the Chinese script created entirely new realities in the evolving consciousness that gradually grew out of the transition from orality to literacy. Because this change effectively took the privileged role of memory away from a class of oral reciters and established it instead as a more broadly enfranchised social benefit, these new realities could result in something as immediately compelling as the creation of new social and political alignments and rankings. Since the creation of texts provides the physical and metaphysical constituents of history, and the material basis for the creation and manipulation of a past and future, the memory involved in literacy is more broadly cultural than narrowly communal in scope. The past is no longer created by remembered or enacted vocalization alone, but by the presence of the object of the text itself, the fact and medium of whose transmission defines culture. Norinaga understood the existence of the *Kojiki*, together with the somewhat later *Man'yōshū*, as a long-lost key whose transmission served to connect his age with the Japanese myths of antiquity and so was central to any redefinition of the present.

The *Kojiki* is not the earliest Japanese text; it is merely the earliest *extant* text, which is perhaps the reason it is so strikingly self-conscious about its relationship both to language and to other texts. In his preface to the work its compiler, Ō no Yasumaro, wrote that Emperor Temmu (r. 673–686), dissatisfied at discrepancies and falsehoods in the existing chronicles, ordered him to set down a true account.[24] Clearly Yasumaro could not rely for his account on existing written records alone if these were considered to be suspect in some manner. But because Japan in the early eighth century was still in transition between orality and literacy, there was also another source Yasumaro could draw upon in creating his document: the oral accounts of the "reciters" (*kataribe*). The reciter in the case of the *Kojiki* was, according to Yasumaro's account, a twenty-eight-year-old man or woman named Hieda no Are.

The dual nature of Yasumaro's sources has several important implications for the *Kojiki*. Until this time the myths, legends, and geneologies of Japan were apparently set down in the entirely foreign medium of literary Chinese, a tradition that continued to be followed in official historiography for centuries to come. The cultural significance of text simply presumed the orthodoxy of its medium. Although we can be sure that this act had occurred countless times before, it is in the writing of the *Kojiki* that we get our first look at one significant locus of the transition from oral to written narrative.

The *Kojiki* is of particular interest not because it was written using Chinese script—all writing, after all, was in Chinese script—but because the Chinese characters are clearly intended for the first time to reproduce the Japanese language rather than the Chinese. That his text represents a conscious use of Japanese, and not merely the sloppy work of a half-educated scribe who had not learned his Chinese satisfactorily, is emphasized by the fact that Yasumaro

---

[24] *Kojiki, KNBT,* 1 : 45–46; Philippi, *Kojiki,* 5 and 41. On the role of Yasumaro in putting earlier oral accounts into writing in a conscious attempt to preserve their oral voice, see Kojima Noriyuki, *Jōdai Nihon Bungaku to Chūgoku Bungaku,* 3 vols. (Tokyo: Hanawa Shobō, 1962), vol. 1, 167ff.

deliberately chose to write his preface to the *Kojiki* in elegant literary Chinese, no doubt for much the same reason that Dante chose to write his *De Vulgari Eloquentia*, a defense of writing in the vernacular Italian, in elegant Latin. If one were going to violate prevailing orthodoxy, it was necessary first to establish one's credentials.

Yasumaro also frequently took pains to render the Japanese readings of certain Japanese words by the addition, albeit somewhat haphazard, of reading glosses in characters used for their phonetic values alone, in order to show exactly how problematic words were to be read. Thus the name of the deity Kuni-no-tokotachi-no-kami is written using characters that signify "deity of the eternally standing (*tokotachi*, 常立) land," and read using the native Japanese words for these semantic values. But the two characters used to represent "eternally standing" might be read in a number of ways in Japanese: *tsunetatsu*, for example, or if read for their phonetic values in Chinese alone, *jōritsu*. Yasumaro therefore provided a phonetic gloss immediately after the name that tells us that he intended these characters to be read as "*to-ko-ta-chi*" (登許多知).

This intentional use of Chinese script to represent Japanese in the *Kojiki* stands in sharp contrast to the elaborate Chinese employed in the closely contemporary *Nihon Shoki* (or *Nihongi*, Chronicles of Japan). Compiled in 720 for the purpose of representing Japan less to itself than to the outside world—that is, to China—as a legitimate and properly civilized country "of mild customs," the *Nihon Shoki* is written entirely in a Chinese script intended to be read *as* Chinese. It covers much of the same material as the *Kojiki*; but because it was written in the language insisted upon for official historiography, the *Nihon Shoki* was to become the first of the early official histories of Japan, the so-called *Rikkokushi* (Six Histories of Japan).[25] The *Kojiki*, on the other hand, with its self-consciously heterodox and innovative attempt to reproduce the living native language by means of a complex hybrid use of the Chinese script, lapsed because of this unorthodox use of script into centuries of relative obscurity. The ironic result is that this text, intended to preserve the ancient matter of Japan in the ancient language, became instead silent and unvoiceable: neither obviously Chinese nor Japanese, the *Kojiki* remained an uncomfortable puzzle to later centuries, an ancient text worthy of reverence that was at the same time paradoxically impossible to read aloud with any authority in the literal sense of the word. It was not until the painstaking work of the eighteenth-century nativist scholar Motoori Norinaga provided a complete and convincingly authoritative reading gloss buttressed by copious commentary that Japan's oldest text finally regained a voice lost for a thousand years.

---

[25] See G. W. Robinson, "Early Japanese Chronicles: The Six National Histories," in W. G. Beasley and E. G. Pulleyblank, eds., *Historians of China and Japan* (London: Oxford University Press, 1961), 213–28, esp. 223, on the implications of the use of Chinese by the Japanese.

In a famous passage in his Chinese preface, Yasumaro commented upon the particular dilemma of the language problem he faced in his attempt to use Chinese characters to write Japanese:

> In ancient times, both language and the reality it signified [*kokoro*, a word with several possible English equivalents] were unsophisticated [i.e., Japanese in contrast to Chinese], so that it is difficult to create sentences to express these matters in writing by the use of Chinese characters. If on the one hand I were to relate everything by using Chinese characters for their semantic values [i.e., to use Chinese *as* Chinese], then the words would not accord with the realities. But if, on the other hand, I were to use the characters for their phonetic values alone to piece together the sounds of Japanese, then my account would be much too long. For these reasons there are times when logographic and phonetic writing are mixed together in the same phrase, while at other times entire events are recorded logographically. When necessary I have used glosses to clarify the meanings of the words when they are difficult to understand; when the meaning is easily grasped, however, I have not provided glosses.[26]

Yasumaro thus faced at least two problems in his attempt to use Chinese script, both important reflections of the state of the adoption of the Chinese writing system in Japan in his time. To take his second point first, to sound out everything using Chinese characters phonetically was not only a waste of space and time; it was even more importantly a waste of the valuable semantic power of the characters to communicate meaning directly. In contrast to their ability to communicate meaning almost automatically, the use of characters as phonetic markers entailed, as an alphabet or syllabary does not, the additional step of decoding the signs of one language (already full of irrelevant meaning, as we have seen) to sound out the words of another—a laborious process, given that in the same time required to memorize the sound of a character one could memorize a semantic value as well. Of course the number of characters one needed to learn simply to reproduce a total of eighty-eight sounds was many times smaller than those necessary to write in acceptable literary Chinese, but scribes were at least ostensibly trained in literary Chinese, even if, as we have seen, their performance must often have fallen far short of perfection. In addition to the attractive semantic power of characters, anyone who has had to struggle with the erratic *Man'yōshū* phonetic transcriptions can certainly appreciate Yasumaro's concern for prolixity.

The other factor involved in Yasumaro's deliberations is that the ease of reading Chinese characters used *as* Chinese had to be balanced against the problem that to write in the language of another culture inevitably distorted the Japanese reality of what he was trying to relate. This problem, far more

[26] *Kojiki, NKBT,* 1:47–48.

important than mere considerations of economy of time or space, was probably shared to some degree by every medieval European writer constrained to use Latin in order to express his most intense inner feelings. The very nature of the foreign mentality inherent in the script itself—the words that reflected another, alien way of thinking—always stood in the way of what one was trying to say at the same time that it provided a means, indeed the only means, of saying it at all. This is precisely the dilemma that Norinaga discovered in Yasumaro's observation of the "unsophisticated" (sunao) nature of the material and language he was trying to relate:

> The myths of our land, transmitted [in the Kojiki] just as they were from the age of the gods, have never been subjected to [Chinese] sophistry, so that they appear on the surface as merely shallow and superficial. In fact, they are of a profundity that cannot be fathomed by such sophistry. The reason that we no longer understand their deepest purport is that very fence of Chinese that has been put up around them. So long as one never ventures beyond that fence, he can spend centuries and millennia in study and achieve nothing for his efforts.[27]

Norinaga went on to note the paradox that the Japanese had no choice but to use Chinese in order to write at all. He realized that as a cultural benefit, Chinese script represented something of great intrinsic power, the ability to communicate ideas, but also that it possessed an inherent evil in its potential to destroy what it was intended to preserve. The resolution to this dilemma was certainly not new to Norinaga, for his answer harkens back centuries, as we shall see in the course of this study. "Since in fact the ancient records are written in Chinese script, we must learn all we can about Chinese," Norinaga stated pragmatically. "But as long as we hold firmly to our national spirit [mikuni-damashii] and do not waver, it can do us no harm." [28] While Norinaga has come to be identified with this chauvinistic appeal to a "national spirit," it had a long history in the ongoing dialectic of the synthesis of Japan/China, or wakan, serving to identify that which can be ascribed to Japan—"spirit" or inner content—in contrast to that which is ascribed to China—external form, technique, learning.

This vision of the harmful effect of long centuries of interpreting Japanese thought through the distorting prism of Chinese is one of the most constant of Norinaga's themes. He lamented the "Chinese mentality" (karagokoro) that he felt had caused such Confucian scholars of his day as Itō Jinsai (1627–1705) and Ogyū Sorai (1666–1728) to misread their own history and literature. Norinaga railed against the "Chinese" readings of Japanese works that would reduce everything to a Confucian or Buddhist point of view and impose a gross foreign

---

[27] Ōno Susumu and Okubo Tadashi, eds., Motoori Norinaga Zenshū (hereafter cited as MNZ; Tokyo: Chikuma Shobō, 1968–1977), "Naobi no Mitama," vol. 9, 58.

[28] Ibid., 59.

model of understanding upon the most delicately Japanese ideas. His remark about *The Tale of Genji*, a work he saw as the perfect expression of what he termed *mono no aware*—that power inherent in things to make us respond not intellectually but with an involuntary gasp of emotion—is justly famous: "To see such a work, written to express *mono no aware*, as intended for Confucian moral instruction, is like chopping down a live cherry tree, whose very existence consists of its beautiful blossoms, in order to make firewood."[29]

One aspect of Norinaga's technique of "holding fast to his national spirit" can be seen in his own fluent and effective use of Chinese script while simultaneously insisting on glossing the characters in their purely Japanese readings. He assiduously avoided even long-accepted Sino-Japanese readings in favor of the purely Japanese, much as if we were to write today in a highly Latinate prose style but insist on giving each word an Anglo-Saxon reading. It sometimes seems that rather than writing in "Japanese," Motoori was in fact thinking in the language of his own day, which was inextricably linked to the use of Chinese characters and ideas, then consciously attributing to the Sinate elements what he thought after careful study of the ancient texts to have been their "original" Japanese readings. This seems less a question of reviving a forgotten native lexicon than of inventing a language that had never existed, somewhat as if we were to write the word "telephone" and, on the model of German, decide to read it with the Anglo-Saxon pronunciation of "farspeaker."[30] To be sure, the Japanese language of his day already made extensive use of Chinese characters, pronounced entirely in Japanese, that made no sense at all if read as Chinese;[31] but a reading like *kotokunifumi* for "foreign writing," for example, instead of the usual *gaikokubun*, while possible, is not actually attested in the spoken language of any period. Even though Norinaga seems often to have employed this sort of process of "reverse Japanization" in giving the *Kojiki* back what he considered its "original" voice, it is likely that the readings he provided

---

[29] "Genji Monogatari Tama no Ogushi," *MNZ*, vol. 4, 225.

[30] The Second World War confronted the Japanese with some of the same problems of language faced by Norinaga. In the early 1900s an enormous number of Western-language words, mainly English but also French and German, had been rapidly absorbed into the modern lexicon, much as Chinese had been during the preceding fifteen centuries. Now that many of these words were identified with the enemy, however, they came under formal or informal proscription, and substitutes were sought using Chinese or Chinese-based neologisms created by the Japanese. Some of these stuck. Thus, while the lexicon of the Japanese national pastime is full of terms like *pitchā*, *katchā*, *sutoraiki*, and *bōru*, the game itself is called *yakyū* (field-ball), and not the expected *bēsubōru*. The Chinese-based neologism for "elevator," on the other hand (*shōkōki*, ascend–descend machine), may never have attained much currency, even during the war. One still rides in an *erēbetā*, for all that the sign indicting its presence in many old buildings still reads *shōkōki*, a word that has gone entirely out of use.

[31] For examples of this use of Chinese in Norinaga's day, see David Pollack, "Kyōshi: Japanese 'Wild Poetry,'" *Journal of Asian Studies* 38:3 (May 1979), 506.

were more often than not much as Yasumaro had intended, since Norinaga for the most part adhered scrupulously to the original text and glosses to produce a consistent if archaic language. It is this technique, then, that served as the practical method by which Norinaga held fast to his "national spirit," enabling him to transcend the confines of that "Chinese fence."

Norinaga's faith in the integrity of the text and its ability to be read, once given a voice, was predicated on his faith in the existence within the imprisoning fence of written text of the authentic native voice of Hieda no Are:

> Though we have other written texts, the ancient spoken language of Japan would have been entirely lost to us today if it were not for this one document that still retains it. Having committed to memory what was based on records written in Chinese, Hieda no Are translated this information back into the ancient language for the *Kojiki*. If he had not done so, the text could never have been read aloud and, transferred only from writing to writing, could never have escaped its Chinese confines.[32]

Norinaga felt that the necessity of inventing some of his "ancient" readings was justified on the grounds that there would inevitably remain unbridgeable gaps in the text that could never be restored to their "original" voice. These places in the text he preferred to patch over with a reinvented ancient language rather than leave silent:

> There is in the *Kojiki* ancient language that, no matter how hard we may puzzle over it, cannot be restored to its ancient readings. The original ancient language has been passed down to us, but in the form of Chinese script. Therefore, though [theoretically] there should be no difficulty in restoring the language, having once been put into Chinese, the original reading was cut off from us and was not in fact passed down.[33]

To Yasumaro, according to Norinaga more than a thousand years later, the lack of "sophistication" of ancient Japanese was amply evident in its lexicon, its artless manner of expression, and in the simple and straightforward nature of its ancient myths. What Norinaga called "Chinese mentality" (*karagokoro*) was on the contrary equally evident to him in two complementary aspects of the Chinese language (*karakotoba*).[34] These are both aspects of the powerfully dense "gravity" of Chinese as an ancient language that I have already mentioned (we are talking about the literary language, or language as expressed in script, since it is meaningless to speculate about the relative antiquity of spoken languages).

The first of these aspects is that classical literary Chinese regularly makes use

[32] *MNZ*, 9:31.
[33] *Ibid.*
[34] *Ibid.*, 32–33.

of an often astounding variety of characters to represent the same meaning, apparently on the principle that repetition of the same character is not only aesthetically displeasing but demonstrates an equally unaesthetic lack of erudition (and we should note that in any literary language the demonstration of learning is clearly an aesthetic ideal in itself). The lexicon of classical Japanese, by contrast, is extraordinarily simple, the same word frequently used in different contexts to mean several different things. Literary Chinese is also an elaborately antithetical language, a fact that seems related to the desirability of using a variety of characters with the same meaning, and in this respect too is quite the opposite of literary Japanese, which shuns the symmetrical orderliness of classical Chinese in favor of a deliberate asymmetry. Again, where Chinese tends to make everything explicit Japanese most often leaves much unsaid or ambiguous, so that while in Chinese prose we always know who is talking to whom, for example, in Japanese we often do not even know whether someone is talking or thinking or whether that thought or speech is being presented in the voice of a character or the author. These aspects of Chinese lexicon and style Norinaga called "Chinese ornateness" (*kara no kazarifumi*), by which he meant elaborate style to no purpose, ornate language used for its own sake, unshaped by any compelling and informing content. This aspect of the Chinese language Norinaga felt had completely obliterated the fragile beauty of the ancient Japanese.

Interestingly, this view of the intrinsic inferiority of elaborate language was shared by Norinaga's European close contemporary, Jean-Jacques Rousseau (1712–1778), who concerned himself in his *Essay on the Origin of Languages* (as the opening of its chapter "On Script" is quoted by Derrida) with the natural development of a literary language over time as it moved away from its source in the vernacular:

> Anyone who studies the history and progress of the tongues will see that the more the words become monotonous, the more the consonants multiply; that, as accents fall into disuse and quantities are neutralized, they are replaced by grammatical combinations and new articulations. But only the pressure of time brings these changes about. To the degree that needs multiply, that affairs become complicated, that light is shed, language changes its character. It becomes more regular and less passionate. It substitutes ideas for feelings. It no longer speaks to the heart but to reason.... Language becomes more exact and clearer, but more prolix, duller and colder. This progression seems to me entirely natural. Another way of comparing languages and determining their relative antiquity is to consider their script, and reason inversely from the degree of perfection of this art. The cruder the writing, the more ancient the language.[35]

---

[35] *Of Grammatology*, 270–71.

Norinaga would not have agreed more, finding as he did in Japanese the simplicity of an ancient tongue, and in the "ornateness" of the classical Chinese
language evidence of that monotonous prolixity, dullness, and coldness of its
own natural genius: a language that no longer spoke to the heart but only to
reason.

Norinaga also located another aspect of "Chinese mentality" in what he called
"Chinese logic" (*kara no kotowari*), by which he meant especially the tendentious nature of Confucian and Buddhist thought that must always interpret the
world in terms of the morality of human relationships on the one hand, or the
working out of karmic destiny on the other. Viewed through the prism of
Chinese thought, with its compelling need to find this sort of philosophical or
religious moral instruction the ultimate purpose of writing, all that was beautiful in Japanese thought was reduced to the uninteresting and meaningless level
of the Confucianist creed adopted as the official political and social philosophical basis of the Tokugawa rule, which amounted to nothing more interesting than "rewarding good and punishing evil" (*kanzen chōaku*). We have
already seen in his figure of the cherry tree reduced to kindling what he thought
of applying this philosophy, based on an alien aesthetic grounded in the
"beauty" of proper human relationships, to the native literature whose more
fragile aesthetic beauty was so easily crushed beneath the weight of this entirely
unsuitable foreign burden.

Norinaga's objections to "Chinese ornateness" and "Chinese logic" places
the notion of the "corruption" of language squarely on the disjunction created
by "otherness." Chinese was ornate because it was a system of signifiers entirely
detached from what they signified. The very compulsion of literary Chinese to
rigid parallelism, antithesis, rhyme, and orderly cataloging demonstrated clearly to him, by this all-absorbing manipulation of the superficial symbols of
language themselves, that there was no longer a link to any vital and informing
root of meaning.[36] Unlike the Japanese beauty of blossoms that bloomed and
died in unpremeditated simplicity, Chinese writing showed clear evidence of
having been uprooted and arranged into the highly ordered and unnatural
ornamentality of a formal arrangement of dead blooms. Indeed, as Norinaga
knew, one of the most common metaphors in traditional Chinese writing
about literature was the floral: writing was "flowers," "petals," "blossoms,"
"blooms," "buds," and the books that contained them were entitled with an
equal number of untranslatable words for "garden." Despite their great formal
impressiveness, these were still flowers removed from their roots and nourish-
ing soil. Their beauty grew out of a logic of formal display whose codes had

[36] Compare Yu-Kuang Chu's comment that "the ancient Chinese did not investigate the
substratum of things, but were only interested in signs and their relations" ("The Chinese
Language," 602).

nothing to do with the life of the flower itself, and everything to do with the mentality implied by the vase.

To this metaphor it might be objected that the Japanese themselves are known for having raised flower-arranging to the level of high art. But from a different point of view, the Japanese art of *ikebana* can be seen as an example of the complex wakan dialectic. *Ikebana* is usually written with the characters for "living flowers," and the Japanese word for what is done to the flowers is *ikasu*, "bringing to life," in significant contrast to our "arranging." This is done by abstracting the flowers from their natural context and rearranging them according to rules of formal representation by a higher code that is itself abstracted from nature. The paradox of the apparent "un-Japaneseness" of this most Japanese of arts can be reconciled if we see in it a philosophical and visual analogue of the relationship between Chinese and Japanese, the wakan dialectic in which the "dead flowers" of visible external form (Chinese words) are abstracted and rearranged in order to give expression to a core of ineffable Japanese meaning. The art of *ikebana* thus becomes representative of an essential Japaneseness that has attained a higher, more complex and subtle nature by the operation of this dialectic than was possible in the simpler and earlier act of merely looking at cherry blossoms. This dialectical operation of "Japanese meaning" and "Chinese form" is a true dialectic, the synthesis of opposites into a new and different state, for it operates simultaneously in both directions. What was all ineffable Japanese signification has been enhanced by formal expression, while what was all empty form has been infused with new life (*ikasu*, brought to life) by that essential meaning. We can thus see in *ikebana* merely one of the myriad crystallizations of the wakan dialectic that is so powerfully embedded within the entire Japanese system of signification.

While Norinaga's twin objections to "Chinese mentality" can scarcely be separated since they contain each other—the "logic" of language influencing its "forms" and vice versa—the objection to "ornateness" seems perhaps the more elemental and damaging within the context of his thought. He saw the ancient Japanese language as growing directly and artlessly out of the compelling reality that informed it, while the very detachment of the Chinese language from its signification demonstrated that it did not. Norinaga identified a unitary complex consisting of *kokoro* (mentality, meaning, signification) and its punning twin affective aspects of *koto* (word) and *koto* (event, thing).[37] He saw not only Japanese but every language as growing out of these same elements, so that the Chinese language was as inseparable from its own "mentality" as Japanese was from its. For this reason, the use of Chinese to describe Japanese reality could never attain to the ontological status of Japanese used for the same purpose, but would always remain at best phenomenological. The *Kojiki* might

---

[37] *MNZ*, 9:6.

seem the sole exception, but Norinaga realized that it was not an exception at all. It had in fact uniquely transcended the problem, its alien script informed directly by the ancient spoken words (koto), and so even in alien guise it could not help but communicate ancient reality (koto). From his point of view, words did not simply "point to" a separate reality but were themselves that reality. Because there was no separation between the words (koto) and the things (koto) they named, to utter the word was to give rise to the reality itself.[38]

This magical power inherent in words to bring forth the very reality that informed them defines the ancient Japanese belief in kotodama, the "power of words." Chinese words might very well bring forth Chinese realities; Norinaga even says as much, although he does not seem to have believed it very strongly. The Kojiki, however, despite its outward Chinese garb, could be made once again to yield its signification directly through the power of kotodama once its original Japanese voice had been restored. This disjunction between the magical power of the spoken word and the alienness of its written form implies that before it can create its reality the theological power of the spoken word as incantation had first of all to be radicalized from its written signifier. Norinaga thus understood that as a precondition of restoring the power of kotodama, logos had to be liberated from text.

The act of reading/writing, rather than merely implying a distinction between name and reality, was therefore at once both congenial and profoundly hostile. In the garden of Eden the existence of the word "naked" itself implied knowledge of good and evil, the polarization that separated men from paradise and would continue to valorize every act of culture, but in Japanese myth the simple facts of human nakedness and sexuality demonstrate no such separation. The problem of good and evil was instead originally implicit in this draping of pristine primitive meaning in the otherness of alien writing. To Norinaga therefore, writing was not merely a "supplement" to logos that, like Rousseau, one might feel a "natural" progression in time. It was at once as necessary and as indicative of shame as the fig leaf, concealing the nakedness of the primitive state at the same time that it so obviously pointed to it and so to the separation of its possessor from that desirable state, the "age of the gods" (kamiyo) that Norinaga wrote of with such passion.

This phenomenon is as potent a figure for Japanese culture as the Fortunate

---

[38] See Miller, "The 'Spirit' of the Japanese Language." Miller's article is based largely on a study by Itō Haku, "Man'yōjin to Kotodama," in Hisamatsu Sen'ichi, ed., Man'yōshū Kōza, vol. 3, Gengo to Hyōgen (Tokyo: Yūseidō, 1973), 46–63. ". . . it was chiefly the direct face-to-face confrontations with the Chinese language that were entailed in the official missions to T'ang China that had the principal effect of reviving the by then almost forgotten cult of the kotodama in the Old Japanese period," writes Miller (284), stressing that it was precisely this defilement of contact with alienness that required the ritual cleansing of kotodama. The idea is thus seen to have existed a millennium before Norinaga revived it.

Fall is for ours. In one sense, the shame that is concealed by the figurative leaf in any culture might be thought to have its origin in the truly revolutionary catastrophe of contact with an alien cultural superiority that makes the less advanced realize for the first time the fact of its inferiority in the face of the "other," the "nakedness" of its former state of blissful unawareness, and the consequent shame that makes concealment both an evil and a necessity.

Norinaga explored the mythic dimension of the primary problem of good and evil in his essay *Naobi no Mitama* (The Power of Rectification), first published in 1771 and subsequently included as part of the introductory essay to his *Kojiki Den*. In this essay he located the source of all evil in the story of the ritual pollution created by the deity Magatsubi-no-kami, whose violent behavior he considered responsible for the perversion of "Chinese mentality" that had run riot through Japanese history violating the true Japanese spirit.[39]

Magatsubi-no-kami appears first in the *Kojiki* as one of two deities who were created from the pollution incurred by the god Izanagi when, searching for his dead wife Izanami, he visited the unclean land of the dead, the underworld called Yomi (the word is written with the Chinese characters for the underworld that mean literally "Yellow Springs"). After his return, Izanagi purified himself by bathing in a river, and as the pollution that he had incurred was removed it took form in a series of deities, the first two of whom were Yaso-magatsubi-no-kami and Ō-magatsubi-no-kami, both of which mean "abundant misfortune–working force." "In order to rectify [*naosu*] these evils" [*maga*, literally "straighten that which was bent"], the *Kojiki* continues, there came into existence the deity Kamu-naobi-no-kami," or "divine rectifying deity," the first of three purifying powers.

Norinaga entitled this important essay, which deals with the meaning of the *Kojiki,* after the sacred power (*mitama*) of the deity Naobi to purify ritual defilement. Most significant for Norinaga, this meant the defilement incurred by contact with China, a place he effectively equated with the land of the dead both by its Chinese name and by its inevitable defilement of whatever was quintessentially Japanese:

> If despite all this [defilement by contact with Chinese] one has the desire to seek the Way of the Gods, he first must cleanse away the impurity of defilement of contact with the Chinese mentality by means of ritual purification. Holding to the pure spirit of our land, he must study the ancient documents [i.e., the *Kojiki*]. As he does this, he cannot but naturally come to know the Way that he is to follow, which is none other than the Way of the Gods. [The Confucian philosophy of our time] that is bandied about has nothing to do with the true Way of the Gods. One must not merely look upon this result of the violent behavior of the deity Magatsubi-no-

[39] *MNZ*, 9:58.

kami without doing anything about it, but make use of the powers conferred by
Naobi-no-kami to set this defilement to rights again.[40]

Norinaga's ultimate aim in this essay was political, and he developed it most
fully in tracing the problem of anarchy within the body politic to a specific
source of "pollution" in the Chinese concept of the Mandate of Heaven
(t'ien-ming).[41] To Norinaga, this fundamental and ancient concept of Chinese
political philosophy was merely an expedient justification for the continual
violent usurpation of power, the Chinese viewing the decline of power as a sign
that its holder was no longer worthy of the "mandate," which would then pass
to its legitimate successor—in actual practice to whomever managed to wrest it
away. Such a philosophy of legitimized anarchy could arise, he said, because the
Chinese, unlike the Japanese, were not in a direct genealogical line of descent
from native deities. The result of this was that history for the Chinese meant
whatever rationalizations mere men were able to impose upon their own brutal
and insensate actions, whether those be Confucian notions of "morality" or
Buddhist ideas of "karma." For Japan, by contrast, history meant the unfolding
story of the deeds of its native gods; thus the roots of Japanese political life lay in
a history that was defined as the will of the gods as evidenced in Japan's earliest
myths.

Norinaga's interpretation of this particular myth thus specifically equated all
Chineseness with ritual pollution that must be purified from Japan. In practice,
as I have shown, he purified the pollution incurred through the use of Chinese
script by applying native readings alone to give voice to the inevitable (and,
we must note, skillfully used) Chinese characters. One could not be defiled
by such contact if he thus "held steadfastly to the national spirit and did not
waver."[42]

The familiar notion of the inseparable good and evil inherent in civilization
that was brought from gods to man in the form of Promethean fire appears as
well in the Kojiki in the form of two kinds of fire, distinguished as the ritually
pure fire of the gods in contrast to the ritually unclean fire of the underworld.
The ritually unclean fire figures in the story of Izanagi's descent into the
underworld in search of his dead wife, Izanami. When he finds her and asks that
she accompany him back to finish their task of creating the world, she replies
that she cannot because she has already eaten food cooked in the unclean fires of
Yomi. This theme, familiar to us from the Greek Persephone story, is of course

[40] Ibid., 62.
[41] For a discussion of the political implications of this essay, published in the year that saw the
largest number of peasant uprisings against the government in an era especially noted for them, see
Shigeru Matsumoto, Motoori Norinaga (Cambridge: Harvard University Press, 1970), 96ff. and
118ff.
[42] MNZ, 9:59.

common throughout world mythology.[43] Norinaga further specifically attributed the evils caused by Magatsubi-no-kami to this use of unclean fire for ritual purposes, so that the light of civilization became corrupted by an evil contamination from an alien source, which is to say from China. "That the fires of our shrines should be even slightly defiled," wrote Norinaga, "is an unacceptable situation that has come about as a result of the spread of that insidious Chinese mentality."[44] By his solution to the problem of defilement, Norinaga was not only "freeing logos from text"; he was pragmatically using the inherent power of Japanese word—the *kotodama*—to neutralize the evil that was an intrinsic and unavoidable part of the text.

Norinaga's attempt to redefine what was truly Japanese in terms of its ancient relationship to what was not, and so was Chinese, can finally be understood as an inevitable reexamination of the very terms of the dialectic that operated to synthesize these opposing terms.[45] By 1800, it was all too clear that those terms could not remain the same much longer. In turning from the familiar problems created by contact with Chinese culture to the new problems that contact with the West was bringing, the Japanese of the nineteenth century were able to see with increasing urgency the terrible price that failure to effect a new synthesis would exact from them. They had before their eyes a final model of China to learn from: an exhausted civilization, unable to find within itself the terms of synthesis with the West, and hemorrhaging its life's blood through opium and the gaping wounds of the foreign concessions. Norinaga's work was a reaffirmation of a Japan that had succeeded in turning an alien mode of expression to meet its own needs without forfeiting its own integrity in the process. Through his recreation of the *Kojiki*, Japan had once again regained life–giving contact with its ancient myths, as it had rediscovered in his vision of *The Tale of Genji* its own ancient native sense of beauty. He achieved a fresh definition of the "Japanese spirit" that, freed from fatally debilitating defilement, would be able once again to meet the challenge of superior foreign technology and achieve yet a new synthesis. And there can be no question that Japan's history of success in adapting Western technical knowledge to its own ends has been as marked as its earlier success in turning the almost impossibly unsuitable Chinese script into a tool that both shaped and was shaped by its culture.

Synthesis comes to an end only when antithesis ceases to appear. For many

---

[43] *Kojiki, NKBT,* 1:64; Philippi, *Kojiki,* 61 and additional note 7, 401.

[44] *MNZ,* 9:62.

[45] Harry Harootunian has argued that "the loss of China's centrality in Japanese discourse prepared the Japanese intellectuals to cope with the urgent problems brought about by contact with the West" ("The Functions of China in Tokugawa Thought," 4), although I must disagree with his statement that "in moral terms outer behavior always took precedence over inner impulse" (11). This subject is further explored in chapter seven.

centuries Japan found its most significant antithesis in China. During the last century and a half the West has been the antithetical term in the dialectic, and as always it has been in that "other" that Japan has sought its own image, peering anxiously for signs of its own identity into the mirror of the rest of the world. After the challenge of Western technology has been successfully met, one wonders what will be left that is "alien," besides the very fact that the historically necessary "other" is lacking. In that case, "Japanese spirit" (*Yamato-damashii*) will find itself face to face with the most frightening "other" of all—its lack—at which point opposition must cease or else feed upon itself.

The fundamental paradigm that for centuries would govern Japan's adaptation of Chinese (and perhaps Western) culture is to be found in the complex adoption and final acceptance of, and a profound alienation from, outward alien form as necessary for the expression of otherwise ineffable Japanese meaning. This was not simply a problem created by Norinaga merely out of hostility to an opposing school of philosophy, as some have seen it. That the problem had existed at least as long as eight centuries before is implicit in the term *Yamato-damashii* that first appears in *The Tale of Genji*, as we shall see in the following chapter. Given the earliest appearance of this radical disjunction of meaning in the Japanese adaptation of Chinese script, it seems likely that the distinction had existed as a cultural problem long before Murasaki Shikibu used these terms in *Genji*. Indeed, Yasumaro's own misgivings in his preface to the *Kojiki* at having to record the myths of Japan (the very soul of his people), in a script whose very words and logic were bound to misrepresent what he felt to be the "true" meaning of the Japanese, is only the earliest *extant* expression of the problem in literary records. It is probable that the scribe responsible for engraving the epigraph of 607 on the aureole of the Yakushi Buddha at Hōryūji in Nara felt something of the same dissonance between what he was trying to say and the means he had to say it—although his would have been a slightly different problem, since the inscription, which reveals an intention to write in Japanese, records the devout hope of Emperor Yōmei that by building Hōryūji Temple and this statue of a powerful Buddhist healing deity he might be cured of his illness. One can only wonder what this new foreign god would have made of being addressed in the heart–felt but, for ritual purposes, rather suspect language of his equally new foreign devotees.

The elemental fracture that thus traverses the entire semiotic field of Japan has persisted through the centuries and spread myriad smaller fissures through the entire cultural continuum, as we have seen in the case of *ikebana*, "flower-arranging." There is little reason to believe that its power is exhausted even today. Once writing was established in Japan it had the immediate effect of creating a new dimensionality, as it does in any culture, for speech unfolds in time, while writing unfolds in space. Because the writing was Chinese, its spatial orientation on a page was vertical, a simple fact that coincides with what has emerged in modern Japan over centuries as the pervasive principle of verticality governing Japanese social relationships.[46] In modern times, the problem of increasingly frequent relations with Westerners has imposed upon the Japanese increasingly close contact with societies whose social relationships and writing are both markedly horizontal. This coincidence of spatial orientations has resulted in a "new" term for Western writing: *yokomoji*, "horizontal writing," in contrast to the Japanese *tatemoji*, "vertical writing." This same principle of dimensional disjunction has naturally been extended to social intercourse with Westerners, so that a Western meal has become *yokomeshi*, "horizontal eating." The term implies that the speaker is under the strain of severe cultural dislocation, a strain that can only be put to rights again by a return to *tatemeshi*, "vertical eating," in the congenial context of home or the company of close colleagues. What was Chinese thus appears only as an entirely integrated element within the Japanese term that is set in opposition to the Western, for nothing is felt to be especially "Chinese" about vertical script today. We might even go further to note that even characters themselves have begun to lose their Chineseness to some extent, as evidenced by the frequent modern use of Chinese characters carefully glossed by their authors with English pronunciations; although they carry their visual semantic burden with them, there are Japanese words that are no longer pronounceable in Japanese. It is interesting to hypothesize that this is one possible direction in which the dialectic might lead in the course of synthesizing modern Japanese and English, together with the ongoing creation of new "Japanese" words from English and other Western languages.

[46] Cf. Chie Nakane, *Japanese Society* (originally *Tate Shakai no Ningen Kankei*, 1967; Berkeley: University of California Press, 1970). The words *tate*, "vertical," and *yoko*, "horizontal," contain some of the same moral implications associated with our "dextrous" (Lat. "right-handed") and "sinister" (Lat. "left-handed"). Matsumoto locates the origins of the all-important verticality of the "parent-child" (*oya-ko*) relationship in Japan in the Japanese insistence that each individual Japanese is vertically descended directly from the goddess Amaterasu (*Motoori*, 115–16, 178ff.). Verticality is implied in the fact that the deities (*kami*) exist "on high" (*kami*), in contrast to men (*shimojimo*) who dwell "below" (*shimo*).

The Informing Image:
"China" in *The Tale of Genji*

"China must be very interesting."
"Very big, China."
"And Japan—"
"Very small."
(Noel Coward, *Private Lives*)

It is difficult to conceive of Japan apart from China; and yet, China seems strangely redundant when we think of Japan. To say that something Japanese was "originally Chinese" is at once to state the obvious and to explain nothing. Noel Coward's tongue-in-cheek send-up of how the British view the Far East seems to epitomize nicely this paradox in the relationship between the two countries. We think of them as a cultural and geographical unit, the Great Tradition and its smaller cultural dependent, of tiny Japan lying fragilely just at the edge of the massive sphere of Chinese cultural influence—just as the Chinese thought of Japan, when they thought of her at all.

And yet, merely having said that China is "very big" seems to exhaust that subject for Coward's characters, who proceed to further explore the fascination of Japan's tininess: one eats raw fish, with chopsticks, with one's shoes off. And this, too, is a perception of Japan from the Sinocentric point of view inherited by Europe—a nation of people who seem not to do things quite right, who always failed to learn their Chinese lessons thoroughly enough. By the Heian period of the late tenth and early eleventh centuries, the *Genji* period, the Japanese had already been long in the habit of regarding China as a civilization of superior resources. The "real" China's occasional inevitable lapses from that superiority were viewed by the Japanese with the same sort of impatient chagrin, nostalgic regret, and finally disappointed truculence that has been reserved in recent years for an equally distressing America. The Tendai monk Ennin, as one example, was appalled as he witnessed the terrible suffering and destruction wreaked by the Chinese government's suppression of Buddhism after 845. As a foreigner traveling in China to gain first-hand knowledge of his religion's origins, texts, and practices, there is an extra edge of horror and disappointment to his reports, so objective in tone, which represent the best first-hand accounts of damage done to the Buddhist establishment in China during the course of the suppression of the Hui-ch'ang era.[1]

When political conditions in China continued to deteriorate, the Japanese court pragmatically decided to cancel an anticipated mission to what remained of the crumbling T'ang polity in 894. This event marked the end of official embassies that had begun in the Nara period, and brought to a close the long era of cultural borrowing from China; at the same time, it signaled the rise of a new era of "Japaneseness." In terms of the symbolism involved, it seems no mere coincidence that the person who petitioned the throne to have the mission canceled was Sugawara no Michizane (805–903), who was to have been Ambassador and was one of the most famous experts of Chinese literature in his time. His own subsequent fall at court and exile to Kyushu in 901 seem to represent symbolically the continuation of this purging of China from Japan, a part of the casting out of China from the new world of the Fujiwara Regents.

For their part, the Chinese were often gratified to know that these "dwarf" barbarians (as their name appears in the dynastic histories) were learning to ape civilized ways, but were not always delighted with what the Japanese were making of prized Chinese treasures. The T'ang poet Po Chü-i, whom the Heian courtiers regarded as the continental mentor of Michizane, had written in a preface to his collected works dated 845 that, aside from the three authorized editions of those works that he was depositing for safekeeping in separate temples (that year saw the start of the Hui-ch'ang suppression of Buddhism—a particularly bad time for keeping things safe in temples) and two others in the hands of relatives, later generations were to ignore especially those editions circulating among the populaces of Japan and Silla. Po was concerned about reports of spurious editions of his works that had made him famous in Japan in his own lifetime.[2] He had already been mortified to discover, as he remarked in a letter to his friend Yüan Chen, that even in China it was the very poems that he considered the most frivolous that were "on the lips of monks, courtesans and unmarried women," rather than the highly moral New Folk-Song Style Poems for which he hoped to be remembered.[3] We can only imagine what he would have thought were he to have learned that the Japanese were paring away from his collected poetry anything that did not adhere to an uncomplicated Six Dynasties and early T'ang taste for courtly elegance, leaving only choice couplets that were clearly lyrical and not particularly edifying. When faced with a choice between the "beautiful" and the "instructive," the Japanese were never to be much impressed by the Chinese insistence that a tone of high moral

[1] See Edwin O. Reischauer, trans., *Ennin's Diary: The Record of a Pilgrimage in Search of the Law* (New York: Ronald Press, 1955), 321ff.

[2] *Po Hsiang-shan Shih-chi* (Collected Poetry of Po Chü-i) (Taiwan; Shih-chieh Shu-chü, 1969), 4.

[3] "Letter to Yüan Nine," included in the *T'ang Shu* biography of Po; *ibid.*, 43. See Eugene Feifel, "The Biography of Po Chü-i," *Monumenta Serica* 17 (1958), 276ff.

seriousness always be the concomitant of lyrical attractiveness. Along with everything else they borrowed from China, they knew exactly what they wanted from Po's poems. Chinese of later centuries would find quite odd the persistent Japanese infatuation for Sung dynasty ceramics over the glossier and more colorful Ming wares, or their preference for the blurred and impressionistic landscapes of Yü Chien and the art of Mu Ch'i, all of whose extant works are remembered in Japanese rather than Chinese records.

To a certain degree, even today we have come to accept the view from the continent that these preferences represent "aberrations" of taste. They do not, of course; it is simply that Japanese perceptions of China were rarely those held by the Chinese themselves. Japanese views began in an entirely native perspective that ranged out selectively over materials within its purview, taking note only of things that resonated with some native aesthetic chord. It is clear that, no less than in the last century, Japan was never dictated to in its tastes, at least not for very long. It is one of the goals of the present study to show that, to the contrary, the Japanese genius for enthusiastically shaping often puzzlingly disparate bits and pieces of imported "superior" cultures to its own ineluctable ends is clearly demonstrated in the uses the Japanese made of Chinese culture throughout premodern history.

It would be wrong, therefore, for us to continue to inquire about "the influences Chinese culture exerted upon the Japanese." Even under the kindest construction, this is still an attitude inherited in part from the Sinocentric sympathies of earlier Western scholarship. We need to inquire instead about those elements that Japanese selected for abstraction from the broad continuum of Chinese civilization available to them at particular historical moments. From this revised point of view, we must pay closer attention to the processes at work in selecting foreign cultural elements and synthesizing them into the native culture. For the purposes of this sort of analysis we must also understand that what we can perceive as a "native" process is itself, in any period from which historical materials exist, already the product of countless earlier syntheses. We are concerned here, in other words, with the dialectic at work in adoption, adaptation, and synthesis, rather than with any particular set of materials— although to illustrate this process at work we shall examine the way particular Chinese materials have been treated in Japan, in this chapter those in *The Tale of Genji*. And even that dialectic must be regarded as part of a continuum that comprises every particular attempt at synthesis, each influenced by earlier and contemporary attempts, and each in turn influencing contemporary and later experiences.

China as a geographical entity was, of course, quite accessible to the Japanese during portions of the Heian period. Since we are concerned with the China that existed in the imaginations of Heian writers, however, what we would normally think of as the the "real" geopolitical entity will concern us very little, except insofar as it corresponds to a need to identify something outside Japan itself, something alien or "other," clearly not Japanese, and while inherently worthy of emulation at the same time threatening, not merely to physical but to cultural identity. Throughout the period with which we are concerned the "dragons" that lurked about the edges of the Japanese mental map of the world were very like those somewhat later and quite "Chinese" dragons that circle the ceilings of the meditation halls of Zen temples like Shōkokuji and Myōshinji in Kyoto, those symbols of the completely awakened mind that define by their alien presence as much what is not Japanese as what is "Chinese." Foreign *meant* Chinese—or Korean, which is very much the same thing—and the terms "Kara," "Morokoshi," and "Koma" seem to have conjured up for the Heian Japanese something of what names such as Xanadu and Cambaluc did for Romantic England, but even more intensely, at once intriguingly exotic and fearsomely different.

It was during the Heian that the dialectic known as wakan (Chinese/Japanese) is first recorded. Indicating the process whereby contemporary Chinese and Japanese elements were brought into accommodation, the term tells us nothing about that process, except that it involved placing elements of both cultures into some sort of relationship to one another, often as crudely as the two characters *wa* (Japan) and *kan* (China) are joined to form a complex concept. Something like wakan clearly precedes the historical record, if only in the sense that elements of Chinese culture were already to be found in comfortable accommodation with Japanese civilization many centuries earlier. I have shown in chapter one that the writing system is perhaps the earliest and most instructive paradigm in its initial awkwardness, its unsuitability for the Japanese language, and the great sophistication and complexity of accommodation over centuries that resulted in the writing system used in Japan today, absolutely inseparable from Japanese culture itself. The operation of wakan was epitomized in the Heian in the expression *wakon-kansai* (or in the reversed native readings of those Sinate words, *karajie-yamatodamashii*), "Japanese spirit, Chinese technique." A millennium later, when the same dialectic was brought to bear upon Western rather than Chinese culture, it would become *wayō* and its operation described as *wakon-yōsai*, "Japanese spirit, Western technique," or, less tendentiously, *wayō-setchū*, "the accommodation of Japanese and Western." Such phrases convey little information about the operation of the dialectic itself; they seem to serve rather as conceptual icons, talismans that protected the writer's sense of cultural identity and integrity from defilement by contact with that which was "alien" to it.

The earliest use of the term *yamatodamashii*, so pregnant for the Japanese in the centuries that followed, is thought to occur in *The Tale of Genji*, where it is used in conjunction with another term for "Chinese learning," *zae* (an earlier reading of *sai*): "It is where there is a fund of Chinese learning that the Japanese spirit is respected by the world." [4] The two concepts "Chinese learning" and "Japanese spirit" do not stand in opposition to each other; rather, as the original passage tells us, "It is precisely against the background of Chinese learning" (*zae o moto to shite koso*) that the elusive qualities of Japan are best defined, the more delicate native patterns emerging most coherently against a background of strong formal design. It is essentially this relationship between Chinese and Japanese that is encapsulated in the term "wakan" in the Genji period.

The practice of combining or setting in some sort of relation to one another Chinese and native Japanese forms in art and literature (as well as in other areas of life ranging from music to governmental institutions) was especially popular in Heian court circles about the middle of the tenth century, the period that serves as the setting for *Genji*. This practice is illustrated by a work like the *Wakan Rōeishū* (1018) of Fujiwara Kintō (966–1041), which places lines of poetry in Chinese, composed by both Chinese and Japanese, together with Japanese waka poems within categories that are similarly a somewhat awkward compromise between those of the Japanese imperial anthologies of poetry and Chinese encyclopedic compilations known as *lei-shu* (fig. 4). However we may choose to account for the popularity of the practice of wakan in this period, the question remains as to exactly how placing Chinese and Japanese forms together functioned in practice.

An answer to this question is suggested by the very structure of *The Tale of Genji* (ca. 1010), in which mention of China is often followed immediately by a clear preference for something native, China brought in as the glittering and impressive background against which a pattern of quiet native Japanese sensibility emerges. A good example of this technique is found in a passage in the "Kiritsubo" chapter early in the novel in which the former "quiet charm" (*natsukashiku rōtage*) of the unfortunate Kiritsubo, the emperor's recently deceased favorite, is contrasted to the lush gaudiness (*uruwashū*) of a painting of the famous Chinese consort Yang Kuei-fei, whose sad story (immortalized for the Heian audience in Po Chü-i's long poem "The Song of Everlasting Sorrow") provides the exemplary classical backdrop against which the unfolding tragedy of Kiritsubo is at once set off and given increased stature (my italics):

> The Chinese lady in the paintings did not have the luster of life. Yang Kuei-fei was said to have resembled the lotus of the Sublime Pond, the willows of the Timeless Hall. *No doubt she was very beautiful in her Chinese finery. When he tried to remember the quiet charm of his lost lady*, he found there was no color of flower, no song of bird, to summon her up. [5]

[4] Yamagishi Tokuhei, ed., *Genji Monogatari*, NKBT, 1:277 and 460, n. 263; Edward Seidensticker, trans., *The Tale of Genji* (New York: Knopf, 1976), 367.

[5] Seidensticker, *Genji*, 12; Tamagami Takuya, *Genji Monogatari Hyōshaku* (Tokyo: Kadokawa Shoten, 1964), vol. 1, 84ff.; *Genji*, NKBT, 4:40.

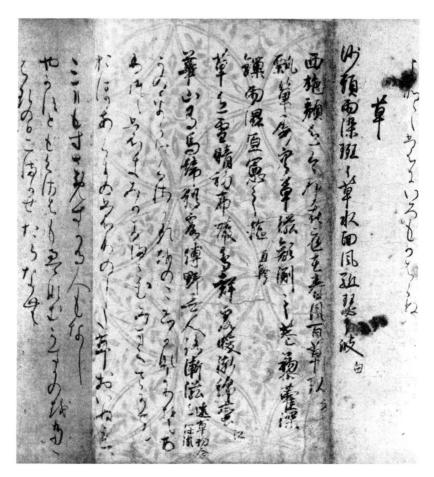

4. *Masudabon Wakan Rōeishū*, calligraphy attributed to Fujiwara Kintō. Heian, eleventh century. From Banba Ichirō, ed., *Sho* (special edition of *Taiyō*; Tokyo, 1979), pl. 18, p. 10. The first Chinese poem in this section on "plants" is by Po Chü-i; the first Japanese poem is attributed to Kakinomoto Hitomaro.

Commentators have long pointed out that the story of Yang Kuei-fei is present from the very opening words of *Genji*, and her tale as told by Po in "The Song of Everlasting Sorrow" has usually been treated as a source for the tale of Kiritsubo. It is not a "source" in the usual sense, for Murasaki Shikibu did not require foreign plots to create her fiction. Rather, it is a metaphoric (from Greek *metaphoros*, "translate") technique whereby Murasaki's plots and characters are endowed with the grandeur of classical archetype. "Translated" to the stature of the magnificent Chinese consort, the tragedy of the otherwise insignificant and merely pathetic Kiritsubo rises to greater heights, and the despair of a rather foolish emperor is given greater dimension. We do not need to find exact correspondence in every part; commentators of *Genji* have also made clear the numerous discrepancies in the stories of the two emperors and their unfortunate loves. Each tale has its roots in its own culture, and must be interpreted in terms of that culture. As third parties, we might be tempted, like Motoori Norinaga, to find the story of Kiritsubo the more satisfactory in its lack of the heavy overtones of Chinese Confucian morality that would blame a ruler's deficiencies in the arts of government on an unbusinesslike eye for the ladies; but this is precisely where Chinese over the centuries have chosen to find the most meaningful framework of construction for the story of Lady Yang. It scarcely mattered to the Japanese, on the other hand, whether the Japanese emperor "went early to court" or not, while from the point of view of Heian beliefs the fact that he did not go in order ostensibly to avoid one of the numerous calendrical or directional taboos could mean everything. From the Japanese point of view, what is important about this story for *The Tale of Genji* is the inconceivable power of karmic cause and effect unleashed by a passion whose very intensity constituted a rupture of the spiritual-temporal continuum, echoed and compounded on the temporal plane by the fatal mismatching in status of an emperor who was a descendent of the gods and a woman of only insignificant backing at court. Because their tragic love resulted in the birth of the Shining Genji, it seems scarcely to begin to state the case forcefully enough to say that from this excessive passion follows all the panoply of generations of life and death through the course of the novel.

Murasaki Shikibu's technique of bringing in China to elevate and set off Japan has echoes and consequences throughout the work. "Yang Kuei-fei as the subject of painting" (*e ni kakeru Yōkihi*), for example, brings to mind the well-known discussion of painting that constitutes part of the "rainy night's discussion of women" (*amayo no shinasadame*) in the Hahakigi chapter, in which a young guards captain compares matters of the heart (*hito no kokoro*) with painting, calligraphy, and artisanry. What is essentially and indubitably "Japanese" in painting, he says, "the things we know, mountains, streams, houses near and like our own," is contrasted with those alien "things no one ever sees ... paradises, fish in angry seas, raging beasts in foreign lands [*Karakuni*,

China], devils and demons." The effect of such outlandish subjects is to "terrify and astonish," while the Japanese subjects give, to the contrary, "a sense of affectionate familiarity" (*natsukashiku yawaraidaru koto*).[6]

Also during the course of the "rainy night's discussion of women" occurs the famous passage about a type of unfortunate woman that Murasaki Shikibu knew well, and whose plight she and others like her—Sei Shōnagon comes readily to mind—were at such pains to avoid, for all were well educated in Chinese, a quality far from desirable in women. This unfortunate woman's education in Chinese had the effect of rendering her so awesomely masculine that her speech alone, larded with three-decker Chinese words (*fubyō* for "a cold," *gokunetsu* for "fever," *sōyaku* for "medicine," and so forth), was sufficient to render her unattractive to men.[7]

"Chinese," in fact, seems often the exact antithesis of "feminine." In the whole of *Genji* there are only ten instances of waka poems composed by women that contain allusions to Chinese poems, in contrast to the countless instances of citations to Chinese poems by the author either as narrator or in the persona of a male character. Obviously it was not thought at all ladylike to make Chinese allusions. Sei Shōnagon did once, very gently, only to show that she had understood an allusion to a line of poetry by Po Chü-i, and all she got for her pains was the unwelcome admiration of the gentlemen and the nickname *kusa no iori*, "Thatched Hut."[8] Even in the single instance when Genji's wife Murasaki appears to have had a Chinese source for a poem in mind, it is generally thought that she was most likely referring not to anything she had gleaned from actually reading Chinese but rather from a screen-painting that "softened" the Chinese scene in Japanese fashion.[9]

[6] Seidensticker, *Genji*, 27; *Hyōshaku*, vol. 1, 199–201; *Genji*, NKBT, 14:68–69. Sei Shōnagon in *Makura no Sōshi* describes a sliding screen (*shōji*) in the Seiryō Palace, "decorated with paintings of the stormy sea and of the terrifying creatures with long arms and long legs that live there," which the court ladies find distinctly unpleasant; the screen was kept in the northeast corner, the direction from which baleful influences were thought to come. See Ivan Morris, trans., *The Pillow Book of Sei Shōnagon* (Baltimore: Penguin Books, 1974), 34; Matsuo Satoshi, ed., *Makura no Sōshi* (*Nihon Koten Bungaku Zenshū*, hereafter *NKBZ*; Tokyo: Shōgakkan, 1974), vol. 11, 84 and 85, n. 24.

[7] Seidensticker, *Genji*, 35–36; Tamagami, *Hyōshaku*, vol. 1, 243; *Genji*, NKBT, 14:83.

[8] *Makura no Sōshi*, vol. 11, 171; Morris, *Pillow Book of Sei Shōnagon*, 89 and 306, n. 190. Among the other women of Empress Sadako's court, however, there was no need to hide her education, and indeed they were constantly testing one another's knowledge. At one winter gathering, for example, Sadako asked Sei, "How is the snow on Incense-Burner Peak?" referring to another line by Po: "To see the snow on Incense-Burner Peak I push aside the blinds." Sei responded by simply rolling up the blinds, an action whose subtlety greatly pleased the assembled ladies (*Makura no Sōshi:*, NKBZ, 11:427; Morris, *Pillow Book*, 241–42). Po's line is indeed in *Wakan Rōeishū*. See pp. 181–182 of this study.

[9] This discussion follows Tamagami, *Hyōshaku*, vol. 1, 68, and Kawaguchi Hisao on the origins of the *Wakan Rōeishū* in Kawaguchi, ed., *Wakan Rōeishū*, NKBT, 73:13–19 (Tokyo: Iwanami Shoten, 1973). See also Kawaguchi, "Wagakuni ni Okeru Daiga Bungaku no Tenkai," in Yamagishi

We are first introduced to such paintings in *Genji*—screen-paintings and the sorts of paintings women are shown perusing in *The Tale of Genji Scrolls* (fig. 1)—in the passage, cited above, in which the bereaved emperor cannot desist from brooding all day over the scroll or screen depicting the story of Yang Kuei-fei. Alien subject matter was made *wa* (softened, Japanized, accommodated to Japanese tastes) in this way. Such screens often treated both Japanese and Chinese subjects together, with appropriate poetic texts written on cartouches (*shikishigata*) affixed to the screen bearing the Chinese and Japanese lines of poetry that provided the sources of the illustrative material. These wakan screens (*wakan byōbu*) were the visual complements of the isolated lines of poetry in Fujiwara Kintō's *Wakan Rōeishū*, and it seems more than likely that each of the lines in that text was capable of evoking its visual counterpart in the Heian imagination.

Indeed, one of the best known of these Heian screens was selected and calligraphed by Kintō himself. The eleventh-century *Kokon Chomonjū* informs us that this particular wakan screen depicted Chinese scenes on its upper part and Japanese on its lower, the two parts separated, appropriately enough, by a central passage depicting water.[10] This screen is closely contemporaneous with the composition of *Genji*, having been presented to the Regent Michinaga's third daughter Ishi (999–1036) upon her marriage to the child emperor Go-Ichijō in 1018. It was doubtless by viewing such screens that the ordinary court lady garnered her knowledge of Chinese exempla and sententiae (to use the familiar Western terms), rather than by anything so noisomely unfeminine as reading Chinese books, as the young guards officer's opinion seems to confirm. There were of course women like Murasaki Shikibu and Sei Shōnagon, both of whose fathers were classical scholars, who were much better versed than the average courtier in Chinese letters and had to live with a certain amount of discomfort all their lives as a consequence. Still, it is quite likely that it was the sort of images she saw on these wakan screens that gave Murasaki, too, her most vivid mental images of such set pieces as the distress of Yang Kuei-fei, Wang Chao-chün, and the other famous Chinese exemplars who stand, screen-like, behind their counterparts in *Genji*.

Tokuhei, ed., *Nihon Kanbungakushi Ronkō* (Tokyo: Iwanami Shoten, 1974), 201–202. In another study, Kawaguchi notes that all sorts of screens concerning Po were popular in the Heian period: see his *Heianchō no Kanbungaku* (Tokyo: Yoshikawa Kōbundō, 1981), chap. 3: "Byōbu no Hyakka Zensho *Wakan Rōeishū*." Murasaki's description of Genji's dwelling-place in Suma is presumably based on lines of Po Chu-i's poetry like those probably once affixed to a cartouche near a hermit's hut on the single such screen still extant from the Heian, the so-called *Senzui Byōbu* in the Kyoto National Museum, thought to show Po in exile meeting his friend Yüan Chen (fig. 5)—this despite the fact that Murasaki herself notes in her diary that she "had to look uncomprehendingly at the Chinese poems affixed to the cartouches above screen-paintings" (202).

[10] Nagazumi Yasuaki and Shimada Isao, eds., *Kokon Chomonjū*, *NKBT* (1966), 84:313.

I have included Wang Chao-chün along with Yang Kuei-fei here, for she figures, if anything, even more significantly than Yang as one of the informing Chinese images that translates Genji to the proportions of archetypal figure. The story of the exile to Suma and Akashi (in the chapters of those names) is an extraordinarily intricate fabric whose involved design is composed of a number of interwoven, self-contained motifs. All the various themes of exile, nostalgia for the court, and encounter on foreign strands in these chapters seem to group themselves around one particularly well known Chinese exemplum of Lady Wang Chao-chün's wretched exile to the land of the Huns as the result of her failure to bribe a venal court artist to do justice to her natural beauty. Her story provides as powerful a structural motif for "Suma" and Genji's exile from the capital as Yang Kuei-fei's does for the tragedy of Kiritsubo and its consequences. Of all the motifs in the Suma chapter, and we shall discuss several, the exile of Lady Wang is by far that which resonates most fully with all the dimensions of Genji's own situation, and sheds the most light on the many disparate facets of the chapter.

In "Suma" we are told several times of Genji's great "crime" (or "sin," *tsumi*) that makes the hero's self-imposed exile unavoidable.[11] This is of course Genji's secret paternity of the Imperial Consort Fujitsubo's child, the future Reizei Emperor, ostensibly Genji's brother, in reality his son. In spite of Genji's constant agony over his terrible deed and the fearful consequences were it to be discovered, no one else in fact knows the truth of the matter, and so it is ultimately not because of this that he is driven into exile. In reality, Genji's true "crime" is the same as Wang Chao-chün's: both were too beautiful for their own good, and both failed to temper their dangerous, naturally radiant beauty with the practical necessity of compromise with political realities, thereby making powerful enemies at court.

Some commentators have found the difference in gender in the two stories to be a problem, but I do not think it is a very large one. In dealing with one crucial and ambiguous passage, Edward Seidensticker, along with translators into modern Japanese, has elected to make Genji's wife Murasaki the object of Genji's thoughts while in exile. His own wretchedness is likened to that of an emperor who has been forced to "dispose of a beautiful Lady."[12] While Genji has indeed been thinking of Murasaki in a passage immediately preceding, however, there follows a marked caesura in the text with the advent of a new season, clearly indicated by the passage that begins "It was winter" (*fuyu ni arite*). More likely, then, the eerie passage that follows refers in fact to Genji himself: it is *he*, not Murasaki, who is being likened to the beautiful Wang

[11] Seidensticker, *Genji*, 221; Tamagami, *Hyōshaku*, vol. 3, 26–29; *Genji*, NKBT, 15:14. See also Seidensticker, *Genji*, 226; Tamagami, *Hyōshaku*, vol. 3, 51 and 54; *Genji*, NKBT, 15:24.

[12] The section begins "*Mashite ikanarikemu ...*" Seidensticker, *Genji*, 240; Tamagami, *Hyōshaku*, vol. 3, 118; *Genji*, NKBT, 15:45.

Chao-chün; and if the Chinese lady's fate was tragic, thinks Genji, then how much more miserable (*mashite ikanarikemu*) must be his own emperor, faced with the prospect of sending someone as beloved as Genji from his side.[13] There follows an allusion to a line of poetry by Ōe no Asatsuna, whose entire poem about Lady Wang was well known to the Heian audience, having been included not as the usual couplet but rather line for line in the *Wakan Rōeishū*:

One sound of the Tartar horn—frost puts an end to her [his?] dreams,
A myriad leagues from the Han Palace—her [his?] heart breaks before the moon.[14]

These lines are ambiguous as is Genji's own situation, and may be understood as referring either to Lady Wang or the Han Emperor. It is likely that any Heian reader, mentally finishing the last two lines of the poem as it continues in the *Wakan Rōeishū*, would have also recognized in this poem the keen recriminations felt by all parties, Chinese and Japanese both:

If only Lady Wang had paid the painter his bribe of gold,
She could have spent her entire life in the service of her lord.[15]

Though such were doubtless Genji's own thoughts at that moment, even at such a time the Shining Genji could never seem anything less than radiant, and it is doubtful that even Po Chü-i, whose poem about Wang Chao-chün heads the seven lines devoted to her in the *Wakan Rōeishū*, could have pictured him in the same ironic light as he did the wretched Lady Wang:

Misery, bitterness, wretchedness and hard labor have left her so haggard,
That now in reality she has come to resemble the portrait that did her such injustice.

Indeed, if we are to judge from the fact that Wang and no other historical personage is given a separate section to herself in the *Wakan Rōeishū*, it seems reasonable to conclude that the story of Wang Chao-chün may have been even more popular in the Heian than that of Yang Kuei-fei.

Later in *Genji*, however, it becomes clear that there is a certain amount of discomfort, within the framework of an entirely Japanese court setting, with Ladies Yang and Wang, both of whom possess certain inauspicious qualities not entirely suited to a Genji who has emerged renewed and triumphant from his ordeals in exile. Early in the "Eawase" (The Picture Contest) chapter, when

[13] See the end of n. 2 in Tamagami, *Hyōshaku*, vol. 3, 118; *Genji, NKBT*, 15:45.
[14] *Wakan Rōeishū, NKBT*, 73:231, no. 702. It is interesting that the confusion over whether the emperor or Lady Wang is to be considered the subject of this poem (as I have indicated by brackets) is found as well in Minamoto Shunrai's (1055–1129) retelling of the story in *Shunrai Zuinō, NKBZ*, 50:237ff. and n. 13.
[15] *Po Hsiang-shan Shih-chi*, 152. See also Eugene Eoyang, "The Wang Chao-chün Legend: Configurations of the Classic," *Chinese Literature: Essays, Articles, and Reviews* 4:1 (January 1982), 3–22.

Genji and Murasaki are found sorting through their collection of narrative stories illustrated with paintings to use in the approaching picture contest, those of the tragic Yang Kuei-fei and Wang Chao-chün are singled out for mention as "particularly interesting," but are quickly rejected for exhibition at the contest (at which the emperor is to be present) as "inauspicious" (*koto no imi aru*).[16] Again, we find that with mention of these two paragons the author has brought in her Chinese backdrop, and immediately thereafter has Genji decide to show Murasaki the paintings he did of his Suma exile, so subtly interwoven with these Chinese experiences. Later in the chapter these same paintings of Genji's win the contest—though apparently not in their original form but rather mounted as elements of a *wakan* screen, that is, as pictures with Chinese and Japanese subjects provided "with captions in cursive Chinese and Japanese" lines of poetry written out on cartouches and affixed by the scenes to which they were related. Given the nature of the other purely Japanese illustrated stories against which Genji's are set in competition, it is not merely the exile but the exile as viewed *against the ground of Chinese archetype* that stands out so impressively from the rest of the images. Genji, after all, has even managed to triumph where Lady Wang had failed. The *wakan* screen is symbolic of Genji's unique ability to mediate in one person between China and Japan, and so stands as a capsule reminder of this metaphoric function in the Suma chapter, and is placed firmly in antithetical relationship to the "inauspicious" Chinese themes as well as the purely Japanese ones.

The "Suma" chapter first begins to weave its patterns of Chinese and Japanese motifs with a reference to the famous exile of Ariwara no Yukihira. This association of "exile" with "Suma" would have occurred almost automatically to any Heian reader, for, as Tamagami Takuya tells us, "When people of the Genji period heard the word 'Suma,' they thought of Yukihira's poem":

Wakuraba ni	If someone should
Tou hito araba	Inquire for me, reply:
Suma no ura ni	He idles at Suma
Moshio taretsutsu	Dripping brine from
Wabu to kotae yo	The sea grass.[17]

Yukihira (818–893) was the brother of the famous poet Narihira (825–880), traditionally held to have written *Ise Monogatari* (Tales of Ise). The well-known episode of his exile appears to have grown up around this poem as a "context" for it, for there is no historical record of Yukihira's "exile" to Suma in other

---

[16] Tamagami, *Hyōshaku*, vol. 4, 35; Seidensticker, *Genji*, 310; *Genji*, NKBT, 15:177. For what follows see also Abe Akio et al., eds., *Genji Monogatari*, NKBZ, 13:378, n. 1.

[17] *Kokinshū*, poem 962; Seidensticker, *Genji*, 231; Tamagami, *Hyōshaku*, vol. 3, 74ff.

sources. There is also a poem in *Tales of Ise* (that appears as well in the *Kokinshū*) to which Genji alludes upon his departure for Suma to Princess Ōmiya, the mother of his dead wife Aoi:

Suma no ama no	Like the smoke
Shioyaku keburi	From the salt-burners' fires at Suma,
Kaze o itami	Agitated by the wind,
Omowanu kata ni	The one I love has drifted off
Tanabikinikeri	In an unforeseen direction.[18]

If Genji's poem looks ahead to the wretchedness of a Suma exile as a native classical *typos*, it looks backward as well by alluding to a poem he has recited at Aoi's funeral, alluding to the smoke drifting from the funeral pyres at the Mt. Toribe cemetery. The poem here thus serves, as does Genji's visit to the princess at this time, both to tie up a loose end and to foreshadow a later event.

There is also the well-known exile that provided the immediate historical model for Genji's, that of Minister of the Left Minamoto no Takaakira, forced into exile in Kyushu in 969 for three years and leaving the capital at precisely the same time of year as Genji.[19] Murasaki's readers would have shuddered with recognition at the thought of Takaakira, whom the Fujiwaras had removed from power with the charge of conspiring against the very emperor whose name, Reizei, Genji's dangerously illegitimate child will later assume upon accession to the throne. The way in which the elegant intricacies of the novel are thus acted out against the blunt realities of the often fatal consequences for those involved in the Machiavellian Fujiwara manipulations at court adds an urgency to Genji's predicament that the Western reader scarcely senses. Indeed, all the colorful and pleasant-seeming pagentry of the picture contest in "Eawase" is played out against the brutal political rivalries of the Genji and Kōkiden factions at court, and the final decision in favor of Genji's paintings of his Suma exile culminates his complete political triumph over his enemies.

If the "Suma" chapter begins with a variety of Japanese allusions, the motifs that the very name "Suma" would have conjured up in the imaginations of Murasaki Shikibu's readers, it is not long before she begins to reveal the Chinese warp-threads into which the Japanese patterns of the exile theme are to be woven, through Genji's frequent allusion to the "other land" whose famous stories of exile were well known to the Heian audience. And the Chinese exemplar whose exiles figure most prominently in "Suma" is, as we should expect, the poet-official Po Chü-i. We discover again in her frequent allusions

[18] Tamagami, *Hyōshaku*, vol. 3, 75; *Kokinshū*, NKBZ, 7:227; Fukui Teisuke et al., eds., *Ise Monogatari*, NKBZ, 8:281 (Tokyo: Shogakkan, 1972).
    [19] Tamagami, *Hyōshaku*, vol. 3, 18ff.

to his poetry how far beyond the ordinary was Murasaki Shikibu's education in Chinese literature.

When Genji sets out for Suma (but a single day's journey from the capital, it should be noted—the distances involved would have made the Chinese laugh), for example, the things he takes along, "only the simplest essentials for a rustic life, among them a bookchest, *The Collected Poems of Po Chü-i* and the like, and a seven-stringed Chinese koto [*kin*]," [20] are clearly modeled on the description of the contents of Po's house in exile at Mt. Lu far in the south of China in what is now Chianghsi Province, which included "a lacquered lute and a few scrolls of Confucian, Taoist and Buddhist writings." [21] It is amusing and instructive to find the Japanese author contracting the wide range of Chinese literature to its Japanese essentials, *"The Collected Poems of Po Chü-i* and the like." Japanese commentators are helpful in locating the sources of such allusions; the fact is, however, that so much of Murasaki's description in this chapter echoes Po Chü-i that it is impossible to limit the sources of her manifold references to a few poems.

We can locate the particular period of exile, however, that appears to have provided the wellspring for most of Murasaki's allusions. This was the period between 815 and 817 when Po was demoted to a low-ranking post in Chiang-chou near Lake Po-yang in the south of China. As Po describes it, this was a place of "yellow fogs and constant dampness," whose aboriginal native populace played music and sang songs that grated harshly on the northern poet's sensitive ears. He called their speech "as incomprehensible as the chirping of birds," just as Genji's friend Tō no Chūjō was to characterize that of the natives of Suma. [22]

The house that Po built during this period of exile, located in an area below Incense-Burner (Hsiang-lu) Peak on Mt. Lu, is clearly the source of one of the two rather contradictory descriptions of Genji's house at Suma, into which Genji moved on the twenty-seventh day of the third month, the same day that Po moved into his. The description of this house that immediately follows the allusion to Ariwara no Yukihira [23] would seem at first to be entirely Japanese; and yet the "brook" that is brought into the "garden," the very "plants" in that garden, and the house's setting deep "in the mountains" all allude to the many poems that Po "Inscribed on the Eastern Wall of His New House below Incense-Burner Peak," [24] in which he describes the dwelling as "deep in the mountains," surrounded by "herb and tea plants," and graced with a brook that the Chinese poet had run into the garden and prized above all else (fig. 5).

[20] Seidensticker, *Genji*, 225; Tamagami, *Hyōshaku*, vol. 3, 48; *Genji, NKBT*, 15:22.

[21] *Po Hsiang-shan Shih-chi*, 69–70.

[22] *Po Hsiang-shan Shih-chi*, 122; Seidensticker, *Genji*, 244; Tamagami, *Hyōshaku*, vol. 3, 132; *Genji, NKBT*, 15:50.

[23] Seidensticker, *Genji*, 231; Tamagami, *Hyōshaku*, vol. 3, 73–74; *Genji, NKBT*, 15:30.

[24] *Po Hsiang-shan Shih-chi*, 177.

5. *Senzui Byōbu*, two central panels of a six-panel screen (Kyoto National Museum). The picture is thought to illustrate Yüan Chen visiting Po Chü-i in exile in his hut below Incense-Burner peak on Mt. Lu. Heian period, eleventh century. From Masao Ishizawa et al., eds., *The Heritage of Japanese Art* (Tokyo and New York, 1981), p. 86, pl. 50.

The other, "Chinese" (*Karameita*), description of the house at Suma is even more clearly modeled on Po's series of poems about his new house below Incense-Burner Peak, with its "fence of plaited bamboo," "pillars of pine," and "stairs of stone," all of which are mentioned in the first of Po's poems.[25] These few allusions merely begin to illustrate the complexity of the intricate fabric of allusion to Po Chü-i that Murasaki Shikibu has woven into the Suma chapter.

The Heian reader, once reminded of Po, would also naturally have been put in mind of his best-known Japanese exponent, Sugawara no Michizane, whose tragic exile by the Fujiwaras, recorded in the *Ōkagami*, provided yet another thematic model for Genji's exile and reinforces the reader's consciousness of the allusions to Po. The relationship between the Chinese and the Japanese poets is echoed especially in two lines of poetry. The first is by Po, addressed to his closest friend Yüan Chen, who was also in distant exile at the time. In this poem Po recounts his thoughts while viewing from the Imperial Palace the most famous moon of the year, that of the fifteenth of the eighth month, which he fears his distant friend will not see since it will be "hidden by the low damps of Ch'ang-ling in autumn."[26] The allusion to a line of Michizane that follows, referring to the Japanese poet's memories of the emperor in the capital, serves to advance the time-frame by its reference to a festival in the ninth month as well as to indicate by Po's thoughts of those at court that Genji is thinking of his own brother, the Suzaku Emperor. The figure also thus alludes, as we have seen in the adaptation of the tale of Wang Chao-chün, to the probable sadness of that emperor in having had to send from his side someone of such radiant beauty. Another reference later to a poem by Michizane about the moon[27] serves to intensify the exile's awareness of the Buddhist sense of finality implicit in the moon's unswerving path through the night sky, ever sinking toward extinction in the west. This same image of the moon returns again at the very end of "Eawase" to illuminate the musical gathering in celebration of Genji's victory, and to bring back to Genji at the height of his triumph this same sudden awareness of his own impermanence in the theme of Buddhist rejection of the world that closes the chapter.

The longing for a distant friend, implied in the reference to poems by Po addressed to Yüan Chen, is eventually realized in "Suma" by the visit of the rather timorous Tō no Chūjō to Genji in exile.[28] When Tō arrived, the two friends "composed Chinese poetry all through the night," and when wine was served "their toast was from Po Chü-i: 'Sad topers we; our springtime cups

---

[25] Seidensticker, *Genji*, 244; Tamagami, *Hyōshaku*, vol. 3, 129–30; *Genji*, *NKBT*, 15:49. The visual analogue of this scene can be seen in the landscape screen mentioned in n. 10. See fig. 5.

[26] *Po Hsiang-shan Shih-chi*, 144; Seidensticker, *Genji*, 238; Tamagami, *Hyōshaku*, vol. 3, 105; *Genji*, *NKBT*, 15:41.

[27] Seidensticker, *Genji*, 241; Tamagami, *Hyōshaku*, vol. 3, 119; *Genji*, *NKBT*, 15:45.

[28] Seidensticker, *Genji*, 243–45; Tamagami, *Hyōshaku*, vol. 3, 128–39; *Genji*, *NKBT*, 15:49–52.

flow with tears.'" The line alludes to a poem written by Po in 819, when he chanced to encounter Yüan again after a separation of four years.[29] At that time, Yüan was en route to a posting near the capital, having been recalled from exile, while Po was traveling in the opposite direction away from the capital to a post in Chung-chou. The two Chinese friends met on the eleventh day of the third month, about a month earlier than Genji and Tō no Chūjō in Suma. The fact that the dates do not agree as well as others suggests that Murasaki found the nature of the occasion of the Chinese poem important enough for her purposes to outweigh considerations of chronology, which she otherwise appears to have taken quite seriously.

It is not my intention to show, by going into such detail, that Murasaki's plot is a patchwork of allusions. To say that is to say nothing at all, for it does not even begin to "explain" the power of the story of Genji's exile; indeed, it explains away all the power of the writing and leaves nothing but a bare and uninteresting skeleton for our contemplation. It is rather to point out the particular method Murasaki employed, a sort of chiaroscuro technique by which she imparted to her figures greater depth and dimensionality, and made them and their actions stand out more clearly against the complexly interwoven designs of plot, place, time, and the working out of karmic destiny. She gave, as it were, Chinese shadows to her events and characters, in contrast to which they stand out all the more strikingly as distinctly Japanese. Such a consciously employed technique would seem to indicate that by the beginning of the eleventh century, the author of *Genji* felt herself distant enough in time and space from an immediate sense of the overwhelming presence of mainland culture that she could feel free to use its matter to lend archetypal significance to the life of her rather claustrophobic little court. And indeed we find in her diary, the *Murasaki Shikibu Nikki*, the same sense of a mind at once intricately involved with the details of court life and able to endow those details with that sense of history and destiny without which detail is no more significant than a mote of dust. In *Genji*, China sets for every aspect of court life the grand pattern against which, like the delicate tracery of feminine *kana* calligraphy against the impressive masculine geometry of prized Chinese writing paper (*karakami*), true elegance of character, the real significance of apparently trivial detail, showed itself to best effect (fig. 2).[30]

But Murasaki Shikibu also shows us in *Genji* that there were those in her day who were not so entirely comfortable in the presence of alien matters. Not everyone mediated between China and Japan as successfully as Genji did, and not everyone could, like Genji, look perfectly at ease in a Chinese robe

[29] *Po Hsiang-shan Shih-chi*, 195–96.
[30] Cf. Seidensticker, *Genji*, 402; Tamagami, *Hyōshaku*, vol. 3, 87, and vol. 5, 118; *Genji, NKBT*, 15:362.

CHAPTER TWO 72

(*karagoromo*);[31] or seem anything less than perfectly apt in reciting a Chinese poem, like the poor rhymers at the banquet in "Hana no En" (The Festival of the Cherry Blossoms);[32] or sound brilliantly talented playing the difficult Chinese seven-stringed koto (or *kin*). Genji himself is permanently identified throughout the tale with this instrument; whenever he reaches for an instrument to play, it is almost invariably this Chinese koto. Entire chapters ("Akashi," for example, and the second "Wakana" chapter) seem to be built upon the playing of koto music, and koto music always seems to crop up whenever we are to learn of great and mysterious depths of character, whether in Genji or in anyone else.

Genji, in fact, might be regarded as a multidimensional improvement on an earlier fictional model, the character Toshikage in *The Tale of the Hollow Tree* (*Utsuho Monogatari*, ca. 960), whose sole dimension was an ability to play the lute. During the course of the picture contest in "Eawase," illustrations from the *Hollow Tree* are pitted against those from the even more ancient *Tale of the Bamboo Cutter* (*Taketori Monogatari*), with Genji's comment that

> Toshikage was battered by tempests and waves and swept off to foreign parts, but he finally came home, whence his musical activities sent his fame back across the waters and down through the centuries. This painting successfully blends the Chinese and the Japanese, the new and the old, and I say that it is without rival.[33]

Genji's own fame, by contrast, is compounded of *all* the senses, part music, part scent, part radiance. Even in music he demonstrates his multidimensionality by playing, just once, the Japanese koto (*wagon*) to good effect in winning the affections of Tamakazura in "Tokonatsu" (Wild Carnations). Genji even contrasts the Japanese instrument to the Chinese with mock humility by belittling its name in a pun: "It may be looked down on as just a 'crude domestic product'" (*yamatogoto to hakanaku misete*), used by "women who cannot know much about foreign things."[34]

In a memorable scene in the second "Wakana" chapter, Genji has assembled his various women on a veranda in the first month to present a remarkable "female concert" for the emperor.[35] Murasaki is to play the *wagon*, the Akashi Lady the *biwa*, her daughter the Akashi Princess the thirteen-stringed Chinese *shō*, and the Third Princess Genji's own seven-stringed Chinese koto. The instrument and music played by each woman are clearly intended to reflect her character. Thus, "The thirteen-stringed koto [*shō*] holds its pitch on the whole well enough . . . but the bridges have a way of slipping in the middle of a concert." Its musician,

---

[31] Seidensticker, *Genji*, 474; Tamagami, *Hyōshaku*, vol. 6, 72; *Genji*, NKBT, 16:80.

[32] Seidensticker, *Genji*, 150–51; Tamagami, *Hyōshaku*, vol. 6, 327; *Genji*, NKBT, 14:303.

[33] Seidensticker, *Genji*, 312; Tamagami, *Hyōshaku*, vol. 4, 40; *Genji*, NKBT, 15:180.

[34] Seidensticker, *Genji*, 444; Tamagami, *Hyōshaku*, vol. 5, 374; *Genji*, NKBT, 16:17.

[35] Seidensticker, *Genji*, 600ff.; Tamagami, *Hyōshaku*, vol. 7, 340; *Genji*, NKBT, 16:342.

the Akashi Princess, is not a worry to Genji on this account, however, since she has often performed in concert before the emperor; and so "the thirteen-stringed Chinese koto, a gentle, feminine sort of instrument, takes its place hesitantly and deferentially among the other instruments." Murasaki's Japanese koto, again deprecated by the term *yamatogoto*, "was most likely to cause trouble," for "everything about it is fluid and indefinite, and there are no clear guides." It is especially intriguing to Yūgiri, Genji's son, always entirely too curious about his beautiful stepmother for Genji, whose conscience over a similar matter is never quite at ease. The instrument that does give Genji immediate reason for concern is the *kin*—it is, after all, the instrument that no one but he can play well, rather like the bow in the sagas that none but the hero can bend, and Genji has been trying to teach it to the little Third Princess, a hopeless task and he knows it.

In the well-known evaluation of music that follows the concert, Genji returns to soliloquize on the difficulties of his own instrument: "The seven-stringed koto is the unmanageable one [a foreshadowing of the Third Princess's disastrous affair with Kashiwagi]. We are told that in ancient times there were many who mastered the whole tradition of the instrument, and made heaven and earth their own, and softened the hearts of demons and gods." Here again Genji refers to Toshikage of the *Hollow Tree*, as well as to a famous Chinese statement concerning the properties of music in the "Great Preface" to *The Book of Odes* (*Shih Ching*). "There was a time," Genji continues,

> before the tradition had been established in Japan, when the most enormous trouble was required of anyone who sought to learn the art. He must spend years in strange lands [*shiranu kuni*, which might be interpreted as China or Korea, as well as the "Hashi" (Chinese *P'o-ssu*, or "Persia") of Toshikage's travels] and give up every-thing, and even then only a few came back with what they had gone out to seek. In the old chronicles there are stories of musicians who moved the moon and the thunders. . . . [and] stars and brought unseasonal snows and frosts and conjured up tempests.

But now the world and Genji are both in decline:

> The seven-stringed koto was the instrument that moved demons and gods, and inadequate mastery had correspondingly unhappy results. What other instrument is to be at the center of things, setting the tone for all the others? Ours is a day of very sad decline. Only a madman, we say, would be so obsessed with an art as to abandon parents and children and go wandering off over Korea and China (*Morokoshi Koma*).[36]

[36] Seidensticker, *Genji*, 604–05; Tamagami, *Hyōshaku*, vol. 7, 362–66; *Genji*, *NKBT*, 16:351–52.

The koto is the single thread that holds the long and rambling *Hollow Tree* together: its discovery in a foreign land after Toshikage's shipwreck en route to China, its journey back to Japan and secret transmission there through several generations, and its final emergence after years of secret teachings as an entirely Japanese miracle of music.[37] This story of a foreign Ur-koto is the very model for Genji, anxious to transmit his own store of esoteric musical knowledge to his children and grandchildren, an anxiety that tells of his own ever-increasing sense of mortality. Toshikage's search is a tale that carries profound implications for Genji, but its significance goes even deeper. We can see in it the very locus classicus of the theme of the synthesis of China in Japan, and not only of music, when we consider the fairly common punning reading of the word *koto* as "word" that occurs, for example, in the "Yokobue" chapter of *Genji*.[38]

There is more than a little cultural chauvinism inherent in this theme: after all, as Genji remarks, Toshikage's achievements were someday to astonish those very foreigners (*hito no mikado*, emperors of foreign lands) from whom the music was first learned. The turnabout theme can be seen in other contemporary sources as well. In the late twelfth-century *emaki* scroll that relates the adventures in China of the Japanese courtier Kibi no Makibi (693–775), for example, the Japanese hero not only defeats the Chinese at every contest they set him—he is also made to outshine his Japanese contemporary Abe no Nakamaro (698–770), an earlier envoy to China who all too servilely gave in to slavish imitation of the Chinese, even going so far as to wear Chinese court robes. Kibi enlists poor Nakamaro's ghost to help him win against the Chinese when they resort to foul play, but only after the gruesome wraith has agreed to don proper Japanese court attire (fig. 6).

If the theme of the voyage to China is in part an odyssey, a reaching out into the terrors of the dark unknown in order to return home with a renewed sense of the secure familiarity of one's own, we inevitably emerge on the other side of this dialectic of the Great Model that elevates the lesser. For the natural concomitant of familiarity was contempt, and of successfully making the quest to foreign lands, the thumbing of one's nose at what had seemed so awful in the first place. The motif was followed: not only was Michizane, a creature of foreign influence, banished from court; even his great Chinese model Po Chü-i would take his lumps in a later century in the nō play *Hakurakuten*, bettered at his own game of poetry by the Japanese deity Sumiyoshi in the guise of an old fisherman, in a Japan where even the birds sing superior poetry. Perhaps from the Japanese point of view there is always a price to be exacted from the superior in a relationship. The words of historian Ernst Robert Curtius in *European*

[37] Kōno Tama, *Utsuho Monogatari Denbon no Kenkyū* (Tokyo: Iwanami Shoten, 1973), 65ff.; Katō Shūichi, *A History of Japanese Literature, vol. 1, The First Thousand Years* (Tokyo and New York: Kodansha International, 1982), 163ff.

[38] Cf. Seidensticker, *Genji*, 661; Tamagami, *Hyōshaku*, vol. 8, 189; *Genji*, NKBT, 17:63.

6. A scene of Kibi no Makibi astounding the Chinese by beating them at their own game. From the Boston Museum of Fine Arts, *Kibi in China: Tales from a Japanese Scroll* (New York, 1977).

Literature and the Latin Middle Ages suggest a striking parallel in the relationship between the Roman Imperium and the new Frankish Empire established under Charlemagne:

> Let us not forget that the "Latin Middle Ages" is nowise limited to the idea of Rome in the sense of a glorification of Rome or of an effort to renew it. The concept of *translatio* [both in the *translatio imperii*, or the transfer of the Roman Imperium to another people, and in the *translatio studii*, the transfer of learning from Rome to Paris], indeed, implies that the transfer of dominion from one empire to another is the result of a sinful misuse of that dominion.[39]

For Japan, of course, "Rome" was always offshore, whether in decline or in reinvigoration, inviting further translation, in every sense of the word, as well as further resentment. The Japanese could not have failed to notice in their studies that the Chinese doctrine of *t'ien-ming*, the Mandate of Heaven, taken

[39] (New York: Harper Bollingen Library, 1963), 29.

from unworthy rulers and passed on to the worthy, was a two-edged sword that cut both ways, and in times of national crisis it is only natural that the barbarians should fail to remember the virtues of a crumbling empire and remember only its "sinful misuse." But just as the harsh realities of a less than ruly peasantry seem as yet only to creep stealthily around the margins of the text of *Genji*, so is a less than ideal China still attenuated, suggested as yet only in those "terrifying creatures" painted on screens that so alarmed the ladies of the court. China in *Genji*, like the pine-tree backdrop of the medieval nō stage, stands in this earlier age as the incorruptible image against which action and plot assume formal significance, a symbol of the immutable and eternal that endows the characters of *Genji* with their most human dimensions.

CHAPTER THREE

"A Bridge Across the Mountains":
Chinese and the Aesthetics of the *Shinkokinshū*

I suggested in the preceding chapter that in *The Tale of Genji* the deepest significance of what is Japanese is brought out against a background of Chinese, with the effect that the Japanese is made to acquire greater depth of meaning by the contrast. At the heart of the image of China in the Heian stood the figure of the poet-official Po Chü-i, whose life the Heian reader knew as the poetry in his *Collected Works* (*Hakushi Monjū*). Indeed, we may even put it the other way around and say that for the Heian, Po's poetry was in a sense the very model of life itself, not as it actually was lived in all its mundane Japanese details, of course, but rather as a kind of elegant ideal for the gentleman poet, whether at court or in exile. In this abstract way Po might be thought of as personifying the Heian courtly ideal, and the many Japanese lives that so intricately intertwine in the "Suma" and "Akashi" chapters of *The Tale of Genji* are in a way but incomplete and comparatively shallow offspring of that one more complete and profound existence.

Po Chü-i is also central to the significance of the *Wakan Rōeishū*, a compilation of Chinese and Japanese poetry nearly exactly contemporary with *Genji*. In each section of this work, lines (usually couplets) selected from Chinese poems are followed by entire Japanese waka poems. The Chinese lines are taken from a variety of sources, with those by Po by far the most numerous. The immediate effect of this juxtaposition is that the Japanese lines are made to stand out in contrast against the Chinese, the Japanese poems acquiring greater stature and depth simply by being placed next to the Chinese.

If this technique of simple juxtaposition seems far from Murasaki Shikibu's complex interplay of Chinese and Japanese, it shows a considerable advance over the technique used by Ōe no Chisato in *Kudai Waka* (Waka Poems Written from Lines of Chinese, 894), in which Chinese poems by Po and others are simply translated literally into Japanese verse form. Clearly a less sophisticated stage in the history of the progressive accommodation of Chinese to Japanese poetry, such a technique accords well with the relatively simple adoption of Chinese themes and poetic techniques of the first imperial poetry anthology, the *Kokinshū* of 905. In the century between the compilation of the *Kudai Waka* and the *Wakan Rōeishū*, Japanese poetry had advanced beyond simply imitating Chinese to a level of sophistication that could comprehend the more subtle relationship involved in the contrast between the two.

Historical events of the two centuries between *The Tale of Genji* and *Wakan Rōeishū* and the publication in 1206 of the eighth imperial anthology of poetry, the *Shinkokinshū*, more than fulfilled the prophetic sense of the end of an era that weighs so heavily in *Genji*. By the second half of the twelfth century the glory of Fujiwara rule was only a memory. The persistent but as yet peripheral mutterings of discontent among the despised, inelegant local governors and rough estate managers that figure so insubstantially in *Genji* had erupted into the terrible civil wars chronicled in the medieval romance of the rise and fall of the Taira clan, *The Tale of the Heike*. The fortunes of the court were in severe decline, and those of a new military class on the rise. China during this period seems for purposes of official diplomacy to have almost completely disappeared, despite the rise of the brilliant culture of the Sung dynasty after 960, and even after 1127 when the still vital Chinese court was forced south by northern Chin Tartar invaders. The Japanese court may have ceased to send official missions to China after 894 out of a sense of fear for the safety of their envoys in a foreign land torn by civil strife; but it was a war-torn Japan, and not China, that forced the Japanese to look inward from the mid-twelfth century.

In spite of the political decline of the court in this period, the Heian traditions of court poetry were maintained as an ideal with remarkable devotion. Still, the ideals of an age can never be immune from political and cultural realities, and in the twelfth century subtle changes were taking place in the theory and practice of poetry that reflect the new contexts in which poetry was thought about and written. We shall see that these changes cannot be entirely accounted for by viewing Japan as staring fixedly inward at her own misfortunes and ignoring the dramatic changes in aesthetic vision that were taking place on the continent. Indeed, the new aesthetic that appeared in Japan about 1200 can best be understood against the background of the new aesthetic vision of Sung China.

The twelfth century saw the rise of important new poetic ideals that inform all of later medieval Japanese waka poetry. *Ushin* (intense feeling), *sabi* ("loneliness," a "withered beauty" devoid of color or richness), *yōen* (ethereal charm), and *yūgen* (mystery and depth) are terms that have come to be associated especially with the poetry and the poetic theory of Fujiwara Shunzei (or Toshinari, 1114–1204) and his son Fujiwara Teika (or Sadaie, 1162–1241), and with the imperially sponsored poetry anthologies for which they were responsible. While these include the *Senzaishū* compiled by Shunzei about 1188 and the *Shinchokusenshū* compiled by Shunzei about 1234, it is rather the poetry of the *Shinkokinshū* (A New Collection of Ancient and Modern Times), commissioned by the retired emperor Go-Toba and completed in 1206 by the work of a committee (Teika among others), that is felt to best represent the ideals of its age. This anthology has given its name to what has become known as the "Shinkokin" aesthetic, informed by those poets who most contributed to the unique qualities that distinguish this collection from others. These poets were for the most part aristocratic courtiers and monks around Go-Toba (1180–1239), both as young emperor (r. 1185–1198) and as abdicated ex-emperor, who at the age of twenty-one first ordered the compilation of the *Shinkokinshū*. Go-Toba himself took an unprecedented imperial interest in the selection of poems, contributing thirty-four poems to the collection. Foremost among the other poets of his circle contributing to the collection were Shunzei (seventy-two poems), Teika (forty-six poems), the monks Saigyō (1118–1190, ninety-four poems) and Jakuren (d. 1202, thirty-five poems), the Tendai Abbot (*Zasu*) Jien (1155–1225, ninety-two poems), and the Regent Fujiwara Yoshitsune (1168–1206, seventy-nine poems). The full list of names would include all those poets whose lives spanned the turn of the century and whose works embody that which is "new" in the "New Collection."[1]

Among the many outstanding poets of this age, Fujiwara Teika stands apart as perhaps the best-known representative of Shinkokin thought and practice. This is in part because of the importance of his poetic theory and practice for his own age, but perhaps even more because of the significance his work held for later poets and theorists. Theorists of the fourteenth and fifteenth centuries looked largely to Teika when they sought the wellspring of their own aesthetics, and the reinterpretation of Teika's poetics constitutes a major current of literary thought through the centuries. In this chapter, I will examine the ways in which the tides of poetic theory and practice were shifting around Teika and the other Shinkokin poets as the practice of poetry began to respond to a new aesthetic vision. In doing so, I shall examine the implications for Shinkokin poetic ideals of some of the contexts of contemporary poetic theory circa 1200, including both native and Sung dynasty Chinese poetic practice and theory, as well as the new currents of Buddhism starting to make themselves felt in Japan around 1200.

In order to understand the aesthetic contexts of the Shinkokin age, we must first turn to the poetics of the poets and theorists Fujiwara Shunzei and Kamo no Chōmei (1154–1216) that provide its basis in theory. Their different concep-

---

[1] According to Minemura Fumito, the works of these poets account for some seven hundred of the 1,979 poems included in the *Shinkokinshū* if only those poets generally identified with the new style are counted; see *Shinkokin Wakashū, NKBZ* (1974), 26:14.

This period of poetry and its concerns is summarized in English in Earl Miner and Robert H. Brower, *Japanese Court Poetry* (Palo Alto: Stanford University Press, 1962), 231–337, who also provide a short but select bibliography (498–502) of works in Japanese and English. Further bibliographical information is available in numerous Japanese works such as the Nihon Bungaku Kenkyū Shiryō Kankōkai, ed., *Shinkokin Wakashū* (Tokyo: Yūseidō, 1980), which appends a bibliography to the collection and the period arranged by subject.

tions, in writings twenty years apart, of what they thought constituted "depth" in poetry reveal these two men as exponents respectively of a "classical" and a "medieval" outlook on the world on the one hand, while taken together they adumbrate a distinction between two elements that make up part of the medieval ethos on the other.

In *Korai Fūteishō* (1197), Shunzei located depth in poetry in terms of a specific metaphysical dialectic that was consciously derived from Tendai Buddhist doctrine. Chōmei in *Mumyōshō* (ca. 1216), however, illustrated it largely in terms of a novel chromatic imagery that involved the attenuation of color.[2] Immediately following his prefatory remarks in *Korai Fūteishō*, Shunzei cited the *Mo-ho Chih-kuan* (J. *Maka Shikan*), a fundamental text by the Chinese T'ien-t'ai monk Chih-i (538–597), as a means of dicussing what he called "depth of meaning" (*kokoro fukaki*) in poetry.[3] This term, which can be traced back to the *Shinsen Zuinō* of the Heian poet and wakan theorist Fujiwara Kintō (d. 1041), has been interpreted as revealing a need, becoming increasingly acute since the early eleventh century, for a significantly new poetics that could account for new developments that were taking place in poetry.

The main thrust of Shunzei's proposal was the proposition that central to both waka poetry and Buddhism—the equation of the two lay at the heart of native attitudes toward poetry in Japan—was the identity of the poetic terms "heart" and "void" (*kororo*, 心, and *kū*, 空), the latter a technical term describing an important tenet of T'ien-t'ai (Tendai) Buddhism. Shunzei further suggested that the concept of depth in both religion and poetry is not something to be thought of as a state or condition, nor even as a dimension, but rather as a dialectical *process* in which Void, the primary principle, is postulated against an antithetical Provisional Reality (*ge*, 仮), and the apparent antithesis resulting in a third, more profound state of Mediated Reality (*chū*, 中) in which the two are brought into reconciliation, not as a duality, but rather within a new synthesis. While this is a great oversimplification of the complex T'ien-t'ai analysis of the nature of reality, it seems at least a fair description of how Shunzei probably understood it.

Shunzei began by asking pragmatically how one is to distinguish between good and bad in a poet's handling of "the words that inform a poem" (*sugata kotoba*), and suggested the following answer:

> In the opening words of the *Mo-ho Chih-kuan* of the T'ien-t'ai sect, Chang-an Ta-shih [Chih-i's disciple, 561–632] wrote that "the illuminating and calming effect of the practice of stillness and contemplation [Ch. *chih-kuan*, J. *shikan*] was not known in the period before Chih-i." But Chih-i was able to infer from the effect of *shikan* the limitless depth and profound meaning of things, a realization that was estimable

---

[2] See Konishi Jin'ichi, "Shunzei no Yūgenfū to Shikan," *Bungaku* 20:2 (February 1952), 108–16.
[3] *Korai Fūteishō*; Ariyoshi Tamotsu et al., eds., *Karonshū*, NKBZ (1979), 50:274ff.

and marvelous. And so too, though it is difficult to express in mere words [*kotoba*], we can distinguish in the light of Chih-i's experience between good and bad in waka poetry through an understanding of "depth of heart" [*kokoro fukaki*].

In the *Mo-ho Chih-kuan*, the order of transmission of the Buddha's Law is first made clear and the Path of the later transmission of the Law made known. Shākyamuni's Law passed to Kāśyapa, and from Kāśyapa to Ānanda, and thence in sequence through twenty-three Patriarchs to Chih-i. Just as a sense of great esteem is instilled in us when we hear of the transmission of the Law, so too we are able to understand the "depth of heart" that is embodied in waka poetry in the course of its transmission from ancient times to our own, in imperial anthologies from the *Man'yōshū* down to the *Kokinshū*, *Gosenshū*, and *Shūishū*.

While the Law that was taught by the Buddha himself has profound meaning, poetry, by contrast, may seem to be mere playing at "empty words and ornate speech." Because poetry, too, reveals the deeper significance of things, however, it can also communicate the Buddha's Way. Moreover, scripture tells us that "even the very desires and attachments themselves are enlightenment," and the *Lotus Sutra* that "even secular works and actions intended to promote life are all in accord with the True Law of the Buddha." The *Kan Fugen Bossatsu Gyōhō Kyō* [Sutra of Meditation on the Bodhisattva of Universal Wisdom] further explains that while we may say that "this is sinful" or "this is good", in fact both "sin" and "good" are unreal, *for the heart itself is Void* [i.e., empty of any reality]. In this sense, we may speak of the Way of "depth" in poetry, too, in the light of the T'ien-t'ai *san-t'i* [J. *sandai*] dialectic of Void, Provisional Reality, and Mediated Reality, for it also communicates the Way of the Buddha's Law.[4]

Shunzei seems to equate himself with Chih-i insofar, he says, as no one who came before understood the true nature of "depth" in things that is made possible by a proper understanding of the Tendai thought contained in the *Mo-ho Chih-kuan*. The import of the second paragraph is to explain why Shunzei has selected a number of poems from the *Man'yōshū* onward to follow his highly abstract theoretical introduction. The crux of his argument comes in the third paragraph, in which poetry is not only given a theoretical basis and a pedigree, but its practice is also sanctioned by a variety of rationalizations cited from the sutras, and the concept of depth in poetry is finally expressly equated with the Tendai metaphysical dialectic. After continuing to explain his reasons for writing and outlining the plan of his work, Shunzei says that although he realizes that he will be thought to be self-serving in making such elaborate rationalizations, and that to write in the hope of fame is vain, still,

---

[4] *NKBZ*, 50:275. The *Kan Fugenkyō* is the text with which the Lotus Sutra closes. In his *Shaseki-shū* (1283) Mujū Ichien also established a rationale for the use of waka poetry as efficacious in stilling and deepening the "heart"; see Watanabe Tsunaya, *Shasekishū*, *NKBT* (1973), 85:222–24.

if as time passes I can come to an understanding of the limitless profundity of the Buddha's Law through an understanding of the profundity of Japanese poetry, I will thereby create the effect of being reborn in paradise and will be able to realize the Boddhisattva's vow to save all living beings. Then, in fact, I will have turned my words of poetry to praise of the Buddha that can travel far and wide to those countries that have heard the Buddha's Law and lead the beings of this world to enlightenment.

While I shall have more to say about the significance of Shunzei's words, it will suffice for the moment to note how utterly his main idea differs from anything that had come before, binding waka poetry firmly to the metaphysics of Buddhist thought in the search for a new profundity in poetry. This dramatic plunge beneath the exterior manifestations of "things" in order to find the deeper significance that informs them is perhaps the clearest sign of the "medieval" mind, and stands in contrast to the typical "classical" concern for lyrical intensity and beauty of pattern so characteristic of the mid-Heian period.[5] This change is often illustrated by Kamō no Chōmei's *Hōjōki* (Record of My Hut, 1212), a short lyrical narrative, based on a Chinese work, that seems to announce the new concern of medieval man with the state of his soul, and from that novel starting point to discover a new sense of order and beauty, a new aesthetic, in the dramatically altered conditions of his times.

Chōmei was concerned, as was Shunzei, with defining this new aesthetic, and especially with the troublesome term *yūgen*, a word with a long history reaching back to early Chinese Taoist thought and now brought into literary discussion to represent something new—exactly what is not always clear—that needed naming.[6] Chōmei wrote that the meaning of this mysterious term gave rise to considerable confusion in his own day, and rather than attempt to define it, he chose instead to provide an illustration:

> On an autumn evening, for example, there is no color in the sky, and although we cannot give a definite reason for it, we are somehow moved to tears. A person lacking in sensitivity finds nothing peculiar in such a sight; he just admires the cherry blossoms and scarlet autumn leaves that he can see with his own eyes.[7]

In other words, beneath the surface of phenomenal reality, the illusion that the colorful things of the world are themselves "real," one finds an otherwise

---

[5] See Yasuraoka Kōsaku, *Chūseiteki Bungaku no Tankyū* (Tokyo: Yūseidō, 1971), 53.

[6] For a complete discussion of the term *yūgen* as it developed in China and was used both there and in Japan, see Nose Asaji, *Yūgenron*, in Nose Asaji Chosakushū Henshū Iinkai, ed., *Nose Asaji Chosakushū* (Kyoto: Shibunkaku, 1981), vol. 2. 199–413.

[7] *Mumyōshō*; Hisamatsu Sen'ichi, ed., *Karonshū, NKBT*, 65:87 (Tokyo: Iwanami Shoten, 1961). Translated in Hilda Katō, "The *Mumyōshō* of Kamo no Chōmei and Its Significance in Japanese Literature," *Monumenta Nipponica* 23:3–4 (October 1968), 408. Chōmei's statement is echoed in a famous passage by Yoshida Kenko (1283–1350) in *Tsurezuregusa* (ca. 1330); cf. *NKBZ*, 27:178.

invisible, more profound reality. This reality, Chōmei said, is sensed in what he called *yojō*, the "reverberations of poetry that are not stated in the words, an atmosphere not revealed by the formal aspects of a poem." It was undoubtedly in sympathetic resonance with this same new way of looking at things, as yet unappreciated by those whom Chōmei described scornfully as "lacking in sensitivity" (*kokoro naki hito*), that the poet Saigyō had written his famous lines included in the *Shinkokinshū* (362):

Kokoro naki	*Even someone like myself,*
Mi ni mo aware	*Lacking in sensitivity,* would understand
Shirarekeri	The sad beauty of it ...

It was not merely in his persona of a Buddhist monk that Saigyō wrote of being devoid of *kokoro*, or "sensitivity," as these lines are customarily interpreted; rather, he was adopting the mock-humble guise of the rustic and unsophisticated poet insensitive to this newfangled sense of beauty. Indeed, it is precisely as a man of religion that Saigyō arrived at this perception. By contrast, Teika's equally famous lines cited above, that immediately follow in the anthology (362),

Miwataseba	Even as I look,
Hana mo momiji mo	The bright colors of cherry blossoms
Nakarikeri	And maple leaves disappear:
Ura no tomaya no	Autumn twilight deepens
Aki no yūgure	Over a thatched hut by the bay.

seem to provide the perfect example of just what it is that the *kokoro aru hito*, "person of sensitivity," should be expected to admire in an autumn sunset. This poem on the topic of "Futamigaura" (Twin-View Bay), composed in 1186 at a poetry gathering in honor of Saigyō when Teika was only twenty-five, takes its method from the double perception demanded by the name of its subject; insisting on a second, deeper "look about," the poet now sees in this scene what no other poet ever had before. It is precisely this "deeper vision" that influenced especially the quality of "color" that so fascinated Chōmei:

> If you look at the autumn hills through a rift in the mist, you catch only a glimpse, and, unsatisfied, try to imagine how pleasing it might be to see the whole of those scarlet leaves—this is almost better than seeing it clearly.[8]

---

[8] *Mumyōshō*, NKBT, 65:87; Katō, "*Mumyōshō*," 409. Hisamatsu notes, as does Nose (see above, n. 6), that this description of the "blurred" aspect of *yūgen* may be traceable to the indistinct epiphanies of goddesses in works such as the "Kao-T'ang Fu" prose poem by Sung Yü and Ts'ao Chih's "Lo-shen Fu," both in the *Wen Hsüan*. The goddess in the "Lo-shen Fu," for example, is depicted as "indistinct as the moon hidden behind light clouds." See also Ōta Seikyū, *Nihon Kagaku to Chūgoku Shigaku* (Tokyo: Shimizu Kōbundō, 1968), 134–44.

We can recognize in Chōmei's stance something of the familiar Heian fascination with *kaima-mi*, the special attraction of something not seen quite clearly or in its entirety, but caught tantalizingly through a gap in some intervening material—fog, blinds, curtains, fences, and the like. But Chōmei was also moving toward a new sort of sensitivity, an aesthetic that emphasized monochromaticity, a reduction of color implying some more profoundly essential reality that stands in contrast to the bright colors characteristic of the superficial world of appearances. "What we can see with our own eyes" he clearly intended to stand in negative opposition to some superior quality that cannot be apprehended by the senses. Here we find one of those polarities that seem so central to Teika's early poetic preference for the appeal of the plain, the simple, the unpretentious, even the drab, the quality that has come to be known as *heitanbi*, in contrast to his later evolution to an emphasis on graceful charm or "ethereal beauty" (*yōenbi*). Saigyō, too, had summed up this same quality in the final two lines of his poem cited above, in an image of the drabbest imaginable nature: a dull, brown, insignificant bird rising from a marsh at autumn twilight:

Sawa tatsu shigi no	. . . A snipe rises from a marsh
Aki no yūgure	In the deepening autumn twilight.

What seems at first a very similar mode of perception can apparently be found two centuries before Chōmei set down his thoughts. In a passage of the "Asagao" (Morning Faces) chapter of *The Tale of Genji*, for example, a preference is explicitly expressed for something *other* than the colors of cherry blossoms and maple leaves—not, however, as in the case of Saigyō or Teika or Chōmei, for the muted tones of autumn twilight, but rather for a Six Dynasties Chinese taste for the brilliance of white moonlight that not only obliterates all color but transcends it as well:

> People make a good deal of the blossoms of spring and the maple leaves of the autumn, but for me a night like this, with a clear moon shining on snow, is the best—and there is not a trace of color in it. I cannot describe the effect it has on me, weird and unearthly somehow.[9]

And what appears at first to be very much the same sort of preference is also found in the *Mumyōshō* in Chōmei's remark that a fine poem "can be likened to the color white, which, although it permits of no gradations of color shades [*kotonaru nioi mo nakeredo*], is the best of all colors."[10] The difference is that while for Murasaki Shikibu it was the "brilliance" (*hikari*) of moonlight that so moved one, for Chōmei it was quite the opposite quality, for, he continues,

[9] Seidensticker, *Genji*, 367; Tamagami, *Hyōshaku*, vol. 4, 294.
[10] *Mumyōshō*, NKBT, 65:89; Katō, "*Mumyōshō*," somewhat emended, 411. We might note that the color "white," and no other, occupies a separate category in the *Wakan Rōeishū*.

"the very highest quality of all things lies in their blandness and lack of particular attraction [*awaku susamajiki nari,* 淡く凄じきなり]."

This last phrase of Chōmei's, which epitomizes the aesthetics of his day, looks to the continent, for it is very nearly a literal translation into Japanese of the contemporary Sung Chinese preference for what was called, among other terms, the "even and bland" (*p'ing-tan,* 平淡) that was already well established in China by this time(that is, the Southern Sung period, 1127–1279). In fact, by the mid-eleventh century Chinese poets were already using a new and radically different vocabulary to describe important aesthetic ideals. Words such as "bland," "dry," "withered," "cold," "lonely," and "thin" so clearly foreshadow the appearance of the new ideal of *sabi* in the Shinkokin period as to suggest a direct influence, the Chinese ideal of *p'ing-tan* yielding in Japanese the aesthetic term now commonly applied to this quality in waka poetry, *heitan.* To understand what these terms might have meant in Japan around 1200, then, we need to look at the evolution of the term as it had developed in China.

Chōmei's own use of the phrase "blandness and lack of particular attraction" is thought to allude to one of the oldest Chinese appearances of the term *tan* in the Taoist text *Chuang Tzu:* "the relations of a true gentleman with others are bland as water," that is, refreshing in contrast to the cloying relations of the "petty man which are sweet as sugar." In other passages from the *Chuang Tzu* and *Lao Tzu* the word is used with similarly positive implications to describe the functioning of the Tao, "simplicity" and "blandness" used as positive attributes to describe Emptiness (*wu,* a Taoist analog and probable precursor of the Chinese and Japanese Buddhist term Void).[11]

The term *p'ing-tan* was first used to describe literary qualities in the *Shih-p'in* of the Six Dynasties theorist Chung Hung (ca. 505). Chung, however, was using the term in a pejorative sense, and it really only came into wide usage as a positive literary term during the mid-T'ang dynasty in the late eighth and early ninth centuries. Po Chü-i's (772–846) characterization of his own poetry as "bland and flavorless," for example, could scarcely have escaped the eyes of Teika and his contemporaries, who were still very much concerned with the Heian tradition of the reinterpretation of Po's poetry.

[11] My discussion of *p'ing-tan* in China follows Jonathan Chaves, *Mei Yao-ch'en and the Development of Early Sung Poetry* (New York: Columbia University Press, 1976), 114–25. See also Yokoyama Iseo, "Sō Shiron ni Miru 'Heitan no Tai' ni Tsuite," Tōkyō Daigaku Kambun Gakkai, *Kanbun Gakkai Kaihō* 20 (1961), 33ff. Most of the passages on *p'ing-tan* in Sung criticism cited below can be found in a section devoted to that term in the important Southern Sung compilation *Shih-jen Yü-hsieh* (Jade Chips From the Poets, preface dated 1244) by Wei Ch'ing-chih, a work well known in medieval Japan. See the edition by Yang Chia-lo (Taipei: Shih-chieh Shu-chü, 1971), 218–19. See also Brower and Miner, *Japanese Court Poetry,* 356–365.

It was only in the Northern Sung dynasty (906–1126), and especially from the middle of the eleventh century on, that what appears to be an entirely new set of aesthetic values appeared in China, not only in the vocabulary of poetry but in that of every art, including painting and ceramics, two areas in which this new aesthetic is most dramatically made visible to the Western eye.

Another important locus of the "even and bland" was the Sung dynasty emphasis on the drinking of tea, a practice that stands in clear contrast to the T'ang preference for alcoholic liquor. While the cult of tea had its origins in the T'ang period, tea appears as the beverage of choice in poetry much more often in the Sung. While wine was the source of inspiration for a great deal of poetry, as well as consolation in difficult times, the blander tea was the meditative drink used especially by Buddhist monks, and the Sung poets were greatly influenced by Ch'an Buddhist practice. Tea seems the very epitome of the "bland" quality so prized in Sung aesthetics, from the drink itself and the bowls that held it to the taste that prized it and the arts that taste informed.

Later important Sung poets and theorists are unanimous in tracing the first regular application of the term *p'ing-tan* to the work of Mei Yao-ch'en (1002–1060), who defined it as referring to poetry that is expressed in understated terms. Mei's requirement that poetic diction be understated is generally interpreted as a reaction to the prevailing lush and overblown style of the Hsi-k'un school of the early Sung, which often amounted to a near-parody of the exotic work of its late T'ang progenitor Li Shang-yin (812–858). Mei Yao-ch'en does not in fact appear to have been entirely consistent in his use of the term *p'ing-tan*, nor is it always a simple matter to discover exactly what is "even and bland" about poems he cites as epitomizing those qualities. What is clear on the whole is that in Mei's day the ideal was not yet fixed but still evolving.

By the beginning of the twelfth century, the qualities felt to embody the new aesthetic had become a fixed canon of critical taste for generations to come, having been endorsed by the great poet Su Tung-p'o (1036–1101). "What is to be prized in the 'withered and bland,'" wrote Su, "is when the outside is withered while the inside is rich, so that something seems bland when it is actually beautiful." This emphasis on the complementary nature of what at first would seem to be opposites is characteristic of mid-twelfth-century Chinese criticism. This critical polarity was further elaborated into a natural seasonal progression, things in springtime and youth "rich," those in fall and winter achieving a matured, "withered" quality. As in Japan, however, Sung critical thought eventually came to place the distinction on one side of a new equation. "With poetry, it is not a matter of being either 'rich' or 'withered,'" wrote the critic Ch'en Chih-jou (fl. 1142). "Things all start out as 'rich' and end up as 'withered.' If there is nothing distinctive within, then the flavor of the idea will emerge spontaneously." And the critic Wu K'o (ca. 1126) held that *p'ing-tan*, as the epitome of that quality of having "nothing distinctive within," represented the culmination of a poet's development, citing as an example the poetry of the T'ang poet Tu Fu, which he said was "flowery" when the poet was young but became "even and bland" as he grew older. "All literature is at first 'flowery and beautiful,' and later 'even and bland,'" wrote Wu:

> In this way, it is like the sequence of the four seasons. In spring, things are flowery and beautiful; in summer, flourishing and ripe. In autumn and winter they withdraw and hibernate, becoming withered outside while rich within.

And K'o Li-wu, a Chinese contemporary of Shunzei, wrote that "if you wish to create an atmosphere of *p'ing-tan*, your writing must first, of its own accord, create beauty. When the blossoms have fallen, the scene thus created will be 'even and bland.'"

Although similar ideas began to make their way to Japan in the twelfth century, we will probably never know exactly by what route or in what form they first arrived in Japan. In contrast to the poetry of Po Chü-i, which historical records tell us was brought to Japan in 838 during the Chinese poet's own lifetime, there is little in the historical evidence to indicate that Japanese poets and theorists of the twelfth century were directly familiar with the critical writings of their contemporary Chinese counterparts. Furthermore, since this period in Japan is usually misleadingly thought of as simply continuing the "reaction" to Chinese learning that began in the tenth century, there has been a reluctance on the part of scholars to examine the nature of Chinese influence at this time, despite the extensive and important work by such scholars as Konishi Jin'ichi on the effect of late Six Dynasties and early T'ang influence on Japanese theory and practice of the *Kokinshū* age (905), and of Sung aesthetics on this and subsequent periods.[12]

This is due in part to a simple lacuna in the historical record. Government-sponsored diplomatic missions to China formally ended in 894 and were not resumed again until the dispatch of the famous "Tenryūji Ship" of 1342. Although there is therefore little of an official record in the centuries to follow,

---

[12] Works by Konishi Jin'ichi that examine Chinese literary theory in the light of its absorption in Japanese literature include: (1) *Bunkyō Hifuron Kō* (A Study of the *Wen-ching Mi-fu Lun*), 3 vols. (Tokyo: Kōdansha, 1948–1953). (2) "Kokinshū-teki Hyōgen no Seiritsu," *Nihon Gakushiin Kiyō* 7:3 (1949), 163–95. Translated by Helen C. McCullough as "The Genesis of the Kokinshū Style," *Harvard Journal of Asiatic Studies* 38:1 (June 1978), 61–170. (3)* "Chūseiteki Hyōgen Ishiki to Sōdai Shiron" (Medieval Japanese Poetic Expression and Sung Dynasty Poetics), *Kokugo* 1:1 (October 1951). (4)* "Chūseibi no Hi-Nihonteki Seikaku" (The Non-Japanese Character of Medieval Aesthetics), *Bungaku* 21 (1953). (5) "Yoshimoto to Sōdai Shiron" (Nijō Yoshimoto and Sung Dynasty Poetics), *Gobun* 14 (1968). (6) "Yōenbi" (The Aesthetic of "Ethereal Charm"), *Kokugo Kokubun* 22 (1953). (7) "Gyokuyōshū Jidai to Sōshi" (The Period of the *Gyokuyōshū* and Sung Poetry), in Jōkō Kan'ichi, ed., *Chūsei Bungaku no Sekai* (Tokyo: Iwanami Shoten, 1960), 151–81. (* These were not available to me in writing this essay.)

it is well known that Japanese merchants and monks in fact continued to travel extensively between the two countries in large numbers, and the Shogun Taira no Kiyomori (d. 1181) is known in part for his vision of an active trade with Sung China as part of a resurgent new Japan. Yet Japanese scholars, for the most part, begin their discussion of the influence of the Sung style upon Japan with the formation of the Gozan, or Rinzai Zen, establishment from the last quarter of the thirteenth century, leaving the erroneous impression that the Japanese knew nothing of Sung Neo-Confucianism until the Zen monk Enni Ben'en returned to Japan in 1241 with a wealth of material gathered during his six-year visit, or of Sung poetry criticism until Enni's disciple Kokan Shiren (1278–1346) wrote his *Saihoku Shiwa*, the first of the extant Gozan treatises on Chinese poetry.

Long before these events, however, the Japanese monk Myōan Eisai (or Yōsai, 1141–1215) had returned from two trips to China (1168, 1187–1191), and the monk Shunjō after him (1166–1227, in China 1199–1211), bearing not only the latest information on the mainland practice of Ch'an Buddhism but a great deal of other mainland culture besides. Eisai, for example, is revered as the founder of the cult of tea (*chanoyu*) in Japan, having brought back not only tea seeds but a first-hand knowledge of tea connoisseurship from China. Eisai and Shunjō are also known as the Japanese "patriarchs" of the style of calligraphy of the Northern Sung poets Su Shih (1036–1101) and Huang T'ing-chien (1045–1105), Huang's influence on Japanese calligraphy still visible in Eisai's holograph of the *Urabon Ippongyō Engi* of 1178.[13] Such records would probably never have been preserved at all except that Eisai, the first politically significant monk to promote the teaching of Ch'an (Zen) Buddhism in Japan, attracted a great deal of attention in his own day and afterward, some of it from the Shinkokin courtiers and most of it hostile, a matter that I shall examine at greater length. Suffice it here to say that Japanese poets and theorists of the twelfth century appear to have been amply familiar with contemporary currents of Chinese thought and practice that were undoubtedly being brought to Japan at that time, albeit in small and erratic waves, by Japanese, Chinese, and Korean monks, merchants, and craftsmen. Much of the Chinese material I have cited seems to have been known by the Japanese long before it appeared at the sinophilic courts of Go-Uda and Fushimi in the form of the Sung compilation *Shin-jen Yü-hsieh* (Jade Chips from the Poets, preface dated 1244 by Wei Ch'ing-chih), although certainly it was in the form of this compilation that particular critical terms and ideas were to enter later literary thought in Japan.

Small but telling hints suggest that the Shinkokin poets appear to have known something of these Sung critical attitudes and were composing their

[13] See Mizuta Norihisa in Mizuta and Rai Tsutomu, eds., *Chūgoku Bunka Sōsho: Nihon Kangaku* (Tokyo: Taishūkan, 1968), 134.

poetry in response to them, though they may not yet have been aware of exactly what it was they were responding to. At one gathering of several of the most important poets of the time at the recently established Poetry Bureau (*wakadokoro*) in the Sentō Gosho palace on the twenty-second of the third month of 1202, for example, Emperor Go-Toba ordered the assembled court-iers, including Teika, Jakuren, and Jien, to write "poetry in three styles."[14] The emperor further explained that by "three styles" he meant that poems on the topics of spring and summer were to be "large and full" (*futoku ōki*), and those on the topics of autumn and winter, "thin and withered" (*hosoku karabi*); the emperor's instructions to his courtiers were recorded this way in one instance by Chōmei in *Mumyōshō*.[15] Teika's diary, *Meigetsuki*, adds to this record the significant detail that what Go-Toba meant by "withered" was "thin and desolate" (*yase sugoki*, interpreting *sugoshi*, 凄し, as meaning the same thing as Chōmei's term *susamajii*, 凄じい, or "lack of any particular attraction").

Of the five works that record this event, the wording of four—Chōmei's *Mumyōshō*, Teika's *Meigetsuki*, Go-Toba's *Go-Toba-in Goshū*, and Fujiwara Yoshitsune's *Akishino Gesseishū*—is essentially the same. Fujiwara Ietaka's (1158–1237) *Minishū*, however, equates the "three styles" ordered by Go-Toba with what seem to be three of the "ten styles" of poetry enumerated by Teika: thus summer and spring he equates with the *taketakaki yō*, a style of fullness and beauty, and fall and winter with the *ushin yō* or style of intense feeling. "Travel and Love Poems," the category of poems to be written in Go-Toba's last style of the three, are to be "charming" (*en*) or "charming and attractive" (*en ni yasashiku*), as described by four of the poets at the gathering. Again only Ietaka's account differs significantly from that of the others: he equates this theme, oddly enough, with the *yūgen tei*, "style of mystery and depth."

Go-Toba's instructions are clearly suggestive of Wu K'o's equation of seasons with different poetic styles. There is something, too, in the wording of the poems Chōmei composed in each category reminiscent of poetry cited in Sung critical works as epitomizing the qualities felt to characterize each season. Thus, Chōmei's illustration of the withered nature of autumn, for example,

Sabishisa wa	A sense of desolation
Nao nokorikeri	All that lingers now:
Ato tayuru	Upon the fallen leaves,
Ochiba ga ue ni	Traces forever buried,
Kesa wa hatsuyuki	This morning's first winter snow.

[14] This event, known as the "Sandai waka," is recorded in Sasaki Nobutsuna, *Nihon Kagaku Taikei* (Tokyo: Kayama Shobō, 1956), vol. 3, 12ff.

[15] *Mumyōshō*, *NKBT*, 65:77–78 and 249, n. 88. For the *Meigetsuki* entry below, see Sekimoto Yukio, ed., *Meigetsuki* (Tokyo: Kokusho Kankōkai, 1970), vol. 1, 249, entry for *Kennin 2/3/28*. See also Yasuda Ayao, *Fujiwara Teika Kenkyū* (Tokyo: Shibundō, 1967), 107ff.; and Minemura Fumito, *Shinkokin Wakashū*, *NKBZ*, 26:19–20.

can be compared with a couplet by the mid-ninth-century poet Wen T'ing-yün that Mei Yao-ch'en had cited as particularly evocative of this season:

A cock crows in the moonlight over the thatched wine shop:
Someone's footprints in the frost on a plank wood bridge.

In the Chinese poem we see the footprints of a traveler up before dawn, his presence marked only by traces that remain in the frost on the bridge leading out of town to the road through the mountains. The Japanese poem, too, calls our attention to the faint traces of footprints that, like the maple leaves' brilliance, have all but disappeared under the first snow of the season. The stark scenes of late autumn emphasize the sense of lonely melancholy implied in the absence of what, until only recently, had been a comfort to the poet.

Mei Yao-ch'en's example was cited by his mentor Ou-yang Hsiu (1007–1072), not with the intention of illustrating what a poem about "autumn" should be like, but rather as an example of what he called a poem whose "idea was felt beyond the words." This quality of poetry, one of the major ideals of the Sung writers, is summed up in the concept that the most important part of any poem was what remained after the words themselves were accounted for. This is of course almost a definition of the medieval Japanese ideal of *yojō*, the "feeling that lingers after the words are exhausted," or, as Chōmei put it, "that quality that is not stated in the words of a poem." In his discussion of the superior "bland" quality in poetry, he refers to a passage in the *Chuang Tzu*, the Taoist text that also contains the classical source of the idea that meaning ultimately lies beyond the realm of "words" themselves: "The fish trap exists because of the fish; once you've gotten the fish, you can forget the trap. Words exist because of the meaning; once you've gotten the meaning, you can forget the words." Mei also stated, according to Ou-yang Hsiu, that the most important thing in poetry was "the ability to write poetry whose meaning is not exhausted by the words, but lies beyond them."[16]

I have rehearsed some of the elements of Sung poetic theory here not to imply that the poetic ideals of *sabi* and *yojō* were simply derived from contemporary Sung practice, but rather to suggest that their sudden importance seems to reflect the court poets' awareness of the new Sung aesthetic *style*, so clearly evident in every other aspect of Sung culture that we should be amazed if the extremely literary-minded Japanese had not perceived it in poetry as well as in the other arts. To the extent that the new continental style was felt to be congenial to Japanese tradition and to contemporary practice, it could scarcely help but make itself felt in the waka poetry of twelfth-century Japan. It seems

---

[16] *Ou-yang Wen-chung Kung Chi*, ed. Ssu-pu Ts'ung-k'an, 128:5a-b; cited in Chaves, *Mei Yao-ch'en*, 111.

more likely, however, that Japanese poets were as yet only vaguely aware of their own response to this style than that they were consciously and enthusiastically embracing it. The latter response was left, on the whole, to the later medieval Zen monks, whose enthusiastic reception of what was felt in other, secular circles to be unacceptably foreign matter was simply a part of the context of their lives.[17] Despite the lack of any officially sanctioned contact with China for two hundred years, a fundamental change of perception, apparently related to new modes of perception arriving from the continent, was beginning to make itself felt in Japanese aesthetics by the end of the twelfth century. Just as Sung Neo-Confucianism, developing since the early tenth century in China, had already begun to reach Japanese soil well before Enni Ben'en returned from China in 1241 with large numbers of works by Sung philosophers, so too had the new styles of poetry, calligraphy, art, and objects of material culture, so radically different from what preceded them, along with the connoisseurship that established their uses.

Also in the air was a new style of Buddhism. The Japanese had been aware of the existence of Chinese Ch'an Buddhism since the seventh century, and in their intense devotion to the works of the poet Po Chü-i, Japanese poets could scarcely have been unaware of his frequent references to the practice of sitting in Ch'an (J. Zen) meditation. A similar form of seated meditation was, after all, a long-established part of Tendai Buddhist practice, the "stillness and contemplation" (Ch. *chih-kuan*, J. *shikan*) that forms part of the title of the *Mo-ho Chih-kuan* cited by Shunzei in 1197 as the metaphysical underpinning of a new understanding of "depth" in poetry.

We know very little of what the Shinkokin courtiers made of this new sect, or how it might have figured in their lives and poetics. They could scarcely have been ignorant of it, for the turbulent decades of the 1180s and 1190s especially saw many developments in the importation of this sect of Buddhism. Evidence suggests, however, that the courtiers were quite antagonistic toward the Tendai monk Eisai, who had traveled twice to China during Teika's lifetime, returning to Japan after his second visit in 1191 to attempt to establish the independent practice of Zen Buddhism there in the face of determined opposition from the leadership of his own Tendai establishment on Mt. Hiei. Eisai's various fortunes in Kyoto are recorded, among other places, in Teika's diary *Meigetsuki* and in the Tendai Abbot and court poet Jien's historical account *Gukanshō* (1220). With regard to one well-known incident in particular, both wrote of Eisai as nothing but a corrupt political upstart who was campaigning for unprecedented honors from Go-Toba and pushing aggressively for recognition as a new religious leader. Eisai, they claimed, wanted to be granted the title of Grand Teacher of Religion (*Daishi*), normally bestowed only posthumously

---

[17] See David Pollack, *Zen Poems of the Five Mountains* (Chico: Scholars Press, 1985).

and by general recognition. So bitterly did Jien oppose this move, and the schism in the Tendai church that it would have recognized, that Eisai finally had to content himself with the lesser title of Bishop; and even that Go-Toba would later say he regretted having bestowed upon him.[18]

For all their apparent antagonism toward the political problems raised by a new sect's challenge to the older established Buddhist structure (and Zen was only one of the new "reform" sects, though the only new sect brought from China), there are clear indications that Chōmei and his contemporaries associated elements of the new aesthetic tastes with the infant Zen religion. Zen itself was only one facet of the entire complex matrix of Sung culture, fundamentally inseparable from its other manifestations in such diverse fields as philosophy, art, poetry, ceramics, landscape architecture, and even tea-drinking. Chōmei noted in his *Mumyōshō*, for example, that in poetry "those who favor the style of the middle period [that is, the conservative Rokujō faction's preference for the style of the *Kokinshū*] regard the *uta* of our own day as nonsensical [*suzurogoto*], deriding and ridiculing it as 'Zen' [literally, *Darumashū*, "the sect of Bodhidharma"]."[19] Elsewhere (lest we should think of Chōmei as a Zen partisan) he describes poetry intentionally made so obscure that even its authors appeared to have lost the drift as being "not within the realm of *yūgen* at all and ought instead to be classified as 'Zen' [*Darumashū*]."[20]

These statements reveal as clearly as anything in the records of the time a tendency to equate the vague term *yūgen* with the popular perception of the Zen style. Teika, too, complained about the fact that his own contemporaries often referred to the poetry he wrote after 1185 as *Darumauta*, or "Zen poetry," a term that had already come to be used in a derogatory sense to mean "nonsense verse."[21] Mujū Ichien noted in his *Shasekishū* (1283) that even by his

---

[18] Tsuji Zennosuke, *Nihon Bukkyōshi* (Tokyo: Iwanami Shoten, rev. ed., 1960–1961), vol. 3, 78–79. Mujū Ichien defended Eisai on the grounds that his actions constituted an acceptable "expedient" that was necessary if Eisai were to be taken seriously in "these latter days of the Buddha's Law"; cf. *Shasekishū*, NKBT, 85:453.

Exploring the political situation around Eisai, Furuta Shokin has proposed the possibility that Eisai was backed in his early rise by Mei'un, who was fifty-fifth and fifty-seventh Tendai Zasu, and about whom Jien (sixty-second and sixty-fifth Tendai Zasu) wrote as disparagingly as he did of Eisai. Embroiled in several political intrigues, Mei'un was stripped of rank and office and exiled in 1177 for his role in the "Shishigatani plot" of 1176. He died on the nineteenth month of the eleventh month of 1193 when Kiso Yoshinaka attacked Hōjūji, the palace of the cloistered Emperor Go-Shirakawa where Mei'un had fled for refuge. Furuta concludes that the loss of Eisai's political mentor at Mei'un's death prevented him from raising the funds necessary to return to China earlier than he did. See *Furuta Shokin Chosakusho* (Tokyo: Kōdansha, 1981), vol. 2, 125ff.

[19] *Mumyōshō*, NKBT, 65:82; Katō, "*Mumyōshō*," 404.

[20] *Mumyōshō*, NKBT, 65:86; Katō, "*Mumyōshō*," amended, 408.

[21] Ishida Yoshisada, *Shinkokin Sekai to Chūsei Bungaku* (Komazawa: Komazawa Tosho, 1972), vol. 1, 118ff., esp. 121ff., "Teika 'Darumauta' no Honshitsu to Seiritsu," cites a passage in the preface of the "Horikawa-in Dai Hyakushū" that calls Teika's "a new style without precedent, Daruma

own day the Zen sect was still the object of the mistrust and envy of the monks of the other sects, whose scholars persisted in ridiculing it with the pejorative term *Darumashū*.[22] Mujū's overriding preoccupation was the promotion of harmony among all sects of Buddhism, which seem to have been quarreling much of the time, but he apparently could not resist citing half in jest a waka poem "by a man of old" in retaliation for what he obviously felt to be an unjust and mean-spirited appellation:

Rachi no hoka	What nonsense!
Daruma o wasuru	It is in fact
Hito o koso	He who speaks ill
Norishirazu to wa	Of Bodhidharma
Iubekarikere	Who knows not the Law!

Teika's early detractors were in excellent company—even Fujiwara Shunzei, as judge of the famous *Roppyakuban* (Six Hundred Round) poetry contest of 1193, agreed with the general opinion that his own son's poems were particularly difficult to understand.[23]

In light of these indications of a general hostility toward Zen on the part of the aristocracy, it seems of considerable interest that in his search for a metaphysics to support his ideas about poetry Shunzei should have felt it congenial or necessary to draw upon the Tendai *sandai* dialectic. The *Korai Fūteishō*, after all, otherwise amounts to little more than a preface to a *catalogue raisonné* of choice poems through the ages. The fact that he should have drawn upon the doctrines of this old and established aristocratic sect that exercised considerable influence at the court of the cloistered Emperor Go-Toba suggests that while Shunzei may indeed have felt the need to turn to the refuge Buddhism offered in those terrible times, he may also have felt himself called upon to defend both Buddhism and Japanese poetry from attack from some quarter.

Exactly what quarter that might have been is suggested by the phrase that immediately precedes his introduction of the *sandai* dialectic: "While the Law that was taught by the Buddha himself has profound meaning, poetry, by contrast, may seem to be mere playing at 'empty words and ornate speech.'" The phrase "empty words and ornate speech" (*fugen kigo*, or more commonly

---

poetry despised by all, noble and base alike." On 289–303, Ishida also discusses Teika's particular sensitivity in adapting Chinese verse in his poetry. Yanagida Seizan, *Eisai* (*Nihon Shisō Taikei*, hereafter cited as *NST*; Iwanami Shoten, 1972), vol. 16, 469–70, also emphasizes that these passages reveal an increasing awareness of mainland Chinese currents.

[22] *Shasekishū, NKBT*, 85:254–55.

[23] Ishida, *Shinkokin Sekai*. Teika's fondness for "Daruma poetry" was clearly part of the indiscretion of youth, and modern scholars seem to have agreed with the aristocratic breeding that ignored it over the centuries in favor of the more important (and respectable) emphasis in his mature verse on the qualities of *yūgen* and *yōen*.

"wild words and ornate speech," *kyōgen kigo*) resounds throughout all of medieval Japanese literary history. Originating in such scriptures as the Pure Land sect's *Sutra of Limitless Longevity (Muryōjukyō)*, it is part of a list of "Ten Evils" among which are "foolish speech" and "ornate speech," usually interpreted to mean poetry intended for the aesthetic enjoyment of the beauty of words alone rather than as an expression of Buddhist principles. Eisai himself wrote in his treatise *Kōzen Gokokuron* (On the Promotion of Zen for the Defense of the Nation) that one should not allow "wild words"—that is, poetic language—to distort "true fact."[24]

The phrase "wild words and ornate speech" first entered Chinese literary discussion in Po Chü-i's famous *apologia pro vita sua* as he, a firm believer and lay practitioner of the tenets of Buddhism, looked back in 840 at the age of seventy-one over a lifetime devoted to the writing of poetry, in apparent violation of this teaching of Buddha. "It was my Original Vow," wrote Po, "to turn my karma of words in this life, my transgressions of 'wild words and ornate speech,' to the cause of praising the Buddha's Law in the world to come and so to turn the Wheel of the Law."[25] The phrase as Po used it entered Japanese literary discussion with its inclusion in Fujiwara Kintō's *Wakan Rōeishū* of 1018, and also appears in the "Buddhist Works" section of the mid-eleventh-century *Ryōjin Hishō*.

What is significant for our own comprehension of Shunzei's intent, and of his sources as well, is that this phrase of Po's that follows Shunzei's citation of the *Mo-ho Chih-kuan* also appears in the *Wakan Rōeishū* immediately after a poetic passage from the *Mo-ho Chih-kuan* that speaks of the importance of metaphor in revealing deeper truths than the human intellect is otherwise capable of knowing. Like Po's reinterpretation of "wild words and ornate speech," this passage offers a justification of what would appear to be a purely literary technique by placing it within the context of religion: "For the moon, hidden by layers of mountains, an open fan serves as a metaphor; of the wind that breathes through the vast sky the movement of trees informs us."[26] Po's justification is thus set, if

---

[24] See n. 28. It is typical that when giving voice to his deepest emotions, however, Eisai should have reverted to his native tongue. Thus, upon learning of the death of his mother in Japan while he was studying in China in 1168, Eisai expressed his feelings in a poem that is entirely and elaborately Japanese:

Morokoshi no	Even the scion in distant China
Kozue mo sabishi	Is saddened by the falling
Hi no moto no	Of the red leaves,
Hahaso no momiji	Dead and returned to dust,
Chiri ya shinuramu	Of the mother oak in Japan.

[25] *Hakushi Monjū*, chap. 27, "Record of the 'Lo Collection' of Po Chü-i"; *Po Hsiang-shan Shih-chi*, 230.

[26] *Wakan Rōeishū, NKBT*, 73:200. The phrase *kyōgen kigo* appears also in the mid-eleventh-century *Ryōjin Hishō*, ed. Shinma Shin'ichi, (*NKBZ*, 25:255; Tokyo: Shogakkan, 1976) as a rationalization for the performing arts in general as Buddhist "expedients."

only by juxtaposition (and we have seen the importance of such juxtaposition in the *Wakan Rōeishū*), in the context of the validity of metaphor for the Heian poet in the metaphysics of both religion and poetry. Once established, this validity continued to find renewed currency throughout medieval Japanese literary theory. Mujū Ichien, for example, and after him many monks much less eclectic in their understanding of their Zen than he, thought of waka poetry as "the *dharani* of Japan," referring to the mystical incantations of the Shingon sect of Buddhism. The native role of Japanese poetry as incantation possessing the magical power of invoking the gods directly was never questioned; these elaborate rationalizations were necessary only when poetry was understood within its alien Chinese and Buddhist contexts.

In terms of literary thought, Shunzei's theoretical formulation can be understood as part of the late Heian search for a renewed sense of the profundity of a poetry that was felt to be in danger of becoming trivialized. But no poetry stands apart from the other concerns of its time, and Shunzei was as much the product of the desperate political fortunes of his age as he was the inheritor of a long literary tradition. So, too, were all the poets around the court of Go-Toba, who "retired" as emperor and took Buddhist orders at the age of eighteen, the year after Shunzei had written his *Korai Fūteishō*, the better to take an active hand in political intrigue and demonstrating a fondness for power beyond his reach that would eventually prove to be his undoing.

Shunzei's unprecedented injection of Buddhist metaphysics into literary theory at this particular time might best be understood in the light of contemporary attitudes of the old and established Tendai institution that three years before, in 1194, under the leadership of Jien as sixty-third Tendai Abbot, had succeeded in persuading Go-Toba to prohibit the infant Zen sect from establishing itself in Kyoto. To do this, the court issued an edict aimed specifically at Eisai, who had only recently returned from his second voyage to China with the intention of teaching Zen for the first time outside the structure of the Tendai church.

Eisai was by no means the first of those desiring to teach Zen to provoke the ire of the Tendai establishment. Indeed, the somewhat earlier monks Nōnin and Kakua, the latter of whom spent the years 1171–1175 in China, were even more aggressive and uncompromising in promoting an entirely independent Zen in Japan.[27] In contrast to these hotter heads, the more syncretistic and congenial Eisai may have appeared all the more dangerous a threat in the long run to the

---

[27] Martin Collcutt, *Five Mountains: The Rinzai Zen Monastic Institution in Medieval Japan* (Cambridge: Harvard University Press, 1981), 35. Yanagida (*Eisai*, 470) says that in his predictions in *Miraiki* (1197) for the future of the Zen sect in Japan, Eisai was trying to separate himself, as the sole authentic propagator of mainstream Sung Ch'an, from the "*Darumashū*" likes of Nōnin and Kakua, claiming that he was the only one of the Japanese monks returning from China to teach Ch'an to have received the Tendai sect's important "Bodhisattva precepts" (*Bossatsukai*).

Tendai sect's prerogatives. Still, if courtiers reacted with hostility to Eisai, we can imagine what their reaction would have been to anyone whose activities appeared even more aggressive. Eventually the court was forced to adopt a modus vivendi with Eisai, taking a pragmatic view of the powerful patronage he attracted from the military government in Kamakura after his return to Kyoto in 1201; for after an absence from the capital of only two years, Eisai was able to return to establish Kyoto's first Zen temple, Kenninji, under the protection of the military government in Kamakura, and there was little the court could do about it.

We have seen that the differences between Shunzei and Chōmei can be understood as reflecting a difference between a "classical" in contrast to a "medieval" outlook. These differences, however, can also be interpreted as being founded less in the metaphysics of literary theory, or even of religious thought, than in the political realities of Japan at the turn of the century. From Go-Toba on down, court aristocrats accepted as much as they comfortably could of the new styles that accompanied the gradual introduction of continental Sung culture into Japan, and took their defense of their increasingly shakily privileged station in the social order where they could find it. The aggressive stance of Zen and its early zealous adherents against "wild words and ornate speech" must have seemed to them to strike at the very heart of their own vocation, court privilege based on hereditary family dominance in waka poetry. In its radical teaching mode, Zen had always espoused direct, intuitive communication between teacher and disciple "from heart to heart," and harshly rejected the written word. Ch'an Buddhism's claim for itself as "a separate teaching beyond the sutras that rejects the written word" first appears in Chinese records in the early-eleventh-century *Wu-men Kuan* (*Mumonkan*) and, even more important for our present interests, first appears in Japanese records in Eisai's famous essay *Kōzen Gokokuron* (On the Promotion of Zen for the Defense of the Nation), written in his own defense against his increasingly antagonistic Tendai rivals.[28]

What seems to us merely a trivial antipathy between religious sects must have looked all the more significant to the courtiers in the context of the political tensions between the military government in Kamakura and the court in Kyoto. Until but a year before the appearance of his *Korai Fūteishō*, for example, Shunzei's own position at court must have seemed entirely secure, backed as he was by the long-powerful Fujiwara (Kujō) Kanezane (1148–1207), brother of Jien and father of Fujiwara Yoshitsune, two of the most important *Shinkokinshū* poets. In 1196, however, Kanezane was removed in a palace coup

---

[28] *Wu-men Kuan*, in Takakusu Junjirō and Watanabe Kaigyoku, eds., *Taishō Shinshū Daizōkyō* (Tokyo: Daizō Shuppan K. K., 1924–1932; hereafter cited as *T*), vol. 48, 293c; *Kōzen Gokokuron* in *T*, 80:4c.

engineered by Minamoto Michichika, a move that effectively diminished Kamakura's influence at court and gave a strong impetus to the restoration movement there.[29] In light of the political implications of this change for Shunzei, and considering his success at court after 1200 until his death in 1204 as doyen of the group that constituted the newly established commission for the compilation of the *Shinkokinshū*, it seems likely that the *Korai Fūteishō* was in fact written consciously to appeal to the powerful elite traditionalist forces centered on the restoration-minded Go-Toba in Kyoto. These forces were staunchly supported by, and were in turn the major patrons of, the still-powerful Tendai establishment in Kyoto. By contrast, the new military government in Kamakura, as much for political reasons as for the other affinities often advanced to explain their alliance, had begun to show increasing interest in the new Zen sect. Even if Shunzei's use of Tendai metaphysics can be construed as politically conservative, however, it was radically conservative, and speaks for the concerns of its age in its very real attempt to find a new dialectic for poetry that could answer the challenges raised by what we can only call the encroaching "metaphysics of style" of the new Zen sect.

We can now turn to a consideration of the elements that constituted that "style." I have already noted that as it developed in China, Ch'an Buddhism was distinguished from other sects in part by an adamant refusal to espouse any particular doctrine based on scripture, going so far as to call itself "a separate teaching beyond the scriptures that rejects the written word." But both Ch'an and Japanese Zen after it did come to develop an extensive written tradition —not traditional scripture, to be sure, but recorded sayings and deeds of its acknowledged masters that took the form of well-known collections of koans (Ch. *kung-an*) such as the *Wu-men Kuan* and the *Pi-yen Lu* (*Hekiganroku*, ca. 1300), made up of stories, sayings, and poems eccentric enough to have easily warranted the derisive appellation of *Darumashū* from Chōmei's contemporaries.

A good example of this sort of "style" in Teika's own day is the answer the zealous Zen monk Kakua gave when invited to court by Emperor Takakura (r. 1161–1181) to explain Zen "doctrine": Kakua simply played the flute in reply, surely bewildering and probably antagonizing the courtiers who were not used to such mysterious and impudent carryings-on. In a way, there was probably little else Kakua could have done, for Zen simply resists logical and coherent formulation. What must have bothered the courtiers even more was the fact that Zen failed to distinguish between privileged "esoteric" and plebeian "exoteric" teachings as Tendai and the other established sects had always

---

[29] Sir George Sansom, *A History of Japan to 1334* (Palo Alto: Stanford University Press, 1958), 333–34.

done. This represented yet another threat to aristocratic prerogative, and the refusal to treat an emperor any differently from a beggar must have carried with it the same unpleasant odor of revolution that marked some of the other "reform" Buddhist movements of the time.

The later Zen monk Gidō Shūshin (1325–1388) was to give the following poem as his own "response to a request to explain the secret teaching of Zen":

If I could explain it to you, it wouldn't be a real explanation,
And if I could write it down, then what would be the "secret"?
At a western window on a rainy autumn night,
White hair in guttering lamplight, asleep facing the bed . . .[30]

What is significant here is that his response alludes not to any Sutra or commentary but rather to a koan in the *Pi-yen Lu* in which a Ch'an master, asked the "real meaning of Bodhidharma's coming from the west" (i.e., from India to China), replied only "To sit long and get sleepy." We shall see that the style of Gidō's response itself, the last half of his poem enigmatically suggesting what seems not quite an answer to a question proposed in the first, is also of considerable importance.

In theory at least, then, Zen Buddhism rejected letters; yet, first in China and later in Japan, the practice of Zen embraced the writing of poetry the imagery and allusions of which were little different from any other sort. This apparent contradiction in Japanese Zen is only a reflection of the same contradiction embraced by Ch'an as it was practiced in Sung China, where a rapprochement had taken place between Ch'an Buddhism and the mainstream of Neo-Confucian thought. In eleventh-century China this synthesis was only one element of a syncretic trend that was also fusing Ch'an with T'ien-t'ai and with Pure Land Buddhism, as well as further blending this increasingly syncretistic Buddhism with Confucian thought to create the basis of the Sung Neo-Confucian synthesis. The Ch'an monk Fo-jih Ch'i-ch'ung (1007–1072), for example, one of many important figures in this eleventh-century process of synthesis, emphasized in his *Fu-chiao P'ien* (Treatise to Support the Teaching, ca. 1060) Buddhism's positive contribution to the usual Confucian interpretation of the religious, social, and political world order. Works like this helped set the stage for the development of what is known as "literati Ch'an," a practice that evolved especially among the upper-class scholar-officials with their vocational concern with literature of all sorts and with poetry in particular.[31]

[30] Uemura Kankō, ed., *Gozan Bungaku Zenshū* (Kyoto: Shibunkaku, repr. 1979; hereafter cited as *GBZS*), vol. 3, 1435–36.

[31] Cf. Ogisu Jundō, *Nihon Chūsei Zenshūshi no Kenkyū* (Tokyo: Mokujisha, 1965), 182; Haga Kōshirō, *Chūsei Zenrin no Gakumon Oyobi Bungaku ni Kansuru Kenkyū* (Tokyo: Nippon Gakujutsu Shinkōkai, 1956), 22–32; and Yanagida Seizan, *Chūgoku Zenshūshi*, in Nishitani Keiji, ed., *Kōza Zen* (Tokyo: Chikuma Shobō, 1968), vol. 3, 90ff.

The fact that the great compendia of Ch'an partriarchs' words and deeds such as the *Ching-te Ch'uan-teng Lu* (Record of the Transmission of the Lamp of the Ching-te Period, 1004) began to take form in this period also testifies to the trend of Ch'an away from the earlier emphasis on "daily life" practice of the T'ang period masters and toward letters and other sorts of intellectual activity instead. Ch'an during the Sung dynasty was, in fact, in the process of becoming less a living practice than a set of ideas, a *style*, whose influence was being sublimated throughout the culture in general. This diffusion both stimulated and reflected the great interest in the study of Ch'an by the literati class in this period. Though it is difficult to determine exactly how much they studied, or exactly how they interpreted Buddhist thought, it is noteworthy that many of the early Neo-Confucian philosophers of the Northern Sung are known to have studied with Ch'an masters. Chou Tun-i (1016–1073), whose sobriquet was "Poor Ch'an Guest," for example, studied with Mei-t'ang Tsu-hsin and Tung-lin Ch'ang-tsung (1025–1091); the brothers Ch'eng Hao and Ch'eng I (d. 1084 and 1107) with Ling-yüan Wei-ch'ing (d. 1117); and, astonishingly enough, even Chu Hsi in later years studied with various Ch'an masters, for all his noted antagonism, eventually regretted, toward Buddhism.

Even more important for our concerns are the extremely influential Northern Sung poets for whom Ch'an had become inseparable from poetry. Su Tung-p'o (1036–1101), for example, studied with the same master as Chou Tun-i, Tung-lin Ch'ang-tsung, and clearly espoused Ch'an teachings in his poetry. His equation of Ch'an and poetry in the phrase "poetry *is* Ch'an" was to serve later poets in China and Japan as a creed. In one poem, he wrote:

I take up a good book of poetry to while away the night:
As I recite each line I am doing Ch'an.[32]

This attitude achieved its most popular statement both in China and later in Japan in the *Ts'ang-lang Shih-hua* (ca. 1225) of the Southern Sung poet Yen Yü (fl. 1187–1230). This seminal work opens with the phrase "To talk of poetry is to talk of Ch'an," and goes on to assert that "the Way of Ch'an is one of sublime enlightenment, and so too is the Way of Poetry," a phrase that is strikingly similar to the equation of the Way of Poetry with the Tendai *sandai* dialectic made by Yen's younger contemporary Shunzei.

Yen Yü's work found its way to Japan by the early fourteenth century with the introduction of the Southern Sung compendium of poetry criticism *Shih-jen Yü-hsieh* (Jade Chips from the Poets), which opens with a jumble of citations from the first chapter of the *Ts'ang-lang Shih-hua* and cites the work frequently thereafter. But the *Ts'ang-lang Shih-hua* did not come into existence in an intellectual vacuum, and such ideas are clearly predicated upon the long devel-

---

[32] *Su Tung-p'o Chi* (Shanghai: Basic Sinological Series, 1940), vol. 4, 80.

opment of the equation of Ch'an and poetry in the minds of Chinese scholar-poets over the course of the preceding century. Yen borrowed the words of the early Sung Ch'an masters, for example, in order to describe what he felt constituted superior poetry: "It is like a sound in the air, the colors in a portrait, the moon in the water, or the reflection in a mirror: when words themselves have come to an end, what is left is the essential meaning."[33] We have already seen that it was a commonplace of poetic theory of both countries in the eleventh century that the deepest meaning of poetry lay in a realm beyond the words themselves. Poetry was already for the Chinese of this period very much the same metaphor for a deeper and otherwise inaccessible reality that it was later to become for Shunzei.

It seems somehow typical of the differences between Chinese and Japanese attitudes toward poetry that while Shunzei was to remain solidly in the mainstream of poetry and poetic theory as a radical conservative, Yen Yü was and still is regarded with some suspicion in China as an eccentric whose fondness for religious metaphor was not really representative of the balanced "humanism" that distinguishes the Confucian outlook. Much the same can be said of the Japanese preference for Po Chü-i over any other T'ang poet, or later for the blurred, impressionistic art of Mu Ch'i and Yü Chien over that of the Sung academicians, or for the starkly elegant "rabbit-fur" and "eggshell" Sung ceramic wares over the glossier Ming styles. We can conclude from these preferences that it is less accurate to speak of "Chinese influences" on Japan than of the Japanese looking in on Chinese culture at irregular intervals to select from the broad continuum of cultural expression only those elements that were felt to harmonize with native tastes. The Japanese may have been fascinated by continental culture, but they were never dictated to by it in their own tastes.

This fact has further implications, for the *interpretations* that the Japanese gave those Chinese values and objects they found congenial were naturally quite different from those of the Chinese themselves. One example of this is the fascination for the Japanese monks and poets of the Shinkokin period with the implications of a particular polarity in Buddhist metaphysics that seems to have interested the Chinese poets relatively little—and here again we find that it is not so much in particular points of religious doctrine as in a "style" of thought that Zen figures importantly in the Japanese poetry and poetics of this period.

This polarity figures most obviously and importantly in a work known as the *Hannya Shingyō* (Heart Sutra). Called in Sanskrit the *Prajñāpāramitā Hṛdaya Sūtra*, the work was first translated into Chinese during the T'ang dynasty and represents the distillation into one brief text of only 177 characters of the difficult *Mahāprajñāpāramitā Sūtra* in six hundred volumes. Along with the *Laṅkāvatāra Sūtra*, said to have been the sole text transmitted by the legendary

---

[33] *Shih-jen Yü-hsieh*, 4.

Ch'an Patriarch Bodhidharma to his disciple Hui-k'o, this brief text was adopted early by the Ch'an sect as especially congenial to its particular vision of reality. This may have had something to do with its extreme brevity, in keeping with the sect's avowed distaste for "words," or with the fact that Ch'an was known as the sect that represented the Buddha's "heart," in contrast to the doctrinal sects held to represent his "words."

More likely, however, even more of its congeniality lay in the way in which this particular text embraces unmediated paradox, a favorite teaching technique of Ch'an and an integral part of its very style. This already brief text can be even more briefly summarized in its famous central teaching that everything is at once *both* Void (*kū*, 空) and verifiable Reality (*shiki*, 色, literally "color"). These two terms represent an unmediated dichotomy alien to the emphasis on mediation in the tripartite Tendai *sandai* dailectic of Void, Provisional Reality, and Mediated Reality. Shunzei's equation of Void with "heart" in poetic theory suggests that the Japanese fondness for the polarity of "Void/Reality" in Zen metaphysics may have been preconditioned by the earlier acceptance of the polarity in poetic discourse of "heart/words" (*kokoro/kotoba*) as it was first given expression by the poet Ki no Tsurayuki in his preface to the *Kokinshū* of 905. In either case the significance of the underlying problem is the same: meaning, which was intrinsically something native and ineffable, necessarily depended upon external form for expression—the dilemma that informs the problem of writing in the *Kojiki*, as I have shown in chapter one.

The Japanese of the early classical period had adopted the Chinese character *kū*, used in Chinese to render the technical Sanskrit term *śūnya*, or "Void," to represent the native Japanese word for "sky," *sora*—a meaning the Chinese themselves attached much more rarely to this character. Similarly, the character for "Reality" (*shiki*) was used in Japan to represent the native word for "color," *iro*, with the further connotations of a fondness for or attraction to sensory beauty, and by extension for sensual or sexual love or desire—again, a connotation generally ignored by the more decorous Sung Chinese in their own poetry (though certainly used often enough in this sense in the following Yüan and Ming periods). Through various extended meanings of the word *iro* and its *engo* or "associated words" such as *someru* (to dye, tint, color) and *utsurou* (to fade, change color) the separate traditions of Buddhism and love poetry were joined in a unique metaphysic of passion—or of passion denied, as illustrated in the following poem by the court poetess Kojijū on "The 'Heart' of the *Heart Sutra*" ("Shingyō no Kokoro," *Shinkokinshū*, 1937):

Iro ni nomi	To the mortification
Someshi kokoro no	Of a heart dyed fast
Kuyashiki o	In the illusory colors of this world,
Munashi to tokeru	How happy is the Buddha's Law
Nori no ureshisa	That resolves it all as emptiness.

The implications of the metaphysical polarity that results from this interplay of the various meanings of the two terms Color and Void (the latter present here in its Japanese reading of *munashi*) become in their full development one of the major tropes of medieval Japanese poetry, whether or not that poetry deals explicitly with such ostensibly religious themes: the slow, inevitable process, as the westering sun in the sky sinks into darkness, of the gradual reduction to stark monochromatic tones of all the lovely but illusory colors of the world. Where earlier poets of the Heian period had argued the merits of the splendors of the pink cherry blossoms of the spring and the crimson maple leaves of autumn, the new metaphysics within which many Shinkokin poets wrote subdued these illusory "colors" (in reality but superficially different aspects of the same Void) equally to their underlying unitary nature by reducing them all to the more profoundly essential monochrome of a sunset "sky" bleached of color in autumn. It was to be moved by this quality, said Chōmei, rather than by any vulgar gaudiness of pinks or reds, that revealed the person of sensitivity.

It is also in this complex change of emphasis that we can locate the most profound significance of the rise of the medieval genre of monochrome ink-painting (*suibokuga*). An art developed by the Zen monks, ink-painting was part and parcel of the new aesthetic taste, with its direct visual ability to reduce all the superficial color and busyness of surface design of the Heian scroll or screen to the stark simplicity of forms generated by the medium of black ink alone. As we see in Kojijū's poem, too, for all this reduction the trope was anything but reductive, as it took on further complications by the emotional overtones of the word *iro* as "feelings," "emotions," "thoughts of love," as well as by the other readings of the character *kū* as *munashiki* (vain, futile) or *itazura* ("for no particular reason"). Her poem also requires us to consider the common extension of the imagery of twilight to include the equally moving twilights of the approaching end of something—of a love affair, or of a year, or of man's own years.

It is interesting that most of the poems in the *Shinkokinshū* that involve the central image of "autumn dusk" are not found in the sections dealing with "Autumn" but rather in those with "Love." To the poets of the Heian period, an autumn dusk was inherently wretched because it signified especially waiting for a lover who did not come—as Teika put it, in another of the poems in the hundred-poem sequence composed at Futamigaura in 1186 (*SKKS*, 1196),

Ajiki naku	Listless,
Tsuraki arashi no	Even the dull sound
Oto mo ushi	Of the storm is vexed—
Nado yūgure ni	Why have we grown accustomed
Machinaraiken	To this anxious waiting at dusk?

The "double vision" (*futa-mi*) here would seem to be the ambiguity of the woman who has fallen into the habit of anxiously anticipating her lover's arrival at dusk, and the storm that is made to wait just as anxiously. In the Shinkokin period, however, the idea of autumn dusk contains an entirely new emphasis: the referent is no longer the strong emotion caused by the absence of love, but rather by the positive *lack* of that absence. That is, *kokoronaki* does not imply a lack of emotion so much as it does some positive quality that is entirely different, although the strength of that quality is the same. Chōmei illustrates this quality in another love poem (*SKKS*, 1318) that seems to perfectly illustrate what he meant when he wrote of a colorless autumn dusk that moves one to tears:

Nagamete mo	Gazing upon it,
Aware to omoe	Think "How moving!"
Ōkata no	The sadness of even
Sora dani kanashi	The most ordinary sky
Aki no yūgure	At autumn dusk.

Here the poet has subtly shifted the sense of pity from himself, the traditional forlorn lover waiting at dusk—"Gazing upon me, think "How sad!""—to the moving quality of the autumn dusk, asking us that we should feel deeply, not on his account but rather for something less personal or specific and more universal.

This same change in emphasis can also be seen in the image of the snipe (*shigi*) as Saigyō used it in the *Shinkokinshū* poem cited above, in contrast to its appearance in the anonymous *Kokinshū* 761 (and its echo by Lady Akazome Emon, d. ca. 1041, in *SKSS*, 1179). In the two older poems the snipe, "writhing," "beating its wings," or "picking at itself" (the meaning of the word *hanegaki* is not clear), is the focus of intense misery; in Saigyō's poem, however, instead of representing torment this drabbest of birds becomes the very embodiment of *kokoronaki*, the colorless and soundless reason why a dusk sky in autumn should cause sadness.

Shunzei's interest in relating poetry to Tendai Buddhism corresponds to an interest in literate society in general in poems on Buddhist themes, especially Tendai themes, as evidenced by the religious cast of the *wasan* (hymnal) poems in the mid-eleventh-century *Ryōjin Hishō*. The first imperial anthology to contain a separate section devoted to Buddhist poetry was the *Goshūishū* of 1086, which contains only nineteen such poems.[34] The category was subsequently abandoned, until Shunzei included fifty-three poems on Buddhist themes in his *Senzaishū* a century later. Among these poems is one by a court poetess, Gishūmon'in no Tango, on the topic "Void is precisely that which is Reality"

[34] See Robert E. Morrell, "The Buddhist Poetry in the *Goshūishū*," *Monumenta Nipponica* 28:1 (Spring 1973), 87–138.

(*Kū soku ze shiki*) from the *Heart Sutra* (*SZS*, 1226). That Shunzei should have
included a poem on what amounts to a Zen theme may seem at first glance to
contradict what I have said of him. While many of the poets in the *Senzaishū* are
also represented in the *Shinkokinshū* (Gishūmon'in contributed nine poems to
that collection), however, the *Senzaishū* itself is a product of the period immediately preceding Eisai's attempt to establish Zen as a separate teaching outside the
Tendai church structure. Zen practice and ideas were not a threat to Tendai as
long as they remained, as they had to this point, docilely within the established
Tendai organization. The very direction of the title of Gishūmon'in's poem
betrays the more optimistic Heian outlook rather than the more profoundly
pessimistic medieval, for she interprets only one half of the Zen formulation,
the half that the Shinkokin poets tended to ignore. While they were concerned,
as I have shown, with the reduction of all the "colors" of the phenomenal
world, usually bright autumnal reds, to the colorless quality of Void, the earlier
poetess instead almost reflexively *colors* her world in springtime green, like
Andrew Marvell very nearly "Annihilating all that's made/ To a green thought
in a green shade":

Munashiki mo	Is it because it understands
Iro naru mono to	That even empty Void itself
Satorebaya	Is one of the illusory colors of Reality
Haru no misora no	That spring should materialize
Midori naruramu	In this aura of bright green?

The poem contains an implicit sense of hope, cloaked in Heian wit, in the
regenerative powers of nature; by contrast, Kojijū invests her hope in the ability
of the Buddha's Law to make new sense of a chaotic world of shattered illusion.

The metaphysical treatment of natural imagery that reads as religious symbolism is so pervasive in poetry by 1200 that we can speak of nature, religion,
love, travel, and the like as metaphors for one another. This mode of symbolism
was already well developed in Japanese poetry long before the Zen monks of
the Gozan established the mode of Sung Chinese poetic perception that begins
to be seen in the Chinese poetry they wrote from about the mid-thirteenth
century. While the Shinkokin poets share a common taste for this as yet largely
unarticulated aesthetic, we can see in the poetry of Teika how this new aesthetic
differs from and yet grows out of what preceded it. Teika, as responsive to the
new style in his younger years as he may have been, was no zealous revolutionary; rather, he sought continuity with the past by carrying on the still vital
tradition of the interpretation of that T'ang Chinese paragon of Heian Japanese
sensibility, Po Chü-i. The long history of the interpretation of this single
Chinese poet in waka poetry would continue as one of the bases of the medieval
aesthetic that emerged after the middle of the twelfth century.

The importance of Chinese poetry and of Po in particular for Teika can be seen from a passage of his *Maigetsushō* (1219) that theorists centuries later continued to find significant for their own work. This passage occurs in Teika's discussion of the style of *ushin-tei*, "intense feeling" (literally, the style of "possessing 'heart' "), which he singled out as the most significant style among the ten he enumerated. In this passage Teika especially emphasizes the need to "clear one's 'heart' " (*kokoro o sumasu*) before one can achieve "depth of 'heart' " (*kokoro fukaki*):

> Although people of the past have warned against the practice of incorporating the "heart" [*kokoro*] and "words" [*kotoba*] of ancient Chinese poetry into one's waka poetry, I do not think that this is such an evil practice.[35] Provided one does not overdo this sort of thing, it has the ability to elevate one's own poetry considerably. I have written elsewhere [*Eika Taigai*, date unknown] that "there is matter for waka poetry all throughout *The Collected Poems of Po Chü-i*, and one should recite these." Chinese poetry has the power to elevate one's heart and make it clear. When one is to compose a waka poem he should first recite Chinese poetry, softly to himself if in the presence of royalty, aloud if he is not. It is my own practice when I compose waka first to clear my heart [*kokoro o sumasu*] thus: I set my heart upon a Chinese or Japanese poem that has kept its interest through the years, and with the power this poem imparts I compose my own.[36]

Teika's dialectic method for achieving "depth of heart," then, seems as radical as Shunzei's in harkening back to the tenth-century court practice of *kudai waka*, the reinterpretation in waka poetry of a line of Chinese poetry—most frequently by Po Chü-i, although a few other T'ang poets were used as models as well. We have seen that this practice was central to the Heian dialectic known as wakan, the juxtaposition in a variety of ways of Chinese and Japanese forms. The *Kudai Waka* (894) of Ōe no Chisato contains 125 waka poems based on lines of Chinese poems over half of which are by Po Chü-i; none of these waka, however, amounts to anything more than a Japanese translation of the Chinese. To a seven-word line by an anonymous Chinese poet, "When in the cold the sounds of geese are stilled, the traveler's melancholy weighs even more heavily," for example, Ōe set the following words:

Naku kari no	When even the voices
Koe dani taete	Of the crying geese are stilled
Kikoeneba	And no longer can be heard,

---

[35] Teika is thought to have been referring here to Shunzei; cf. *NKBZ*, 50:528, n. 2. That Teika disagreed freely with Shunzei and nearly everyone else in matters of poetry is attested by Emperor Go-Toba's arch observation that "seeing that he thinks so little even of his great father's poetry, one can imagine what he thinks of others' " (*Go-Toba-in On-kuden, NKBT*, 65:148).
[36] *Maigetsushō, NKBT*, 65:136ff.

Tabi naru hito wa   The traveler's heart is all the more
Omoimasarinu   Lost in melancholy.[37]

We can understand how completely Teika's use of Chinese poetry differs from this simple mode of translation by examining a poem he wrote in 1218 in response to an imperial order to compose one hundred waka poems on topics from Po's *Collected Works* (J. *Hakushi Monjū*). In this collection of waka, known as the *Monjū Dai Hyakushū* (One Hundred Poems Set to Poems from *The Collected Works of Po Chü-i*), one of the themes by Po was a poem entitled "Village in Snow: Sitting at Night" (*Hakushi Monjū*, chap. 6):

At a southern window I sit, lamp turned to the wall,
While windblown hail blows wildly in the darkness;
As the stillness deepens in the village night,
The cry of a goose that remains behind is heard through the snow.[38]

To this poem, then, the Japanese poet was to set his own. Teika was more interested in the "heart" of Po's poem than merely in the "words," those superficial constituents of meaning that had served earlier court poets in the composition of their poems. To be sure, Teika used the word "hail" (*arare*) and matched the Chinese rhyme word, "hear," with its Japanese translation, *kiku*, apparently in acknowledgment of certain rules imposed for the occasion that governed the way the poems were to be composed.

Of much more importance to Teika than these superficial rules was the "heart" of Po's poem, the world that existed beyond the words themselves that one had to enter if one was to match the poem in Japanese. It was clearly his understanding of the importance of Ch'an meditation in Po's poetry—his Heian predecessors had altogether ignored this uncourtly practice—that led him to locate the "heart" of Po's poem in the experience of sitting in meditation. This, after all, is what the word "sit" usually meant in the context of T'ang poetry, but earlier Japanese poets seem to have been entirely unaware of this connotation. In the course of this experience, the mind naturally focused first on such superficial, external sounds as the rattle of hail blown by the wind against the roof; as night, silence, and meditation deepened, one came to hear more "deeply," until through the receding sound of wind and hail there finally came the sound whose significance informed and gave essential meaning to the experience: the cry of a lone goose coursing high over the world. To this "heart" of "hearing more deeply," Teika then set his own poem:

[37] Kaneko Hikojirō, *Heian Jidai Bungaku to Hakushi Monjū* (Tokyo: Baifūkan, 1943), 218. In recent years a revised and expanded version in three volumes was published of this excellent work that eliminates the author's earlier jingoistic language (Kamakura: Geirinsha, 1977).

[38] *Po Hsiang-shan Shih-chi*, 58; see *Kokka Taikan*, suppl. vol., 31ff., no. 56; cf. Andō Tsuguo, *Fujiwara Teika* (*Nihon Shijinsen*, vol. 11; Tokyo: Chikuma Shobō, 1979), 256–57.

Kaze no ue ni	In the light of
Hoshi no hikari wa	Stars that gleam
Saenagara	Coldly above the wind
Waza to mo furanu	I hear the sound of hail
Arare o zu kiku	Scarcely falling.

At first glance, the poem simply seems to say that the poet hears hail falling although the night sky seems clear. We can make a case for a much deeper meaning, however, for Teika was clearly playing upon the idea of turning away from the lamp the better to hear, an oxymoron found often in Po's own poetry. The poet hears less the almost inaudible sound of the sparse hail itself so much as the synesthetic "sound" made by the cold light of the stars gleaming in the wintry sky like myriad pieces of falling hail. His poem therefore embodies, as did Po's, the Ch'an idea that "the mind [or "heart"] hears more clearly than the ear." Teika shows us the experience of listening with a mind (heart, *kokoro*) cleansed of the superficial dust of the mundane world; starlight glittering coldly in the wind is the last thing we should have expected to hear, but in the end the hail, attenuated to the point of inaudibility, is transformed into starlight itself. This same conceit would later provide the metaphysical wit underlying a famous poem by the cloistered Emperor Fushimi (1265–1317). In his exploration of the same *sandai* dialectic that Shunzei used to discuss the problem of "depth" in poetry, Fushimi considered the paradox that "the three teachings [*sandai*] are not one, nor are they three," which is to say that reality must be understood as a dialectical process comprising the mediation of contradictory terms (*Fūgashū*, 2057):

Mado no to ni	The better to hear
Shitataru ame o	The rain that falls dripping
Kiku nabe ni	Against my window,
Kabe ni somukeru	I turn my midnight lamp
Yowa no tomoshibi	To the wall.

In much of the Shinkokin-style poetry of Teika and his contemporaries we sense the conflicting pull of two currents, one flowing back into the past Heian modes of wit and decorum, and another, newer and deeper current that speaks of a new "heart" swelling toward the future. This new vision alongside the old can be summed up in (perhaps even hinges upon) a vision such as that of an autumn dusk by the young Teika. His description of the scene sets both halves of the old Heian argument—cherry blossoms or maple leaves?—on one side of an implied equation, and places on the other a startlingly new vision: the stark drabness of a thatched hut fading into the darkness of autumn dusk. This sort of vision seems very much in the style of the puzzling answer that Teika's contemporary Kakua had given Emperor Takakura five years earlier when asked to court to explain Zen to the emperor and his assembled courtiers. Kakua too had simply set all the distinctions implied by the emperor's question—this against that, something as opposed to something else—on one side of a radically new equation, and on the other, enigmatically, only the sound of a flute. Among Kakua's few extant works is a poem that clearly alludes to that occasion:

Raise your fist, yell, jump around—
But saying "is" or "isn't" will get you into muddy water;
No making distinctions between things—stop pointing at commentaries!
Nothing comes back but the sound of a flute: la, la, lee . . . [39]

Teika was not, of course, solely responsible for the new style in waka poetry that corresponds to such a reply. This was the so-called "distant" (soku) style in which a train of thought stops at the end of the third of the five lines and is followed by another idea in the last two lines that appears to be only very "distantly related" to the first. This technique forces the reader to search for meaning not at the superficial level of the words (kotoba), but rather in the "heart" revealed in the yawning gap between the two halves of the poem. The soku style was used by many of the poets of Teika's circle, most notably by Saigyō and Jakuren, but was bitterly opposed by the more conservative factions at court—undoubtedly those who felt that such outlandish disregard for continuity in verse constituted "Daruma poetry." The fifteenth-century poet and theorist Shinkei would equate this technique with the "Zen style," contrasting it with lines that were "closely related" (shinku) and therefore more akin, as he saw it, to the older styles of Buddhism that relied on the logic of words. He described the soku style as "throwing out the form [sugata] and words [kotoba] and linking by heart [kokoro] alone," citing as authority Teika's opinion that "most superior poems are in the soku style." [40] The first of Shinkei's several illustrations of the soku style in waka poetry is a poem by Teika on the subject of dawn, drawn from the same series of one hundred waka composed on the topics of poems by Po Chü-i:

Sato tōki	In the first sounds
Yagoe no tori no	Of the birds that call
Hatsugoe ni	From a distant village:
Hana no ka okuru	A mountain breeze
Haru no yamakaze	That brings the scent of blossoms.

To say that the song of far-off birds on a spring dawn is what brings the scent of plum blossoms certainly seems enigmatic enough to qualify the poem's two

[39] *Dai Nihon Zoku Zōkyō* (Kyōto Sōgō Shiryōkan edition, undated), 2/2/10:144b.

[40] *Sasamegoto*, NKBT, 66:154–55; Shinkei was citing two works, *Sangoki* and *Guhisshō*, both dated 1217 and attributed to Teika; the attribution and date may be spurious; see 259, n. 19.

halves as "distantly related." The last two lines create meaning in the mind of the reader more by their odd juxtaposition with the first three than by any logic that flows straight through the poem from start to finish. Shinkei included one more poem by Teika among his other examples of the *soku* style in waka:

Sagi no iru	Snipe at
Ike no migiwa ni	Pond's edge,
Matsu furite	Ancient pines:
Miyako no hoka no	The feel of anyplace
Kokochi koso sure	Not Kyoto.

What both poems have in common in translation is the need for a colon or a dash, some marker of discontinuity between the first and second halves, for there is no other way to relate them syntactically in any meaningful fashion. Meaning emerges not from linear argument, but rather from the dialectical mode into which the mind is forced in its attempt to create a single poem of two such disparate parts. It is altogether understandable that the term *Darumashū* could have been used in a pejorative sense to refer to poetry that used such a technique; the very antagonism that the Shinkokin courtiers felt toward this new style speaks of the ways in which the new Zen style was making itself felt in Japan around 1200 as but one facet of the new stylistic complex from the continent.

And yet, one also feels that there is always a limit, never very clearly defined, to just how far Japanese sensibilities were willing to carry the burden of unmediated paradox so central to this style, whether in poetry of elsewhere. Indeed, there were clearly limits to the extent that even the best-known—perhaps especially the best-known, as we shall see in chapter four—Japanese Zen monks, Musō Soseki for example, were willing to accept the demands of the Sung style of Zen. In this sense, Shunzei's turn to the Tendai dialectic of mediation in search of new profundity of meaning in poetry seems somehow, in its reemergence into the world of everyday experience, more in the mainstream of Japanese thought. Congenial as it may have been to the Chinese, the tensions created by the antithesis of unmediated paradox seem finally alien to Japanese thought. Indeed, the elaborate arabesques of tropes that court poets wove around the stark polarities of Void and Phenomenal Reality would have seemed congenial to a Donne or Marvell, and can be read as testimony to an inability to live comfortably with that tension. Throughout the history of poetic theory in Japan, the renewal of meaning at the level of apparent reality (*kotoba*, words) was always the goal of the attempt to deepen awareness of the ineffable and ineluctable source of that reality (*kokoro*), never its polar opposite.

In more than one way, then, the Shinkokin aesthetic can be seen as bridging two worlds: the differences between Heian and Kamakura, classical and medieval, tradition and innovation, old and new, even China and Japan, seem somehow to depend on it as the crucial link in the span from one to the next. Perhaps the age is therefore best summed up in Teika's own image of a "bridge across the mountains" occurring in a poem that, although in the *soku* mode, is not itself a radical departure from earlier styles. Rather, the poem itself can be seen as a bridge, a span carrying tradition, in the persona of a traveler, forward as securely as possible into a future at once inevitable and perilous (*Shinkokinshū*, 953):

Tabibito no	Caught in the autumn wind
Sode fukikaesu	That blows back
Akekaze ni	The traveler's sleeves:
Yū hi sabishiki	A bridge, suspended across the mountains
Yama no kakehashi	In the lonely light of the setting sun.

CHAPTER FOUR

"Chineseness" and "Japaneseness" in Early Medieval Zen: Kokan Shiren and Musō Soseki

In chapter three we saw that Sung Chinese aesthetics, and especially what I have called the "style" of the Ch'an (Zen) sect of Buddhism, had already begun to make itself felt in Japan by 1200. This will undoubtedly seem something of an anachronism to those who accept the established view that nothing of Sung culture was known in Japan before the arrival half a century later of the first of the Chinese Ch'an teachers who founded the great Kamakura monasteries of the early Gozan or medieval Zen establishment. In fact, Japanese Zen monks had long been at work preparing the ground for the arrival of the Chinese and at the request of their patrons, the Hōjō rulers, finally went to actively seek them out in China. The Chinese monks who accepted these invitations were not likely to have departed their homeland simply because of the stick of Mongol invasion had the carrot of eager Japanese ruling-class patronage not been extended as well. Among the most famous of these early Chinese masters to come to Japan were Lan-hsi Tao-lung (who arrived in Japan in 1246), Wu-an P'u-ning (1260), Ta-hsiu Cheng-nien (1269), and Wu-hsüeh Tsu-yüan (1279).

The establishment in Kamakura from the middle of the thirteenth century of the large Zen temples and monasteries built on the Chinese model and headed by émigré Chinese monks is usually interpreted as initiating the existence of a very Chinese organization on Japanese soil. Indeed, the Japanese themselves have tended to think of the entire Zen institution in Japan—more specifically, the Rinzai-dominated Gozan (Five Mountains) that began in the Kamakura temples—as a monolithic entity whose content and form were entirely Chinese, enforced by stern Chinese masters upon their Sinicized Japanese students. This picture of the Zen establishment does not stand up well under close scrutiny, however. Even among the émigré Chinese monks were some who, like Ming-chi Ch'u-chün (1261–1336, arrived in Japan in 1330 together with Chu-hsien Fan-hsien) during his short six-year existence in Japan until his death, appear to have become quite Japanese in their way of thinking. I-shan I-ning (1247–1317, arrived in Japan 1299) even wrote poetry about such Japanese personalities as Kōbō Daishi and Shōtoku Taishi. The other extreme may be represented by the Chinese monk Wu-an P'u-ning (d. 1276), who returned embittered after only five years in Japan to the China he felt he should never have left.

If the Chinese masters were a heterogeneous group, the Japanese Zen monks can also be separated, at the very least, into two broad groups: those who actually made the difficult voyage to China to study, often remaining there a decade or more before returning, and those who for various reasons never left Japan. Kokan Shiren (1278–1346), representative of the latter group, sometimes wrote lines of "Chinese" poetry that seem more Japanese than Chinese in the sources of their inspiration. For example, his line

Hearth smoke deepens over thatched huts
    On a rush-covered islet in a bay of reeds.[1]

is so reminiscent of the last lines of the famous poem by Fujiwara Teika on autumn dusk included in the *Shinkokinshū* that it seems almost consciously modeled upon it:

Autumn twilight deepens
    Over thatched huts by a bay.

It may seem odd that the poetry of a Zen monk, and especially one as famous for his Chinese scholarship as Kokan, should echo Chinese poetry less than it does a Japanese poem written a century earlier. It is a fact, however, that the Chinese poems of the Gozan monks as often reflect the new tastes in waka poetry that evolved during the late twelfth and early thirteenth centuries as they do the Sung tastes with which the monks were presumably very familiar. In fact, such poems can be interpreted satisfactorily from the point of view of either culture in terms of entirely native aesthetic developments in poetry. For this reason, it is often difficult to decide whether to trace such lines to the spare, muted, and "flavorless" quality of *p'ing-tan* that is made so much of in Sung critical treatises, or to the subtle and elusive *yūgen* and *sabi* that became important in Japanese criticism from around 1200, in the development of which Shunzei and Teika had been so important.

When a Japanese Gozan monk like Tetsuan Dōshō, a contemporary of Kokan, wrote in a poem of about 1320 that

To the rest of the world this life seems cold and sour—
I, however, find it thin and bland.[2]

---

[1] Uemura, *GBZS*, 1:85. For a study of Gozan poetry, see the introduction to my *Zen Poems of the Five Mountains.*

[2] *GBZS*, 1:375.

he was writing in the language of Sung dynasty aesthetics: *han* (寒, cold) and *suan* (酸, sour) employed as a common synecdoche for poverty, *po* (溥, thin) and *tan* (淡, bland, flavorless) as positive attributes perhaps best defined in contrast to their opposites—that is, *not* rich, gaudy, substantial.

Yet in other poems, Dōshō and other Gozan monks regularly employed Japanese *utamakura* (place names used widely in waka poetry for their rich associations) as subjects for Chinese poems, written in diction that reflects Chinese less than it does the native Japanese models of the *Man'yōshū* and *Kokinshū*. Such practices suggest that poets like Dōshō, who received aristocratic educations and never felt the long voyage to China to be necessary, were inclined toward a particular aesthetic vision in their poetry as much by their sensitization and preconditioning in the native literary arts as they were by any Zen-inspired allegiance to "Chinese" tastes. When we consider the fact that they were often trained in the literary arts of the court long before they were in those of the Zen temples and monasteries, the frequent assertions of Japanese Zen monks to the effect that they knew little and cared less about their native literary traditions becomes a pose at once disingenuous and self-serving.

We can find the Japanese poet concealed within the guise of the Chinese even in a monk like Jakushitsu Genkō (1290–1367), who spent the years 1321–1326 traveling and studying in China. Born a Fujiwara, Jakushitsu was sent to study at Nanzenji in Kyoto under the Chinese émigré master I-shan I-ning from 1317 before departing for China. One mode of his "Zen" poetry is authentically grouchy, the equivalent in verse of a master's shout or a rap on the pupil's head, as we see in his "Poem to Show to My Pupils":

To do Zen you've got to be tough,
Body and mind tempered like forged steel!
Look at all the Patriarchs who came before—
Which of them ever fooled around like you?[3]

And yet, this same monk, widely admired for his "Chinese" qualities, was capable of writing poetry in Chinese that reads for all the world like contemporary Japanese verse rather than Chinese:

A monk comes knocking at my brushwood gate
Wanting to discuss weighty matters of great Zen import;
Excuse this mountain priest, too lazy to open his mouth,
But warblers are singing all over the blossom-strewn village.[4]

Except for the fact that Jakushitsu's bird is a warbler (*uguisu*) rather than a cuckoo (*hototogisu*), the final trope might have been suggested by Ōtomo no

[3] *T*, 81:104b.
[4] *Ibid.*, 105b.

Tabito's poem in the *Man'yōshū* (no. 1437):

Tachibana no	The days are many
Hanachiruzato no	When I, like *the cuckoo*
Hototogisu	*In the village*
Kataomoshitsutsu	*Strewn with orange blossoms,*
Naku hi shi zo ōku	*Cry* over unrequited love.

That there should exist this range of differences between what appear to be more "Chinese" and more "Japanese" elements within the ostensibly (but obviously impossibly) homogeneous Gozan is all the more significant for the monks' denials that such distinctions existed at all. I shall now turn to the question of these differences in "Chineseness" and "Japaneseness" as they figure in the lives and writings of two well-known Japanese Zen monks, Kokan Shiren and Musō Soseki, both of whom were among the large and important group of Japanese Zen monks who omitted altogether what had been, and still continued in their time to be, the customary pilgrimage to China.

Perhaps no other Japanese Zen monk of the fourteenth century was as familiar with the implications of Sung Chinese Neo-Confucian philosophy for Buddhism as Kokan. His mentor Enni Ben'en (1202–1280) is traditionally held to have been the first to bring the study of Neo-Confucianism from China to Japan; but it was Kokan, following in Enni's line to become Abbot of the Gozan Tōfukuji temple in the south of Kyoto in 1332, who studied most closely and tellingly the implications of Neo-Confucian thought for Japanese Buddhism.

The work of few scholars in either Japan or China embodied to the degree Kokan's did the famous dictum of the Chinese Neo-Confucian writer Ch'eng I (1033–1107) that "a student must first of all learn to doubt." [5] Kokan was widely read not only in Buddhism but in Chinese classics, poetry, and the broad range of commentary on these as well. His collected works, the *Saihokushū*, contain his opinions on poetry and poets, as well as on the anecdotal body of critical opinion concerning the practice and theory of poetry that is known in Chinese as *shih-hua* (J. *shiwa*). [6] Kokan adopted from the very outset the rational skepticism of the early Chinese philosopher Wang Ch'ung (27–100?), adopting his *Lun Heng* (Opinions Weighed in the Balance) as the model for his own *T'ung Heng* (*Tsūkō*, Received Opinions Weighed in the Balance). Kokan began his first essay in poetic criticism with an unprecedented frontal attack upon received Chinese wisdom:

> It has long been held that the Duke of Chou wrote only two poems, "Ch'i-hsiao" and "Ch'i-yüeh"; that Confucius did not compose any of *The Book of Odes* but

[5] *Erh-Ch'eng Ch'üan-shu, ed., Ssu-pu Ts'ung-k'an, Wai-shu,* 11:2b.
[6] Kokan's *Saihoku Shiwa* is found in *GBZS,* 1:228–41.

merely compiled the poems; and that poeple after the Han and Wei dynasties wrote so much poetry because they were frivolous. These things are not true.[7]

Kokan gave as his reasons for these opinions that it was higly unlikely anyone would have written only two poems in his lifetime, so that the Duke of Chou clearly had to have written more; that no one could have edited the *Odes* so well had he not himself been a poet; and that while there may indeed have been frivolous poets after the Wei dynasty, which ended in A.D. 265, certainly not all the poets during that long span could have been frivolous. These may not seem like terribly weighty arguments to us today; but to anyone familiar with the terms of traditional Chinese literary criticism, his comments reveal a habit of thinking plainly and sensibly about subjects that often occasioned a great deal of petty hair-splitting in China. In dealing with the question of why there were no other extant poems by the Duke of Chou and Confucius, Kokan's suggestion that their works perished in the infamous book-burnings conducted by the first Ch'in emperor Shih-huang-ti seems at once lame and likely.

Having set this tone of rational skepticism—a stance that no Japanese had adopted so clearly toward China before, it should be noted—Kokan turned to his most important point regarding poetic theory: the Neo-Confucian advocacy of the primacy of *li* (理), or "innate principle," as a critical concept to which all other critical considerations were subordinate:

Sung dynasty critical theories of poetry are not exhaustive in their emphasis on such terms as "plain" [*p'u*], "antique" [*ku*], "even" [*p'ing*] and "bland" [*tan*], while belittling such terms as "unusual" [*ch'i*], "artificial" [*kung*], "dynamic" [*hao*], and "beautiful" [*li*]. Poetry need not be "antique" or "bland" in its diction any more than it need be "unusual" or "artificial"—it need only accord with innate principle [*li*]. Ancient poetry is generally of a simpler nature and so is closer to being "plain" and "antique." From the Middle period on [i.e., the Six Dynasties], however, poetry came to contain emotions that the poets were not actually feeling when they wrote, so that their works are closer to being "unusual" and "artificial." From time to time, a Sage has given voice to feelings of protest in poetry, and in so doing has given new life to true emotions. How then are we to be constrained by such terms as these? Such men merely wrote in accordance with *li*, and so there are ancient poems that are "plain" without being true, and true poems today that are not "plain." How could we evaluate everything on the basis of terms like these?[8]

Rather than rehearse here separately each of Kokan's attacks on what he clearly considered the critical deficiencies of his mainland mentors, let us turn to the very last of these essays in poetic criticism, in which Kokan expressed his own ideas about the composition of poetry. Kokan suggested that rather than

[7] *Ibid.*, 228.
[8] *Ibid.*

rules and regulations, instruction for the novice should begin in what he called the "purity" and "integrity" of the young child, innate qualities that, once developed, could later with practice be polished to maturity:

> I have some pupils who fool about, joke, chaff, and won't recite their lessons. When I prod and scold them to write poetry, they say "But we don't know the rules of tone and meter." When I tell them to forget the rules and just write out lines with the correct number of syllables, they grumble and complain. But I do not become upset, and in spite of themselves, they present me with some lines. Their poems may be halting, uneven, doltish, and clumsy, and sometimes make no sense at all; but still, they are often filled with a self-possessed purity and integrity that make me marvel.
>
> Again, when I would have them study calligraphy, they complain, saying "But we don't know the techniques or styles." So I tell them to forget about techniques and styles, and simply try to make their characters look like the models. As usual they grumble and complain, but I do not get upset, and in spite of themselves, they present me with a few sheets of calligraphy. Their characters may look like wriggling worms or like crows flapping wildly about, and sometimes don't even resemble characters at all; but still, the strokes often have a purity and integrity that astonish me.
>
> For these reasons, I can only sigh that those who would study such arts as poetry or calligraphy only do themselves harm by concentrating on such notions as "artifice" or "unusualness." They never attain to the realm of actual creation this way, and only end by making empty distinctions. That these children can be so frightfully untutored and yet have something essentially pure and integral within them results from their simple natures. Thus I have come to the conclusion that if a student of poetry does not have the purity of a child, he cannot speak of "poetry"; and if one who studies calligraphy does not know the purity of a child's brush-strokes, he cannot speak of "calligraphy." And this applies not only to these two arts, for no Way is any different. In studying anything, one must first establish a pure and integral mind and then improve it with practice. Only in this way will he easily achieve his goal.[9]

Kokan's priorities would probably have seemed wrong-headed or even eccentric from the point of view of contemporary Chinese criticism. His preference for the state of untutored childlike innocence is a familiar Taoist one, of course, found in the ancient philosophical texts of the *Lao Tzu* and the *Chuang Tzu*. But it can also be thought to echo certain tendencies in contemporary Japanese critical attitudes, of the sort that had earlier led Kamo no Chōmei, in explaining the new "*yūgen* style" of waka poetry, to comment that he "would compare this style to the speech of a lovely child, awkward and

---

[9] *Ibid.*, 241.

without any clear perception, but lovable in all its helplessness and worth listening to."[10] While one hesitates to credit such sentiment to any particularly Japanese mode of thought, we might recall that even Genji himself had raised the child who was to become his wife Murasaki, finding it more desirable to train childish innocence to a state of maturity than to attempt to impose impossible standards upon the already mature. This preference for the pure sincerity of youth over the sullied cynicism of age is a recurring theme in Japanese aesthetics.

At any rate, it is interesting to find the clear preference in Sung dynasty critical texts for what was called the awkward or clumsy (*cho*, 拙) over clever contrivance, related or not to Taoist thought, or for the bland or withered over the beautiful, rejected as irrelevant in Kokan's view: poetry should simply accord with *li*, or "innate principle." Not content merely to theorize about such things, Kokan also put his theory into practice in hundreds of small poems that focus sharply on individual objects. These poems follow a Chinese genre, popular during the Sung, known as *yung-wu shih* (*eibutsushi*, poems about objects). Like the Sung poets who wrote in this genre, Kokan seems to have been attempting through these poems to arrive at a more profound insight into the operation of *li* by attending as closely as possible to its individual manifestations in "objects" or "things" (*wu*, 物). Consider, for example, the minute focus in "Evening Stroll in a Summer Garden":

My room so miserable with heat and mosquitoes I can't do zazen,
I kill the time pacing the gravel paths, hands behind my back;
Nothing in the inner garden—something catches my eye—
I look more closely: a single strand of spider web stretches across the path.[11]

Again and again in these poems Kokan insists on the second look, the closer attention that provides the basis for new and more profound perceptions. Thus, his concentration is actually a kind of meditation, a Zen *samadhi*, that results in new ways of seeing the world, as for example his novel insight into the nature of the season in aural terms in a poem on "The Start of Autumn":

The heat's full intensity hasn't abated one whit,
So why now this feeling of coolness?
I take my time, concentrate, listen again:
Falling paulownia leaves and chirping crickets have joined in a new sound.[12]

It is very Japanese to fret as Kokan does over the failure of the Chinese agricultural calendar to accord properly with the Japanese seasonal markers;

[10] *Mumyōshō*, *NKBT*, 65:87.
[11] *GBZS*, 1:95.
[12] *Ibid.*, 96.

again and again in his poems we are confronted with autumns that begin without cool weather, springs that start without plum blossoms. In order to account for these discrepancies (which, we might note, are the result of alien Chinese norms used to express native Japanese realities), the poet must discover some less superficial, more essential indication of the new season. In this case, he finds it not in the weather, or even in the fact that leaves are falling or crickets chirping—presumably they have been doing so since late summer. Rather, it is in the way that these sounds have combined in a new synthesis that the poet senses the deepest meaning of the arrival of an otherwise imperceptible autumn. To Kokan, such perceptions were always the result of the state of deep concentration brought about by *zazen* meditation:

To escape the heat I sleep upstairs
Where a slight coolness grows in the night:
  Frogs croak in a stone basin,
  Moonlight patterns through bamboo blinds;
Accepting every sight and sound that comes,
The more detached I grow, the more I see and hear.
  This time of night is so truly still
  I no longer notice the mosquitoes buzzing round my ears.[13]

    Set in such terms, Kokan's practice of Zen meditation is very much like the Neo-Confucian meditation practice of "investigating things" (*ko-wu* 格物), popularly known through the story of the Ming philosopher Wang Yang-ming's attempt to arrive at a more profound understanding of the nature of bamboo by sitting in meditation before a clump for several days. Wang eventually became ill from exhaustion, and his failure at this attempt, which finally led him to reject Buddhist practice in favor of the Neo-Confucian formulation, illustrates the nature of the difference between Neo-Confucian and Zen meditation. Kokan's poetry can be understood as reflecting his under-standing of the Neo-Confucian reinterpretation of the Zen Buddhist dialectical principle of Void and Phenomenal Reality, represented in the complementary technical terms *kū* and *shiki*, as this dialectic was integrated in China into the revised framework of a supreme moral universal organizing "principle," *li*, and its manifold expression in "things," *wu*.

    Kokan's philosophical and literary priorities, eccentric as they may appear from the point of view of traditional Chinese thought, come as a breath of fresh air to anyone familiar with the loosely and often unquestioningly used terms of traditional Chinese literary criticism. His Chinese scholarship seems especially remarkable in light of the fact that he never went to China. In 1300, at the age of twenty-two, Kokan did begin initial preparations for "the journey south," as

---

[13] *Ibid.*, 74.

travel to China was called, prompted by an acute sense of shame that "only the most mediocre Japanese monks were going to China" and determined "to let them know that there are good men in Japan."[14] Kokan was apparently constitutionally weak from birth, however, and given the rigors of the voyage across the sea, he decided at the last moment to stay in Japan to look after his aged mother—an unusually Chinese sort of filial piety, and curious especially in a Zen monk.

Several of Kokan's disciples would later make the voyage. Shōkai Reiken (1315–1386), one of the best known, returned from a stay of twelve years, having studied under the most famous Chinese Zen masters of the day, to report that in all those years he had never found a Chinese master the equal of Kokan.[15] Shōkai's evaluation may be discounted as loyal exaggeration, and there is no question that loyalty to one's Zen master in Japan (as contrasted, for example, with filial piety toward a parent) was a matter of supreme importance in the Japanese temple world where it was not in the Chinese.[16] Still, Shōkai's assertion is only an early example of numerous statements that were to come from Japanese monks who, in increasing numbers, were failing to find what they had gone to China for. Their attitude is summed up in a complaint in 1323 by Kempō Shidon (d. 1361): sending Japanese monks to China for instruction, he said, was tantamount to "trading Japanese gold for Chinese gravel."[17] To be sure, the omission of the expected pilgrimage to China was less common in

[14] *Zoku Gunsho Ruijū* (Tokyo: Zoku Gunsho Ruijū Kangeikai, 1926), vol. 9b, 463a. See also Makita Tairyō, "Zekkai Chūshin to Minsō to no Kōshō," *Zengaku Kenkyū* 57 (1970), 167.

[15] *GBZS*, 2:1237–38.

[16] The Japanese have periodically raised the question of the alien quality of Chinese thought that emphasized *kō* (*hsiao*, filial piety) over what the Japanese prized as *chū* (*chung*, loyalty to one's superior), never terribly important in Neo-Confucian thought. In the second novel of Yukio Mishimas's tetralogy *The Sea of Fertility*, *Honba* (Runaway Horses), for example, the eccentric patriotic scholar Masugi Kaidō makes precisely this distinction between alien Buddhist and Confucian thought in contrast to native Japanese (trans. Michael Gallagher; New York: Knopf, 1973).

Chūgan Engetsu (1300–1375) offers a good example of what might happen to a Gozan monk who was considered disloyal to his teacher. Chūgan had studied in Kamakura for several years with the Chinese Sōtō monk Tung-ming Hui-jih (of the only Sōtō line besides that of Dōgen, one that became part of the Rinzai-dominated Gozan). Leaving Japan in 1325, Chūgan spent a year in China from 1330–1331 studying with the famous Chinese Ch'an master Tung-yang Te-hui. Upon returning to Kamakura in 1339, Chūgan had a falling-out with Tung-ming and announced that he intended to follow Tung-yang's line instead. As a result he was immediately ostracized by the Kamakura monks, one of whom even set upon Chūgan with a sword. As long afterward as 1362, a monk fired an arrow at Chūgan causing him to suffer a nervous breakdown so severe that he had to resign his post as Abbot of Kenninji. See Tamamura Takeji's biographical account of Chūgan in *Gozan Bungaku Shinshū* (hereafter cited as *GBSS*; Tokyo: Tokyo Daigaku Shuppankai, 1971), vol. 4, 1205ff.; and his interesting article on Chūgan as heretic, "Zenshū ni Okeru Itan no Mondai," in his *Nihon Zenshūshi Henshū* (Kyoto: Shibunkaku, 1981), vol. 2 (pt. 1), 373–745.

[17] Tamamura, *GBSS*, suppl. vol. 1:423.

Kokan's day than it was to be from the middle of the fourteenth century onward.

It comes as no surprise to learn that the Japanese monks who did go to China and stayed there for any length of time appear relatively less eccentric in their acquired tastes, and more conventionally "Chinese." Those immediate or near contemporaries of Kokan who lived in China for a significant length of time— one thinks especially of monks like Sesson Yūbai, Betsugen Enshi, Ryūzan Tokken, Chūgan Engetsu, and Zekkai Chūshin as only the most famous examples among many—wrote poetry that was more consistently "Chinese" than that written by monks who never left Japan. While the Chinese scholarship of Japanese monks who had studied in China was generally held in high esteem by their Japanese colleagues, even these more Sinicized monks were viewed with something less than complete enthusiasm by the Chinese themselves, as we see for example in the Ch'an monk Ju-lan's astonished and somewhat backhanded admiration, in a colophon dated 1403 written for the collected poems of Zekkai Chūshin, that his very talented Japanese colleague's poetry should "bear no trace of Japanese."[18] The Chinese were undoubtedly flattered when "barbarians" managed to ape Chinese culture with any degree of success; and the Japanese back home were always gratified by whatever compliments they could prevail upon the Chinese literati to write for them (many of whom supplemented their meager official stipends with the fees Japanese were willing to pay for such "prefaces").

But to the degree that such Japanese Zen monks were able to appear Chinese, they interest us less than their counterparts who remained in Japan and never attempted to conceal their essential Japaneseness. That even their colleagues in Japan seemed to feel that Japanese should act like Japanese is suggested in a humorous poem by Gidō Shūshin (1325–1388) entitled "Watching a Crow Bathe" (the Zen monk in his shapeless black robe was often likened both in poetry and in painting to a black crow):

I've watched you bathe for quite some time, old crow,
But try as you may, you'll never be as white as a gull;
Why not just stay your usual pitch-black self,
And avoid making the other birds suspicious?[19]

It is to these Japanese monks who never went to China that we must turn if we want to understand the role that the Zen monks played within the broader cultural context of the relationship of the Zen establishment with the rest of Japan, rather than merely the degree to which they were familiar with Chinese theory and practice.

---

[18] Makita, "Zekkai Chūshin to Minsō to no Kōshō," 175 and 178. For Sung Lien's equally backhanded compliment to Jorin Ryōsa, who accompanied Zekkai to China in 1368, see Itō Shō, *Rinkō Chōsho* (Kyoto: Kyoto Sōgo Shiryōkan, 1838), 2/1:34a–35a.
[19] *GBZS*, 2:1351.

Kokan Shiren became famous as a scholar of Buddhist history, and is still best known for his history of the religion in Japan, the *Genkō Shakusho* of 1322. In the introduction Kokan states that he was shamed into writing the work by the astonishment professed by his teacher, the Chinese émigré monk I-shan I-ning, that there was still no such history in Japan. Kokan began to study with this Chinese monk soon after the latter's arrival in Japan in 1299 as an official envoy of the Yüan government, which was aware on the evidence of the large numbers of monks flocking to China that Japan represented itself as a Buddhist country.

Kokan and I-shan appear to have gotten on well, and it was Kokan who eventually composed the best-known biographical account of I-shan's life. From this account the world was to learn that I-shan was apparently as devoted to literary pursuits as he was to the practice of Zen:

> The Master was of an infinitely gentle and compassionate nature. Other Chinese Zen masters in our time have tended to be severe and strict as befits their religious duties, not sparing the rod. The Master, however, sat alone in his chair and did not permit visits. Newly arrived from abroad, he came and went ceaselessly. When others insisted on coming to him for instruction, it was not his style of Zen to probe for deeper meaning, but merely to keep them busy about the temple [literally *yüan/en*, 苑, "garden"]. There are many who use secular writings as a detriment to Zen life, and the Master wished to promote logical principles [*li*] in order to set aside doubts. But since his spoken Japanese was poor, he spent his days and nights poring over the most minute aspects of temple correspondence, dashing off replies in his harmonious and graceful style. He was widely versed not only in the texts of the Buddhist canon, but also in the writings of the Confucian and Taoist philosophers, classical and vernacular fiction, and even the sorts of tales told by storytellers.[20]

This then was the personal style of Kokan's teacher, a well-meaning and well-read man of broad literary interests, forced to rely more than he might otherwise have on written rather than oral communication. At about the same time that Kokan began his studies with I-shan, another young monk, Musō Sōseki (1275–1351), also made his way to Engakuji Temple in Kamakura, attracted by reports of the fame of the newly arrived Chinese Zen master. Like Kokan, Musō was born into the aristocracy, a fact that has important implications for the religious atmosphere that prevailed in the Kyoto Zen temples of their day, for the children of the aristocracy were usually exposed to Tendai and Shingon Buddhism long before they embarked upon the study of Zen.[21] Five years before Musō came to Kamakura, his teacher, a great favorite of the young

---

[20] *T*, 80:332b–c; *GBZS*, 1:221–22.

[21] See Tamamura Takeji, *Musō Kokushi* (Kyoto: Sara Shobō, 1977), 6–10, 14, 16ff. On Musō's Tendai and Shingon background, see also *T*, 80:498b–c.

man's, suffered a stroke that left him, as Musō was to write later, "unable to write even a single character," a perception that speaks of Musō's early literary orientation. Shocked by this event, Musō entered a period of asceticism that finally ended in the Zen monasteries of Kamakura, where he became one of approximately forty Japanese I-shan finally accepted for study after weeding out the numerous candidates by means of an examination in Chinese versification.

   The ability to write Chinese well was undoubtedly a requisite for study with the émigré Chinese Zen masters, for as we have already seen in I-shan's case, the common written language usually had to serve as the medium of communication between the master and his pupils. The custom of what was called "brush talk" (*hitsuwa*) had already been in long use between Chinese and Japanese, the usual verbal give-and-take of Zen training carried out in writing instead. As the Ch'an monk Ming-chi Ch'u-chün put it in a poem to his Japanese patron Ōtomo Sadamune,

I've come ten thousand leagues across the sea to these shores
Knowing nothing of the language that you speak:
Able to make out only a babble of "ba-ba-ba,"
I can't catch more than a lot of "ri-ri-ri"![22]

With brush and ink as a substitute for the spoken word, Ming-chi continued,

To communicate my feelings, I take up a brush to say what is on the tip of my tongue,
And you catch my ideas by listening to my words with your eyes.

   I-shan's method of selecting his students is the first known example of a Chinese monk's actually setting would-be students examinations in Chinese poetry, a long-established practice in the Chinese civil-service examinations. Musō was one of only two candidates that I-shan placed in what he called his "top grade" of students, for his facility in Chinese poetry, one can only presume. But it was not long before Musō began to experience difficulties with his practice of Zen, and by 1303 he was in serious distress over what he took to be I-shan's stern and inhumane insistence on maintaining the unyielding style of Zen, often called the "pure Sung style," preferred in the Kamakura Zen monasteries, all of which were founded by Chinese masters. The Zen practiced in those monasteries could scarcely be called "pure" any more than Ch'an Buddhism as it was practiced in China was free of admixtures of elements from T'ien-t'ai and Pure Land Buddhism. In comparison with the styles of Zen that were developing within the Kyoto temples patronized by the court nobility, however, the Zen of Kamakura probably did seem harshly alien to the Japanese of Musō's day, so that "Chinese" would seem a more appropriate label than

---

[22] *GBZS*, 3:2026.

"Sung." In view of Kokan's later evaluation of I-shan's "gentle and compassionate" nature, it may be that the Chinese monk had simply not yet lived in Japan long enough to have had the sharp corners of his alienness smoothed down, and so seemed needlessly abrasive.

Whatever the case, when Musō eventually came to I-shan for encouragement and answers to his questions, the Chinese monk only responded in the best Ch'an manner: "There is no word, no Law, that I can give you." Musō begged for "compassion, some expedient," but I-shan only responded, "No compassion! No expedients!"[23] This dramatic episode reveals a side of I-shan's character that we do not see in Kokan's biography but is supported by other historical material. On one occasion of the traditional lecture to the assembled monks of the temple on the Festival of the Ninth Day of the Ninth Month, for example, I-shan, as was the custom, prefaced his talk with a poem suited to the occasion, full of traditional Chinese imagery. After I-shan had recited his poem,

there suddenly appeared a monk who objected, "You aren't talking about Zen Buddhism! You're only talking about literary matters!"

"Blind fool," retorted I-shan. "It is you who do not see the Way! I recite my poetry for those who can understand it!"[24]

Musō, however, was never to resort to the traditional Zen style of refusal, paradox, shouts, and blows. Rather, his own Zen was affable, chatty, simple, and accommodating, qualities that helped draw Japan's new Ashikaga rulers to him. These were provincial warriors, men without much sophistication in matters of Buddhism but with great aspirations to aristocratic culture and ready to learn.[25] The distinction Kokan drew between the demeanor of I-shan and that of the sterner Zen monks of his day would have applied as well to Musō, the many extant statues and portraits of whom reveal a gentle-looking man of extremely courtly bearing, almost comical with his long face and pointed dome, looking as though he could not harm a fly, in contrast to the awesome and even ferocious faces that so often glower from such likenesses.

In no mood for blows or riddles from I-shan, Musō turned in his distress to the more congenial Zen style of the Japanese monk Kōhō Kennichi (1241–1316), then in residence in Kamakura. Kōhō, as we might have expected, was also born into the aristocracy (he is said to have been a son of Emperor Go-Daigo). Like Musō too, Kōhō had never been to China. Perhaps it was because

---

[23] T, 80:498c.

[24] Bussho Kankōkai, ed., *Dai Nippon Bukkyō Zensho* (Tokyo: Nippon Bukkyō Zensho Kankōkai, 1956), vol. 95, 429.

[25] Tamamura, *Musō Kokushi*, 121ff. The question of Musō's dilution of Zen practice and of his competency in general is summarized in English in Akamatsu Toshihide and Philip Yampolsky, "Muromachi Zen and the Gozan System," in John W. Hall and Toyoda Takeshi, eds., *Japan in the Muromachi Age* (Berkeley: University of California Press, 1977), 322–29.

of their similar backgrounds that the two seem to have gotten along well; whatever the case, in 1306 Musō received Kōhō's seal in confirmation of his enlightenment.

Tamamura Takeji has interpreted Musō's failure under the tutelage of I-shan as an inability to deal with Zen in its "Chinese" form.[26] We have already seen, however, that I-shan's style, as abrasively alien as it may have seemed to Musō, was scarcely free of all sorts of admixtures ranging from esoteric Buddhism to Neo-Confucianism. In fact, I-shan's style eventually proved so congenial to courtly Japanese sensibilities that in 1313 he became the first Chinese monk invited to head any of the Kyoto Zen temples patronized by the court aristocracy, in this case Nanzenji. Nor did I-shan's style, apparently in the traditional mainstream of Zen practice if we can believe the following anecdote, appear to frighten Musō's teacher Kōhō, whose amusing encounter with I-shan in 1299 is recorded in the Japanese monk's biography:

> I-shan was placed in charge of Kenchōji [in Kamakura]. One day Kōhō went to pay him a visit. I-shan asked him, "What sort of instruction do you usually give your pupils?" Kōhō replied, "In my cave the colors of the mountains are beautiful in any season! The sounds of all the creeks beyond the clouds are cold!" I-shan asked, "Doesn't that sort of thing dazzle people these days?" Kōhō replied, "It increases the value of the Treasury of the Eye of the True Law [*Shōbōgenzō*]!" I-shan shouted "*Chieh!*" [Japanese *katsu*, a traditional Zen shout, here indicating approval]; Kōhō shouted back. After they had drunk some tea, I-shan asked, "Is the grass sweet to the water-buffalo?" Kōhō replied, "It's slept its fill and the sun is setting, but I can't get it to go back home." I-shan said, "It just needs a sharp whipping!" Thereupon, Kōhō roared, put his head down, and butted I-shan, bowling him over. I-shan laughed uproariously.[27]

For all of the very Zen-like behavior, shouts, and enigmatic repartee that liven this passage, we have seen that Kokan's description of I-shan lingers (approvingly, we might imagine) on the Chinese monk's familiarity with a broad range of literature. Yet even with his penchant for setting his pupils to meditating on poems instead of koans, I-shan was far from the most literary of the Chinese masters in Japan. Kōhō Kennichi's own master, Wu-hsüeh Tsu-yüan (who came to Japan in 1279), for example, is reported to have attained enlightenment at the age of twelve upon hearing lines of poetry—a fitting start for the man usually considered the founder of the most literary Zen line in all Japan.[28]

---

[26] Tamamura, *Musō Kokushi*, 20ff.

[27] *T*, 80:283a.

[28] *Ibid.*, 244a, and *Dai Nippon Bukkyō Zensho*, vol. 95, 388, contain these lines of poetry. For Wu-hsüeh's position in the history of Gozan literature, see Tamamura Takeji, *Gozan Shisō* (*Nihon no Zen Goroku*, vol. 8; Tokyo: Kōdansha, 1978); chart F3 at the end of the book gives an idea of the relative size of Wu-hsüeh's faction in Japan.

Kōhō was well trained in the native literary arts as a young man, and left a number of waka poems still known today because of their inclusion in such imperial anthologies as the *Fūgashū* (1346) and *Shinzoku Kokinshū* (1433). His waka poems were also compiled in a private collection by the well-known fifteenth-century waka poet Kazan'in Nagachika (known as Kōun). His poems, far from monkish, follow in the tradition of earlier non-Zen poet-monks like Saigyō, Nōin, and Jakuren, thoroughly of their time in diction and allusion. While some of his poems express an uncourtierlike familiarity with meditation in isolated mountain retreats:

Ware dani mo	The white clouds
Sebashi to omou	On the mountain-tops
Kusa no io ni	Poke halfway into this thatched hut
Nakaba sashiiru	I had thought too cramped
Mine no shiragumo	Even for myself.[29]

others seem quite at home within the established modes of court poetry:

Yo mo sugara	If you would inquire
Kokoro no yukue	Of my heart's whereabouts
Tazunereba	Throughout the night:
Kinō no sora ni	Where are the traces of birds' flight
Tobu tori no ato	Through yesterday's sky?[30]

The latter poem belongs to what Teika had called the *soku* (distantly related) style, in which the last two lines do not seem easily related to or to follow logically from the first three. It was Kōhō who instilled a taste for this kind of poetry in his pupil Musō Soseki. Like Kōhō, Musō wrote—even more significant, did not care if others knew that he wrote—waka poetry that, like his teacher's, was collected in the *Fūgashū*, as well as in a private collection. Both men were well known in their time as renga (linked-verse) poets, and the famous renga theorist Nijō Yoshimoto, who included several of Musō's renga stanzas in his *Tsukubashū* of 1356, states that the two "composed renga night and day."[31] Such proclivities for the native literary arts were undoubtedly instrumental in commending Musō to Emperors Go-Daigo, Kōgon, and Kōmyō, to influential courtiers like Reizei Tamesuke and Nijō Yoshimoto, and to powerful military leaders like the Ashikaga brothers Taka'uji and Tadayoshi.

This point has been generally overlooked by scholars in their attempts to account for Musō's eventual success, after a few false starts, as the single most important figure in the political history of the Gozan establishment. His success

---

[29] *Fūgashū*, 1747.

[30] *Ibid.*, 2065.

[31] *Tsukuba Mondō*, *NKBT*, 66:82; in this section Yoshimoto discusses the affinity between renga and Buddhism.

lay in his devotion to the task of making Zen accessible and meaningful to the ascendant Ashikagas, while at the same time guaranteeing the perpetuation of the established temple system under his own line during the difficult transitional period after the split of the court into northern and southern factions after 1331. It is doubtful that the Ashikagas, who met frequently with Musō at Saihōji in the western outskirts of Kyoto to exchange waka poems with him and be pleasantly instructed in a not terribly rigorous Zen, would have bothered to spend much time with any monk who persisted in bewildering them with alien and uncongenial Chinese poetry and thorny, uncomfortable Zen riddles. Of course, it seems equally unlikely that any Zen monk who wrote only waka and renga poetry could ever have cut much of a figure within the Zen temple world of this period, as many were in fact able to do in the fifteenth century.

When we consider his background, it is not surprising that Musō's waka poetry should seem more polished and erudite than his poems in Chinese, more in touch with tradition with their up-to-date language and frequent knowledgeable allusion to earlier waka poems. Even his Chinese poems often seem to reflect Japanese rather than Chinese traditions. Consider, for example, one waka poem whose headnote states that "for some years [1320–1323], I lived in a retreat I built at Yokosuka, on the Miura Peninsula in Sagami Province where the sea meets the land":

Hikishio no	There is a sound
Ura tōzakaru	As the tide draws far out
Oto wa shite	Into the bay,
Higata mo miezu	But I cannot see the tidal flats—
Tatsugasumi kana	A rising mist has covered them.[32]

If we compare this Japanese poem with lines of a Chinese poem that Musō wrote at about this time, we find that the Chinese poem seems to follow less from Chinese tradition than from the Japanese context within which such a waka could have been composed:

I thought that with a hide tough as bark I could live beyond the waves of the world,
But busy mouths that could melt iron followed me everywhere;
Just when I had muted my emotions to the hues of pale mist,
My sweet, dark dreams were shattered by the sound of the evening tide
    going out . . .[33]

Musō refers in both instances to a period of extreme political precariousness in his career following his resignation as Abbot of Nanzenji—a position delicately balanced between two feuding imperial factions—and his return to

---

[32] *Gunsho Ruijū*, vol. 15, 360b.
[33] *T*, 80:477a.

the Kamakura area. Even while keeping himself as distant as possible from potentially dangerous political involvements, however, Musō was not exactly living in isolation. Among several other important guests Musō received at his Yokosuka retreat Hakusen-an (Moored Boat Retreat) in the summer of 1321 was Reizei Tamesuke (1263–1328), a great-grandson of Fujiwara no Teika, and, after the success in 1291 of the famous lawsuit brought before the Kamakura authorities by his mother, the nun Abutsu, the acknowledged legal heir to Teika's literary legacy. Musō wrote the following rather conventional Buddhist poem upon seeing Tamesuke to his boat:

Kari ni sumu	Putting on the face
Iori tazunete	Of someone who owns the place,
Tou hito o	Again I see off
Arujigao nite	A visitor who has come calling
Mata okurinuru	At this temporary dwelling.[34]

Tamesuke's reply is, if anything, even more conventional than Musō's poem, with its rather stale image of tears and the play on the name of Musō's retreat:

Tōkaranu	At today's parting
Kyō no funaji no	The paths of our boats
Wakare ni mo	Are not really so very distant,
Ukabiyasuki wa	But they float so easily
Namida narikeri	Because of our tears.

Despite his earlier troubles under the tutelage of I-shan, and an episode of "false enlightenment" in 1304 at the age of thirty, Musō, much to his dismay, became a focal point for students attracted by his particular style of Zen. In 1311 he built a retreat called Ryūsan-an; hounded by would-be students, he abandoned it in 1312 to live at Jōkyoji, at that time headed by Kōhō. From there Musō left for Mino province the following year to lodge at Eihōji (the "mountain designation" of which was Kokeizan, "Tiger Valley Mountain"), again in order to escape the hordes of students who had arrived to seek him out. "I tried to hide at the Keizan Temple in Mino," he wrote. "And even though it was so deep in the mountains that there was not even a real road of any sort to the spot, much to my annoyance people kept calling to study Zen with me":

Yo no usa ni	It would be merciful of people
Kaetaru yama no	Not to come calling and disturb
Sabishisa o	The loneliness of these mountains
Towanu zo hito no	To which I have returned
Nasakenarikeru	From the sorrows of this world.[35]

[34] *Gunsho Ruijū*, vol. 15, 362b.
[35] *Ibid.*

This poem is clearly an "allusive variation" (*honkadori*) on a famous poem by the poet-priest Saigyō:

Tou hito mo	If it were not for the loneliness
Omoitaetaru	Of this mountain village
Yamazato no	Where people have given up calling on me,
Sabishisa nakuba	It would probably be
Sumiukaramashi	Too wretched to live here.

Musō here follows the long native poetic tradition of the hermit-priest, for whom any dwelling at all is merely a reflection of the impermanence of life on earth; the true significance of life lay in something other than these temporary structures, built on one's journey only to be abandoned without attachment. As Musō wrote in a Chinese poem on the same topic,

A drifter my whole life, I never save a thing;
The clouds in the mountains and moon in the creeks have been my carpets.
East to west, I tread this narrow path in vain—
What I seek for isn't in the dwellings along the way.[36]

The waka poem he wrote subsequently "upon abandoning the hermitage I had built in Shimizu in Mino province" reflects even more accurately than this Chinese poem the language of the waka tradition that was Musō's source for such a topic:

Ikutabi ka	How many times
Kakusumi sutete	Have I left abandoned,
Idetsuramu	Living hidden away like this,
Sadamenaki yo ni	A temporary dwelling built
Musubu kariio	In an uncertain world?[37]

In the imagery of Musō's poetry, as in Saigyō's, it is the path of Buddhism that the poet followed as he "returned home" to his original nature that was important, and not the temporary stopping places along the Way. In a waka poem that takes its title from the Zen saying "To put one foot after the other is to follow the Way," Musō makes clear that the "road home" is not to be interpreted as taking any particular topographical direction:

Furusato to	At those times
Sadamuru kata no	When I cannot decide the way
Naki toki wa	Back where I came from,
Izuku ni yuku mo	Anywhere I go
Ieji narikeri	Becomes the road home.[38]

---

[36] *T*, 80:456c.
[37] *Fūgashū*, 1783.
[38] *Ibid.*, 2053.

The sharp difference between these conventional poetic attitudes of other-worldliness and noninvolvement in the affairs of this world on the one hand, and on the other of Musō's extraordinary gregariousness, so well attested in the historical records as well as in poems to and from important people like Reizei Tamesuke, makes us wonder how Musō was able to reconcile the contradiction. As with many other problems of apparent contradictions in Buddhist theory and practice, one fruitful approach to this problem lies in the province of what was known as "expedient measures" (*hōben*), a technical term in Buddhism. Musō always claimed that he was only unwillingly involved in the writing of poetry, as had so many Zen monks before him, especially the Chinese masters like I-shan and Wu-hsüeh. This pursuit, which we have seen was condemned in Buddhist texts centuries earlier as "wild words and ornate speech," Musō rationalized as only one "expedient" among many that could serve to lure others toward the practice of religion. Perhaps the best-known Buddhist rationalization for the use of "expedient measures" to this end is found in the "parable of the burning house" of the *Lotus Sutra* (*Saddharma-puṇḍarīka Sūtra*; *Myōhō Renge Kyō*), in which a man must resort to promises of rich gifts in order to lure unconcerned children from a burning house and save their lives. The use of "expedient means" thus implies an awareness of different levels of audience, someone mature enough to fully realize his perilous situation not requiring the lures necessary for the still immature.

In this sense, Musō's poetry speaks directly to the needs of his as yet benighted secular counterparts among the warrior and noble classes. To his own Zen students, though, Musō delivered stern warnings to forebear from such perilous distractions and to stick to their meditation mats. In one statement on the subject, Musō divided his pupils into three grades:

> Those who have zealously cast off all worldly ties and singlemindedly pursue enlightenment to the exclusion of all else—these are my first grade. Those whose Zen is not pure and who cultivate a taste for scholarship—these are my middle grade. Those who are blind to their own spirituality and are fond of any drivel of the Patriarchs—these are my lowest grade. Then there are those who, besotted with poetry, conceive of their vocation as a literary one—these are shaven-headed laymen, not worthy of inclusion in even the lowest grade. Nay, they are stuffed with food and stupid with sleep, vagrant time-passers I call frocked bums! The ancients had another name for them: "robed ricebags." They are not monks, and certainly no disciples of mine![39]

This division into three grades reflects I-shan's own division of his students into three groups depending, apparently, upon their aptitude for Chinese poetry.

[39] *T*, 80:503c. See also Tamamura, *Musō Kokushi*, 19 and 23, n. 3. This division into groups of three permeates all of medieval Japanese aesthetics; see among other examples Seigan Shōtetsu on tea aficionados (*NKBT*, 65:230–31) or Bashō on haikai poets (*NKBT*, 46:430–31).

This system of ranking had even earlier precedent in China. The important
Sung dynasty Ch'an monk Ta-hui Tsung-kao (1089–1163), for example, wrote
in 1127 of the Ch'an master Fa-hsiu, who divided students into three grades
according to the following test:

> On a snowy day, the top grade are found seated in meditation; the middle grade are
> grinding ink and wetting brushes to write poems about the snow; and the third
> grade are sitting around the fire eating and talking.[40]

Musō also borrowed Ta-hui's unusual term for poetry, "the technique of
calling to the maid," for the poems he used as "expedient measures" to attract
others' attention. The Chinese expression refers to a poem about a woman who
calls to her maid, not because she actually requires attention but because she
needs some indirect means of letting her lover know she is available.[41]

Because of this approach to Zen, Musō was inevitably the target of the
frequent criticisms of his contemporaries. Shūhō Myōchō (1282–1338), founder of the important non-Gozan "Ōtōkan" (Daitokuji-Myōshinji) line of Zen,
for example, complained that Musō's methods seemed to have more in common with those of Tendai and Shingon Buddhism than they did with Zen.[42]
And indeed, Musō's experience with I-shan suggests that his inability to deal
with the stark contradictions of the more traditional Chinese Zen style within
the context of his ascendency to power in the Gozan is the crux of an important
change in the Japanese interpretation of Zen. The problem of "styles" is
particularly vexing insofar as it tends to be dependent on personalities; and yet,
it is from the occasional, if blurred, vision of human personalities that emerges
from the anonymity of dry historical record that we often seem to find our best
understanding of the shifting directions of human institutions.

I would interpret Musō's response as representing the truly native Japanese
pattern asserting itself in the historical process of assimilation and adaptation of
what was instinctively felt to be alien. His style can be summed up by the word
"mediation," or more specifically the reduction of the tensions created by the
clash of cultural values. In this sense, we might locate the deepest meaning of the
ancient wakan dialectic in the *wa* element's native Japanese reading of *yawara-
geru*, "to soften, mollify," the bringing of two things into "harmony," the
reduction of tension by accommodation.[43] On the surface this problem ap-

[40] Tamamura, *Musō Kokushi*, 108.

[41] *Ibid.*, 102; *Zoku Gunsho Ruijū*, vol. 96, 529a.

[42] Akamatsu and Yampolsky, "Muromachi Zen," 322–24.

[43] See, for example, Haga Kōshirō, *Higashiyama Bunka* (Tokyo: Hanawa Shobō, 1962), 201, for a
discussion of the chanoyu (tea ceremony) as an "artistically softened" (*geijutsuteki ni yawarageta*)
derivative of the *sarei* tea ceremony practiced within the Zen temples. It is clear from the
subheadings of this section—"The Nature of the Chanoyu as a '*Wa*' Art," "The '*Wa*' of the
Concept of the Chanoyu"—that by "*wa*" Haga means more than merely "Japanese."

peared to Musō's contemporaries, and so to later historians, as the contradiction of an unacceptably "Japanese" devotion to letters, especially to poetry, in the person of someone theoretically committed to the ancient Zen formula of "no reliance upon the written word." It was especially in the sense of mediation, of *wa*, that Musō was so crucial a figure in medieval Zen and poetry, as well as in other arts, as we shall see in chapter five. The truly Japanese pattern that he seems to exemplify can be located precisely in the equation of religion and poetry that, as I suggested in chapter three, was beginning to be made by 1200. This equation seems to have suggested itself in the obvious parallel between the current terms of religious and critical discourse. Poetic criticism from the tenth century on had developed the complementary polar terms of ineffable "heart" (*kokoro*) and the "words" (*kotoba*) needed to give it expression. We have also seen that the Zen metaphysics that had begun to color the aesthetics of the Shinkokin age centered on a similar polarity between an ineffable Void (*kū*) and its manifestation in the Colors (*shiki*) of the phenomenal world. This parallel between the necessary complementarity of essentially formless meaning (*kokoro*; *kū*) and meaningless form (*kotoba*; *shiki*) serves also to mediate between the disjunctive terms of the "fracture of signification" proposed in chapter one. Earlier Japanese poetic thought held that heart and words, while obviously different, were inseparable aspects of the same unity. Zen metaphysics, too, insisted upon a simultaneous identity and distinction between Void and Color. If carried to its logical conclusion, then, the equation implies that not only is meaning formless and form meaningless; meaning is also to be found in form itself, and form in meaning.

That this equation is fundamental to the Japanese pattern can also be seen in Mujū Ichien's *Shasekishū* of 1283. Mujū, who represents the very different style of a different time and personality, was someone of whom less "Chineseness" was expected, for all that he was a Zen monk of the Gozan Jufukuji in Kamakura and Tōfukuji in Kyoto. His loquacious anecdotes and gossip, recounted in the manner of a born storyteller, were therefore less likely to be regarded as a serious religious failing. Underlying the *Shasekishū* from its preface on is a strong attempt to provide a theoretical basis in earlier Chinese works, already well accepted in Japan, for a reconciliation of the contradition between a stark and very un-Japanese silence on the one hand, and the poetry and storytelling that Buddhist doctrine had labeled at once both "sins of the mouth" and acceptable "expedient means" on the other. Mujū found this theoretical basis precisely where earlier poets and monks had for over four centuries, in the T'ang poet Po Chü-i's fervent defense of "wild words and ornate speech to serve the cause of praising the Buddha's Law in worlds to come with the effect of turning the Wheel of the Law." [44]

---

[44] *Shasekishū*, *NKBT*, 85:58, n. 9, and 509, n. 3; also 218–20. For Mujū's equation of waka with Shingon *dharani*, see 222–25 and 513, n. 42.

When Musō wrote waka in what the Tendai monk Shinkei was to call a
century later the "Zen-like" *soku* mode of "distantly related verse" that came
into fashion around 1200, we find him as adept at bleaching the phenomenal
landscape of illusory Color and reducing it to its essential Void as any *Shinkokinshū* poet:

Kurenu yori	Even before the darkening sky
Yūbe no iro wa	Can be touched with crimson,
Sakidachite	The colors of the evening are gone
Kikage suzushiki	With the water flowing in the mountain
Tanikawa no mizu	rills
	Under the cool shade of trees.[45]

That he may not have been particularly pleased that as a Zen monk he was, if
only by the exigencies of protocol alone, expected to equate this congenial
aesthetic vision with the Zen mode of viewing reality is suggested by the
following poem in Chinese:

Autumn's colors drop from the branches in masses of falling leaves,
Cold clouds bring rain into the crannies of the mountains:
Everyone was born with the same sort of eyes—
Why must *mine* see these as a Zen koan?[46]

Musō clearly felt it more congenial to explore the implications of this
metaphysic—one he seems to have felt to be very Japanese—in native rather
than in alien terms.

Kokan Shiren, appearing to reach out toward China, found it somehow
lacking and insufficiently "rational"; as we read his explorations in Chinese
thought and letters we feel everywhere the fundamental ambivalence of his
attitude toward China. The same ambivalence can be sensed in his biography of
the Chinese monk I-shan; we are never really sure whether Kokan is praising or
condemning I-shan's gentleness where there ought to have been sternness, his
silence where there should have been guidance, his poetasting and reliance on
literature where others insisted upon koans. While there may be some argument over the integrity of the text (the original of which disappeared in a fire at
Tōfukuji in 1393, according to a colophon dated 1407), this very ambiguity
accords so well with Kokan's general view of everything else Chinese that we
sense in the end that this distortion of I-shan's portrait can only be attributed to
the superimposition of Chinese spectacles over Japanese vision.

Indeed, Kokan was much less ambiguous with those among his Japanese
colleagues who did not seem to him to act sufficiently like Zen monks. We feel

[45] *Gunsho Ruijū*, vol. 15, 361b.
[46] *T*, 80:480c.

the chill of his scorn, for example, for what he cleverly derided as "*kana* [仮名] monks." A fine three-level pun that can also be translated as "false name" monks, the term simultaneously suggests Zen monks like Musō who had abandoned the proper world of Chinese (*mana*, 眞名) learning for frivolous fame in the courts of Japanese cursive (*kana*) writing.[47] The word also carries heavy implications of Tendai Buddhism, for the word Kokan uses is also the technical term used in the Tendai *sandai* dialectic to mean "Provisional Reality," and so implies a willingness to accept the superficial world of phenomenal illusion as absolute Reality, and an unwillingness to see it simultaneously, as Zen insists, as Void. Kokan seems to be aiming his attack at monks like Musō whom he thought to be more involved with Tendai and Shingon Buddhism than with Zen.

Musō, to the contrary, found the Chinese master I-shan altogether too alien: his Chinese poem cited above seems to be saying, Why must *he* insist on seeing everything as Zen riddles when *I* see a beautiful Japanese sunset? Musō's attitude is reflected, by and large, in his entire line, the largest and most important in the Gozan in the century that followed. But even a Japanese as Sinicized as Musō's younger contemporary Chūgan Engetsu (1300–1375) could feel the uncomfortable tug between the outward "Chinese" forms of his vocation and something undeniably Japanese within. A poem by Chūgan sums up the problem as it must have been felt by many a Japanese Zen monk:

The older I get, the more I detest affectation—
In fact, every now and then, I *like* the pretty things of the world!
Giving in to my true nature, I open the window onto the small pond,
And, chin on fist, gaze into the infinity beyond:
Blown by the breeze, butterflies flit through sweet-smelling grasses,
Dragonflies everywhere rest on open lotus flowers—
  If the "cold and tasteless" in these seem so sweet to me,
  What am I doing living in a Zen temple?[48]

[47] *GBZS*, 1:235.
[48] *GBZS*, 2:902.

CHAPTER FIVE

Wakan and the Development of Renga Theory in the Late Fourteenth Century: Gidō Shūshin and Nijō Yoshimoto

The minor art of poetry isn't worth a copper—
Best just to sit silently in Zen meditation:
"Wild words and ornate speech" don't cease to violate Buddha's Law
Just because he died two thousand years ago.[1]

So Gidō Shūshin (1325–1388) wrote near the end of his life to the well-known renga theorist Nijō Yoshimoto (1320–1388), suggesting, "humorously" as the title of the poem informs us, that in the two millennia that had elapsed since the death of the Buddha, poets were continuing to find sophisticated and elaborate rationalizations for their pursuit of poetry, contrary to the warnings of the Buddha himself. There is some irony in Gidō's words: of the many famous men of letters who followed in the Zen line of Musō Soseki, Gidō himself, renowned in his own day as a poet, was among the most prominent.

From the time he began religious studies, Gidō had been aware that the young monks of the Gozan often spent more time composing poetry than they did in Zen meditation. No exception himself, Gidō was already enough of a scholar to understand that contemporary poetice practice in the temple world was based on inaccurate and corrupt texts of Chinese models.[2] At the age of

---

[1] *GBZS*, 2:1540.

[2] That the Gozan monks often knew their Chinese literature from badly corrupt texts is suggested by a colophon by the most eminent of the Chinese then in Japan, Chu-hsien Fan-hsien, to the collected poetry of a monk named Kotoku, which mentions the popular Yüan dynasty collection *Chiang-hu Feng-yüeh Chi* (compiled by Sung-po Tsung-hsi) containing the poetry of Ch'an monks written between 1260 and 1321 (*GBZS*, 1:723):

> When I was in China I once saw this *Chiang-hu Chi*, which monks young and old alike delighted in following as a paragon of clever words and phrases. ... The situation here is exactly the same. Day and night the young and old pore over this book instead of busying themselves with their Zen studies. However, nine of every ten words in the book are misprints, and one cannot make out what they mean. Nor can I make out the gist of even one or two in ten of these monks' poems. Alas! ... How tragic that men should take up [this text] in their search for poetic subjects. It is for this reason that I have added this colophon.

twenty-two, therefore, he compiled an anthology of what he considered proper Chinese poetic models. His *Jōwashū* (Collection of the Jōwa Era, 1347) contains some three thousand poems by Chinese monks of the Sung and Yüan dynasties. One might well wonder in which of his "three grades of students" Musō would have classified so literary a pupil; the Master, however, was apparently impressed with his young student's zeal. One record says that Gidō regularly volunteered for latrine-cleaning duties, and even went so far as to use his fingernails for scrubbing the woodwork. Apparently concluding from this sort of behavior that Gidō had the proper attitude toward literature as an "expedient" in attracting others toward Zen practice, Musō in 1351, the last year of his life, gave the young monk his seal of enlightenment.

For all of his lifelong devotion to poetry, Gidō was as severe with his poetaster pupils as Musō had been. In 1371, for example, he reprimanded some pupils in Kamakura who had failed to attend a sutra lecture because they had been writing poetry:

> I warn you to dissociate yourselves henceforth from these secular activities! If you fail to do this, I shall be forced to gather up all the non-Buddhist writings in the monastery and burn them in the central courtyard as an offering to God.[3]

Like Musō, Gidō would undoubtedly have been able to cite as precedent for such a drastic course the action taken by the important Southern Sung monk Ta-hui Tsung-kao (1089–1163), known as one of the most influential thinkers in the accommodation of Ch'an Buddhism to the literary interests of the Chinese ruling class. In one of those actions so common in the lives of the Ch'an masters, and so bewildering to posterity, Ta-hui burned the printing blocks of the *Pi-yen Lu* (*Hekiganroku*, Blue Cliff Records), a collection of koans compiled in 1150 by his own master, Yüan-wu K'o-ch'in. Ta-hui explained that he found intolerable the fad that this famous collection had created for what was known as "literary [*k'an-hua*] Ch'an" among the scholar-bureaucrats.[4] It is ironic, and indicates how little Gidō was prepared to carry out such a threat, that his own restoration of the text of the *Jōwashū*, which had perished in a fire at Tenryūji in Kyoto in 1358, would become the obsession of his last years, demanding so much of him physically that it probably shortened his life.

After Musō's death in 1351, Gidō moved to Kenninji in Kyoto, a Gozan temple then headed by the Japanese monk Ryūzan Tokken (1284–1358), recently returned from an unprecedented forty-five year sojourn in China. Of

---

[3] Tsuji Zennosuke, ed., *Kūge Nichiyō Kufū Ryakushū* (Tokyo: Taiyōsha, 1938), 61, entry for 9/28/1371. Gidō uses the Chinese word *t'ien-ti* (literally, Heavenly Emperor) for "God"—very unusual diction for a Zen monk.

[4] Cf. *T*, 48:1036b, "Letter to Chang Tzu-shao"; also Yanagida, *Chūgoku Zenshūshi*, 98ff.; and Araki Kengo, "Confucianism and Buddhism in the Late Ming," in William T. de Bary, *The Unfolding of Neo-Confucianism* (New York: Columbia University Press, 1975), 54–56.

the forty monks accepted by I-shan I-ning for study when he first arrived in Japan, the formidable Ryūzan had taken first place, while Musō placed second. Following Ryūzan to Nanzenji in 1354, Gidō records an encounter that year with the older monk that provides a good illustration of the sort of stern "Chinese" attitude toward literary composition Japanese monks could adopt when they had lived a considerable time in China:

> In the first month of 1354, I paid a visit to Abbot Ryūzan, taking with me my collection of Chinese verse in the "old" and "regulated" styles to ask for his suggestions. But Ryūzan merely attacked my poems, saying "Dabbling in poetry is nothing a Zen monk should be doing!" I left feeling quite upset. The next day, however, he invited me back for tea and explained, "Poetry is one of the Six Arts. Beginning with the three hundred poems of *The Book of Odes*, one must apply oneself with utmost diligence for ten, twenty, even forty or fifty years, studying day and night, before one can write well. But Japanese Zen monks seem to think one can write poetry with no study at all!" [5]

Gidō may well have felt abashed, considering the contrast between Ryūzan's forty-five years in China and his own complete lack of first-hand experience. But Gidō's later importance within the Gozan as a representative of Musō's line places him almost by definition within the group of Zen monks who were never to go to China (what can only be called a half-hearted effort to go in 1342 collapsed when he discovered, as he wrote in his diary, that travel by boat made him seasick). Gidō and most of Musō's other disciples would, however—unlike Musō—draw the line at writing in Japanese. Their attitude toward Japanese letters was somewhat like that which Confucius is said to have taken toward ghosts: although there was certainly no denying that something of the sort existed, the true gentleman did not deign to take notice of them. Just enough of other poets' waka and renga compositions are recorded in Gidō's diary, the *Kūge Nichiyō Kufūshū*, to indicate that he was without a doubt familiar with their composition. We shall see in the discussion that follows that his knowledge of Japanese poetic theory and practice went far beyond what one would expect of a Zen monk.

When we read Gidō's poems in Chinese, we find them to be generally witty and adept, but far too voluminously occasional and slight to indicate truly great talent, or at least to have been very good for the talents he did possess. Rather, his poems reflect in their extremely social cast his political importance among

---

[5] *GBZS*, 2:1645–46. I should note that Ryūzan seems to have been much more concerned that Gidō was unfamiliar with the latest Chinese styles than that he was writing poetry. The traditional enumeration "Six Arts" (*liu-i*) includes Rites, Music, Archery, Horsemanship, Calligraphy, and Mathematics; Ryūzan is referring, however, to the "Six Classics," which include the *Book of Changes, Book of Odes, Book of Documents, Spring and Autumn Annuals, Book of Rites,* and *Book of Music.*

the court and military aristocracy. His real forte was small poems intended for inscription on ink fan-paintings illustrating small scenes, a favorite genre of the Muromachi period:

FAN LANDSCAPE

In mist-bordered pine woods, a Buddhist temple,
At the water's edge, willow trees and fishermen's huts;
Zen monk's bowl empty in the afternoon,
Old fisherman's nets drying in the setting sun.[6]

INSCRIBED ON A FAN

Night mists begin to disperse, dew not yet dry,
From the dark, chill sea the round ball of sun emerges;
Somewhere a traveler, anxious to make good time:
On the horizon, a homeward-bound sail sweeps the dawn cold.[7]

The Zen monks in general favored the shorter Chinese genres such as these four-line *chüeh-chü* (cut-off lines) or the eight-line *lü-shih* (regulated verse) when they wrote Chinese poetry. This preference may indicate the influence of the brief native waka poetry on the one hand, and on the other some discomfort with the long, untamed stretches of the forms more favored by the Chinese such as *p'ai-lü* (extended regulated) and *ku-shih* (old-style verse). Few Japanese poets wrote well in these longer forms, or even bothered much to use them at all, with some notable exceptions who, like Chūgan Engetsu, had spent a considerable amount of time in China. One sometimes gets the impression reading Gozan poetry from about the middle of the fourteenth century on that meaning tends to spill over the ends of lines and couplets more in the manner of the linear, hypotactic progression of thought that characterizes waka poetry, rather than the rigid parataxis that results from (or alternatively results in) the antithetical parallelism characteristic of end-stopped Chinese verse.

This reduction in the scale of the formal elements of poetry is paralleled by a reduction in scale of the natural world depicted in the Zen monks' poems. The horizonless stretches of sky and water of Chinese verse remain—these are after all as much a part of the Japanese landscape as of the Chinese. But conspicuously missing are the abrupt scarp and towering peaks typical of Chinese karst formations, or the sandy wastes and subtropical badlands that figure in so much Chinese poetry. The monks' landscapes tend rather to resemble the gentle and numinous hills and bays of Japanese *utamakura*, scenic spots hallowed by

---

[6] *Ibid.*, 1349.
[7] *Ibid.*, 1432.

mention in earlier poetry. For all that the Gozan monks conceived of their world as a "Chinese" one, the scene in the poetic near-distance is often conspicuously un-Chinese: no city walls, no loft-storied buildings, no wail of barbarous Tartar flute or screech of monkeys in river gorges. These alien sights and sounds are replaced in Gozan poetry by thatched village farmhouses seen over low hedgerow fences, the aristocratic thrum of a koto, the twittering of a bush warbler. Inside the temples of the Chinese poetry written by Zen monks, as in the temples of the Gozan itself, cushions and tatami mats take the place of Chinese-style chairs and hard earthen floors, and the study alcove with its sliding window of translucent paper assumes the importance in poetry that it did in the new *shoin* styles of aristocratic residences.

Gidō himself noted this transformation from Chinese to Japanese content, for example, in the following poem about a Chinese festival known in Chinese as *Jen-jih*, or People's Day (celebrated on the seventh day of the first month), a name that provides the pun in the first line:

This antique scene may add to "people's days,"
But each passing year subtracts some teeth;
Not for bald Zen monks, those Chinese palace coiffures—
Someone else will have to wear colorful hair ornaments.
Nowadays we eat Japanese tangerines instead of mandarin oranges,
Unable to pronounce the traditional Chinese herb, drink tea instead.
What better image could one find for this lingering cold
Than a shivering Chinese passion flower?[8]

After the typically Chinese remark that each year finds him with fewer teeth, Gidō sets about exploring the dissonances of the Chinese festival as it was then celebrated in Japan: there can be no colorful hair ornaments for bald Zen monks; the traditional Chinese word for the mandarin orange (read in Japanese as *karatachi*) has become the more congenial Japanese *mikan* tangerine or *tachibana*; and the traditional herbal infusion is no longer made from an obscure Chinese herb but from ordinary tea, the character for which is similar to the archaic and by then quite unfamiliar character for the Chinese plant. The "passion flower" of the last line is literally a "flower of Tu-ling," a Chinese expression for the female entertainer who in China would have livened the holiday festivities; the English translation must serve to render an untranslatable pun. This and many similar poems nicely demonstrate how uncomfortable Chinese conventions could become even within the supposedly "Chinese" world of Japanese Zen temples, revealing a certain ironic distance from alien matter, a distance that was only to grow greater with time.

For all his attention to the proper models of Chinese prosody—and some of

[8] *Ibid.*, 1466.

his poems are very fine indeed—Gidō's poems in Chinese are at least as Japanese as they are Chinese. In this regard, they stand in marked contrast to poems by his friend Zekkai Chūshin (1336–1405). The two monks came to be linked in traditional evaluations, and are still thought of as the "twin pillars"—a very "Chinese" sort of phrase—of Gozan literature. As personalities, however, they might more accurately be said to have complemented each other as opposites. Unlike Gidō, Zekkai spent more than ten years in China (he left Japan in 1368, the year the Ming dynasty was established), returning home with praise from eminent Chinese, including Emperor T'ai-tsu, with whom he had exchanged poems. Zekkai also appears to have reserved his poetry for moments of deeply felt emotion or inspiration, a trait that seems rather more Chinese than Japanese. One result is that Zekkai left a corpus of poetry less than a tenth the size of Gidō's, much of whose poetry is social verse of relatively slight literary merit. On the other hand, the existence of so much poetry based on human intercourse and relationships suggests something of Gidō's eventual importance within the Gozan as one of the major diplomats of Musō's line. Recognized while still a young monk for his tact, Gidō was dispatched early in his career to help oversee the establishment of a politically important and extremely sensitive branch of Musō's faction in Kamakura. He remained there for two decades, patching over potentially dangerous ruptures with other factions of the Gozan, as well as between various tendentious groups within his own.

After his return to Japan in 1378, Zekkai, apparently less comfortable in the ruling-class world of Muromachi Japan than in that of Ming China, and ill at ease with the life led by the Shogun Yoshimitsu with its astonishing variety of aristocratic amusements, fled to the provinces around Kyoto and could not be prevailed upon to return to the capital. In a poem written during this period, Zekkai alludes to Yoshimitsu as a "haughty prince," and his poems in general show him in the unyielding stance of a crusty and eccentric Zen hermit. By 1383, however, Gidō had somehow managed to lure his friend out of the hills, and by 1386 Shogun and monk had improved their relationship to the point where Zekkai agreed to return to Kyoto to head the Ashikaga family temple, Tōji-in. Following Gidō's death in 1388, Yoshimitsu came to rely increasingly on Zekkai for the sorts of advice he had earlier sought from Gidō, and by the time of the suppression of the Meitoku Rebellion in 1391 it is reported that the Shogun actually rode forth to battle dressed in Zekkai's own Zen robes.

Gidō spent two decades in Kamakura trying to keep the peace among the various Zen factions there before he was finally recalled to Kyoto in 1380, at the order of the Shogun Ashikaga Yoshimitsu, to head the Ashikaga family burial temple, Tōjiji. Within a month of his arrival in the capital, Gidō found himself drawn into the very active literary circle around Nijō Yoshimoto (1320–1388). Yoshimoto, the most important of the Shogun's aristocratic advisors and soon to be appointed Regent (*sesshō*), was already the most famous exponent of the art of renga poetry. Gidō took part in frequent literary gatherings with Yoshimoto in much the same way, and for the same reasons, that Musō Soseki had participated in such gatherings half a century earlier—monk hoping to draw ruling-class patron into deeper involvement in Zen practice, as well as to further the interests of his own line within the competitive world of the Gozan temples.

While in Kamakura Gidō had often participated in gatherings with other monks at which renku (linked-verse poetry in Chinese, or *lien-chü*) was composed.[9] With the move to Kyoto and the broadening of his contacts among the leaders the of the noble and military classes, Gidō was introduced to wakan-renku gatherings, then in vogue in the capital, at which a hybrid form of renga linked-verse poetry was composed in alternating Japanese (*wa*) and Chinese (*kan*) stanzas.

Here we shall pause briefly to review the history of experimentation and practice of wakan poetry since the Heian that lead to this development.[10] There had of course been various waves of interest in the ways that Chinese forms might be accommodated to Japanese that extend back into the dawn of history. The Japanese seem to have first become truly self-conscious about their cultural response to China during the Heian period, and I have shown in chapter two that experimentation in this sort of accommodation, known as wakan, was an important part of Heian aristocratic life from the middle of the tenth century on. Chinese culture endowed with a gloss of imported attractiveness whatever was mundanely Japanese, while also helping to define an emerging "native" aesthetic by providing a contrasting "foreign" background. Helen McCullough has aptly described the first part of this practice as it figured in ninth-century literature:

> Japanese poets were not incapable of creating topics, techniques and images of their own. But they felt an increasingly explicit desire to refine the waka, to invest it with an aura of sophistication, and to elevate it to the status of Chinese poetry, and one way of achieving those goals, they believed, was to use words, phrases, images and techniques that by their very antiquity, their encrusted connotations, conjured up, like some richly patinated bronze vessel, the whole glorious span of Chinese civilization.[11]

[9] See David Pollack, "Linked-Verse Poetry in China: A Study of Associative Linking in *Lien-chü* Poetry with Emphasis on the Poems of Han Yü and His Circle" (Ph.D. diss., University of California at Berkeley, 1976). For a close study of one Chinese linked-verse poem, see David Pollack, "Han Yü and the 'Stone Cauldron Linked-Verse Poem,'" *Journal of Chinese Studies* 1:2 (June 1984), 171–202.

[10] The importance of wakan gatherings in this period has been pointed out by Haga, *Chūsei Zenrin*, 418–22. Haga's work is central to any understanding of the role played by the Gozan monks in the larger context of Japanese literature.

[11] Helen C. McCullough, trans., *Tales of Ise* (Palo Alto: Stanford University Press, 1968), 33–34.

In contrast to earlier gatherings at which the composition of Chinese and Japanese verse simply went on side by side, gatherings at which wakan linked-verse poetry was composed first appear in Japanese records in 1035.[12] The Shingon monk Ryōki notes in his *Ōtaku Fukatsushō* (ca. 1278) that wakan-renku was popular in his day, a fact that accords well with the pronounced interest in the "Chinese" culture of the Zen monks at the courts of Go-Uda (r. 1274–1287) and Fushimi (r. 1288–1298), both as emperors and as cloistered emperors (*in*).[13] It seems reasonable to assume that the increasing interest at this time in finding grounds for a rapprochement between Japanese and Chinese poetry was related to the arrival in Japan of such émigré Chinese monks as Wu-hsüeh Tsu-yüan, who left China in 1279 to establish the most literary line of Zen in Japan. It was only natural, after all, that the courtier and warrior patrons of these important Chinese monks would want to find ways to include them at their gatherings at which the composition of poetry played so large a role.

The occasion that most clearly marks the rise of wakan-renku to popularity among the elite during the medieval period is the elaborate gathering held at Saihōji Temple in Arashiyama by Musō Soseki during the late spring of 1346 to celebrate a particularly ancient cherry tree. This gathering was attended by several important Gozan monks as well as by prominent members of the military and court nobility.[14] The linking of Chinese stanzas was headed by the most eminent of the monks present, the Chinese Chu-hsien Fan-hsien (Chikusen Bonsen, 1291–1348, arrived in Japan 1329), while Musō himself characteristically wrote only lines in Japanese.[15] Musō was now at the peak of his career, and it would be interesting to know what the other monks must have thought of this unmonklike participation in the Japanese rather than the Chinese side of public life.

While Gidō, unlike his ambidextrous mentor Musō, appears never to have actually written poetry in Japanese, Nijō Yoshimoto wrote poetry in both Japanese and Chinese, and frequently called at Gidō's residence to ask him to judge and comment formally on his contributions to renku and wakan-renku gatherings. During the eight years following his arrival in Kyoto until his death in 1388, Gidō recorded some eighteen wakan-renku gatherings in his diary at which both he and Yoshimoto were present. Yoshimoto's name appears about thirty times in those parts of the diary still extant, and twenty-three of these

---

[12] Kidō Saizō's chronology of renga developments shows renku-renga (an earlier term for wakan-renku) beginning from 1035. See *Rengashi Ronkō*, 2 vols. (Tokyo: Meiji Shoin, 1973), 862.

[13] Kaneko Kinjirō, *Tsukubashū no Kenkyū* (Tokyo: Kazama Shobō, 1965), 756ff.

[14] *Ibid.*, 619ff.

[15] *Ibid.*, 631. Kaneko asserts that the linking at the 1346 gathering is that of the *kotobazuke* (word-linking) style, calling it "flat and monotonous," and finds the linking in the twenty-four examples included in the *Tsukubashū* little improvement (636ff.). Surprisingly, he finds no subsequent improvement in the linking demonstrated in the examples included in the *Shinsen Tsukubashū* compiled in 1494 by Sōgi and others.

entries are concerned with wakan-renku; it seems likely that a good many less formal wakan-renku sessions were simply never recorded.

Few complete wakan-renku poems remain from this period; the best known is a solo (*dokugin*) performance of one hundred stanzas by Emperor Go-Komatsu in 1394.[16] The longest extant sequence that includes stanzas by both Gidō and Yoshimoto is a fragment that comprises only the first nine stanzas of the original one hundred, set down in Gidō's diary in an entry dated the last day of the eleventh month of 1384.[17] That day Gidō had invited Ashikaga Yoshimitsu to attend the opening of a subtemple at Daiji-in in Nara:

> The Shogun arrived in his carriage and I went forth to welcome him. . . . In the retinue accompanying him were the Regent [Yoshimoto] and some five others, as well as the monks Fumyō Kokushi [Sessō Fumyō], Shōkai Reiken [a disciple of Kokan Shiren], Taisei Shōi, and some ten others. After we had taken a light meal, we assembled at the Pavilion of the Southern Branch to compose a hundred-stanza wakan-renku poem.

Gidō mentions in his diary that a few days before this gathering he had prevailed upon the Shogun to write the characters for the name of the pavilion, Southern Branch, on a plaque which was to be installed over the entrance. The day following the gathering, he paid a visit to the residence of Sasaki Dōyo, where he was called upon to explain the significance of the Chinese story known as "The Dream of Han-t'an" (also known as "A Record in a Pillow") written by the T'ang dynasty writer Li Mi (722–789). This request would seem to have been suggested by the theme of the previous day's verse-linking, for "The Dream of Han-t'an" is very similar to another T'ang tale known as "The Story of the Governor of Southern Branch" by the T'ang writer Li Kung-tso (770–850). Both stories concern events that happened in the course of dreams. At least from the scant ten percent of the poem that remains, however, these T'ang dynasty tales would appear to have nothing to do with the wakan-renku poem in question. The poem may also have drawn upon a purely Japanese association of the phrase "southern branch": in a well-known story in the medieval chronicle *Taiheiki*, the beleaguered Emperor Go-Daigo (r. 1318–1339) dreamed of a tree whose branches, pointing south, led him to his stalwart defender Kusunoki Masashige, whose family name (楠) is a rebus composed of the characters "south" (南) and "tree" (木).[18]

[16] The 1394 *dokugin*, or "single-author linked-verse poem," by Go-Komatsu is reproduced in its entirety in Nose Asaji, *Renku to Renga* (Tokyo: Kaname Shobō, 1950), 168–75, who analyzes the poem on 176–86 and discovers "Bashō's sort of *nioizuke* [linking by indirection]" (186); see however Kaneko, *Tsukubashū no Kenkyū*, 538–639, who does not.

[17] The preface and poem that follow are cited from Tsuji, ed., *Kūge Nichiyō Kufū Ryakushū*, 203. See also Kageki Hideo, *Kunchū Kūge Nichiyō Kufū Ryakushū* (Kyoto: Shibunkaku, 1982), 324.

[18] *Taiheiki*, NKBT, 14:96–98. See also Morris, *Nobility of Failure*, 111.

In the first nine stanzas of the poem, however, the allusion to a "southern branch" refers more immediately to a passage from an encyclopedic work by Po Chü-i, the *Po-shih Liu-t'ieh*. Under the heading of "Flowering Plum," it says:

> The blossoms of the plum trees of the Ta-yü mountains fall from the southern branches while those on the northern are just opening, so different is the warmth on the former and cold on the latter.[19]

This passage had long been known in Japan, having been included in the mid-eleventh-century anthology *Honchō Monzui* as well as in the earlier *Wakan Rōeishū*, where it appears under the heading "Early Spring" and set in opposition to lines from Po Chü-i's poem "Early Spring Scene." It is these Heian anthologies of wakan sensibility that are most often the sources of allusions underlying the linking association of the poem that follows in Gidō's diary. Later, in discussing Yoshimoto's theoretical writings about wakan-renku, we shall see that he considered wakan anthologies the primary locus for any Japanese poet's knowledge of "Chinese" sensibility.

Probably in deference to Yoshimoto's stature as a linked-verse expert, the Shogun yielded to him the place of honor at the start of the poem. I shall simply translate the nine extant stanzas first, and then look into the question of the linking between stanzas afterward.

1. *Yoshimoto*
   Kazu ya chiyo   Famed for countless generations,
   Na mo tamamatsu no   Its very name evokes
   Kasumi kana   Mists in the jeweled pines.

2. *Gidō*
   歳晩喜回春   In the evening of the year
                                  It is gladdened by the returning spring.

3. *Yoshimitsu*
   Chiru koro no   Its blossoms, as they scatter,
   Hana ya yamaji o   Will soon conceal
   Kakusuran   The mountain paths.

4. *Gidō*
   鞋香草欲匂   Our sandals with fragrant grasses
                                  Will soon be redolent.

5. *Yoshimoto*
   Yuki no ayumi wa   One will find no longer then
   Ato mo shirarezu   Any trace of these walks in the snow.

---

[19] *Wakan Rōeishū, NKBT*, 73:49 and notes.

6. *Yoshimitsu*

    Kesa mitsuru   The blossoms, so haggard

    Hana wa mukashi ni   This morning, will have

    Chirinashite   Long since scattered.

7. *Fumyō*

    春遊跡易陳   These traces of our spring outings

                          So easily lend themselves to poetry.

8. *Yoshimoto*

    Aki no ta no   The Kingdom of Shining Rice

    Mizuho no kuni mo   Too, with its autumnal fields,

    Osamarite   Is peacefully gathered.

9. *Taisei*

    晃旒拜紫宸   These crown jewels are revered

                          In the imperial handwriting.

It is nearly impossible to gauge the skill of the poets or the success or failure of the poem as linked verse on the basis of this fragment of nine links, representing little more than the *omotte hakku*, or first eight stanzas written on the first fold of the first sheet of paper of a hundred-stanza sequence. Still, from these few stanzas some generalizations might be sustained.

It is striking that not only is the first link typically gratulatory, but also the eighth and ninth as well. From the tone of the eighth and ninth stanzas one might even imagine that the "Northern Court" backed by the Ashikagas and the "Southern" following the line of the rebellious Emperor Go-Daigo had already been reconciled, an achievement that would have to wait another eight years. Although the gathering was held in the eleventh month, during the period called Lesser Snow in the adopted Chinese agricultural calendar, the poem from the first link addresses itself to spring, giving the clear impression that the scene before the assembled poets is one of a plum tree unseasonably in bloom, a seasonal discrepancy in keeping with the idea of the "southern branch" of early-blossoming plum from Po's encyclopedia. While Taisei's stanza clearly alludes to the jewellike plum blossoms, it may allude as well to one of the three Sacred Treasures of the Imperial Regalia, the jewel Yasakani no Magatama. With neither side possessing all three Treasures, the dispute over the legitimacy of contending emperors could in theory never be resolved. Perhaps the early flowering of the plum blossoms suggested to the participants an omen of the unification of the Northern and Southern Courts, by association with Po Chü-i's vision of a single tree of earlier-blooming "southern" and later-blooming "northern" branches.

A closer look at the participants' understanding of one another's allusions reveals that Gidō was surprisingly well versed in Japanese poetry, certainly more than Yoshimoto was in Chinese. An example or two of the allusions in each link will suffice to show the extent to which the Japanese poets were aware of Chinese allusions and the monks of Japanese.

Yoshimoto's first stanza, in its felicitous connotations of longevity, alludes to spring with the word *kasumi*, "mist." While its primary reference is to *Man'yōshū* 113, it alludes as well to a waka poem by the Heian courtier Minamoto no Muneyuki that is anthologized in the *Wakan Rōeishū* and appears also in the Spring section of the *Kokinshū* (1:24):

Tokiwa naru	Even the greenery
Matsu no midori mo	Of the evergeen pine,
Haru kureba	Now that spring has come,
Ima hitoshio no	Has turned a deeper
Iro masarikeri	Shade of color.

as an adaptation of this poem in the *Shinchokusenshū* (ca. 1234), poem 461:

Tokiwa naru	Even the branches
Tamamatsu ga e mo	Of the *jeweled pines*,
Haru kureba	Now that spring has come,
Chiyo no hikari ya	Seem to gleam with the brilliance
Migakisōran	Of *countless generations*.

What is particularly interesting about Gidō's succeeding stanza is that in the phrase "returning spring" he appears to indicate that he is aware of the words *haru kureba*, "Now that spring has come," not actually used by Yoshimoto but present in both the poems to which he alludes. This stanza perfectly complements the first, receiving it in accord with its seasonal connotations and continuing with little disrupting change. Gidō reveals here a sensitivity we would not have expected from a Zen monk toward the nuances of waka poetry he claimed to know nothing about.

His next stanza, which echoes a line by the Sung poet Tai I, is also interesting, less for any particular sensitivity to tradition—the word "sandals" simply continues the theme of "travel" suggested in the "mountain paths" (*yamaji*) of the preceding stanza—than because he ends his line with the Chinese character *chün* ("equal" or "uniform"), which as it stands makes little sense except that it satisfies the requirement of a unified rhyme throughout the Chinese lines. It is only when we understand that the character is in fact intended to represent the similarly drawn Japanese graph (not used in Chinese) for *nioi* (匂, fragrant, redolent) that the meaning of the line emerges. This illustrates the sort of thinking that wakan linked verse stimulated as it forced the participants to find ways to adapt Chinese forms to the exigencies of Japanese signification and vice versa.

In the fifth stanza Yoshimoto appears to have had in mind a poem in the *Wakan Rōeishū*, linking a traveler in a "Chinese" line found there to the unseen footprints of the traveler in Gidō's preceding stanza:

In mountains that recede into the distance clouds bury all trace of the traveler;
In pines that grow increasingly cold blows a wind that shatters the traveler's dreams.[20]

The first line of this couplet has a Japanese counterpart in a waka poem included in the *Shingosenshū* (ca. 1303; 557) that turns the clouds themselves into "travelers":

Iwane fumi	As they tread the base
Kasanaru yama no	Of mountain ranges,
Tōkereba	Receding into the distance,
Waketsuru kumo no	*The white clouds, as they depart,*
Ato mo shirarezu	*Leave not even a trace behind.*

Yoshimoto states explicitly in several places in his theoretical works what he felt the practice of wakan-renku could contribute to the art of renga poetry. In so doing, he throws a certain amount of light as well on the larger question of what the contributions of "Chinese" things in general might be to the development in this period of a new aesthetic that was and still is felt to epitomize something quintessentially "Japanese."

When Gidō returned to Kyoto in 1380 after a twenty-year absence from the capital, he was a newcomer, albeit one much sought after, to the modish wakan-renku gatherings then in fashion. Yoshimoto, however, had already considered wakan-renku a significant literary genre for more than twenty years, if we may judge from the fact that he had included twenty-four examples of it in his renga anthology *Tsukubashū* of 1356. Those examples, spanning the years 1329–1349, include several stanzas composed at the 1346 Saihōji gathering sponsored by Musō Soseki. Yoshimoto had also already written about the practice and theory of wakan-renku in such critical works as *Tsukuba Mondō* (1372) and *Kyūshū Mondō* (1376), both composed while Gidō was still in Kamakura. Gidō's partially extant diary, *Kūge Nichiyō Kufūshū*, however, is our principal source of information about Yoshimoto's participation in wakan-renku gatherings between 1380 and 1388, a subject we know almost nothing about before Gidō arrived in Kyoto to take an interest.

Best remembered today as advisor to Ashikaga Yoshimitsu in matters Chinese, Gidō lectured frequently to the Shogun and his circle on such topics of current interest as how Neo-Confucianism was to be interpreted both in theory and in governmental practice, the correct ways of composing Chinese poetry, and the sources and meanings of Chinese classical allusions. He clearly expected that by cultivating this powerful audience he would eventually succeed in bringing his interlocutors to a deeper appreciation of Zen and, perhaps more

---

[20] *Ibid.*, 152.

pragmatically, in insuring their continued support for Musō's line within the Gozan. But he was also realistic enough about such people to understand that they were usually most interested in whatever information he could impart in the area of practical political philosophy or, at the other extreme, in acquiring a sophisticated patina of imported culture. Gidō was very likely not altogether surprised, then, to discover that Yoshimitsu and Yoshimoto often put his solicitous instruction in philosophy and literature to uses that he had probably never intended.

Although they met nearly every day, Yoshimoto mentions Gidō only infrequently in his own writings. In the *Jūmon Saihishō* of 1383, for example, Gidō is simply cited as the authority for a reference to Chinese traditional poetic theory that Yoshimoto apparently included to support his view that renga poetry developed naturally from the native waka, an idea that he based on the Chinese critical notion of *pien-t'i*, "evolved form."[21] An examination of Yoshimoto's use of Sung dynasty theoretical works reveals that he frequently cited bits and pieces of works like Yen Yü's (1180–1235) *Ts'ang-lang Shih-hua*, especially as they are excerpted in the important and popular Southern Sung anthology *Shih-jen Yü-hsieh* (Jade Chips from the Poets, compiled ca. 1244 by Wei Ch'ing-chih and brought to Japan before 1324), less from any profound understanding of the Chinese theoretical concepts involved, or from any attempt to apply these concepts in a systematic way to his own theories, than as ornament that lent authoritative prestige to buttress his own innovative ideas about renga poetry.[22] We need only recall that renga, a form with deep roots in noncourtly and nonelite practice, was still in the process of becoming the elite literary genre that would be at the fore of poetic practice and theory in the fifteenth century (along with nō drama, another as yet uncouth entertainment) to understand why Yoshimoto should be so anxious to establish an acceptable pedigree for it in earlier native and Chinese theory and practice.

In view of their close relationship between 1380 and 1388, it is likely that Yoshimoto was familiar with the general range of Gidō's opinions on Chinese literature. One of these opinions, found in a number of Gidō's writings, held that the T'ang dynasty (618–906) had been the golden age of linked-verse poetry in China (*lien-chü*), especially in the late eighth and early ninth centuries, the age of Han Yü and Po Chü-i. Much as Fujiwara Teika had reaffirmed the importance of Po's poetry for the composition of waka in his own time, Gidō now held up Po's linked-verse poetry as the best model for renku poetry in Japan. But Chinese linked-verse (renku) as practiced by his own Japanese contemporaries, wrote Gidō, had fallen into a degenerate pastime of unimaginative superficiality, the poets doing little more than linking together stanzas in the

---

[21] *NKBT*, 66:113.
[22] Konishi Jin'ichi, "Yoshimoto to Sōdai Shiron," *Gobun* 14 (1968), 1–9; see also 135.

Chinese manner using conventional words in conventional antithesis, "linking 'yellow' to 'white' and 'wind' to 'moon.'" [23] This comment accords well with Yoshimoto's view that waka poets in his day "merely toy with 'blossoms,' sport with 'wind,' and show not the least refinement or elegance [*fūga*]." [24] Yoshimoto's response to this deplorable situation lay in part in adopting Chinese models to provide new depth in poetic practice, much as Teika had done two centuries earlier.

In his early treatise *Renri Hishō*, written when he was twenty-nine, Yoshimoto had listed what he considered to be the fifteen different types of linking possible in renga poetry. Included among these were the two categories of "word-linking" (*kotobazuke*), or superficial association, and "heart-" or "mind-linking" (*kokorozuke*), or more profound association. By the time he had reached the age of fifty, Yoshimoto had elevated the distinction between these two types of linking to a position of central importance in his theory of renga poetry, in a new emphasis on the primacy of *kokorozuke* that was taken up and elaborated by later theorists. [25] Yoshimoto's emphasis on the crucial distinction between complementary opposites also parallels Teika's earlier emphasis on the distinction between what he called the "style of possessing 'heart'" (*ushintei*) and the rest of the "ten styles" he enunciated in his *Maigetsushō* of 1219. [26]

Yoshimoto's elevation of linking by heart over linking by words can be seen in the section of the *Tsukuba Mondō* that deals with judging renga. It was naturally in evaluation and judgment, more than in any other activity, that theory came to the fore, and Gidō recorded in his diary Yoshimoto's frequent visits to his temple to ask the monk's judgment of a Chinese poem, renku, or wakan-renku. "In the composition of renga poetry," Yoshimoto wrote,

> one may make associations [*yoriai*] with Chinese literature as well as with matters of the mundane world, and therefore a man who would be a judge must have broad experience in literary practice [*keiko*]. These days it is usual to make associations to the *Wakan Rōeishū* and other collections of poetry set to music. *The Book of Odes*, the very source of Chinese poetry, also provides interesting associations as well as [what Confucius called] "the names of plants and animals." These sorts of things appear so often in waka poetry that if a poet is not well versed in the ancient poetry and matter of Japan he will certainly find allusion to those of other countries too much for him. It is especially the heart [*kokoro*] of ancient poetry that is of interest in

---

[23] *GBZS*, 2:1642; a convenient compilation of Gozan monks' comments on renku poetry can be found in Ōno Kitarō, "Gozan Shisō no Renku," in *Hattori Sensei Koki Shukuga Kinen Ronbun* (Tokyo: Hōzanbō, 1943), 195–202.

[24] *Tsukuba Mondō, NKBT*, 66:81.

[25] *Ibid.*, 50–52.

[26] *NKBT*, 20:514–17.

the practice of wakan-renku poetry. As I have written before, *in wakan-renku poetry one should always link by heart rather than by word.*[27]

Yoshimoto is discussing here the importance of not merely keeping one's eye on the points that could be scored by superficially witty word-association (*kotobazuke*), which he called "a trivial business" (*kitanaki mono*),[28] but having instead the cultivation and refinement that alone would enable the poet to probe beneath the surface of words to discover the true nature of the underlying world created in a line of poetry. In his *Kyūshū Mondō* four years later Yoshimoto restated somewhat more elaborately the ideas set forth in the *Tsukuba Mondō*:

> *The Book of Odes* may be called the original model of all Chinese poetry . . . and so it is of special interest for the practice of wakan-renku poetry. Besides the *Odes*, also of interest for wakan-renku are the styles of the *San-t'i Shih* [Poems in Three Styles, an anthology compiled by the Sung author Chou Pi] and the works of poets like Li Po, Tu Fu, Su Tung-p'o, and Huang T'ing-chien. If in linking stanzas one takes the *words* of Chinese poetry as one's basis for linking, one should be careful to use only those that show delicacy and *yūgen*—words that are jarring should never be used. In the case of wakan-renku poetry, moreover, there is the additional matter of what I have called "rejecting the words in favor of adopting the heart." It should be one's general practice in wakan-renku linking to *reject the surface meanings of the words, and to link one's lines instead to the heart of the previous line.*[29]

These passages suggest that Yoshimoto found wakan-renku poetry valuable as a kind of "practice of an art" (*keiko*) that could broaden one's familiarity with the "ancient matter" especially of China, as well as of Japan. Placing Japanese poetry near the more ancient and stately Chinese encouraged the elevation of tone he felt was essential if renga were to be given serious consideration as high art rather than be treated as merely a vulgar amusement. Rather than the term *keiko*, however, Gidō preferred, and often used, the term *shugyō* (practice of religion) in the same context when discussing poetry. But as Gidō well knew, men like Yoshimoto concerned themselves little with religious matters.

Given the almost daily necessity of including formidably Sinicized monks in their literary circles, it is also clear that the aristocracy felt a knowledge of Chinese versification and allusion would be helpful in keeping them from appearing foolish at such mixed literary gatherings. This sort of knowledge was also of pragmatic value in preventing the linking association from one stanza to the next in wakan-renku sessions from running aground on the shoals of

---

[27] *Tsukuba Mondō*, NKBT, 66:91.

[28] *Ibid.*, 90.

[29] Cited in Haga, *Chūsei Zenrin*, 420.

linguistic and cultural ignorance, for obviously the *kotoba* or diction permitted in Japanese and Chinese poetry were alien enough to each other to cause severe problems, especially in the crucial matter of tone, as we have seen in the lines of the wakan-renku poem translated above.

It remains to ask just what Nijō Yoshimoto, a well-known theorist of renga poetry, could have expected to gain by such intense involvement in the ungainly hybrid genre of wakan-renku linked verse. One possible response to this question lies within the larger framework of the changing concept held by monks, nobles, and warriors alike of "China" and its cultural artifacts. A generation earlier, Musō Soseki, for all of his involvement in the composition of waka and renga poetry, had waxed quite indignant in his assessment of the new uses to which tea-drinking was being put in what he termed "scandalous" tea gatherings, severely condemning as well the newfangled zeal for connoisseurship in poetry, music, and landscape gardening (*sansui*, an area in which Musō was acknowledged a master). "These are elevated pursuits," he wrote,

> that can regulate the evil in men's hearts and give rise to a refined elegance. But the way they are carried on these days, they amount to little more than artistic accomplishments [*nōgei*] that give rise to egotism, and as such are detrimental to the Way of refinement and a source of evil.[30]

What he found so objectionable, Musō continued, was that like the tea that had traditionally been used in the temples to stimulate drowsy minds to greater effort and concentrate scattered attention, and had even been used as a medicine, Zen monks were beginning to turn poetry as well to uses for which it had not originally been intended within either Chinese or Japanese temples. Musō located this change of emphasis within the context of the degeneration of the concept of *kufū* (工夫) a word that originally included any activity performed within a religious context, and in both China and Japan still meant "work" or "effort" expended in practice of the Way. By Musō's time, the Chinese (and so the Japanese Gozan monks) had begun to use the word to refer to what one did in one's "spare time away from work" (the word *kung-fu* is still used in Chinese to mean "free time," while in Japanese it appears to have developed along its original lines to mean "devise a plan, project, or scheme").[31] Musō's criticism

---

[30] *Muchū Mondō*, ed. Karaki Junzō, *Zenka Gorokushū* (Tokyo: Chikuma Shobō, 1969), 152–53. Muso's use of the term *sansui* has sometimes been interpreted as "ink-painting" or even as "appreciation of nature"; that he clearly meant "landscape gardening" can be seen from an earlier part of the same passage in which *sansui* is described as "building mountains, erecting rocks, planting trees, creating streams" (150–51).

[31] The *Ch'a Ching*, or "Classic of Tea," by the T'ang author Lu Yü, the most important early work on tea in China, describes "*Kung-fu* tea" taken in tiny cups, a style of drinking that must indeed have required a certain amount of "free time."

of tea-drinking, along with anything else that smacked of connoisseurship for its own sake, is evident from his complaint in his *Instructions for Rinsenji Temple* (*Rinsen Kakun*, 1339) about "monks who do nothing but hold tea-gatherings and chat all day"—an item that precedes in appearance and so in importance the usual injunction against eating meat and drinking alchohol ("even if lay guests are present").[32] The difference, wrote Musō, lay in whether such activities as tea-drinking were part of the context of one's daily religious "work" (*kufū* here identified with *dōshin*, 道心, "keeping one's mind upon the goal of enlighten-ment") or merely performed in the spirit of "connoisseurship" (*shiai*), "artistic accomplishments" (*nōgei*), and so forth, To him, the terms *shugyō*, *kufū*, and *keiko* all meant the same thing; he would probably have been appalled at the comparison Seigan Shōtetsu made a century later between the appreciation of *waka* poetry and connoisseurship in tea, intended to garner for the older poetic tradition something of the glamor of the new fashion in tea.[33]

Poetry written in Chinese, too, was in this period coming to be regarded much like any other *karamono*, or "Chinese object"—such as the tea bowl whose original homely function was to all but disappear in the increasingly stylized ritual and connoisseurship of chanoyu; the Chinese brocade that served to lend an atmosphere of rich ceremony to various sorts of formal display, including the nō stage; calligraphy whose provenance and style rather than content lent a touch of elegance to the new *kaisho* styles of ornamentation that centered on the focus provided by the emerging space of the *tokonoma* (display alcove); and the new painting styles, modeled after the Chinese, commissioned to decorate the equally new spaces provided by screens, sliding doors, and wall panels of the new *shoin*-style architecture of residences of the military elite. In other words, cultural and artistic forms once thoroughly alien to the Japanese were in this period in the process of being emptied of their Chinese content and replaced with entirely Japanese signification. Ironically, Musō himself may even have inadvertently contributed to the growing demand for Chinese goods through his personal sponsorship of the "Tenryūji ship." Dispatched to China in 1342 in the expectation of trade profits to help underwrite the cost of completing Tenryūji, a temple Musō was building in the western outskirts of Kyoto, this ship represented the first trade mission to China to be officially sanctioned by Japanese authorities since the Mongols' attempted invasion of Japan in 1281.

In much the same fashion that other Chinese cultural artifacts were being subjected to new interpretations within a Japanese context, poems written in Chinese (*kanshi*), as their composition spread beyond the confines of the temple

---

[32] *T*, 80:501c.

[33] *Shōtetsu Monogatari*, *NKBT*, 65:230–31.

world, were also becoming objects to be esteemed more for their ceremonial and ornamental qualities than for their traditional functions within an earlier religious context. The traditions of Chinese poetry and ink-painting especially were largely in the keeping of the Gozan monks, along with the most recent information from the mainland on their composition and critical theory. Thus, it was inevitably to the Gozan monks that the creators and consumers of the new cultural tastes had to turn in this period, Nijō Yoshimoto among them, for the poetry itself and the difficult rules that governed its composition. Even more important, they turned to the Gozan monks in order to understand the elements of what men like Yoshimoto thought of as the atmosphere of *fūga*, "elegance and refinement," evoked by Chinese poetry.

The practice of wakan-renku poetry seems clearly related to a need, beginning to be felt in the Nambokuchō period and growing acute during the rule of Ashikaga Yoshimitsu, to bring an atmosphere of aristocratic refinement to literary gatherings, of the sort that was then generally believed to have permeated the gatherings of the Heian court nobility. It was felt that Chinese cultural artifacts especially lent the desired element of elegance and refinement to all such group cultural activities. At first, the glamour of imported continental culture simply overshadowed the Japanese. It was inevitable, however, that eventually the need would arise to accommodate what was essentially alien to what was essentially Japanese, as an increasing awareness of what was properly "native" provoked a heightened sensitivity to what was "foreign," and vice versa. The process that appears to have occurred in such cases was that the two elements were at first simply placed side by side in a variety of hit-or-miss attempts at finding harmony between them. We can see this early stage in the gaudy and indiscriminate, or so-called *basara*, styles of *karamono* display that were common through 1400. This stage was followed by a gradual assimilation or subordination (*wa*, harmonization) of the foreign to the native, Japanese (*wa*) needs determining the ways in which Chinese (*kan*) forms and materials found expression.

The fondness for *karamono* that developed in the late Muromachi period to a high point around 1480 in the Higashiyama culture of Ashikaga Yoshimasa (so called after his villa in the Higashiyama, or Eastern Hills, of Kyoto) is a reflection of the Ashikaga Shoguns' yearnings for courtier sensibilities of *fūga*, "refinement and elegance," what was "Chinese" serving also to point up by contrast what was peculiarly "Japanese" about the new aesthetic. This development of a new aesthetic is epitomized in the frequent pun that followed the transformation of a taste for imported "Chinese" (*kara*) elements into a taste for the "withered" or "dry" (*kara*, *kare*) that came so completely to dominate late-Muromachi aesthetics.[34]

[34] See the interesting study by Nagashima Fukutarō, *Ōnin no Ran* (Tokyo: Shibundō, 1965),

In this context, it is not difficult to understand how incorporating lines of Chinese verse written by Zen monks into the Japanese milieu of the linked-verse gathering may have been felt to contribute to the cultivation of an atmosphere of refined elegance, held by contemporaries to have been the classical ideal of such gatherings in Heian times, and now felt to be sadly lacking. The participation in poetry gatherings of such a major figure as Musō had served to mediate within the same society between Chinese and Japanese elements that until then were unacceptable as literary partners, thereby greatly helping to banish much of what even the Chinese called the "smell of pickled vegetables" that emanated from the poetry of monks, and rendering more palatable what Japanese of all periods have considered the indigestible quality of things Chinese in their unmediated state, whether they be food, the written language, or poetry.[35] Kokan Shiren's earlier pointed use of the phrase "*kana monks*" (仮名僧; cf. p. 133) may indicate that Musō's participation in Japanese letters was not to the taste of all Gozan monks; but it was Musō and not Kokan who was more in the mainstream of contemporary medieval Japanese culture. Men like Yoshimoto and Zeami were for their part delighted by the opportunities presented by accommodating and solicitous monks like Gidō, and took pains to cultivate them, a matter that will be considered more fully in chapter six.

It was natural for Yoshimoto, having devoted his life to raising the practice of renga poetry to the level of high art, to be concerned with that aura of elegance and refinement that Chinese poetry might lend the native genre. But the practical question inevitably arose as to exactly how the apparently irreconcilable forms of Chinese and Japanese poetry could meaningfully be brought together. Working from the context of an intense involvement with the traditions of Japanese poetry, Yoshimoto required a collaborator—no one as unacceptably alien as a Chinese who spoke little Japanese and had less sensitivity to the requirements of native Japanese literary concerns, of course, nor even a Japanese monk as uncomfortably "Chinese" in culture as Zekkai Chūshin. Rather, Yoshimoto found his ideal collaborator in Gidō, a fellow Japanese who, having

---

241–68: "Ōnin no Ran to Higashiyama Bunka"; and the central importance of the wakan dialectic, 262–66: "Wakan no Kon'yū." See also Haga, *Higashiyama Bunka*, 73ff., on the term *kara-sansui*, "Chinese landscape garden," as a punning near-homophonic equivalent for the term *kare-sansui*, "dry [waterless] landscape garden," found for example in an important Gozan text of 1446. Medieval literature contains many similar examples of the word *karabu*, 枯らぶ (withered, dry) written as 唐ぶ, "Chinese." There is, for example, Zeami's discussion in *Fūshikaden* of the simplicity of appearing Chinese when acting Chinese roles: "If one simply acts in some 'Chinese' manner or other in order to appear to others as Chinese-like ["Karabitaru (唐びたる) yō ni yosome ni minaseba"], one will soon seem to *be* Chinese" (*NKBT*, 65:356).

[35] For the expression "smell of pickled vegetables" in Chinese criticism, see the "Ch'an-lin" section of *Shih-jen Yü-hsieh*, 443.

already succeeded in assimilating a great deal of Chinese culture within a Japanese framework, could be uniquely helpful in the task of further assimilation into the mainstream of warrior-aristocrat cultural life. Musō Soseki, who was equally active in both traditions, would have been the perfect choice for such a task, and Musō's interest in waka and renga had clearly opened the way for later experiments such as Yoshimoto's. But Yoshimoto, whose earliest extant critical treatise dates from 1349 when he was only twenty-nine, was still only thirty-one when Musō died in 1351. Nor had the all-important climate of interest in things Chinese among literary and other circles in mid-fourteenth-century Kyoto yet risen to the hothouse levels that were to accompany Ashikaga Yoshimitsu's infatuation from 1378 onward with the luster of mainland culture.

Gidō's return to Kyoto in 1380 coincided with this new climate fostered by Yoshimitsu in the capital. Working from what would be thought of as the "Chinese" side of Japanese cultural concerns, Gidō was primarily committed to the task of involving his new circle (the powerful patrons of Musō's line among the noble and military elite) in Zen, which meant in both the politics and the culture of the Gozan. If they seemed to want the glitter of Chinese culture rather than the more profound understanding of Zen that he held out to them, Gidō was realistic enough to cooperate with them in the hope that some Zen might rub off in the process.

The result of this collaboration can be seen especially in the wakan-renku gatherings of the day. It was, after all, highly unlikely that Gidō as a Zen monk would be invited to gatherings of renga poets, though in the fifteenth century Gozan monks would be deemed appropriate members of such circles. What Yoshimoto thought of wakan-renku gatherings, however, is made clear in his theoretical writings: in the course of the search for a meaningful way to relate Japanese lines of poetry, Japanese poetic thought, to Chinese, a poet would necessarily develop the broader, deeper cultivation that came from having to steep oneself in a more ancient tradition, and at the same time his art would acquire something of the patina of antiquity.

Yoshimoto was quite aware of the paramount and obvious obstacle that lay in the path of any attempt to adapt Chinese forms to Japanese ends: the apparently irreconcilable differences between Chinese poetic diction on the one hand and the *kotoba* or diction considered permissible in Japanese poetry on the other. Although the languages of Japanese speech and poetry had always evolved in dialectical response to Chinese, for long centuries the existing corpus of waka poetry was felt to be the only proper "word-hoard" of Japanese sensibility. In the terms of native Japanese poetic discourse, however, a problem involving *kotoba* necessarily involved its complementary aspect of *kokoro*, or "heart." This critical polarity had evolved in theoretical discourse since at least the start of the tenth century, and may even be traced back centuries to the punning use of the word *koto* in the *Kojiki* to mean both "things" themselves as well as the "words" that stood for them. Progress in waka poetry had always been motivated by the awareness of successive generations that the words of earlier poets no longer sufficed to represent new realities. In response to this dilemma, poets invariably turned to a "deepening of *kokoro*" to provide the still deeper well from which fresh *kotoba* would spring anew.

If there was now a problem with *kotoba*, then, the proven remedy was to experiment with *kokoro*, and this is exactly what Yoshimoto did. He felt that if one probed beneath the superficial level of "words," one would discover the "heart" or realm of underlying ideation from which they came, a realm in which essential similarities became clear as apparent differences disappeared. If one were then to match one's *kokoro* to that which informed a line of Chinese poetry, one's own *kotoba* would necessarily "harmonize" with it and at the same time be made more profound by the effort.

This was the goal of what Yoshimoto called "linking by heart" (*kokorozuke*). In a famous comparison, the later theorist Shinkei was to call linking by heart the "Zen" style in renga. In fact, its operation recalls more closely the Tendai process of mediation that Shunzei had adopted in *Kōrai Fūteishō* (1197) as part of the theoretical context for the evolution of a new aesthetic, discovering in the operation of this dialectic a means by which the poet could probe beneath the level of the superficial in order to reemerge into a new and more profound synthesis. We saw in chapter three that Teika had appealed to the power of Chinese archetype, embodied in the Heian enshrinement of the poetry of Po Chü-i, to calm the mind, elevate the spirit, and provide the ground against which the true significance of Japanese pattern might best emerge. To Yoshimoto "China" clearly held out much the same possibility for this needed renewal of "depth" that it had to Teika.

To speak of the emergence of design against background is necessarily to be reminded of the important contrast in medieval theory between "ground" (*ji*, 地) and "design" (*mon*, 文), a critical concept considered especially important in the composition of hundred-stanza renga sequences. This effect was achieved by placing a few striking "design" verses among a much larger number of intentionally unimpressive "ground" verses so that the full impressiveness of the former might emerge more clearly. The origin of this technique has been attributed, like nearly everything else in later medieval aesthetics, to Teika, who is said to have emphasized the importance of the ground/design contrast in the teachings of his father, Shunzei.[36] Whatever the actual origins of this concept, it was clearly of great interest to Yoshimoto in the development of his renga theory. "What requires skill," he wrote, "is to create a quiet, subdued renga sequence that includes a 'design' stanza only every four or five links. This creates a superior style that makes itself felt immediately when one so much as looks at

---

[36] See *KNBT*, 66:250, n. 21.

the page, since the stanzas without 'design' do not leap to the eye." [37] And again, "It is a sign of great skill when at a single session there are no more than two or three superior stanzas that make one prick up one's ears." [38]

The distinction between "heart" and "words" could with some justification be located within the context of Ch'an-influenced Chinese critical theory. The uniquely Japanese contrast between "ground" and "design," however, had no counterpart in Chinese thought, for it never occurred to the Chinese to find such dialectical contrast inherent in or intrinsic to the creation of meaning, which they regarded to be a purely Chinese matter. But this Chinese indifference to the idea of contrast did not prevent Yoshimoto from drawing on the impressive weight of Chinese archetype to help illustrate his point. In a passage whose moral relativism would surely have bewildered the Chinese, he wrote:

> Of old even the time of the Sage Emperors Yao and Shun was not entirely devoid of evil, nor were the reigns of the Wicked Emperors Chieh and Chou entirely devoid of good. Still, on the whole we distinguish between "Sage" and "Wicked" Emperors. In people, too, though good may predominate, we must accept that there will also be some bad—this is not something that is limited to the art of renga alone. [39]

This was intended as a pragmatic response to the problem that even the most skilled poet might on occasion find himself without resources and, under pressure to create an unobtrusive "ground" stanza, might only create an obtrusive and grating stanza instead. Yoshimoto's more general concern for the problem of ground and design can be seen too in the twenty-four examples of wakan-renku linking he chose for inclusion in his anthology *Tsukubashū*. In each case a Chinese stanza is followed by a Japanese one, Japanese "design" thus deliberately set off against its Chinese "ground." This treatment has its visual analogue in the heightened contrast of the graceful and delicate linear flow of the cursive Japanese script set side by side on the page of wakan-renku with the more cumbersome and block-like appearance of the Chinese characters (fig. 4).[40] Although contrasting, neither element predominates on the page, each alternating as ground and design much as background and foreground seem to alternate in the familiar modern figure, used to illustrate the principle of gestalt perception in psychology textbooks, of the vase created by the space between two facing profiles of a human head.

At this point the principle of ground/design contrast was still in embryonic

---

[37] *Ibid.*, n. 20.

[38] *Tsukuba Mondō, ibid.*, 87.

[39] *Ibid.*

[40] Examples of the appearance of wakan in poetry manuscripts can also be seen in John M. Rosenfield and Edwin H. Cranston, *The Courtly Tradition in Japanese Art and Literature* (Cambridge: Fogg Museum of Art, Harvard University, 1973), 138–47 and plates 45–47.

form, not to attain its full importance in renga theory and practice until the fifteenth century. Its role in the development of fifteenth-century aesthetics forms part of the discussion of chapter six. Since I shall have more to say about renga too in the following chapter, I have restricted myself here to an exploration of the significance of the intense interest in wakan-renku before 1400, during what has become known as the Kitayama era of Muromachi culture. From his writings, we find that Yoshimoto seems to have developed his clearest idea of what renga *was* by consciously opposing the Japanese form to what it was *not*, which is to say Chinese poetry. Although it continued to be practiced well into the sixteenth century whenever Zen monks gathered with other groups of poets to write poetry together, wakan-renku remained an ungainly hybrid form, by its very nature impossible of complete assimilation into the mainstream of Japanese literature. While some of it is actually quite good as poetry, its primary interest for us lies in its significance within the context of the overall development of Muromachi aesthetics.

Like any form, wakan-renku can be thought of as "self-referential," as a formal sign, that is, that points as much to itself as to any particular content. In this sense, wakan-renku can be understood in semiotic terms as being "about" the age-old imperative of Japan to define itself against and in terms of the "other"—China—and, by establishing itself in dialectical relation to the other, to give expression to a more profound meaning than could otherwise have been achieved.

CHAPTER SIX

Wakan in Literary Theory in the Fourteenth and Fifteenth Centuries: Zeami, Shōtetsu, Shinkei and Sōgi

The idea of a complementary polarity of "words" and "heart" in poetry did not originate with Nijō Yoshimoto, but can be traced back through Japanese literary theory through Teika at least as far as Ki no Tsurayuki's preface to the *Kokinshū* (ca. 905): "The poetry of Japan has its roots in the human heart and flourishes in the countless leaves of words." [1] In earlier chapters I have suggested that this consistent understanding of meaning as a dialectical synthesis of antithetical terms can be traced to the earliest fracture of signification in the *Kojiki* into the complementary polarities of ineffable native content on the one hand and inadequately meaningful alien form on the other.

Tsurayuki's criticism of Ariwara no Narihira's (825–880) poetry as "excessive heart and insufficient words," and to the contrary that of Henjō for "adequate words but insufficient substance," suggests his emphasis on the balance and essential complementarity of the two elements of his formulation, a balance that continued to dominate Heian literary theory. Fujiwara Kintō in the next century stated in *Shinsen Zuinō*, however, that "when difficult to realize both heart and form [*sugata*, which is to say "words"], one should give preference to heart." [2] Teika, too, while likening heart and words to "the right and left wings of a bird," felt that in the last resort "rather than that heart should

---

[1] *NKBT*, 8:1. See Earl Miner, *An Introduction to Japanese Court Poetry* (Stanford: Stanford University Press, 1979), 18ff. The source for Tsurayuki's formulation was undoubtedly Po Chü-i, who remarked in his most important theoretical document (the letter to Yüan Chen of 815) that "poetry has its roots in the emotions, its sprouts in words, its flowers in sound, and its fruit in meaning" (*Po Hsiang-shan Shih-chi*, 41; see also Feifel, "Biography," 276). His words are also reflected in the "Chinese preface" (*manajo*) to the *Kokinshū*: "Poetry has its roots in the heart and puts forth its blossoms in forests of words." It is interesting to observe how quickly the Japanese managed to transform what had originally been a simile of organism in China into a dialectical process.

[2] *NKBT*, 65:26.

be lacking, better let the words be clumsy."[3] Despite the apparent influence here of the important Sung Chinese emphasis on the "clumsy" (*cho*), the idea of balance remained the mainstream of critical thought.

It was only after the development of a strongly Zen-influenced mode of thought in Japan about the beginning of the thirteenth century that the scale began to tip decisively on the side of heart, and by Yoshimoto's time the distinctions of Tsurayuki's earlier botanical metaphor had taken on radically new ramifications and exfoliations. The notion that the most profound understandings are communicated not by "words"—that words in fact betray meaning—but rather through the "heart" or "mind" had been sublimated throughout Japanese culture. This idea, originating in the fundamental Ch'an Buddhist antipathy to words, can be summarized in the sect's byword that Ch'an "does not use words or letters" (*pu-li wen-tzu*), understanding being "transmitted directly from one heart [or mind] to another" (*yi-hsin ch'üan-hsin*). The phrase was long a cliché by Yoshimoto's time, and he cited it in his *Tsukuba Mondō* as it had been adapted in China to poetic criticism by the Sung writer Yen Yü in *Ts'ang-lang Shih-hua*: "Poetry, like Zen, communicates directly from heart to heart."[4] He simply extended this concept to embrace renga poetry as well.

Much the same formulation was elaborated in the work of many later theorists. Among these, perhaps the best known is the renga theorist Shinkei's (1406–1475) attribution in *Sasamegoto* (Murmurings, ca. 1450) to the late Heian poet-monk Saigyō the dictum that "the Way of poetry is the Way of Zen," discovering in poetry "the shortest path to sudden enlightenment."[5] Of even more importance for the development of renga theory was Shinkei's equation of linking of the "distantly related verse" (*soku*) type—a natural development in renga linking of the concept of "heart-linking" (*kokorozuke*)—with the religious style of Zen Buddhism, in contrast to that of the "closely related verse" (*shinku*) type, which he likened to the style of the Tendai and Shingon sects.[6] The implication of this statement is that verses linked "distantly" were those related not by any mundane, easily comprehended sort of logic, but rather in some more profound manner divorced from superficial considerations: "linking by *soku*," explained Shinkei, "means to reject the form and words of the preceding stanza and to link by *kokoro* alone."

From this analogy one might imagine that Shinkei was clearly championing the use of *kokorozuke* over *kotobazuke*; indeed, in *Oi no Kurigoto* (Mutterings in

---

[3] *Ibid.*, 130.

[4] *Shih-jen Yü-hsieh*, 8; *NKBT*, 66:94.

[5] *Ibid.*, 182.

[6] *Ibid.*, 187. Shinkei was himself a Tendai monk and at one time abbot of Shōgoin Temple in Kyoto; see Ōta Seikyū, *Nihon Kagaku*, 180–81.

Old Age, 1471) he even went so far as to state that "there should not be stanzas that are not linked by *kokorozuke*."[7] While these sorts of formulations certainly appear to lead in the direction of establishing a "Zen" orientation for renga theory, it is clear from other sections of *Sasamegoto* alone that Shinkei, who was a Tendai monk, had in fact no desire to limit renga either in theory or in practice to anything so narrowly circumscribed as a mere expression of "Zen" ideas. When we look more closely at the context of his analogy, similar statements by earlier syncretic theorists make Shinkei's assertion seem rather less one-sided. In *Shasekishū* (1283), for example, Mujū Ichien had cited the fifth Hua-yen patriarch in China, Tsung-mi Ch'an-shih of Kuei-feng (779–841), to the effect that "the Instructional sects [T'ien-t'ai, etc.] represent the *words* of the Buddha, the Ch'an [Zen] sect the *heart* [or mind] of the Buddha," but added that these were two complementary aspects of the same unity, neither aspect inherently better than the other.[8]

Indeed, if worked out to its logical conclusion, renga practiced by means of *kokorozuke* alone would be terribly limited in its range of expression. Yoshimoto's point in making such a distinction between the two sorts of linking in renga, as we have seen, was rather to underscore the fundamental importance of finding new ways by which one might continually deepen one's practice, and thereby rescue one's art from lapsing into superficiality. If a poet *were* to link by word-association, Yoshimoto had observed, then it was important that his words be of the sort that a truly profound "heart" would promote: fresh, delicate, graceful, and, above all, imbued with *yūgen*. What was wrong was to slip into the well-worn rut of merely associating by means of puns and word-play, and it was this that Yoshimoto's emphasis on *kokoro* was intended to prevent.

For the later renga master Sōgi (1421–1502), too, the overriding consideration in all renga practice was the need to elevate one's art above the level of the mundane, not petty adherence to elaborate rules. In his *Azuma Mondō* of 1470, Sōgi follows Yoshimoto in insisting on the importance of Chinese poetry and the practice of wakan-renku in helping the poet to maintain that "loftiness" (*taketakaki*) that alone could prevent him from becoming mired in what he called "triviality" (*kokorokitanaki*):

> The general level of practice of renga poets today is absolutely trivial because they think detail more important than loftiness. If this is regrettable in renga, how much more so is it when one composes a wakan poem with writers of Chinese verse. When one's heart is trivial, what interest can there possibly be? One must never fail to keep one's heart lofty and not become mired in detail. Tailor your lines large,

[7] Hayashiya Tatsusaburō, ed., *Kodai Chūsei Geijutsuron* (*NST*, 23; Tokyo: Iwanami Shoten, 1973), 418.
[8] *NKBT*, 85:174 and 255.

strive for emotion and expanse of vision, and never even in a single line permit yourself to be trivial. Whether in renga or wakan-renku, you must write loftily.[9]

It comes as no surprise, considering that Yoshimoto was less gifted a renga poet than he was a theorist, that the examples he chose to illustrate wakan-renku linking in his *Tsukubashū* should seem to show more linking by word than by heart, the stanzas bound tightly together by imagery and word-association.[10] Nor can Yoshimoto be expected at age thirty-six to have developed his theoretical formulations very far from his earlier balanced treatment of various types of linking in the direction of his later mature emphasis on the distinction between these two types alone. While Sōgi, too, stressed as a theorist the cultivation that would enable a poet to deal with the full range of complexities in Chinese and Japanese literary allusion, he was also a brilliant poet.

In one section of the *Azuma Mondō*, Sōgi provides an excellent example of the way in which a good poet (as so often in his work, his admired older contemporary Sōzei) might be expected to deal with the problems posed by Chinese allusion when it cropped up in renga poetry, and so with the entire problem of how a poet accommodated *kan* to *wa* in general. "How," he asks, "does one go about linking a Japanese stanza to one that contains a Chinese literary allusion?":

> After two successive stanzas that contain references to Chinese allusions, one can scarcely continue on in the same vein, for to do so entails the same problem as carrying an idea over into third stanza. In such a situation, then, one should link with a Japanese allusion. Consider the following example:
>
> | Kuruma no migi ni | He rode at the right of the carriage |
> | Norishi kaerusa | When it was time to return. |
> | | |
> | Hito no miru | It is now past the season |
> | Mumaba no hiori | For the horse race |
> | Toki sugite | Where he saw his beloved. |
> | (Sōzei) | |
>
> The first stanza alludes, as did the one that preceded it, to [the Chinese Sage] T'ai Kung-wang, 太公望. The stanza by Sōzei that follows alludes to the poem by Narihira about that day of the horse race at the Ukon Racegrounds when, falling in love with a woman whose carriage was standing next to his, he wrote the poem "*Mizu mo arazu ...*" Thus, to the word "right" [右, *migi*] Sōzei linked the "U" of the word "Ukon Racegrounds" [右近馬場]; and to the word "carriage" [車, *kuruma*] he linked the carriages of the pair of spectators there. In this way Sōzei linked the words [*kotoba*] "past the season" [or "time"] to the difficult allusion

[9] *NKBT*, 66:233.
[10] Kaneko Kinjirō, *Tsukubashū no Kenkyū*, 631.

"returned riding," without losing the heart [*kokoro*] of the allusion in the former line. It is very important for a poet to be able to do this sort of thing, for similar allusions are always arising to the likes of Wang Chao-chün or Yang Kuei-fei, and when they do one must know how to deal with them.[11]

The allusion to T'ai Kung-wang (Lu Shang) that Sōgi has in mind appears in the chapter of the *Shih Chi* (Records of the Grand Historian) that deals with "The Generations of the Family of Duke T'ai of Chi" in which the biography appears, and in particular to the following passage:

> Feng Hsiu-fu was the person who was to ride at the right in the chariot of Duke Ching of Chi. The Duke said to him, "Drive quickly! After I have defeated the Chin army, I want to return in time for the banquet!"[12]

The person who sat to the right of a nobleman in his chariot was considered the bravest of all his warriors, and it was his responsibility to protect his lord in battle. Normally a chariot would have held the driver flanked by two warriors; when a high-ranking nobleman went out, however, he was accompanied only by his "right-hand man."

To this extraordinarily thorny allusion—how many Japanese renga poets after all could be expected to be so thoroughly familiar with the *Shih Chi* as to recognize such an obscure passage?—Sōzei recalled the Duke's urgent desire to "return in time" and, interpreting this as the heart (*kokoro*) of the passage, says in his stanza that it is now "past the time" (the word *toki* usually means "season"). If Sōgi is correct in his identification of the Chinese allusion, and it would appear he is, then this is indeed an excellent example of one sort of linking by heart. Sōzei had identified a concern with timeliness as the *kokoro* of the Chinese allusion, and responded in his own stanza, as Sōgi notes, with a line whose *kokoro* matched well.

This is not to say that Sōzei did not make excellent use of word-linking as well: not only has the Duke's chariot called to mind the two Japanese carriages (the character for "chariot" and "carriage" is, of course, the same), but exactly *whose* carriages he had in mind was apparently determined by the word "right," which Sōzei transmuted into the former Ukon or "Right Guards" Raceground at Ichijō Ōmiya in Kyoto. This allusion is based on a story in the *Ise Monogatari* (99):

> Once, on the day of the horse races at the Ukon Raceground [i.e., the competition held there on the festival day after the Fifth Day of the Fifth Month], an officer of the guards [that is, Narihira] saw faintly, through lowered rush blinds, the face of a woman in the carriage next to his, and wrote her the following poem:

[11] *NKBT*, 66:229–30. Cf. my discussion of the roles of Wang and Yang in chapter two.
[12] *Shih Chi*, *chüan* 32; "Ch'i T'ai-kung Shih-Chia," in *Erh-Shih-wu Shih* (Hong Kong: Wen-hsüeh Yen-chiu She, 1959), vol. 1, 125b.

Mizu mo arazu	It is not that I have not seen you,
Mi mo senu hito no	But, having fallen in love
Koishiku wa	With one I cannot see,
Ayanaku kyō ya	Must I now waste the entire day
Nagemekurasamu	Longing for a longer look?[13]

In his later work *Oi no Susami* (Diversions of Old Age, 1480), Sōgi also commented on what he saw as still another effective use of "heart" and "words" in renga achieved through association with a line of Chinese poetry:

Tsuki samushi	The cold moon—
Toburai kimasu	And will someone else
Hito mo ga na	Come to visit?
Nodera no kane no	Distant on an autumn night
Tōki aki no yo	The bell of a temple in the fields.

These stanzas are linked by the line of Chinese poetry that runs, "From a temple in the fields a visiting monk returns girded in moonlight." While the "heart" of the Chinese line may be different, the word "visit" in the upper stanza caught the second poet's attention and so he took the Chinese poem as his linking association. The "heart" of the link here is an autumn night made lonelier by the sound of a distant bell from a temple in the fields. a visitor arriving just when the moon at dawn is at its most desolate and chill—how full of sad beauty it is! While the "heart" of both the Chinese and the Japanese lines are used, the words are used separately as "related words" [*engo*] and the "heart" of the lines are linked independently of them.[14]

The primary source of the association between stanzas is, as Sōgi says, the word "visit" (*toburai*) in the first stanza, although it seems obvious that the poet's recollection of the Chinese poem was prompted at least as much by the presence of the word "moon." The concatenation of the two words apparently brought to mind a couplet in the *Wakan Rōeishū* by the T'ang poet Pao Yü (the poem is not found in Chinese sources):

From a temple in the fields a visiting monk returns girded in moonlight,
While in the fragrant woods friends arm in arm doze intoxicated among the
    blossoms.[15]

The "heart" of the Chinese line, which depends on the meaning of the entire couplet, is the loneliness of the monk that is emphasized as he returns from his

[13] *NKBZ*, 8:218–19.
[14] Nose Asaji, "*Oi no Susami* (Sōgi Renga Ronsho) Hyōshaku," in *Nose Asaji Chosakusho* (Kyoto: Shibunkaku, 1982), vol. 7, 395ff.
[15] *NKBT*, 73:205.

visit through woods filled with merrymakers on a spring night outing. Sōgi therefore says that its heart is "different" from that of the Japanese stanza, which speaks not of spring but of late autumn, prompted by the mention of a cold moon. The real heart of the lines, however, is not to be found merely in the season itself, but rather in the perverse sense of loneliness that the beauty of the season lends the scene. The monk in the Chinese couplet is contrasted to secular carousers inebriated at their evening cherry blossom-viewing parties under the full moon, and Sōgi observes that the sound of a temple bell in the chill autumn moonlight, denoting the small hours of the night, serves to make the figure of the lone monk all the more "full of sad beauty" (*awarebukai*). In this example, as in the one discussed above, the poet has succeeded in finding a way to link the "words" while simultaneously matching the "heart" of his allusion in a true tour de force of wakan association.

Yoshimoto's experiments in wakan-renku took place within the early part of what is called the Kitayama era of Muromachi culture, a period powered largely by the Shogun Yoshimitsu's driving desire to identify himself with the culture of the aristocracy. As the art form that best represents the achievements of the period, however, one would certainly not choose wakan-renku, or for that matter even renga, which was not to reach its high point until the mid-fifteenth century. Rather, it would be the sudden rise of the nō drama, whose spectacular development during Yoshimitsu's late years began under the direction of Kan'ami Mototsugu (1333–1384). Yoshimitsu's support for the not-quite-elegant "*sarugaku* nō" from about 1374 was a shift from that which previous Shoguns had given "*dengaku* nō." [16] In a moralizing discussion with Yoshimitsu in 1381 on the observation of the anniversary of Ashikaga Taka'uji's death, Gidō noted that while Ashikaga Moto'uji had excelled in the art of government, as well as in Buddhism and the "proper arts," he had also shown an untoward fondness for such "improper amusements" as *dengaku* nō and dog-shooting from horseback (*inuōi*). Ashikaga Tadayoshi, however, "had disliked the theater as inimical to good government" (at this point, Gidō reports, the Shogun looked somewhat ashamed of himself).[17]

Especially important in so strongly attracting the Shogun's eye to the new theatrical entertainment was the physical beauty of Kan'ami's twelve-year-old son Zeami (1363–1443?).[18] Young "Fujiwaka," as the Shogun affectionately

[16] Omote Akira, ed., *Nōgaku Ronshū*, NKBZ, 51:204–05.

[17] *Kūge Nichiyō Kufū Ryakushū*, 185, entry for 3/30/1383.

[18] Yoshimitsu's notorious fondness for handsome young men extended to Gozan monks as well. One monk, Taihaku Shingen (1357–1415), noted in 1386 that the twenty-nine-year-old Shogun was in the habit of inviting young, good-looking monks along on his lavish outings, and that to be included in the Shogun's retinue was considered a great honor by the monks (*GBZS*, 3:2231–32). See also Kageki Hideo, *Gozan Shishi no Kenkyū* (Tokyo: Kazama Shobō, 1977), 295–96.

called him, also quickly drew lavish—some scholars say fulsome—praise from Yoshimoto, who appreciated the lad's ready talents at court football (*kemari*) and in renga poetry. Yoshimoto's theories of literature are thought to have been influential in the early shaping of Zeami's aesthetics of the nō drama as it developed over a span of thirty-six years, beginning in 1400 with the first three parts of the *Fūshikaden*.[19]

It seems significant that Zeami should have come so suddenly to Yoshimitsu's attention at the age of twelve, in light of Zeami's own theories about the stages in the training of a nō actor. To Zeami there was something special about the child as actor; as he wrote, "Whatever a boy actor [*chigo*] does will be imbued with *yūgen*." He defined the stage of *chigo* as lasting from the age of ten until the capping ceremony that took place when his boyish locks were cut at twelve or thirteen years old.[20] He also wrote that the foundation for all *yūgen* in the performing arts that was to follow in one's life was established in the training in song, dance, and mime that one received from about the age of ten.[21] Of course, training in any of the artistic accomplishments (what Musō had called *nōgei*—the inversion of the same characters, *geinō*, today means "performing arts") naturally began with the still pliable limbs and brain of the child, and developed through stages appropriate to each age. One is struck by the similarity between Zeami's insistence on what comes naturally to a child without coaching and must be carefully guided to maturity and Kokan Shiren's concern for those natural endowments, found only in children of this age, that must be carefully developed to maturity and upon which rigid standards must not be prematurely imposed. In the interest of developing such talent naturally, wrote Zeami, a boy of twelve may not yet wear a mask and is to be costumed appropriately for his age. Only after the capping ceremony is he to be allowed to wear the masks and costumes appropriate to the various roles, and to begin training in the styles of performance of the generic roles of the Old Man, the Woman, the Warrior, and so on.

The power behind the Shogun's drive toward a new cultural aesthetic with which he might identify his rule is apparent enough in its ability to encompass the disparate likes of Yoshimoto, a representative of the old aristocracy, and Gidō, a representative of the "Chinese" culture of the Gozan. If Yoshimitsu's circle had included only these men, however, the social and cultural parameters involved in these associations would not have gone beyond those of the close association enjoyed earlier by Ashikaga Taka'uji and Ashikaga Tadayoshi with monks like Musō Soseki and aristocrats like Reizei Tamesuke. The new element

---

[19] *NKBZ*, 51:205–06. For a detailed examination of the evidence for the relationship between Yoshimoto and Zeami, see Ijichi Tetsuo, "Zeami to Nijō Yoshimoto to Renga to Sarugaku," in Nihon Bungaku Kenkyū Shiryō Kankōkai, ed., *Yōkyoku, Kyōgen* (Tokyo: Yūseido, 1981), 28–32.

[20] *Fūshikaden*, *NKBT*, 65:344.

[21] *Shikadō*, *Ibid.*, 400–01.

in the Kitayama era was, of course, the inclusion of members of a new urban social class previously unrepresented in the cultural activities of the elite, and now represented by actors like Kan'ami and Zeami, men of socially insignificant origins. The abrupt flowering of nō as a fully developed art form during the relatively brief period between 1375 and 1420, in contrast to the slow ascent of renga to its peak a century later during the Higashiyama cultural era circa 1480 that centered on Ashikaga Yoshimasa, might well be accounted for in part by the fact that the drama was unencumbered by the restraining burden of centuries of court traditions. We must also remember that like Sōgi, Kan'ami and Zeami were both known as great artists, while Yoshimoto, as we have seen, was not as significant a poet as he was a renga theorist.

Scholars generally divide Zeami's theoretical writings into three periods. The first, from age thirty-eight in 1400 to age forty-six, ending with the death of the Shogun Yoshimitsu in 1408, includes the first three parts of Fūshikaden. The second, from age forty-seven to the death of the Shogun Yoshimochi in 1428 when Zeami was sixty-six, includes such works as Kashō, Shikadō, Ningyō, Nōsakushō, Kakyō, Yūgaku Shūdō Fūken, and Goi. The last, from age sixty-six to Zeami's death, after his return from exile on Sado Island at age eighty-one in 1443, a year after the death of the Shogun Yoshinori, includes Kyūi, Rokugi, Shūgyoku Tokka, Go-on, Zeshi Rokujū Igo Sarugaku Dangi, and Kyakuraika.

It was especially from the middle period that Zeami began to cite with increasing frequency Chinese sources ranging from Confucius to the Ch'an masters. Konishi Jin'ichi has called Kyūi (Nine Ranks) "smothered in Chinese allusion," but even an earlier work such as Goi (Five Ranks, 1425–1426) is heavily dependent upon Chinese sources, the five ranks epitomized by citations from the T'ien-t'ai patriarch Miao-lo Tai-shih, The Book of Odes, the critical Sung text Shih-jen Yü-hsieh, Mencius, and finally the Odes again.[22]

The marked increase in Zeami's critical treatises not only of Chinese allusion but of a specifically Chinese Buddhist vocabulary as well from the middle period on strongly suggests the influence of Zen.[23] Certainly his constant reference to the actor's discipline as kōan indicates that he saw his art in the context of what Zen called kufū, the work of daily life focused within a religious context. At this stage in his life Zeami began to treat Chinese terminology quite idiosyncratically, using words to mean what he decided they should mean for each particular occasion. It may be possible, as Konishi has suggested, that this use of language is associated with the practice of the Zen "question and answer" (mondō) session between master and pupil "in which one must answer each time in one's own words," Zen having no use for any other sort of response. This

---

[22] Nishio Minoru, ed., Nōgaku Ronshū, NKBT, 65:313–26; Konishi Jin'ichi, Zeami (Nihon no Shishō, vol. 8; Tokyo: Chikuma Shobō, 1970), 10.

[23] Konishi, Zeami, 16ff.

interpretation is bolstered by Zeami's later emphasis on the need to adapt each performance to its own particular circumstances, a concept he termed *sokuza wago* 即座和合.[24] In *Shūgyoku Tokka* he illustrated this concept with an anecdote from the Ch'an compilation *Wu-teng Hui-yuan*, upon which early Japanese Zen works such as Dogen's *Shōbōgenzō* also drew:

> A philosopher asked the Buddha, "What Law did you preach yesterday?" The Buddha replied, "The same Law as always." "And what Law will you preach today?" "Not the same Law as always." "Why?" "Because what was 'the same Law as always' yesterday is not 'the same Law as always' today."[25]

While a general "Zen influence" seems obvious, the question of Zeami's actual relationship to the Zen establishment of his day is made problematic by lack of documentation. Yasuraoka Kōsaku, among others, has noted his apparent familiarity with the teachings of such Zen monks as Getsuan Sōkō (1326–1389) of the nonmetropolitan (*ringe*) line of the Daiō faction of Daitokuji temple, which was not part of the Gozan temple establishment.[26] Getsuan remained outside Kyoto all his life and died when Zeami was still only twenty-seven, but even so it is not improbable that the two might have met. Indeed, Getsuan's writings were obviously well known to the dramatist, for Zeami cites the monk by name in *Shūgyoku Tokka* (1428) and also cites a koan of Getsuan's in *Kakyō* (1424).[27] Yasuraoka has also hypothesized that what he calls Zeami's "relationship" with Daitokuji temple (otherwise unexplained) may have led the fifty-nine-year-old dramatist to Getsuan's writings after the monk's disciple Kōrin Sōkan became Abbot of Daitokuji in 1421. That this may not entirely account for Zeami's contacts within the Gozan can be seen in yet another scholar's suggestion that his knowledge of Zen was heavily indebted to acquaintance with the Gozan monk Giyō Hōshū (1361–1424), who became Abbot of Tenryūji in 1415.[28] What is clear is that despite the uncertainty about the circumstances of Zeami's training in Zen matters, he was unquestionably better informed and more serious about Zen than Nijō Yoshimoto had been, regardless of the earnest attempts of Gidō Shūshin to instruct Yoshimoto in Zen. To understand this requires that we look more closely at the way that Zeami incorporated Chinese and especially Ch'an sources into his evolving theory of nō drama.

In *Yūgaku Shūdō Fūken* (The Styles of Practice and the Way of Nō Perfor-

---

[24] *NKBT*, 65:454ff.

[25] *Ibid.*, 456 and 563, n. 9.

[26] *Chūseiteki Bungaku no Tankyū*, 220–30 and 82ff. As Yasuraoka notes, it was predominantly the non-Gozan Zen monks who were patronized by men of Zeami's social class at this time.

[27] Konishi, *Zeami*, 219–21 and 312.

[28] Cf. Morisue Akira, "Tōgen Zuisen no *Shikishō* ni Miru Zeami," in Shiryō Kankōkai, ed., *Yōkyoku, Kyōgen*, 44ff., reprinted from a 1967 article.

mance) Zeami discusses the stages of development of the actor's art in terms of the pattern of "slow introduction, medium development, fast finale" (*jo-ha-kyū*) that he had worked out earlier in the *Kadensho*.[29] He adopted this pattern, originally used in the terminology of dance and musical structures, to describe units ranging in size from a single play to the entire series of plays performed in a single day, and even to the development of an actor's art over an entire lifetime.[30]

Zeami began by citing from *The Confucian Analects (Lun-yü)*: " 'There are sprouts which never flower, and flowers which never come to fruition.' From this maxim we can understand the three stages of *jo-ha-kyū* in the practice of one's art over a whole lifetime." [31] Zeami then elaborated this basic metaphor into an analogy: one's art begins as a "sprout" (*nae*), which he equates with the slow introductory period (*jo*). There follows the long developmental "flowering" (*hiideru*) of the middle *ha* stage. And finally, provided there is not too little or too much sun or water and conditions are just right, the "fruit" will set in the final *kyū* stage and can be harvested.

Earlier in *Fūshikaden*, Zeami wrote that the "flower" of "heart" originated in the "seed" of "performance," a botanical model of development he borrowed from *The Platform Sutra (Dankyō)* of the Sixth Ch'an Patriarch Hui-neng, which likens the Buddha-nature latent in all people to "seeds" that require the "rain" of the Buddhist Law to open the "flower" of enlightenment. Zeami then quoted the following *gātha*, or Buddhist poem, with which Hui-neng summarizes this simile:

The ground of the heart contains the seeds
That all begin to sprout in the universal rain;
When the flower of sudden enlightenment has become one's very nature,
Then the fruit of Buddhahood will form naturally.[32]

In his later years Zeami came to formulate the stage of *kyakurai* (sometimes read as *kyarai*), the final transcendence of even superior art in which one "returned again" to artlessness. This concept evolved naturally from his em-

---

[29] The date of *Yūgaku* is unknown, but Konishi places it in the middle period, in part because it emphasizes such terms as *mu* and *myō* in much the same way that the middle-period works *Shikadō* and *Kakyō* do, and in part because the later concept of *kyakurai* is not yet present. For *Kadenshō* see *NKBT*, 65:359.

[30]*NKBT*, 65:417, 442ff.

[31] *Ibid.*, 442. This phrase from the *Analects* was part of the common currency of aesthetics in this period; it is also used, for example, by Shinkei in *Sasamegoto* (*NKBT*, 66:196).

[32]*NKBT*, 66:367–68 and 548, n. 7; Cf. Philip B. Yampolsky, *The Platform Sutra of the Sixth Patriarch*, 178 (New York: Columbia University Press, 1967). We should note here the possibility that Zeami may have been familiar with Yoshimoto's earlier distinction between "flower" and "fruit"; see *Tsukuba Mondō*, *NKBT*, 66:114. The polarity of "fruit/flower" used as an exact equivalent to "heart/words" can be traced to Teika's *Maigetsusho* (*NKBT*, 65:130).

phasis in his middle period on *ran'i*, the stage in which an actor has mastered the techniques of producing *yūgen* (mystery and depth) and returns in performance to non-*yūgen* as a still higher stage of development. Konishi has called the concept of *kyakurai* "Zen" insofar as it seems clearly predicated upon the Zen concept of the enlightened man who does not stop at enlightenment but goes on to transcend the duality implicit in that egotistical awareness to return again to his preenlightened self. This return of the individual who has already attained his own salvation to help all living beings is the Zen equivalent of the concept of the Bodhisattva, and so partially justifies Zen's claim to belong to the main-stream of Mahāyāna Buddhism. Zeami also wrote that "the more enlightened one becomes, the more one becomes the same as he was before he was enlightened," a Zen adage that appears in several sources including the *Wu-teng Hui-yuan*.[33] He then followed this citation with an adage by the Sung dynasty Ch'an monk Tzu-te Hui-hui (d. 1183) in a considerably simplified version of the original Chinese text: "One finally detaches oneself from one's previous existence, and having detached oneself is reborn again, taking on a physical form appropriate to one's development," which seems to mean that, as the famous koan of "Pai-chang and the Fox" (*Mumonkan*, case 2) says, though one may never be so enlightened that he is entirely free from the karmic cycle of death and rebirth, still within this greater cycle one can evolve to higher stages of development. It was this evolution to a higher plane that Zeami equated with *kyakurai*, the return to one's original self.

Having elaborated the three stages of artistic development that precede this stage, Zeami continued in his *Yūgaku Shūdō Fūken* to an important transition:

> The *Heart Sutra* says, "All Phenomenon is itself Void, and all Void itself Phe-nomenon." Every artistic Way, too, has these two aspects. When one has passed through these three stages [sprout-flower-fruit] and has finally achieved the state of being entirely secure in one's art [*an'i*, or *yasuki kurai*], then one's performance will have attained to the full style of "concrete realization of the conceptual ideal" 意中の景 in which it may be said that "all Phenomenon is itself Void."[34]

The latter phrase, we have seen, originates in the *Hannya Shingyō* (Heart Sutra), a text especially favored by the Zen sect for its use of unmediated paradox in its central teaching, which is summed up in the phrase "All Phenomenon is itself Void, and all Void itself Phenomenon." It is with these words that Zeami opens this section of his work.

---

[33] *Ibid.*, 460 and 565, n. 28. While it has often been noted that the same passage is cited in Dōgen's *Shōbōgenzō*, it is not clear that this was Zeami's source. What Zeami called *kyakurai* seems to have been part of literary theory by the mid-fifteenth century. Shinkei in *Sasamegoto*, for example, says "The beginner enters from the shallow into the deep, and once he has attained the depths, he emerges again into the shallow" (*NKBT*, 66:187).

[34] *NKBT*, 65:443–44 and 550, n. 4.

By "concrete realization of the conceptual ideal," Zeami means the ability to give expression freely and effortlessly to whatever idea that enters one's mind. He borrowed the expression from a Chinese treatise on literary criticism, most likely by way of its inclusion in *Shih-jen Yü-hsieh*: "In every conceptual ideal lies the concrete realization, and in every concrete realization the conceptual ideal" (意中有景, 景中有意).[35] Apparently finding suggestive the similarity of these phrases from Buddhist sutra and Chinese critical treatise, Zeami adapted these complementary ideas to his theory of dramatic representation. Thus, it is only when one has reached the stage of being able to freely express any conception, he wrote, that one's acting can realize the Zen principle that "all Phenomenon is itself Void."

But precisely because this is so, Zeami continued, it is especially necessary at this point to guard against the danger of shortcomings that arise from a still inadequate understanding. Only the actor who is so mature that he no longer needs to bear such considerations in mind can also simultaneously realize the complementary Zen principle that "all Void is itself Phenomenon."

Having brought the rigorous Zen dialectical method this far, Zeami obviously realized that it could never be abandoned. In *Shūgyoku Tokka* he pointed out that only when one understands the world in terms of this dialectic will one be able to present both complementary aspects of reality simultaneously in performance. To illustrate his point, he drew upon the phrase "flying blossoms and falling leaves" (*hika rakuyō*) that Yoshimoto and other contemporary theorists also used to illustrate the primary Buddhist principle of *mujō*, or impermanence:

> It is because they bloom that we find blossoms appealing, and because they fall that we feel them to be precious. In response to the question "What is impermanence?" We can reply "Flying blossoms and falling leaves." But to the question "What is unchanging [*jōju fumetsu*]?" we can *also* reply "Flying blossoms and falling leaves." There is no fixed meaning, then, in that moment of awareness in which we perceive these things to be "appealing."[36]

The last sentence means that the observation of the fact that the cherry blossoms are flying or the maple leaves falling, while the archetypal sources of man's feelings of *aware* (the pathetic beauty implied in the heightened awareness of the transiency of such a moment), has in itself no such meaning. Rather, a true understanding of these facts embraces the paradox that there is simultaneously "impermanence" in the constant changing of things and "permanence" in the

---

[35] *Shih-jen Yü-hsieh*, 11, which in turn cites the phrase from the Sung work *Pai-shih Tao-jen Shih-shuo* by the poet Chiang K'uei.

[36] *Shūgyoku Tokka*, NKBT, 65:456.

fact that blossoms and leaves will inevitably fall. Zeami revealed his understanding of this paradox when he cited the Buddha's observation that "what was 'the same Law as always' yesterday is not 'the same Law as always' today."

By comparing this statement with Yoshimoto's own understanding of *hika rakuyō* as epitomizing impermanence alone, we can see how truly relentless was Zeami's drive, conditioned by the Zen dialectical technique, to see simultaneously the pattern in ground and the ground in pattern. Yoshimoto wrote:

> In renga there is no connection between what comes after and what came before. The way that rise and decline, joy and sorrow, follow each other in renga is no different from the way that they do in this floating world. While we brood on yesterday, today is already gone; as we dwell on spring, it is already autumn. In our concern for the cherry blossoms, we fail to notice the leaves turning red. The principle of "flying blossoms and falling leaves" operates relentlessly. People of old clung too much to the Way of poetry: some prayed fervently for "just one good poem," and some even died if their poetry was criticized. But renga is not like that. Because its meaning lies only in the moment of composition, there is nothing to which one can become attached in this manner, and since the participants have no time for such concerns, there is no opportunity for evil ways of thought to take hold.[37]

To Yoshimoto, the practice of renga poetry was justified in Buddhist terms as a model of the creation and extinction of worlds that have no reality in themselves, but only in relation to the world they result from as "effect" and the one they give rise to as "cause." As epitomizing cause and effect, the concept of *mujō* thus becomes the aesthetic representation of the action of karma over time. In one sense, then, "impermanence" becomes the Buddhist definition of time itself, and so of history. And because in Buddhist thought attachment to what is impermanent is the cause of all suffering, renga can be understood as a practical exercise in nonattachment that can lead to enlightenment. Indeed, Yoshimoto seems to have found his justification against Gidō Shūshin's accusation of "wild words and fancy phrases" precisely on the grounds that renga's most fundamental technique epitomizes the Buddhist principle of nonattachment.

But Yoshimoto did not go on to the step that a more profound familiarity with Zen dialectics would have insisted upon, and that Zeami found especially important because of what he called "the dangers of shortcomings that result from inadequate understanding"—the danger, that is, of becoming attached to the idea of nonattachment itself and of seeking a permanent condition in impermanence.

---

[37] *Tsukuba Mondō*, NKBT, 66:82. Yoshimoto echoes Teika's warning in *Maigetsushō*, NKBT, 50:516. For the incident mentioned in Yoshimoto's text concerning Fujiwara Nagatō, who died because his poetry was criticized, see *Shunrai Zuinō*, NKBT, 50:253–54.

For all that Zeami's writings from the middle period on often seem a crazy quilt of citations from Chinese Ch'an texts, he considered an understanding of the vitality of dialectical reality to be ultimately of greater importance than Yoshimoto's aristocratic sort of vision of what constituted higher art. We have seen that Yoshimoto's final appeal was not to the deeper meanings of the Chinese texts he cited so much as to the support that they, as Chinese objects to be prized by the connoisseur (*karamono*), might lend to his endeavor to create of renga an art form worthy of the aristocracy—an endeavor, we might note, upon which his very position in society depended. Zeami, on the other hand, an actor of insignificant social origins whose art could not appeal to aristocratic roots in waka alone as Yoshimoto's could, had to create for the much less reputable drama the solid theoretical basis and the mystery of secret traditions that waka had taken centuries to evolve. Drama by its very nature could not rely for its elevation to the status of art upon the juxtaposition of Japanese and Chinese forms, as renga could and did with wakan-renku. After all, while Chinese and Gozan monks participated in poetry and tea gatherings, they did not perform drama, nor does the very active contemporary Chinese drama of the mainland appear to have served as a model for the nō theater.

Art and literature can be interpreted in many different ways at different levels. If, for example, we consider the structure of all art forms as reflecting essentially linguistic models, as I have assumed from the outset that they do, then such an interpretation will necessarily reflect aspects quite different from those that mimetic, myth-critical, or political analysis, for example, might evoke. The earliest work on the linguistic structure of Indo-European, by the Sanskrit grammarian Pānini, analyzed language into four interrelated levels, a methodology that is still useful in the analysis of art forms as well, provided that we understand that such an approach does not lead to judgments of the nature of beauty or to the discrimination of good and bad (that is, to aesthetic or ethical judgments), but rather to an awareness of certain structural principles that inform all art.

Pānini's model of language progresses, as it moves from deeper to more superficial levels, from "semantic" to "deep syntactic" to "surface syntactic" and finally to "phonological" structures, each level characterized by different linguistic structures.[38] By applying this model of linguistic structure to nō drama and renga, it is possible to resolve Zeami's several apparently conflicting systems of description into a greater structure that possesses a high degree of internal coherence.

---

[38] This theoretical construct is derived from Paul Kiparsky and J. F. Staal, "Syntactic and Semantic Relations in Pānini," *Foundations of Language* 5 (1969), 83–117, as adapted in Masayoshi Shibatani, "Grammatical Relations and Surface Cases," *Language* 53:4 (1977), 789–809.

At the phonological level are the superficial constituents of communication, or what are termed phonemes in descriptive liguistics. At this level we can identify the elements of what Zeami referred to as the *nikyoku santai*, or the "two fundamental musical forms" of dance and chant and the "three fundamental mimetic styles of performance" of the Old Man, the Woman, and the Warrior.[39] They are more "superficial" in the sense that Zeami perceived these rather general structures as containing the multitude of sensory elements that create our most immediate experience of nō as a complex of song and words (*ongyoku*), dance (*mai*) and gesture (*hataraki*), mime (*monomane*) and story (*monogatari*). Each of these general structures, of course, comprises in turn unique but ultimately unanalyzable (in the sense that further analysis leads to considerations of structure rather than of expressive content) structures such as pitch, rhythm, mode, alliteration, movement, archetypal character, and plot (further analyzable into myth, legend, etc.). Zeami's earlier theory of "flower" (*hana*) was formulated primarily at this phonological level of art, and reformulated at progressively deeper levels as his understanding matured.

It seems to have been in the interest of finding an overall structure that could at once give these disparate smaller structures unity while still permitting to each its characteristic mode of expression that Zeami came to develop what we can call the "surface syntactical" structure of *jo-ha-kyū*. This structure originated in the natural structure of dance and music, whose elements could thus be termed "surface syntagmemes." We have seen that Zeami extended the principle of *jo-ha-kyū* as the controlling structure of not only the entire nō play but also of the series of plays that make up a day's performance, and finally of the development of the actor's art over an entire lifetime. Brazell and Bethe have pointed out the modular nature of the several constituent elements of nō drama, each operating independently of the others and simultaneously coordinated by larger structures of *jo-ha-kyū*.[40] Zeami found the theoretical model for his extension of this overall tripartite structure in the Ch'an Buddhist botanical analogy of spiritual growth in which the "seeds" inherent in human nature, watered by the rain of the Buddhist Law, open into "flower" to finally produce the "fruit" of enlightenment.

But we have also seen that Zeami went on to identify a level even more profound than this tripartite structure and to which he ultimately subordinated it. What we can call this "deep syntactic" level is summed up in the Zen notion of a dialectical reality that can only be considered in both its antithetical aspects at once: "All Phenomenon is itself Void, and all Void itself Phenomenon."

[39] *Shikadō*, *NKBT*, 65:400ff.

[40] The polysemic and multistructured nature of nō is discussed in Karen Brazell and Monica Bethe, *Nō as Performance: An Analysis of the Kuse Scene of Yamamba* (Ithaca: Cornell University East Asia Papers No. 16, 1978), 19, 21ff.

Analogous to this were the inseparable complementary aspects of the "conceptual ideal" (Chinese *i*, 意, equivalent to Japanese *kokoro*) and "concrete realization" (*ching*, 景, or *sugata*). This structure is more profound than the cyclical *jo-ha-kyū* in that it functions as a dialectic—not one and then the other, but both at once defining each other. Also at this level are located the complementary aspects in renga theory of "heart" and "words," and of "ground" and "design." While Yoshimoto found the deepest meaning of renga in "impermanence" (*mujō*) alone as a poetic representation of the function of karma in the world and a practical exercise in detachment, Zeami developed the Buddhist concept of *mujō* at this deeper level, finding it meaningful only when paired with "permanence" to function in the dialectic he termed "flying blossoms and falling leaves."

In this four-level structural model it remains to account for the semantic level, which lies below not only the recognizable structures of artistic expression and their principles of arrangement, but below the deeper dialectical relations as well, in the primary structures of meaning themselves. It is especially at this level that the gestalt principle operates in the Japanese insistence on defining itself against the ground of "otherness," which, I have proposed, was invariably China. I have said in chapter one that at the deepest linguistic levels Japanese can be described as polysyllabic, agglutinating, and highly inflected when considered in contrast to Chinese, which is monosyllabic, isolating, and uninflected. The contrast between the poetic structures of these two languages, considered in the light of semiotics as signs that point to themselves as much as they serve on another level to structure content, suggests that at this deepest level of structure both nō and renga "mean" the extraordinary polysemy of the Japanese language when considered in contrast in Chinese—in other words, the way in which the native Japanese perception of universal structure is aware of itself as distinct from any other. Nō seems, more than any other form of aesthetic expression, to positively exhalt the particular Japanese characteristics of polysemy at every level. This is most apparent to us at the superficial level on which the complex interplay of the structures of poetry, music, dance, and mime convey a rich, polyvalent yet coherent sense of meaning. But this celebration of the principle of polysemy is apparent as well, if increasingly less obvious at deeper levels, in the complex interplay of constituent modular structures, in the unitary dialectical embrace of antithetical religious and critical principles, and finally in the definition against the ground of alterity of the most Japanese structures of meaning themselves.

This "structural" analysis of nō drama, which I am the first to admit is a difficult and problematic one, can be extended to renga as well. If at a more superficial level renga seems to be "about" the Buddhist principle of impermanence, it can also be seen at the semantic level as a formal amplification into poetic structures of the primary linguistic devices of the Japanese language that structure polysemy. These are, as discussed in chapter one, the "pivot-word" (*kakekotoba*) and the tendency to extreme hypotaxis in modification, as well as the high degree of controlled ambiguity afforded by the techniques of "close" and "distant" linking. These structures function to provide a certain degree of temporal linearity while simultaneously permitting the insistent play of poly-semy or polyvalence of meaning that is the primary characteristic of the language that asserts itself in distinction to Chinese. By so obstinately opposing itself to considerations of permanent content, renga points to itself in semiotic terms as a code of transformation that serves to formally structure content. Both renga and nō can thus be understood as codes whose primary structure is the bivalent principle of Phenomenon/Void, a Buddhist and particularly a Zen concept that can be rephrased in terms of semiotics at the semantic level as "all signs are empty" (that is, they are self-referential in that they are devoid of content) and "all emptiness is sign" (that is, meaning inheres not in any particular content but rather in the code itself). The expression as it is used in Japanese theory is itself bivalent, denoting the Buddhist concept on the one hand, and on the other all attempts to express "meaning" with "form," and so all art. Renga, nō, chanoyu, ink-painting, all have in common the group creation (which the medieval Japanese termed *za*) of an object—poem, play, drink, painting—that is at the same time a metaphor for the unfolding ritual of its production, the *michi* or Way of the art, identical with the aesthetic produc-tion of meaning itself. Renga and nō are on one level as much "about" polysemy—about Japan setting itself off from China—as they are on other levels "about" religious ideas, particular themes, or aesthetically pleasing con-structs. In this sense, chanoyu, ikebana, and painting seem as much "about" the synthesis of Chinese forms with Japanese meaning as they are "about" their uses within ritual contexts or as aesthetic objects.

We have seen that Musō Soseki resisted the development of a chanoyu that moved outside the context of Zen practice. Tea-drinking began in China, of course, and arrived in Japan still largely contained within the context of its use in Sung dynasty Ch'an monasteries. At the same time, what had originated as something of a cult of aesthetics in T'ang China was becoming by the middle of the Sung dynasty a medicinal aid, a gastronomic delight, or a conscious exercise in antiquarianism. The Chinese would ultimately find meaning in the historical value of tea utensils such as bowls, braziers, and water jars within the context of the philosophy of *k'ao-ku*, the "investigation of antiquity" which can be understood in part as a new way of interpreting history in the light of the reexamination of the significance of ancient material objects. The Japanese, to the contrary, beginning with the fad for the imported object, came eventually to locate the central meaning of tea-drinking in the ritual (that is, the code of transformation we can call *chadō*, the Way of Tea) in which all the "furniture" of apparent content was entirely subordinated to the generation of intensely native meaning through the medium of alien forms. This is certainly not to deny that Chinese poets often emphasized the meditative aspects of tea-drinking, nor that the Japanese were often greedy collectors of tea objects; it is simply to point out that each culture emphasized greater significance in the contrary case. Indeed, one can understand Kawabata Yasunari's novel *Senba-zuru* (Thousand Cranes, 1949–1951) as a paradigm of the evil of chanoyu considered as inheritable "property" rather than as a ritual code than means only itself, an aesthetic involving the filling and emptying of form. The tea bowls in Kawabata's novel, epitomizing attachment rather than nonattach-ment, take on a karma of their own to which the destinies of their owners become frighteningly subordinated.[41]

The conceptual dialectic of wakan continued to be central to the develop-ment of the new aesthetics during the Higashiyama era as well as the Kitayama, most notably in the marked preference for the "dry" and "withered." This taste evolved within the context of chanoyu under the tea-master Murata Shukō (or Jukō, 1422–1502), whose use of terms like *hiekareta* (chill and dry) and *hieyaseta* (chill and thin) are considered forerunners of the critical term *wabi* that is used, for instance, in the tea term *wabicha*.[42] These terms, like those used by Yoshi-moto and Shinkei, can ultimately be traced back to the Sung critical vocabulary of works like the *Ts'ang-lang Shih-hua*, where they are used in a much more literal sense to describe the stark poverty of the T'ang poets Chia Tao (788–843) and Meng Chiao (751–814) and so by extension the spare, lean style of poetry those men wrote.[43] From about 1400 on such "Chinese" terms became increas-ingly part of the aesthetic vocabulary of a wide variety of masters of the arts including renga, waka, ink-painting, tea, interior decoration, and so forth, all of whom could lay a claim of some sort to the Chinese cultural heritage that, from the outbreak of the Ōnin War in 1467, was almost literally looted from the smoking ruins of the once-flourishing Zen temples and dispersed through the culture at large. Many of these masters were men trained within the Gozan but on equally—if not even more—familiar terms with the native cultural tra-ditions through the sorts of contacts with the elite classes afforded them by the

[41] See Yasunari Kawabata, *A Thousand Cranes*, trans. Edward Seidensticker (New York: Knopf, 1958).

[42] See the discussion in H. Paul Varley and George Elison, "The Culture of Tea: From Its Origins to Sen no Rikyū," in George Elison and Bardwell L. Smith, *Warlords, Artists and Commoners: Japan in the Sixteenth Century* (Honolulu: University of Hawaii Press, 1981), 250ff.

[43] Cf. *Shih-jen Yü-hsieh*, 129, 328–29, 331–32, etc. The source of the characterizations of Chia and Meng's poetry is Su Tung-p'o's "Eulogy to Liu Tzu-yü," cited in *Hsü Yen-chou Shih-hua* (332). Shinkei cited Su's phrase verbatim in *Sasamegoto*; see Ōta, *Nihon Kagaku*, 177ff. For a study of these terms in China and Japan, see also Konishi Jin'ichi, "Hie to Yase," *Bungaku Gogaku* 10 (November 1975), 12–29, esp. 26ff.

cultural gatherings of the Ashikagas, and men like them, that brought together for the first time the worlds of court, camp, monastery, and town.

Since mid-fifteenth-century high culture was of a piece, and the same critical terms current everywhere, we might take note here of Zeami's less often remarked upon but significant use of the terms *sabi* and *hie* in the generation that preceded Shinkei and Shukō. In *Kakyō* (1424), following his discussion of the "nō that proceeds from sight" and that which "proceeds from sound," Zeami discusses the "nō that proceeds from the heart":

> As for the nō that proceeds from the heart: in the most skillfully performed *sarugaku*, after a full day's performance, the performance of a nō play that is not as brilliant in song, dance, mime, and plot but rather is subdued and unimpressive [*sabisabi to shitaru uchi ni*] somehow possesses something that reaches the heart. This may be termed the "nō of chill performance" [*hietaru kyoku*].[44]

And in a discussion of the contemporary *dengaku* actor Sōa in *Zeshi Rokujū Igo Sarugaku Dangi* (recorded by his second son, Motoyoshi, in 1430), Zeami is quoted as saying, "In the nō drama *Shakuhachi* [now lost], Sōa plays the bamboo flute with one hand and sings brilliantly. There is nothing else remotely like it. It is the most chill of the chill [*hie ni hietari*].[45] Zeami was so impressed with Sōa that he placed him in the third category of the highest of his nine classes in *Kyūi*, the "Style of the Refined Flower" (*kankafū*), Zeami's metaphor for which—"snow heaped in a silver bowl"—is one of his best known and most mysterious apothegms.[46] This figure also serves as a strikingly concrete illustration of what Zeami may have intended when he used the word "chill." The idea of "a silver bowl filled with snow" did not originate with Zeami, however; like so many of his descriptive images, this one can be traced back to the Chinese Ch'an masters, in this case to Tung-shan Shou-ch'u (ca. 900). When we think today of the highest expression of medieval aesthetic sensibility, it is Zeami's emphasis on a new kind of *yūgen* and images like the "silver bowl filled with snow" that first come to mind.

Inevitably less concerned with Zen practice as the decades passed, for reasons suggested above, monks like Zeami's close contemporary Seigan Shōtetsu (1381–1459) of Tōfukuji, nominally a mere scribe (*shoki*) in the temple hierarchy, found greater satisfaction in what must have seemed the obviously more attractive and rewarding world of Japanese arts, a world in which the lowly monk Shōtetsu was hailed as a master of waka poetry. It is therefore inevitable that he should have come to view his religious vocation with some irony:

[44] *Kakyō*, NKBT, 65:432.
[45] *Ibid.*, 488.
[46] *Kyūi, ibid.*, 448.

The desk where the sayings of the Zen patriarchs should occupy the place of honor is strewn with waka manuscripts; on the floor where I should be seated in meditation upon my mat, I lie reading *The Pillow Book*. On hot days I forget to put on my unbearable Zen robes; greedy for the fine things of life, I revel in wine and meat. The extreme of wanton selfishness, I do not cease from these things the whole day long.[47]

The formidable weight of learning and culture implied by examples drawn from Chinese works was part of the stock in trade of such men. They were astute enough to perceive the futility of setting their ambitions on fame within the crumbling world of the Zen temples and the better fortune that beckoned from the salons of the wealthy as teachers of the new and ancient Japanese literary arts. Such attitudes were paralleled by a growing belief among even the most dedicatedly "Chinese" monks of the Gozan in what they called the "identity of Zen and poetry" (*Zen-shi itchi*) prompted by the need then reasserting itself to justify poetic activity in terms of the long revered and sanctioned Way of waka poetry of native Japanese provenance.[48] That Shōtetsu himself was greatly concerned with the knowledgeable ability to blend and harmonize Chinese and Japanese elements that played so crucial a role in the development of the new aesthetic of the period can be seen from a passage in his *Shōtetsu Monogatari* (ca. 1450), in which the art of calligraphy serves as the vehicle for the discussion of broader aesthetic concerns:

> The calligraphy of the retired emperor Fushimi [r. 1287–1298] is thoroughly steeped in wakan [*wakan ni tsūjitaru mono nari*]. When we put it next to calligraphy by Chinese like [Chao] Tzu-yang [1254–1322] and [Chang] Chi-chih [1186–1266], we find the emperor's way of using the brush in no way inferior to theirs. We can liken Fushimi's calligraphy, in its blending of *wa* and *kan* elements, to the modern style in which we hang a triptych of monks' paintings in a *tokonoma* [*toko-oshiita*], or set out the Three Utensils [incense-burner, flower-vase, candle-stand] in a *zashiki*-style room [i.e., *kaisho*] against a screen painted with silver foil.[49]

Shōtetsu went on to add that the effect of the "Chinese" element in Fushimi's calligraphy was to lend it an aura of "masculine vigor," in contrast to the "feminine charm" of the purely Japanese style of the emperor Go-Kōgon (r. 1352–1370). It was not any antique "masculine" (*masuraoburi*) character of Fushimi's calligraphy that Shōtetsu seems to have admired, however, so much

[47] *Nagusamegusa*, cited in Haga, *Chūsei Zenrin*, 400.

[48] The idea that "the way of poetry is the Way of Zen" also had venerable roots in certain aspects of Sung dynasty thought, and can be seen most notably in the work of Su Tung-p'o; cf. *Shih-jen Yü-hsieh*, 8ff.

[49] *Shōtetsu Monogatari*, NKBT, 65:200ff. The Shogunal advisor Nōami made the same observation in his *Kundaikan Sayū Chōki* of 1454; see Hayashiya, *Kodai Chūsei*, 434.

as the singular and purposeful lack of any "charm" that made it at once superior in kind to anything else and entirely inappropriate for novices to attempt to imitate:

> Fushimi's calligraphy is like a withered tree, without the slightest beauty. Since it makes no attempt at all to be ornamental [*chitomo fude o tsukurowazu asobashikereba*] it should not be imitated.[50]

Shōtetsu's disciple Shinkei [1406–1475] is even better known for his partiality for this taste for the "withered" aesthetic that, he said, represented the very highest realm of beauty, and the one most difficult to attain to:

> Once when one of the ancient poetic geniuses was asked how a waka poem ought to be written, he replied with the lines

| Karino no susuki | Pampas grass on a withered moor |
| Ariake no tsuki | In the pale dawn moonlight. |

> What he meant by this is that one should turn one's "heart" toward the part that is not expressed in words, and in this way one will come to understand that which is "chill and desolate" [*hiesabitaru*]. It is only the lines of poets who have entered the most exhalted realm of poetry that can create this effect.[51]

Shinkei also recalled, albeit rather imprecisely, Yoshida Kenkō's echo in *Tsurezuregusa* (137) of Kamo no Chōmei to the effect that

> the moon, blossoms—these are things that are seen only with the eyes. It is rather when we are lost in thought through a rainy night, or in the shadow of a tree whose blossoms are all scattered and withered [*chirishioretaru kikage*], that our thoughts turn to things that are no longer.[52]

This sentiment is reminiscent of many similar scenes in *The Tale of Genji*, the study of which had become so important in this period. Consider, for example, the description of the dawn at the mansion of the Minister of the Left just before Genji departs the capital for exile in Suma:

> The moon in the first suggestion of daylight was very beautiful. The cherry blossoms were past their prime, and the light through the few that remained

[50] *NKBT*, 65:167–68. The most well-known extant example of Fushimi's calligraphy (which is also described as "withered and elevated" by Shōtetsu) is the fragment of a poetry scroll known as the "Hirosawa-gire"; see Shimonaka Kunio, ed., *Shodō Zenshū* (Tokyo: Heibonsha, 1957), 19:84–85.

[51] *Sasamegoto*, *NKBT*, 66:175; the "ancient poetic genuis" is the Heian wakan poet Fujiwara Mototoshi (1060–1142; cf. ibid., 261, n. 23). See also Nagashima, *Ōnin no Ran*, 243ff.

[52] *Sasamegoto*, *NKBT*, 66:178. Shinkei's imprecision in quoting Kenkō can be seen by comparing *Tsurezuregusa*, *NKBZ*, 27:200.

flooded the garden silver. Everything faded together into a gentle mist, sadder and more moving than on a night in autumn.[53]

Here again we find the preference for the "whiteness" of a scene—the only color category included in the *Wakan Rōeishū*, as I have noted—over any other color, and the profound emotion that this wash of silver evokes. The "silvery" quality of the dawn is also of special interest here, recalling as it does the later evocation of this color in the two similes of Shōtetsu's discussion of calligraphy—the triptych hung in a *tokonoma*, the vessel against a silver screen—particularly arresting as they bear directly on the art of interior decoration, whose evolution in this period was to have great impact on the development of such allied arts as *suibokuga* ink-painting and chanoyu. During the Higashiyama era, new styles of decoration followed the new spaces and surfaces created by temple-influenced *shoinzukuri* architecture and the emergence of *kaisho*, rooms of new design evolved from Zen temple architecture that were specifically intended for cultural gatherings. The preference for tryptich arrangements (*sanpuku-ittsui*), popular both in *karamono* display and in art (in the latter instance usually involving a central religious motif flanked by landscapes or bird-and-flower figures), was itself an example of wakan, a uniquely Japanese style of arranging Chinese objects and paintings that evolved together with one of the *kaisho* architectural style's central elements, the *oshi-ita*, or movable display board that was the forerunner of the *tokonoma*. Nōami's *Gyōmotsu On'e Mokuroku* of 1470, for example, also remarks on the new tryptich style of hanging paintings in a *tokonoma*.[54] The other decorative element that Shōtetsu mentioned, the arrangement of precious *karamono* utensils against the backdrop of a Japanese screen painted with burnished silver foil (*ibushigin*), also suggests the fascination that developed in this period with the use of this ornamental material as a major component of art and decoration.

The major theme that runs through all of Shōtetsu's work is his acknowledgement of the debt he felt he owed Fujiwara Teika in waka poetry. Shōtetsu harkened back to the master, too, when discussing the importance of wakan in poetry, citing, for example, a poem composed by Teika in 1196 as the embodiment of the very "heart" of a couplet by Po Chü-i:

Ranshō no	Through fading memories
Hana no nishiki no	Of the flowery brocades

[53] Tamagami, *Hyōshaku*, vol. 3, 31; Seidensticker, *Genji*, 222.

[54] Tanaka Ichimatsu, *Japanese Ink Painting: Shubun to Sesshu*, trans. Bruce Darling (Tokyo: Weatherhill/Shibundō, 1974), 135, states that the *tokonoma* "originally served as a kind of altar for the display of religious painting." For a discussion of Nōami's comments and the evolution of the trypitch style of displaying art, see Gail Capitol Weigl, "The Reception of Chinese Painting Models in Muromachi Japan," *Monumenta Nipponica* 35:3 (Autumn 1980), 257–72, esp. 259 and 270.

Omokage ni	In the orchid-blazoned ministry
Iori kanashiki	Comes the cold drizzle of autumn
Aki no murasame	To sadden my thatched hut.[55]

The poem by Po Chü-i whose world Shōtetsu says Teika explored so well was known widely in Japan because of its inclusion in the *Wakan Rōeishū*, the waka poem based as usual on a single Chinese couplet:

You are there beneath the brocade hangings of the orchid-blazoned ministry,
I here in this thatched hut on Mt. Lu on a rainy night.[56]

The first word of the waka poem, *ranshō* (orchid-blazoned ministry), is almost shockingly Chinese in the context of a medium like waka poetry that self-consciously shunned such raw Sinate words. Teika's blunt use of it here is obviously intended to convey, by its impressive sound and weight, a sense of solid massiveness against which the fragile Japanese thatched hut (*iori*) becomes all the more insignificant and pathetic.

In citing Po's couplet, Shōtetsu left the first line in its original "Chinese" state—uninflected, that is, by Japanese *kana*—but wrote the second in Chinese characters mixed with Japanese script (*kana-majiri*), the way such a "Chinese" line would normally have been read, whether silently or aloud, by any Japanese (italics indicate Sinate readings):

Ranshō kaji menchō ka
Rōzan no amayo, kusaio no naka

The form of this particular citation gains special significance when we recall Shōtetsu's professed lack of clerical diligence and his preference for reading *The Pillow Book* of Sei Shōnagon over seated meditation. This preference is confirmed by the way he cites Po's couplet, for the peculiar stylistic mixture of the citation in fact reflects a passage in *The Pillow Book* in which Sei is sent the first line of this same couplet in Chinese—simply written out, that is, in the Chinese characters alone—by the courtier Fujiwara no Tadanobu (the line is reproduced by Sei as if she were reading the text aloud: "ranshō no hana no toki no nishiki no tobari no moto"—an awesomely cumbersome gloss), and is asked if she knows the next line.[57] She knew it, of course, for Sei was second to no one at court when it came to a knowledge of Chinese allusion. To reply in overly

---

[55] *Shōtetsu Monogatari, NKBT*, 65:225 and 282, n. 25. Another poem by Teika composed on the second line of this couplet is found in *Kokka Taikan*, supp. vol., 32, no. 68.

[56] *Wakan Rōeishū, NKBT*, 73:191. Yūasa Kiyoshi has suggested that this poem and the entire *Wakan Rōeishū* may have been influential in the development of Shinkei's concept of *hie*; see *Shinkei no Kenkyū* (Tokyo: Kazama Shobō, 1977), 357ff., esp. 368.

[57] *Makura no Sōshi, NKBZ*, 11:171; see Morris, trans., *Pillow Book of Sei Shōnagon*, 89 and 306, n. 190. I have already cited a similar story in chapter two, n. 8.

Chinese language, however, would have been too shockingly unladylike a thing to do, a predicament we have seen illustrated in the figure of the comically pedantic lady in the "Hahakigi" chapter of *Genji* whose terribly Sinicized speech occasioned the gentlemen such mirth. Sei therefore wisely chose to reply in such a way as to appear both ladylike and knowing, with the last lines of a waka poem that merely allude delicately to the line of Po's that follows:

Kusa no iori o   Who might it be that would visit
Tare ka tazunemu   This poor thatched hut?

And still for all her pains Sei only succeeded in garnering, along with the somewhat unwelcome admiration of the gentlemen of the court, the unlovely nickname "Thatched Hut." Shōtetsu's citation of the couplet as a line in Chinese followed by one in Japanese gloss would seem to indicate that it was its appearance in *The Pillow Book*, rather than in *Hakushi Monjū* or even *Wakan Rōeishū*, that came most readily to mind when he recalled Teika's poem.

What impressed Shōtetsu most strongly about this sort of well-wrought adaptation of Chinese to Japanese was, as it had been for Teika, precisely the effect that the Chinese verse could exert upon the Japanese, elevating the mundane native form to a higher plane of artistic endeavor. Sōgi, we have seen, had nothing but praise for the abilities of his older contemporary Sōzei to capture the *kokoro* of a Chinese allusion in a Japanese verse. Shōtetsu too felt that Chinese had the power to translate art to a higher plane, not only when one transferred an idea from Chinese into Japanese, but by the sheer power of Chinese poetry to ennoble one's *kokoro*—especially if the poetry were by the peerless "Po Chü-i":

Teika wrote that when one is trying to devise a waka poem, one should recite Po's couplet

In my old home my mother sheds tears in the autumn wind,
In this inn on the road are nothing but ghosts in the evening rain.

When one recites these lines one's heart is elevated and one will write better waka poetry. One can also recite the lines about "the orchid-blazoned ministry ... "[58]

As it happens, Shōtetsu was mistaken: this lovely and haunting "Chinese" couplet was composed not by Po Chü-i but by the Japanese courtier Minamoto no Tamenori (d. 1011). What is important is that Shōtetsu thought it was by Po, and clearly via the *Wakan Rōeishū*. This is finally beside the point, however, since Teika did indeed make use of the couplet's *kokoro* in a way that Shōtetsu found worthy of praise. For after the death of Teika's mother, he continues, the

---

[58] *Shōtetsu Monogatari*, *NKBT*, 65:213. Just where Teika mentions these lines is not known, but the practice is suggested in his *Maigetsushō*, *NKBT*, 65:137, and in *Eika Taigai, ibid.*, 115.

poet visited her former house at a time when the autumn wind was blowing and, greatly saddened, sent the following poem to his father, Shunzei:

Tamayura no	Neither glittering drops
Tsuyu mo namida mo	Of dew or tears will cease
Todomarazu	In the autumn wind
Naki hito kouru	That keens through this dwelling
Yado no akikaze	For one no longer here.[59]

The line in Chinese about "sleeping alone in an inn on the road while the rain drips down" is truly forlorn, and this waka poem about "The autumn wind/That keens through this dwelling/For one no longer here" accords perfectly with the heart of the occasion.[60]

Shōtetsu's critical remarks are especially interesting because his life spans the period between the aesthetic tastes of the Kitayama and Higashiyama cultural periods. Born during Yoshimitsu's long rule, he was twenty-seven when the Shogun died in 1408. He was one of the last generations of mainstream Gozan monks—men like Josetsu, Oguri Sōtan, and Shūbun in art, Shōtetsu in waka poetry, and even the eccentric Ikkyū Sōjun of the non-Gozan Daitokuji-Myōshinji line of Zen—to play an influential role in the new developments in native Japanese aesthetics; and Shōtetsu, as we have seen, and no doubt the others to one degree or another, scarcely thought of themselves any longer as monks.

Rather, they considered themselves part of that very broadly defined category known as *tonseisha* (hermits) that included everything from men of religion to men of taste (in other contexts called *suki*) usually of other than elite origins, often of the equally ill-defined new wealthy middle class (*machishū*) emerging during the Muromachi period in the urban centers of Kyoto and Sakai. Identification with some respectable religious organization permitted this otherwise disenfranchised plebeian group legitimate claim to participation in the new culture as "advisors" (*dōbōshū*) or "teachers" (*wakashi, rengashi,* etc.).[61] Their most famous representatives were poets like Sōgi (1421–1502), *dōbōshū* like Nōami (1397–1471), and artists (although in his case the plural scarcely seems credible) like Sesshū (1420–1506). These men mingled so freely with the elite of the military and noble classes and with the Gozan monks that their actual social affiliations blur even as one looks at them.

---

[59] *Ibid.,* 212.

[60] *Ibid.,* 213.

[61] In the interest of simplicity and accuracy I refrain from going here into the thorny question of the often-mentioned relationship of the *dōbōshū* to the Ji sect of Jōdo Buddhism. For an interesting study in English of the relationship of these "advisors" as members of the Ji sect to the evolution of the nō drama, however, see Toshio Akira, "The Songs of the Dead: Poetry, Drama, and Ancient Death Rituals of Japan," *Journal of Asian Studies* 61:3 (May 1982), 485–509.

To men such as these the concept of wakan meant two separate but related things. First, it provided a refined atmosphere, an elegance that served to raise native practices, especially those without former pedigree, to the level of high art. Second, it provided them with a vocabulary, derived in part from Sung Chinese aesthetics and criticism as expounded in Japan by Gozan monks from works like the *Shih-jen Yü-hsieh*, a language that was useful in describing the developing tastes as well as in defining them.

In practice, wakan meant placing "Chinese" and "Japanese" side by side, with the effect first of elevating the Japanese by contrast with the "superior" culture, then of deepening one's craft (*keiko*) by the effort required to reconcile one with the other and to effect a meaningful synthesis, and finally, of emphasizing that which was uniquely and essentially Japanese by contrast to that which was Chinese. If "Chinese" meant, as Shōtetsu put it, the manly vigor of the courtier in his brilliant court robes in contrast to the feminine charm of the court lady retiring in the shadow of the curtains, it also suggested that "Japanese" meant the quiet mystery of that lady brought out by contrast with those gaudy court robes.[62] Far from being weakened by such contrast, this was a beauty that instead took its strength from it.

Murata Shukō also recognized the centrality of the wakan dialectic to his own art when he wrote one of his students that the single most important aspect of the chanoyu was the "harmonizing of 'Chinese elements' [*kan*] and 'Japanese elements' [*wa*]."[63] But he wrote this by way of criticizing those who were already, inevitably, coming to emphasize that prized new rough or "withered" quality in Japanese tea-ware, the essence of *wabi* taste, over the delicate balance that was achieved only when neither Japanese nor Chinese tastes, neither "withered" nor "gaudy," predominated, but served instead to define each other in an ongoing dialectic of ground and design—a dialectic so fundamental to the maturity of Zeami's later theory of nō drama as well as of renga poetry in Sōgi's day.[64] This preference for the new aesthetic that quickly emerged in tea-taste can be seen as one of the forces at work that was to rapidly carry renga into *haikai no renga*, and to emerge again during the Edo period in the new style of linked-verse poetry perfected by Bashō. An exploration of the continuing concern for the importance of wakan in the arts of Edo Japan, and its role in achieving new syntheses in the arts, is the subject of the next chapter.

[62] *NKBT*, 65:201.

[63] Nagashima, *Ōnin no Ran*, 257ff. This letter from Shukō to Furuichi Chōin (1452–1508), a wealthy Naniwa merchant turned monk, is an important document in the history of medieval Japanese aesthetics. See Hayashiya, *Geijutsuron*, 448. The letter has been translated and studied in Dennis Hirota, "Heart's Mastery: *Kokoro no Fumi*, The Letter of Murata Shukō to His Disciple Chōin," *Chanoyu Quarterly* 22 (1979), 7–24.

[64] That Hirota ("Heart's Mastery," 12) is working backwards from the reverence in which Shukō is held by modern tea practitioners as a founder of *wabicha* can been seen in his opinion that Shukō is advocating the use of Japanese bowls, when in fact he is clearly upset over an increasing lack of wakan balance in the new tastes.

CHAPTER SEVEN

The Intellectual Contexts of Tokugawa Aesthetics:
Itō Jinsai, Ogyū Sorai, and Genroku Culture

Kusuwashiki	How wretched,
Kotowari shirazute	Without understanding our principle
Karahito no	Of the mysterious,
Mono no kotowari	To expound the Chinese
Toku ga hakanasa	Principles of things.
	(Motoori Norinaga)

The bourgeoisie is a state of mind ... the stomach and gross intestines of the body politic and social, as distinct from the artist, who is the nostrils and the invisible antennae.
(Ezra Pound)

The ways in which the intellectual and cultural life of the Edo period (1603–1867) was influenced by China are too well known, too overwhelmingly obvious, to require elaborate restating. At the same time, the dynamic that governed the relationship between Chinese and Japanese ideas in this period is too complex and subtle a subject, and too often misunderstood, to be taken for granted. I should reiterate here the caveat I have hoped to keep before the reader all along: we are not concerned so much with Chinese "influences" on Japan—if indeed we are dealing with such at all—as with a constructive dialectic, carried on over the centuries, that took the form of a Japanese monologue with itself about China. I have tried to show how Japanese thought consistently referred the question of signification back to China, with the result that a dynamic and dialectical concept of meaning developed as something composed of the interplay of two terms, the Japanese term emerging into meaning only as its content took form against the background of China. In terms of medieval aesthetics, for example, this dialectic entered literary practice and theory as the appearance of native "pattern" (*mon*) against the alien "ground" (*ji*) of China. At the same time, as I have shown, this construction of the terms of meaning arrogated to itself the element of dimensionality, especially of depth, somewhat in the way that one might first become aware of the

7. *Winter Landscape*, by Sesshū (Tokyo National Museum). From Masao Ishizawa et al., eds., *The Heritage of Japanese Art* (Tokyo and New York, 1981), p. 121, pl. 88.

severe linearity of the Japanese horizontal handscroll, all patterned surface and no depth, only when it was set in contrast to the nonlinearity of a Chinese vertical landscape painting that seems, to the contrary, all depth and no surface.

Continuing this metaphor of culture as artistic style, we can begin to leave the medieval period through what amounts to a rent in its aesthetic fabric that appears in the shape of a brush–stroke crack, nearly wide enough to walk through, that seems to split open the oddly abstracted *Winter Landscape* ink-painting by Sesshū Tōyō in the Tokyo National Museum (fig. 7). The work of this remarkable painter at the end of the fifteenth century symbolizes many changes, among them a shift of interest away from China, where Sesshū had traveled and studied between 1468 and 1469. In the famous inscription on the so-called *Haboku* (literally, broken or flung ink) *Landscape* painting dated 1495 (Tokyo National Museum), Sesshū stated that he regarded the Japanese monk-painters Josetsu and Shūbun as his real teachers, and gave but scant mention to the two contemporary Chinese masters with whom he had studied in China.[1]

The undated *Winter Landscape*, in the style influenced by the harsh, abstract contours of Hsia Kuei, is based on a smaller study in the style of Hsia (Asano Nagatake Collection, Tokyo) among a group of four that Sesshū did in con-scious imitation of the styles of four Chinese masters. While the study seems a fair representation of Hsia's style, the larger painting is all angles and empty planes suddenly cross–hatched by busy angular strokes and punctuated by splashes of ink that do not seem to care whether they land on scenery to connote vege-tation, or in space to become nothing at all. Everything in the composition and technique of the painting conspires to draw the viewer's eye to the surface. The lone figure of a monk walks toward a temple in the background, but the entire scene is dominated—tyrannized, really—by the odd, slashing vertical crack that looms above. Appearing to have begun in the middle of the painting as the outline of a foreground mass, which indeed it is in the study, it suddenly flies straight up for no apparent reason to rive open the empty sky. That single craggy, vertical brush-stroke continually forces our attention, contrary to the conventions of Chinese-inpired ink-painting, back to the surface of the work; it simply cannot be made either visually or conceptually a part of the scene to which it is supposed to belong. Even without it, the rest of the painting, with its bleak and forbidding aspect appropriate to winter, would have been unsettling. But of this careless crack down the middle, one scarcely knows what to make. It

---

[1] The question of the relationship of Sesshū's style to the Chinese art of his time is too complex to be addressed here. Of the career and painting of Chang Yu-sheng we know nothing. Li Tsai (fl. 1426–1435), however, was one of the leading artists of Hsüan-tsung's court. James Cahill, *Parting at the Shore*, 7, 27–28, 45ff., and 101ff., discusses the Chinese styles current in Sesshū's day that clearly influenced his work. What we should note here is that while the stylistic flattening of depth and the return to the surface was merely an eccentricity in Ming China, it was central to the development of Japanese painting.

8. Haboku Landscape in the style of Yü Chien, by Sesshū, dated 1495 (Tokyo National Museum). Inscriptions on the top two-thirds of the painting by Sesshū and others are not shown. From Tanaka Ichimatsu and Nakamura Tanio, *Sesshū, Sesson*, vol. 7 of *Suiboku Bijutsu Taikei* (Tokyo, 1973).

is as if, having come this far with the outline of a monumental foreground cliff, the artist finally demurred, taking objection with the alien sense of style; the depth imparted by conventional Chinese perspective that began at the bottom of the painting simply disappears into flat decorative planes at the top.

This painting seems to begin where what Cahill calls Li Tsai's "two-dimensional zigzag pattern" (p. 45) leaves off, and is reminiscent of the stylistic excesses of the later Che eccentric Wu Wei (1459–1503). The *haboku* landscape painting of 1495, on the other hand, is almost a parody of the impressionistic and blurry style of the Chinese master Yü Chien (fig. 8). Together with its inscription by the artist—who says he drew it as a parody for a student to remind him that his *real* lineage is Japanese, not Chinese—it seems to bring to an end yet another Chinese style that had been extremely popular in Japan. It was not many years afterward that Sesshū painted the revolutionary depiction of the landscape at Ama-no-Hashidate (ca. 1503, Kyoto National Museum), a soft yet detailed horizontal composition suffused with light colors in what has been hailed as a new and entirely Japanese style, a development that clearly leads toward the "townsman-painter" (*machi-eshi*) decorative style of the "beach and pines" (*hamamatsu*) screens of the Tosa school.

Hindsight tells us now that what was rent open by the ink-stroke crack in the *Winter Landscape* was nothing less than the aesthetic and intellectual fabric of a world that for nearly a millennium had been given its order and coherence by Buddhism. Indeed, as the eye follows the line back down the paper, we can see that much of the anxiety the painting evokes stems from the fact that all the chaos and disorder implied in that line descends upon the lone monk and the Buddhist temple in the distance that is his goal. By eliminating depth, its effect is to collapse both geological and iconongraphic structures, cutting the one irrevocably off from the other.

This reading would seem consistent with the widespread destruction of the Ōnin Wars of 1467–1477 that left little intact of the enormous Gozan institution that had dominated the Japanese geographical, cultural, and political landscape so entirely for more than two centuries. The major temples of Kyoto were burned to the ground, their monks dispersed to the countryside in search of whatever shelter, peace, and patronage they could find. The temples would be rebuilt and reinhabited soon enough, though their days of glory were over. But the political fabric of Ashikaga rule had been hopelessly damaged, and with its end came also, part and parcel, the end of Gozan influence in Japanese culture.

As I have shown, the great innovations in the arts in this period were already being achieved largely outside the temple world by men of obscure origins. Like other Gozan monks, Sesshū too took up residence in the countryside, and the scattering across the land at large of these accomplished men opened their arts to new and previously unknown contexts. For many monks of this period, religious cultivation meant possession of knowledge that had a certain mar-

ketable value. Just as Sesshū thrived on commissions for paintings in various Chinese styles, ordered to decorate the dwellings of wealthy samurai and
townsmen, others made successful careers by means of their extensive knowledge of Neo-Confucian statecraft or of the composition of Chinese literature
and poetry.

Before closing the door on the Muromachi period, I would like to turn to one
further example of what might have become of a Zen monk at the end of the
fifteenth century. Living in this difficult transitional period soon to slip into
near political anarchy that would persist for much of the next century, Banri
Shūkyū (1428–1502) in many ways symbolizes the end of the world of the Zen
temples at the same time that he prefigures the start of a new, secular order.

Banri was originally trained at Tōfukuji but moved to Shōkokuji at the age
of fifteen; such a move was almost unheard-of in an age of extreme factional
partisanship in the world of the Gozan temples.[2] When Shōkokuji was burned
to the ground in 1467 by marauding soldiers, he fled to Ōmi, then in 1469
to Mino, and finally in 1470 to Owari. During this time he remained in close
contact with monks of the Shōkokuji faction, further antagonizing those of
the Tōfukuji faction. Caught in the middle of this pointless feud, Banri took
what must have seemed a logical step in a direction that had become increasingly clear, and abandoned his vocation altogether to return to lay life.

Gozan monks reacted in a variety of ways to the unsettling years of the Ōnin
Wars. Some fled into reclusiveness, never again to return to the world of the
urban temples. For others like Ikkyū Sōjun, who had already given up on the
Zen establishment well before the Ōnin years, the bad times were just another
stage in what many had already come to regard as the increasingly rapid slide of
institutional religion into final depravity. Banri was apparently already sufficiently inclined toward the lay life that his reaction to the surprise of unfolding
political events both inside and outside the Gozan was simply to permit himself
to drift into a way of life that did not accord well with remaining a monk. By
1472 we find him already married and the father of two children (Senri and
Hyakuri), although he did not live with his family but rather in temples of the
Shōkokuji faction. In 1480 he finally built a retreat on the grounds of a temple in
Mino into which he settled with his family.

Banri still maintained an active role in the literary side of temple life—by far
the largest part of temple life by this time, it would seem. His expenses were
defrayed in part by the temple, in part by lay patrons for whom he played the
role of poetry teacher and literary advisor, leading a life practically indistin-
guishable from that led by the professional *dōbōshū* (aesthetic advisor to the
samurai elite) or renga master of the day. He lectured regularly on Chinese

---

[2] The following biographical information is based on Tamamura Takeji's study of Banri in
GBSS, 6:1139–65.

subjects, and by 1482 had completed his *Tenkahaku,* an enormous annotated edition of the Sung poet Su Tung-p'o's collected works. Such commentaries are still valuable today, less for the light they shed on Chinese texts than for what they reveal of late-fifteenth-century Japanese attitudes toward the relationship to China (they are also important primary sources for the study of Muromachi Japanese language).[3] Banri was invited by patrons to lecture on his scholarship, an activity that became his main source of economic support.

In 1485, at the invitation of the samurai poet Ōta Dōkan (1432–1486), Banri left Mino for Edo Castle to be in attendance on the *daimyō* Uesugi Sadamasa (1442–1493), Dōkan's liege lord. With such powerful backing Banri was able to devote full time to cultivating his new role of *suki* (professional man of taste), and soon found himself so comfortably settled that he summoned his family to join him in Edo.

In 1486, however, Banri's patron Ōta was assassinated by Uesugi on the basis of a rumor of treason. Banri tried to leave Edo immediately, but was detained and found himself with little to do and even less inclination to do it. He was finally given permission in 1488 to return to Mino, and en route stayed for some time at the military camp of Ōta's son. During his return journey Banri was accompanied by a large entourage composed of his wife, children, monks, attendants, and at least one concubine. Back in Mino, he continued to live the life of a successful scholar and teacher of *kanshi* until his death in 1502. That year also saw the deaths of the renga-master Sōgi and the tea-master Murata Shukō, and so may serve as a convenient marker for the end of one cultural era and the start of another.

Despite the setback in Edo, Banri's life is not untypical of what was becoming of the monks of the Gozan at the end of the fifteenth century. They possessed specialized knowledge of the sort that wealthy patrons found useful and necessary in the conduct and enjoyment of a full life. That many of these monks entered to one degree or another into the mainstream of Japanese life at this time is an indication of the breakdown of the temple world and the concomitant insecurity of the religious vocation, increasingly less attractive than the appeal of a more secular calling under the relatively secure patronage of local military strongmen.

As political anarchy increased during the sixteenth century, Neo-Confucian philosophy proved one of the most attractive of the Zen monks' areas of specialized knowledge. Sung Chinese Neo-Confucianism began to enter Japan

---

[3] For an interesting discussion of the interpretation of the Gozan monks' commentaries on Chinese texts in the late Muromachi period, see Yoshikawa Kōjirō, "Toshi Shōshō" (A Commentary on Commentaries on the T'ang Poet Tu Fu"), in *Yoshikawa Kōjirō Zenshū* (Tokyo: Chikuma Shobō, 1975), vol. 22:62.

late in the twelfth century along with Japanese monks returning home from study in China. Since it had over the course of six centuries developed a central relationship to the exercise of political power in Japan, Buddhism at that time still provided the primary context for the importation of Chinese cultural materials. It was central to the themes and symbols of aesthetics as well: we have seen, for example, that by the close of the twelfth century Fujiwara Shunzei had for the first time made art and religion explicit metaphors for each other.

As I have shown in chapter three, Neo-Confucian thought was only one among many elements of the Sung Chinese cultural continuum. Other elements such as the theory and practice of poetry, ink-painting, ceramics, and tea-drinking were also gradually synthesized into the mainstream of Japanese cultural life. I have shown in chapter four something of how the Gozan monk Kokan Shiren received and interpreted contemporary Neo-Confucian thought, especially in the area of poetic theory and practice. It was becoming increasingly important in his time to reconcile the new mainland interpretation of the relationship between political and cultural thought and institutions with the budding relationship of the Zen institution in Japan to central political authority. In his work Kokan was able to draw upon excellent first-hand contemporary Chinese materials in the library at Tōfukuji that Enni Ben'en, his teacher and founder of the Tōfukuji line, had collected in China and brought back to Japan.

From its inception, one of the main activities of the Gozan institution was the assimilation of Chinese Neo-Confucian ideas within a Japanese context. That Neo-Confucianism should be nurtured within Zen Buddhist temples was simply a part of that Japanese context, though the contradiction would probably have startled any Chinese who heard of it. We have seen that in their capacity as advisors to the Shoguns, monks like Gidō Shūshin provided instruction not only in Zen Buddhism but, as experts in Chinese subjects in general, in the interpretation of Chinese Neo-Confucianism as well. As the Zen content of Gozan monastic training after 1400 declined, the amount of time spent by the monks on Neo-Confucian and other nonreligious studies increased. And as we have seen in the case of Banri Shūkyū, writing and lecturing on Chinese texts of every sort would become the most important of the monks' activities after the Ōnin Wars.

By 1500 two conditions were developing simultaneously that, in conjunction, were to create the environment for what was to become Tokugawa period Neo-Confucianism. First, the collapse of the Ashikaga Shogunate had brought with it that of the Gozan, which is to say the end of the long history of close association between state authority and Buddhism, and especially of the interpretation of state authority as something that properly existed within and was legitimized by the Buddhist world-order. From the start, Zen Buddhism in

Japan had appealed to its ability to provide legitimacy to and protect temporal authority, most notably in Eisai's essay entitled *On the Promotion of Zen for the Defense of the Nation* (*Kōzen Gokokuron*), an appeal that must have later seemed both validated by and rewarded with the repulsion of the attempted Mongol invasions of Japan in 1274 and 1281. Musō Soseki had succeeded in guaranteeing the perpetuation of the Zen sect's political importance only by tying its existence firmly to the Ashikaga dynastic rule, an act whose wisdom is still debated in Japan. No one of equal skill appeared in the mid-fifteenth century, however, to guide the Gozan to new patrons, nor for that matter was there much by way of a viable alternative authority to which the Buddhist world-order might reassert its claims. Buddhism continued to exist as a faith, of course; but the Buddhist polity that had been a central part of the legitimization of state authority for seven centuries was dead.

Second, as I have already shown, the interpretation of Neo-Confucianism that had been developing within the Zen establishment had reached a degree of assimilation after three centuries of gestation such that, with the crumbling of its confining temple environment, it could emerge as an independent entity, an entire ethical system of attractive political utility in a new secular and politically confusing age, ready to assist in the administration of government as Zen once had.

We must also take into account, along with the vagaries of political power, the new internal social contradictions that were rendering Buddhism increasingly inadequate to make sense of new social realities. It was only in this age that thinkers seem to have begun to see for the first time the obvious fact that Buddhism had in general a profoundly pessimistic and negative outlook on the world. Even the promises of eternal and glorious salvation held out to the adherents of various sects could not hide the fundamentally dim view that Buddhism held of the still living as temporary agglomerations of fugacious emotions and transient physical properties, doomed to nothing happier than the possibility of ceasing to be reborn into this vale of tears, the "snuffing out" of Nirvana. The extension of this sad dynamic in time constituted the Buddhist view of history, whose inner meaning was thus revealed to be the unpromising premise that decay was the inevitable lot of society. Contemporary mankind seemed always to be in a "Final Stage of the Law," the gloomy *mappō* that had persisted with such durability over the centuries.

This view may have sufficed to make sense of the political and social upheavals at the end of the twelfth century, to endow the fall of the Taira clan with an aura of tragic inevitability, or to herald a novel spirit of stoicism in Kamo no Chōmei's newly profound view of the changed circumstances of his hermit's hut. But by 1500 the power of Buddhism to make sense of one more wrenching social and political upheaval appears to have diminished to the point that it no longer seemed very relevant to the way that men now saw the world. For whatever reasons, those who would achieve an enduring political stability found little help in it—found it necessary in fact to destroy what was left of its annoyingly substantial temporal power. Everything about Neo-Confucianism, to the contrary, promised to be of great help to the would-be prince—and not least that it offered no temporal or spiritual competition to authority.

Perhaps most significant, Buddhism's negative and pessimistic view of man accorded poorly with the single most important fact of life from the sixteenth century on: the rise of a bourgeoisie, an urban entreprenurial class dedicated to the improvement in life promised by materialism and the solvent power of a money economy to break down former barriers, and imbued with a concomitant spirit of positivism and optimism. The warrior who dedicated his life to a glorious extinction may have found comfort in the idea of the world as illusion, life as a dewdrop, and Nirvana as salvation; to the man who loaned out capital at a good rate of return, however, the idea of tomorrow suggested a very different sort of interest. Where *shiki* (色) in the context of Buddhism had denoted "the manifold illusory appearances of reality that are in fact empty," in the context of pragmatic Edo hedonism the same character, in its native reading of *iro*, meant, simply, "sex." In short, where Buddhism had always denied humanity, thought in the Edo period tended generally to affirm it in all its fascinating variety.

In many respects, Neo-Confucianism was remarkably similar in its outward formal aspects to Zen Buddhism, having incorporated a great deal of it in its initial formation as a reaction to Buddhist thought. Thus its emphasis on "quiet sitting" (*ching-tso*) for the purpose of stilling the mind is clearly analogous to Zen's "seated meditation" (*zazen*). The Neo-Confucianist emphasis on scholarly study similarly seems very much like that of the monks who were the great scholars of the medieval period, especially, as we have seen, scholars of Neo-Confucianism. Finally, the long experience of the Gozan monks as advisors to rulers clearly prefigures the active political involvement of Neo-Confucian scholars in the Edo period. This is not to minimize the differences that have been already noted, of course, especially the profoundly negative and pessimistic Buddhist view of man, in contrast to the Neo-Confucian emphasis on the perfectability of what was already an essentially good nature—the Edo adoption of this Mencian premise was nearly universal, even if the state seemed to take a more narrowly Legalist position. In Neo-Confucianism, then, the Japanese found a system that, nurtured for centuries in the context of the Zen Buddhist institution, could scarcely help but show close correspondences to earlier forms.

My portrait of Banri Shūkyū as representative of the Zen monk at the end of the fifteenth century can now begin to give way around the start of the Edo period to that of another former Zen monk whose interests and talents coincided with an age that was, in contrast to Banri's, infinitely more receptive to them. Like Banri, Fujiwara Seika (1561–1619) abandoned a vocation at Shōkokuji Temple in Kyoto in order to devote himself to the Neo-Confucian studies, primarily the punctuation and exegesis of Chinese texts, that were the standard fare of scholarship in the temple world. In so doing he was, as William T. de Bary has written, a representative of the change from medieval to early modern Japan:

(1) As a former Zen monk, he represents the abandonment of medieval religiosity for a new spirituality with a strong ethical emphasis; (2) as a sufferer from the violent final paroxysms of the Warring States period, he felt a compelling need for a philosophy and a way of life on which to establish peace and construct a new polity; (3) as a consequence both of his personal situation and his exposure to the works of Ming thinkers, he stressed practical ability in everyday life and the subjection of all learning to the test of personal experience; (4) as both ex-Zen monk and Confucian convert, he expressed the need for a synthesis of religious and moral disciplines which would reconcile the claims of moral duty and spiritual freedom . . . ; and (5) as one involved in the international relations of his day (with China, Korea, Annam, and the West), he manifests the universalistic drive to find the common human ground in all teachings and thus to arrive at a deeper humanism.[4]

The concerns of the new man, then, can be summarized as ethical, political, positivist, eclectic, and humanistic. Two aspects of Seika's thought in particular seem most germaine to our interests. The first is the careful balance of two complementary aspects of the world—the manifold details of physical reality and their uniting principles—in which we can see the reflection of the age-old Zen insistence on the simultaneous operation of the polarities of Void and Reality. "There is a unity of principle [*li*]," he wrote, "that pervades the multiplicity of things and facts [*wu*]. Between self and things there should be no separation." He then went on to adopt a tactic common to the development of all schools of Neo-Confucianism in Japan (indeed, common to all Japanese attempts to absorb things Chinese), and attacked the very model of his methodology as a way of distancing himself from it: "To insist on the unity of principle is to follow in the ways of Buddha with his leveling of things and his purely expediential view of them . . . [On the other hand] to dwell exclusively on the particularity of things inevitably leads to the egoism of Yang Chu [i.e., unprincipled hedonism]." He thus insisted on the simultaneous "unity of principle and the diversity of its particularizations."[5] As it developed, however, Edo cultural and intellectual thought was, as we shall see, especially prone to dwell on the "particularities of things" while relegating "unity of principle" to the more abstract realm of philosophical discourse.

The other pertinent aspect of Seika's views is his postulation of a strictly

[4] William T. de Bary and Irene Bloom, eds., *Principle and Practicality: Essays on Neo-Confucianism and Practical Learning* (New York: Columbia University Press, 1979), 25–26.

[5] *Ibid.*, 131.

hierarchical relationship between the Way and literature, advocating Chu Hsi's own view of this relationship: "The Way is the root of literature, literature the branches and leaves of the Way. Only because it is rooted in the Way is all of literature also the Way." [6] At the same time, the context of Neo-Confucianism, with its methodology of "the investigation of things" (ko-wu) and "questioning the ancients" (k'ao–ku), provided the framework of a new historical methodology that Buddhism had denied, and this is one of the most significant developments in the Japanese adoption of Chinese Neo-Confucianism. To state this same idea the other way around, only an emerging bourgeois view of history as revealing material progress could have permitted the turnabout from an earlier and essentially aristocratic view of the passage of time as revealing only decay. However we account for this new diachronism, Seika perceived it as fundamental to, and most clearly illustrated in, his interpretation of literature:

> Someone said that "poetry changes over time and differs from one poet to another. Those who think that poets today are the same as those of antiquity, or think that all poets can be lumped together, are like a boat on land or a wheeled vehicle in the water—either crazy or stupid."
>
> My response to this is that while it is naturally true that people change over time, it does not follow that this accounts for a poet's being good or bad. How can something be one thing or another on the basis of being modern or ancient? Pears and oranges are not alike either, yet each has its own particular appeal. Just because one of them might not appeal to someone, he says it doesn't "taste right." But these differences in flavor are exactly the same as the differences in poets over time. Poetry that appeals is good, and that which doesn't is not. [7]

While his emphasis is somewhat different, Seika's argument is remarkably similar to Kokan Shiren's critique of Chinese poetic theory nearly three centuries earlier. According to Seika, historical change was a natural process that was not to be confused with ethics: past and present were one thing, value judgments entirely another. Along with this incipient historicism, then, was introduced a new sort of relativism in the context of which it was to become increasingly difficult to defend the view of the past or of China—especially of China *as* revered antiquity—as something inherently "good," and of a similarly categorized Japanese present as inherently "bad," thereby setting the stage for an entirely new interpretation of Japan's inherent moral worth with respect to China.

Seika's view of poetry, utilitarian as it may have been[8] (and one feels that he was not really very interested in poetry), also introduces another important

---

[6] Matsushita Tadashi, *Edo Jidai no Shifū Shiron* (Tokyo: Meiji Shoin, 1972), 196.

[7] *Ibid.*, 199.

[8] Donald Keene, *World Within Walls* (hereafter cited as *WWW*; New York: Grove Press, 1976), 537.

element that later generations would seize upon and amplify: the notion that poetry has its origins in human emotions and is their most legitimate (read also "sincere," "true," or "real") expression. "Words are the expression of the heart, and writing is the essence of words. Therefore words that are simple and plain coming from a sincere heart never fail to move us. But how could we ever be moved by ornate and overwrought words coming from an insincere heart?" [9] Seika felt that the sincerity (*makoto*) of the poems in *The Book of Odes* moved, by means of an empathic emotional reaction, a corresponding sincerity in the individual.[10]

Where Kokan Shiren had reduced all critical evaluation to the single element of "principle," Seika's analysis of poetry and any other literature was much more complex, requiring a balance of four elements:

> Although there are many different genres, there are but four elements from which they all derive. In setting forth one's heart, therefore, one must look to these four elements, each of which follows naturally from its appropriate subject matter to unite with the other three. Thus, if literature lacks "mind" [意] it will be coarse; if it lacks "scene" [or "setting," 景] it will be withered; if it lacks "emotion" [情] it will be phony; and if it lacks "fact" [or "detail," 事] it will be empty [虚]. Setting forth one's heart must unite these four elements.[11]

Seika recognized what Chu Hsi had called the "material aspect" (*ch'i*, 気) as a necessary and complementary counterpoise to the nonmaterial aspect of "heart/mind" (*hsin*, 心) in poetry. Used as one of the terms defining this nonmaterial aspect, "mind," when considered as the opposite of "coarse," means that which makes poetry "refined," the cultivated mental activity or wit that shapes raw emotion to give it effective artistic form. Seika also insisted on the element of "scene or "setting" to instill the sense of vitality without which poetry will seem withered; on "emotion" to provide "sincerity"—obviously the opposite of "phoniness"; and on "fact" to prevent the appearance of "emptiness."

Here we already find in embryonic form a number of potential oppositions that would become further clarified and polarized as Edo thinkers became more familiar with the intricate literary debates of their mainland mentors and, more important, as they continued to impose Japanese preferences upon these Chinese schema. The traditional Neo-Confucian polarities of spirit/material or substance/function seem to have interested later Edo poets and thinkers little, as though these distinctions were either too obvious or too obscure, or at any rate too alien to Japanese concerns, to be remarked upon. The elaborate Chinese

---

[9] Matsushita, *Shifū*, 196.
[10] *Ibid.*, 196–97.
[11] *Ibid.*, 197.

metaphysics of epistemology, of how the mind perceives and is related to external reality, seems largely taken for granted; what validated the two, and was the really important element in their equation, was almost universally felt to be the sincerity of the human emotional response.

If the Chinese term *i* is taken to mean "play of wit" that lends "elegance" (*ga*, 雅) to emotion, then by "coarse" Seika seems to have meant what later theorists identified as "common" or "vulgar" (*zoku*, 俗), which was to become one of the most important terms of mid-Edo aesthetics. We have seen that "withered" had been used as a positive term in Sung critical theory and made to bear great significance in Muromachi aesthetics. But Seika uses it here in a negative sense to mean that which is literally "lifeless," brought about as the result of too little "scene," the lack of atmosphere that results from inadequate description. Later, as we shall see, this term would be set into opposition with "emotion," and "lacking fact" (i.e., "emptiness" or "fictitiousness," 虚) made to oppose "reality" (i.e., "fullness" or "truth," 実).

This still unsystematic, loosely defined and freely used set of terms was woven into a more coherent system of ideas in the thought of Itō Jinsai (1627–1705). Jinsai's philosophy can be understood as the product of the times he lived in, the vital and ebullient society of the Genroku period (1688–1704) that produced such famous men as the *haikai* poet Matsuo Bashō (1644–1694), the dramatist Chikamatsu Monzaemon (1653–1725), the novelist Ihara Saikaku (1642–1693), the Rimpa school artists Ogata Kōrin (1658–1716) and Ogata Kenzan (1663–1743), and the early woodblock artist Hishikawa Moronobu (d. 1714). Jinsai's family also had important connections with the cultural lineages of the time as well as among the Genroku elite. His mother, for instance, was the daughter of the famous poet and linked-verse master Satomura Jōha (1527–1602); and Jinsai himself married into the Ogata family in 1670, his wife a cousin of Kōrin and Kenzan and a niece of the founder of the Rimpa school style, Hon'ami Kōetsu (1558–1637).

Perhaps the most obvious difference between Jinsai and earlier Edo philosophers lay in their respective notions of the relationship between literature and the Way. Fujiwara Seika's view of this issue, carried on in even more extreme form by Hayashi Razan (1583–1657) and Yamazaki Ansai (1618–1682), was the usual Neo-Confucian treatment of the two as hierarchical, literature regarded as entirely subordinate to the Way (literally *honmatsu*, "having the relationship of root to branch"), and worthy of notice only insofar as it could be shown to validate it.[12]

---

[12] Nakamura Yukihiko, ed., *Kinsei Bungaku Ronshū* (Tokyo: Iwanami Shoten, 1973), *NKBT*, 94:448, n. 1, compares Chu Hsi's, Razan's, and Ansai's views on this matter. Cf. Nakamura Yukihiko, *Kinsei Bungei Shichōkō* (Tokyo: Iwanami Shoten, 1977), 63.

Jinsai, however, emphasized instead the *complementary* nature of the two: precisely because literature was that which revealed the ancient Way to man, without literature there could be no Way. In arriving at this conclusion, Jinsai took the unprecedented step of equating the Way with "human emotions" (人情, Ch. *jen-ch'ing*, J. *ninjō*), locating in *The Book of Odes* the textual source for the authentic emotions of the ancient Sages. In further stark contrast to the views of Hayashi Razan, who saw in the *Odes* and later poetry only a vehicle for ethical morality,[13] Jinsai explicitly denied that poetry served any such purpose:

> Poetry tells of human emotions and human nature. No matter how many people there may be in the world—and those who have lived from ancient times to the present are without number—there is no human emotion that is not contained in the *Odes*.[14]

He based his denial on the grounds that there was nothing in the *Odes*, contrary to received opinion, that was either "proper" or "licentious" of itself, but that their interpretation was entirely a matter of relativity:

> When the elevated see them they consider the *Odes* from an elevated point of view, and when the lowly see them they consider them from a lowly point of view. They are round or square according to one's circumstances, great or small depending on how one sees them.[15]

This relativism has profound significance, for it suggests not only, as in Seika's case, that China is no "better" than Japan, or antiquity "better" than the present, but also that neither can that conventional quality in poetry called the "elevated" be considered as any better than the low, the humble, or the common. Jinsai extended his concept of "humanity" even to the all-too-human. He saw the only difference between the elegant and the common to be the fact that the former was fettered by stale convention, while the latter was able to express emotions with unhindered and fresh immediacy. Although the common was of even greater value as a key to understanding literature, and by extension of understanding the Way, Jinsai insisted on the necessary complementarity of the two:

> What makes *The Book of Odes* a classical text is its incorporation of both the elegant and the common, its jumbling together of both good and evil. It is like mixing

---

[13] Matsushita, *Shifū*, 231.

[14] *Ibid.*, 330. For a study of the path Jinsai may have traveled in arriving at his central and heterodox formulation of "emotions," see Samuel Hideo Yamashita, "The Early Life and Thought of Itō Jinsai," *Harvard Journal of Asiatic Studies* 43:2 (December 1983), 453–80.

[15] Yoshikawa Kōjirō and Shimizu Shigeru, eds., *Itō Jinsai, Itō Tōgai* (Tokyo: Iwanami Shoten, 1971), *NST*, 33:86–87.

black and white in the same garment, or like keeping ice and coal in the same container: the good looks even better [against the contrasting evil], the evil even worse. This is why it can stimulate the good in people's hearts and keep errant intentions in line.[16]

Despite his insistence on their complementarity in theory, Jinsai frequently seems to tip the balance in favor of the common (*zoku*): "The Way of every-day life is the exhalted Way.... there is nothing in daily life that meets the eye or ear that is not the Way.[17] "There is no Way that exists outside the common, nor anything common that is outside the Way."[18] Here he carried a step further Razan's acceptance of Chu Hsi's notion that "there is no Way that exists outside of literature, nor any literature that exists outside the Way."[19] Jinsai felt that nothing in human society, no matter how humble, should be despised; rather, by striving to understand its role in the human fabric, he affirmed in its entirety all that Buddhism had consistently denied. As if in response to the undeniable sensual appeal of his times, he saw human beings and their society as vital and in constant motion, alive because they were endowed with the original creative force that suffuses the universe, "drinking, eating, talking, discoursing, looking, listening, moving, and creating without pause to their very end,"[20] and saw "heaven and earth as one great living thing."[21] Neo-Confucian metaphysics made a great deal of this primal energy, and the intricacies of the philosophical polarity between its material as opposed to its formal aspects (Ch. *ch'i*, 気/*li*, 理; J. *ki*/*ri*) were well known to the spectrum of Edo Neo-Confucian thinkers. Jinsai's unique contribution to Edo thought was his view of human emotions as the clearest manifestation of this energy made material in culture.

We have seen that Fujiwara Seika felt that if literature lacked "scene," "setting," "atmosphere," it would appear to be dried out and withered; if it lacked "emotion," it would be phony; and if it lacked "fact," it would be empty. Partly accepting and partly rejecting the terms of Chinese critical terminology, Jinsai recombined these elements, building from a foundation of human emotion as the only firm reality a philosophical structure well suited to the materialism of his time. Because human emotions contained the authentic response to whatever moved the heart, he said, they were all for this reason *jitsu*

[16] Matsushita, *Shifū*, 330.

[17] *Ibid.*, 231.

[18] *Ibid.*

[19] *Ibid.*, 58.

[20] Ienaga Saburō et al., eds., *Kinsei Shisōka Bunshū* (Tokyo: Iwanami Shoten, 1966), *NKBT*, 97:237.

[21] *Ibid.* It is interesting that in this passage Jinsai explicitly equates life with good and death with evil, suggesting that a nativist Shintō preference may have been operating even in the realm of Neo-Confucian metaphysics.

[実], "true," "real," "factual." [22] This central element of his thought would appear to represent an absolute volte-face from conventional Chinese theory that inevitably equated "scene" [景] with reality, and "emotion" [情] with falsehood or fiction.[23] In a move that suggests how far the Japanese idea of mimetic reality is from our own, he rejected the clever depiction of "scene" in poetry for its own sake, "skillfully made to appear right before one's very eyes," for it served no purpose other than to create the illusion of a world, uninformed by the reality of emotion. Therefore, contrary to received Chinese ideas, "scene" had rather to follow from "emotion" in order to be real; otherwise it was false or fictitious. "In poetry," Jinsai wrote, "there are 'emotions' and 'scene,' people considering 'scene' as 'real' and 'emotion' as 'fictitious.' In my opinion, however, all poetry from the *Odes* to that of the Han and Wei dynasties is 'emotion.' From scene [i.e., outside objects acting on the heart] comes emotion, emotion expanding into scene." [24]

From Jinsai's point of view, whatever was "low" (*hi* 卑, meaning the same as *zoku*, 俗) was also "real," and whatever was "elevated" (*ga*, 雅 or 高) was "fictitious." [25] He must have realized just how far his views had diverged from conventional Neo-Confucian metaphysics, for in his *Answers to Children's Questions* (*Dōjimon*, 1693) he has a "pupil" ask, "Your discussion of the Way so far has been truly excellent—but aren't you carrying this 'low' business a bit too far?" Jinsai responded,

What is low is of itself real, while what is elevated is of itself fictitious. The scholars of ancient times did not disdain the low and near-to-hand, and those who look down on it now do not understand the Way. The Way is like the great earth. In the whole universe there is nothing as low as the earth. Therefore nothing can be separated from the earth and still stand on its own. It bears up the highest mountains as if they weighed nothing, contains great rivers and oceans without spilling a drop. Since it can carry all things, how can one be disdainful of the humblest thing that is permitted to dwell upon it?... If you are not ashamed of the Way in these two words "low" and "near-to-hand," then your Way will progress, your scholarship will be enlightened, and you will not end up somewhere far removed from the Way.[26]

[22] *NKBT*, 97:254.

[23] This ethical equation is perhaps one of the most powerful of all Chinese hermeneutical principles and has its roots deep in classical Chinese thought. Its operation is responsible for, among other things, the principles that determine the boundaries of "fact" and "fiction" respectively, and so of what can legitimately be included in writing intended as "factual" (e.g., history) in contrast to that intended as "fictional" (e.g., poetry). For a discussion of some of the dimensions of these aspects, see Jaroslav Prusek, "History and Epic in China and the West: A Study in Differences in Conception of the Human Story," *Diogenes* 42 (1963), 20–43.

[24] *NKBT*, 97:73–74.

[25] Cited in Nakamura, *Kinsei*, 60.

[26] *NKBT*, 97:73.

We have seen in chapter four that the Chinese Zen monk I-shan I-ning was said by his biographer, the Japanese monk Kokan Shiren, to have been well versed not only in the expected Buddhist and Neo-Confucian texts but, somewhat more dubiously in Kokan's view, in the vernacular fiction and poetry of Sung China as well. To Jinsai's eyes, conditioned as they unquestionably were by prolific Genroku fiction, this sort of thing, far from suspicious, was in fact admirable:

> When you comprehend the principles that pervade the Four Classics, then you will discover that ultimate principles exist even in romances and novels 野史卑說 and that the most sublime Way is to be found even in poetry and drama 詞曲雜劇. Neo-Confucian scholars know only about principles in that which purports to have them, but do not know about principles in that which does not purport to have them. *That* is what is "vulgar!"[27]

It seems highly unlikely that Jinsai could have arrived at this complex and unorthodox position as the result of the theoretical manipulation of Neo-Confucian metaphysical abstractions alone. That he himself took an active interest in what he termed "romances and novels" is revealed in an entry in his diary for the end of 1683, which contains the first recorded mention in Japan of one of the great Chinese collections of contemporary fiction, Feng Meng-lung's (1574–1645) *Stories to Rouse the World* (*Hsing-shih Heng-yen*, 1627).[28] It is also well known that his son Tōgai (1670–1736), who succeeded Jinsai as head of his school (the Kōgidō, or Hall of Ancient Meanings), was also widely read in Chinese vernacular fiction, and that several writers of popular Japanese fiction were students of their school.[29] Again, the fact that almost the only contemporary biographical notice of the great novelist Ihara Saikaku is a notice in *Kenbun Dansō* by Jinsai's younger son Baiu (1683–1745) suggests that the school's interest in fiction was not restricted to works in Chinese, as Jinsai's own views on the equality of China and Japan would seem to indicate.[30]

Jinsai's novel reorganization of Neo-Confucian terminology suggests a debt both to Muromachi Gozan scholarship and to the wide variety of often mutually conflicting theories of poetry then current in China. The most obvious sources of his interest in the relationship between "emotion" and "scene" are popular Sung works on poetics, the best known of which in Japan was *Poems in Three Styles* (*San-t'i Shih*, ca. 1240) by the Sung writer Chou Pi (fl.

[27] *Ibid.*, 157 and 152 n. 3.
[28] Nakamura, *Kinsei*, 58–59.
[29] Keene, *WWW*, 376.
[30] Nakamura, *Kinsei*, 56; Keene, *WWW*, 174. There is also Bashō's reference to Saikaku (his almost exact contemporary) as cited by Kyorai: "Then there are those who write about human emotions, searching out wisdom in every nook and cranny of life—thus does Saikaku plumb the depths of the lower side of human existence" (*Kyoraisho, NKBT*, 66:355).

1225–1265). The preface to this work specifically equates "scene" as verifiable external description with reality, and "emotion" as internal and unverifiable with fiction.

The *San-t'i Shih* is not, however, unique among Sung works on poetic theory in making this equation, which can be found as well in other Sung works popular in Edo Japan, for example Fang Hui's (1227–1306) *Ying-k'uei Lü-sui*.[31] One reason for the early and enduring interest in these works, along with *Shih-jen Yü-hsieh* by Wang Ch'ing-chih discussed in chapter five, and the later *T'ang-shih Hsüan* by Li Yü-lin (P'an-lung, 1544–1570) and *T'ang-shih P'in-hui* by Kao Ping (1350–1423), is their usefulness as handbooks in which discussion of poetic theory and practice, rules, examples, and critical commentary were conveniently gathered together in one work under appropriate headings. The *San-t'i Shih*, for example, discusses poems by 167 poets in three major poetic forms, further arranging the poems into four categories depending on whether the four middle lines of a *lü-shih* poem (or the four lines of a *chüeh-chü* poem) are considered to be all "fact," all "fiction," the first couplet "emotion" and the second "scene," or the first couplet "scene" and the second "emotion." The work's most interesting observation in light of its influence in Japan is that poetry is what serves to "transform the objects in a scene into emotion."[32]

While works went in and out of style, the *San-t'i Shih* seems to have endured in the mainstream of literary interest from the time it was introduced into Japan. It is thought to have been brought to Japan by the Gozan monk Chūgan Engetsu (1300–1375) when he returned from China in 1332. The work had been introduced to Chūgan by another Gozan monk in China at the time, Ryūzan Tokken, who was not to return to Japan until 1350. We have seen in chapter five that one of Ryūzan's early pupils in Japan was Gidō Shūshin, whom Ryūzan had counseled at an interview in 1354 to write no more "old-style poetry"; if he *had* to write poetry, Ryūzan continued, he should concentrate instead on the "new styles" demonstrated in the *San-t'i Shih*.[33] Gidō later recommended the work to Nijō Yoshimoto and wrote a treatise on it himself, *On the Methodology of the "San-t'i Shih"* (*Sandaishi Hōshō*).[34] After 1400, in fact, it seems difficult to find a monk who did not write or lecture on this extremely popular Chinese work.[35]

Jinsai's reinterpretation of these polar critical terms is perhaps the most striking adaptation of Neo-Confucian thought of his time, reversing as he did long-accepted Chinese ideas on the basis of his own culturally conditioned belief in the material reality of human emotions. It was poetry based on

---

[31] See Yoshikawa Kōjirō, *Sōshi Gaisetsu* (Tokyo: Iwanami Shoten, 1971), 237ff.

[32] Ōta Seikyū, *Bashō to To Ho* (Tokyo: Hōsei Daigaku Shuppankai, 1971), 211ff.

[33] See chapter five, p. 136, n. 5.

[34] Tsuji, *Ryakushū*, entry for 8/25/1381.

[35] Haga, *Chūsei Zenrin*, 294.

considerations of "scene" or narrative description for its own sake, rather than on sincerely felt emotion, Jinsai wrote, that was properly considered "empty" or "fictitious," and not the other way around. This seemingly minor change is in fact central to the development of Edo Neo-Confucian thought, and can be seen as the statement in philosophical terms of the mid-Edo understanding of "human emotions" (*ninjō*) as inner native Japanese reality, expressed in terms of its opposition to an external, alien fiction of "the principle of restraint" (*giri*), a term whose further ramifications in the realms of public and private discourse are explored below.

The modern scholar Nakamura Yukihiko has attempted in numerous works to demonstrate the heuristic value of this relationship, examining in some detail the expression of the *giri/ninjō* polarity in Edo literature against the background of Jinsai's philosophical ideas. His main thesis, that Jinsai's Kōgigaku school provided the theoretical basis for what Nakamura calls Genroku "humanism," however, seems to me to misrepresent the relationship between philosophical speculation and aesthetic expression in any period. It seems unlikely that one philosopher could have exerted so enormous and uniform an influence on society at large that he can be held responsible for the creation of such a multitude of new and aesthetically consistent artistic forms.

Rather, we should understand Jinsai's philosophical insights as the reflection in the high-culture philosophical discourse of his day, whose language was borrowed from China, of the social and cultural realities of the world in which he lived. We need not attribute to him creation of the opposition of *giri* and *ninjō*, although he did require that human emotion be given shape by the Confucian forms of rites and music before it could truly be held to be the basis of the Way. To Jinsai, the material vitality of the universe was manifested in human terms by the emotions that they evoked. Such Confucian abstractions as *i* and *li* (J. *gi* and *ri*) were by contrast "dead," "empty," or "fictitious" alien concepts that were necessarily imposed upon native content in the service of giving it formal expression. The formulation of this opposition in more rigorous philosophical terms had to await Ogyū Sorai, in whose thought the posteriority of philosophical speculation to cultural reality becomes more evident.

We can locate a contemporary aesthetic equivalent to Jinsai's conception of emotion as shaped by formal considerations in statements by the dramatist Chikamatsu Monzaemon (1653–1725), as they were recorded in the *Naniwa Miyage* (Souvenirs of Osaka, 1758) of his friend Hozumi Ikan, a disciple of Jinsai's Kōgigaku school:

> I consider pathos to be entirely a matter of *giri*. Since it is moving [*aware*] when all parts of the art [*gei no rikugi*] are controlled by restraint [*giri*], the stronger and

firmer the melody and words are, the stronger will be the impression created [*aware naru mono*].[36]

Chikamatsu here states clearly that the dramatic effect of emotion is strongest when shaped by the constraints of *giri*, this term obviously used in its narrower philosophical meaning of "the principle of restraint" as I have discussed it rather than in its broader social currency. That is, *giri*, as "the principle of the formal aspects of artistic expression," is not simply the contrary of *ninjō* and *aware*, but rather must be regarded as their necessary complement.

The usual interpretation of *giri* is "duty" or "obligation," and so required elaborate glossing when Keene translated the term in this passage into English. The word of course is generally understood to be the opposite of *ninjō* in that opposition of human feeling and duty thought to lie at the very core of the dramatic dilemma representative of Edo, especially Genroku, plays and novels. And at the level of language of low culture discourse this is quite true. The masses, unequated with and uninterested in the subtleties of Neo-Confucian discourse, may have borrowed their terminology from such technical debate— a feature of the expression of mass aesthetics in any age, one would presume; but they could hardly have been expected to identify themselves with the dilemma of a hero torn, say, between the demands of "intuition" (心) and "reason" (理), terms that are thought of as marking one of the major lines of cleavage in the history of Neo-Confucian debate, whether in China or in Japan. These terms had to be quite literally translated into Japanese, both in intellectual discourse by the exegesis of Chinese philosophical texts on the one hand, and in cultural representation by the translation, dissemination, and imitation of contemporary Chinese fiction and drama in Japan on the other.

Nakamura schematically represents the *giri-ninjō* opposition as bifurcated in cultural representation, especially in drama, on two levels: that of the audience, whose goal is what Chikamatsu called "entertainment" (*nagusami*), and for whom dramatic representation could be reduced to the level of fiction (*uso*) as opposed to fact (*jitsu*); and that of the artist (*geisha*, "performer," although I think we should substitute here "playwright" or "author"), whose goal is instead "art" (*gei*) and whose representational tools, using the terms of Chinese critical discourse, are divided into the twin components of the "affective aspect" (興象) in contrast to the "descriptive aspect" (景象).

[36] The text is reproduced in Nakamura Yukihiko, "Kyōjitsu Hiniku Ron" (originally published in 1963), in Nihon Bungaku Kenkyū Shiryō Kankōkai, ed., *Chikamatsu* (Tokyo: Yūseidō, 1976), 70ff. The English translation is that of Donald Keene, *The Battles of Coxinga* (London: Taylor's Foreign Press, 1951), 95ff. Puzzled by this use of the term, Keene comments, "The word I have translated here as 'restraint' is *giri* 義理. The word normally means 'propriety' or 'duty,' but in the context, 'restraint' seems to be the meaning indicated, although it is not a recognised meaning of the word" (178, n. 21).

Between these two extreme modes of expectation in artistic representation lie the congruent terms of philosophical discourse whose equation I have already noted: "emotion" in contrast to "scene," and "fiction" (on this level of discourse to be read not as *uso*, 嘘, but as *kyo*, 虚) in contrast to "truth." [37] That Chikamatsu was familiar not only with the terms of mass cultural reference—categories that in fact may have been imposed upon his work by the demands of mass culture—but of high-culture discourse as well is suggested by a passage in *Naniwa Miyage* on the necessity of suffusing what he calls "descriptive passages" (風景) with "emotion" for effect. In this passage he uses the Chinese critical term that I have translated as "affective aspect" (and Keene as "evocative power") in contrast to the term "descriptive aspect" (景象), which appears in the next sentence:

> When one says of something which is sad [*aware*] that it is sad, one loses the implications, and in the end even the impression of sadness is slight. It is essential that one not say of a thing that it is sad, but that it be sad of itself. For example, when one praises a place renowned for its scenery [風景] such as Matsushima by saying, "Ah, what a fine view!" one has said in one phrase all that one can about the sight [景象], but without effect. [38]

Perhaps a less satisfactory but more informative translation for what Keene has translated here as "sight" would be the cumbersome philosophical term "descriptive aspect of the scene," since Chikamatsu clearly intended it to stand in contrast to the term "affective aspect" in the following passage of *Naniwa Miyage*:

> Even descriptive passages like the *michiyuki*, to say nothing of the narrative phrases and dialogue, must be charged with feeling or they will be greeted with scant applause. This is the same thing as is called evocative power in poets [lit., "called 'the affective aspect' (興象) in Chinese critical theory"]. For this reason, it should be borne in mind that feeling [情] is the basis of writing. [39]

We have seen that Jinsai reversed the usual equation of these philosophical terms and, rather than opposing them, equated "emotion" with "truth" or "reality," and "scene" with "falsehood" or "fiction," with the further observation that the function of poetry was to "transform the objects in the scene into emotion," art effectively transmuting what was an external and therefore unverifiable fiction into internal and therefore verifiable reality. Near the opening of *Naniwa Miyage*, Chikamatsu provides us with a marvelously con-

---

[37] Nakamura, "Kyōjitsu," 71.

[38] Keene, *Coxinga*, 94. Compare Shinkei's statement of two centuries earlier: "There is nothing interesting in merely saying of something moving that it is 'moving'" (*Shinkei Sōzu Teikin*, in *Zoku Gunsho Ruijū*, 17b:1125).

[39] Keene, *Coxinga*, 94.

crete example of how this is achieved in a passage in *Genji Monogatari*, and also tells us how this technique affected his own art:

> Once, when I was young and reading a story about the court, [i.e., *Genji Mono-gatari*], I came across a passage which told how, on the occasion of a festival, the snow had fallen heavily and piled up. An order was then given to a guard to clear away the snow from an orange tree. When this happened, the pine tree next to it, apparently resentful that its boughs were bent with snow, recoiled its branches. This was a stroke of the pen which gave life to the inanimate tree. It did so because the spectacle of the pine tree, resentful that the snow has been cleared from the orange tree, recoiling its branches itself and shaking off the snow which bends it down, is one which creates the feeling of a living, moving thing. Is that not so? From this model I learned how to put life into my *jōruri*.[40]

This artistic technique of "giving life to the inanimate," or in more abstract technical terms imbuing "scene" with "emotion" so that the former is made to embody the latter, is complemented in Chikamatsu's view by the necessity of a detailed and accurate representation of social reality as it immediately concerned the audience:

> Inasmuch as the nobility, the samurai, and the lower classes all have different social stations, it is essential that they be distinguished in their representation from their appearances down to their speech. Similarly, even within the same samurai class, there are both daimyō and retainers, as well as others of lower rank, each rank possessed of distinct qualities; such differences must be established. This is because it is essential that they be well pictured in the emotions of the reader.[41]

This emphasis on mimetic exactitude in fiction has its equivalent expression in every age, of course, each social class concerned with the unique details of its own existence. Thus, *Genji Monogatari* is full of the subtleties of scent, writing paper, and color combinations of robes that mean nothing to the reader today; the *Heike Monogatari* describes at length the various parts of a warrior's armor and tells us exactly how each of his arrows was fledged; and in the Edo period Ihara Saikaku reports the prices of *hatsumono*, those costliest early produce of each season so dear to the hearts of conspicuously consuming townsmen, in detail that could delight only the economic historian. The degree to which Edo writers were interested in every aspect of everyday life—the aspect they called the *zoku*, or "common," "vulgar"—can be seen as representative of a new spirit of positivism, fostered by and reflected in Neo-Confucian philosophy, especially in the concept of the "investigation of things," which was to serve as the scientific basis for the deduction of "principle." Jinsai in his writings

[40] *Ibid.*, 93–94. Cf. Seidensticker, *Genji*, 125.
[41] Keene, *Coxinga*, 94.

intentionally contrasted this positivist mode of deduction of abstract principles from concrete reality with what he saw as a scurrilous imposition of "dead" foreign abstractions upon "living" Japanese realities.

Yet Chikamatsu understood that realistic representation alone was inadequate to the demands of art, "which lies in the slender margin between the real and the unreal" in Keene's translation[42] or, if we translate more literally, "in the interval between truth and fiction, a relationship like that between skin and flesh." [43] That is to say that art is not something that "lies between" two realms, but rather is composed of two elements that exist in the complementary relationship of inner content to outer form. This means, then, as Chikamatsu understood it, that "realism" in art cannot be so readily and superficially equated with the faithful representation of fact, nor "fiction" with its opposite:

> In writing *jōruri*, one attempts first to describe facts as they really are, but in so doing one writes things which are not true, in the interest of art. To be precise, many things are said by the female characters which real women could not utter. Such things fall under the heading of art; it is because they say what could not come from a real woman's lips that their true emotions are disclosed. If in such cases the author were to model his character on the ways of a real woman and conceal her feelings, such realism, far from being admired, would permit no pleasure in the work.[44]

In dramatic illustration of this point, Chikamatsu's remarks end with the story of a woman who, longing for her absent lover, had a doll made of him that was so utterly lifelike that it finally turned her love to revulsion.

Chikamatsu's practical understanding that "fact" or circumstantial verisimilitude does not necessarily add up to artistic truth (that is, that "scene" cannot lead to "emotion") accords well with Jinsai's unique reversal of the usual Chinese metaphysics of aesthetics that simply equated the two. Art was rather a matter of understanding that realism lay instead in the human emotional response invested in its environment. If detail failed to grow organically from its foundation in the audience's empathic response to the characters' emotions, it would be perceived by the audience as false. This was also the foundation of Zeami's art of mimetic representation in the nō drama, a mimesis that we know owed very little to the naive attempt to depict "reality" as composed of a multitude of tiny, circumstantial details as we usually perceive it, but one that insisted that reality grew instead out of a more profound view of how it was actually understood and reacted to by human beings.

[42] *Ibid.*, 95.

[43] Accepting Nakamura's reading of 皮膜 as *hiniku*; "Kyōjitsu," 64.

[44] Keene, *Coxinga*, 95. We might wonder if such an attitude is related to the often-made argument that a male actor is better able than an actress to portray women, even when we know that women were early banned from the kabuki stage by government fiat.

That Chikamatsu saw his art as an attempt to return to the level of Zeami's, from which it had fallen, is seen in his remark that "the old *jōruri* was just like our modern day street storytelling and was without 'flower' or 'fruit,' " [45] using Zeami's technical terms *hana* and *mi* that, as we have seen in chapter six, were so important in his organic metaphor for the taxonomy of his artistic concepts. In this, as Keene has observed, Chikamatsu was preceded by the chanter (*daiyū*) Uji Kaganojō (1635–1711), "known especially for his determination to elevate *jōruri* to the level of Nō by borrowing from its language and themes.... 'In *jōruri* there are no teachers. You should consider Nō as the only parent of your art.' " [46] Chikamatsu's determination to set right the order of things in China where they had gone awry is evident not only in his aesthetic preferences but even in the theme of his play *The Battles of Coxinga* (*Kokusenya Kassen*, 1715). By all accounts the greatest dramatic success of any play in its own time, the play concerns the determination of its hero—not incidentally the offspring of a Chinese man and a Japanese woman—to restore the Ming rulers to the throne of China and overthrow the Manchu Ch'ing invaders. We have already seen China depicted in the *Kibi no Makibi* scroll, the romance *Utsuho Monogatari*, the nō play *Hakurakuten* (Po Chü-i), and elsewhere as a country where Japanese realities were turned on their heads, with the implication that it was up to the Japanese to stand those realities back on their feet again, usually at home, if not even in China itself.

Once this crucial equation between "reality" and "human emotion" (and the power of emotion to create a "true" reality that, lacking this basis, is otherwise "false" and "unreal") is understood, it is not difficult to perceive in other aspects of Genroku culture at large many of the same concerns I have shown in Jinsai's philosophical and Chikamatsu's dramatic writings.

These seemingly rather abstract relationships can be observed, for example, to inform the very structure of Matsuo Bashō's (1644–1694) masterpiece *Oku no Hosomichi* (1694). This work is composed of a series of narrative passages written in extremely compact and allusive art-prose, each passage usually containing or ending in one or more poems, that relate the poet's journey into the region of Oku or northern Japan in 1689–1690.[47] Only with the discovery in 1943 of the journal of the trip kept by Bashō's traveling companion and disciple Kawai Sora (1649–1710) did the world discover that Bashō appeared to have had a puzzlingly free interpretation of the relationship between truth and fiction. It has often been noted since that some of the individual passages of the work are structured in the manner of a renga sequence, a fact that indicates that

[45] *Ibid.*, 94.

[46] Keene, *WWW*, 241

[47] General introductions to issues raised by this work are found in Keene, *WWW*, 98ff., and Makoto Ueda, *Matsuo Bashō* (New York: Twayne, 1970), 137ff.

the poet reordered somewhat the events of his journey, perhaps even invented others, in order to make each passage fit the strict rules of renga that governed its place in the sequence. This theory is weakened, however, by the fact that while such structures can be seen in certain passages, they cannot be found to operate through the work as a whole, as they would if the work were indeed structured on the model of a renga sequence. Also, Bashō was traveling in commemoration of the five hundredth anniversary of the death of the great poet-monk Saigyō (d. 1190), a circumstance that would naturally influence the selection and ordering of the "facts" of his journey. Indeed, so many different kinds of artistic structures large and small have been pointed out in the work that it scarcely seems any wonder if Bashō's text should finally bear little relation to geographical or chronological "reality" as we expect it—especially in view of the fact that he spent four years tinkering with his text before it was finally published in 1694.

The title of the work itself makes it abundantly clear that this "journey on the narrow path into the far depths" of art was intended to explore, as did much of medieval poetry, below the surface of quotidian reality.[48] "Oku" thus exists not only as an actual geographical locus in northern Honshū but as an analogue of *kokoro* ("heart" or "mind") in its dialectical aspects of "emotion" and "scene." Since it was both a philosophical and an aesthetic commonplace in this period that what was "real" were the emotions, and that narrative flowed organically from them, it seems only natural that the poet should have re-structured narrative detail to accord with them.

Scholars have located several specific instances in which Bashō appears to have sacrificed literal truth to fiction in the interests of art. With the foregoing in mind, we can restate this observation to say that Bashō structured his narrative details so that the form of his work would flow naturally from the exigencies of emotion (*ninjō* or *kokoro*). Thus, since lavish receptions and substantial donations by wealthy patrons along the way did not accord with the emotional reality of the itinerant poet-monk, mention of them is eliminated and harsh treatment sometimes substituted where in fact there was none; if coming upon a harbor in the rain did not accord with the emotions evoked when an earlier poet had seen it in sunshine, the weather was changed; the emotionally charged descriptions of two holy sites required a lighter interlude between them, so Bashō added a nonexistent day to the month so that he could stay with the simple and devout innkeeper "Jack Buddha";[49] and if the emotional tenor of a poem by the Sung poet Su Tung-p'o required clearing weather during the day

[48] Keene, *WWW*, 99–100; Ueda, *Bashō*, 137 and 141, n. 1.

[49] "Hotoke Gozaemon"; the wonderful English rendering is that of Cid Corman and Kamaike Susumu, *Back Roads to Far Towns: Bashō's Oku-no-Hosomichi* (New York: Grossman, 1968), 23. See also Keene, *WWW*, 103, and Sugiura Seiichi et al., eds., *Bashō Bunshū* (Tokyo: Iwanami Shoten, 1961), *NKBT*, 46:72, n. 1.

for an outing on a boat, Bashō had the weather clearing, even though Sora insists prosaically that in fact it rained all day and cleared only after supper.[50]

It is also well known that the entire Hiraizumi section, together with the opening and the sections on Matsushima and Kisagata considered the emotional high points of the work, can be seen by comparison with the mundane "facts" of Sora's journal to be a veritable tissue of fiction. The contrast of the gorgeously "orientalized" Chinese grandeur of the Hiraizumi episode with the stark native simplicity and "commonness" of the surrounding scenes, often remarked upon as examples of Bashō's concern for the element of *zoku*, seems intentionally devised to echo the renga mode of "patterned" stanza set off against "ground." But it may also simply be that the "truth" of art required the reordering of what we usually take for reality, for fear, as Chikamatsu said, the audience would have otherwise greeted the work with scant applause. Bashō's disciple Kagami Shikō (1665–1731) recorded the Master's comments about such matters in his *Haikai Jūron* (1719), reminding us of what I have called Bashō's "free interpretation" of the relationship between truth and fiction:

> What is called the "Way of *haikai*" means primarily that by the free interplay of fiction and truth [*kyojitsu jizai*, 虚実自在] one sets the demands of logic [*rikutsu*, 理屈] at a distance and can thus freely enjoy the Way of elegance.[51]

And in another passage, Shikō cited Bashō as saying

> All poetry is skillfully told untruth [*jōzu ni uso o tsuku*]. When truth appears as falsehood, we call it literature, while falsehood in the guise of truth we call ordinary worldly wisdom. Truth in the guise of truth belongs to the realm of philosophical discourse. Rarely do we encounter falsehood appearing in the form of falsehood.[52]

Ueda Makoto, in his discussion of Bashō's late critical term "lightness" (*karumi*), cites a statement by Bashō in a letter to Itō Fugyoku (d. 1697), who was one of his hosts in Sakata during the *Oku* trip: "Poems of recent times look heavy because they make too much use of sentiment [i.e., "emotion"]. To avoid this, I depend on 'scenery' in most of my verses."[53] If this would seem to

---

[50] *NKBT*, 46:120, n. 59, and 123, n. 102.

[51] Cited in Nakamura Yukihiko, *Bashō no Hon*, vol. 1, *Sakka no Kiban* (Tokyo: Kadokawa, 1970), 116. Keene, *WWW*, 145, calls Shikō an "unscrupulous figure" who was self-serving, which may suggest that his citations of Bashō's words may be less than accurate. The word in the text that I have translated as "freely enjoy" (*asobu*) is much closer to the modern French critical term *jouir* in all its senses than to the inadequate English word "play." For an interesting discussion of further aspects of the relationship between "truth" and "fiction" in Bashō, see Kuriyama Riichi, *Haikaishi* (Tokyo: Hanawa Shobō, 1966), 134ff.

[52] Kuriyama Riichi, "Bashō Hairon no Kōzō," in Nihon Bungaku Kenkyū Shiryō Kankōkai, ed., *Bashō* (Tokyo: Yūseidō, 1977), vol. 2, 237.

[53] Komiya Toyotaka, ed., *Kōhon Bashō Zenshū*, 10 vols. (Tokyo: Kadokawa Shoten, 1959–1962), vol. 7, 420–25. See Ueda, *Bashō*, 159–60. Cf. *NKBT*, 46:447.

suggest that, as in Chikamatsu's view, the often unbearable weight of emotion sometimes requires the fiction of description as leaven, we can see Bashō putting this theoretical requirement into practice in the "Hotoke Gozaemon" episode of *Oku no Hosomichi*.

Part of Bashō's poetic power lay in his ability to elevate the level of his work by frequent allusion to Chinese poetry, which modern scholarship reveals he did far more often and skillfully than other poets of his day. The journey in *Oku* thus unfolds both on the horizontal continuum of geographical space-time, structured by the actual points of the journey, and on a vertical continuum of artistic and historical space-time, structured by allusion to Japanese poets like Saigyō and Sōgi and to Chinese poets like Li Po and Tu Fu.[54] This is only a part of Bashō's great debt to China, however, and although it stands out so clearly in his work, it merely continues the medieval technique, which I have examined at some length, of attempting to achieve new depth in poetry by setting contemporary work against a Chinese background.

Bashō understood "the Way of elegance" not simply as "refinement," but rather as the dialectical relationship between the elevated (*ga*) and the mundane (*zoku*). A statement cited by Kyorai makes it clear that Bashō regarded the use of the Chinese language itself as something "elevated," in contrast to the "ordinary" use of Japanese:

> The Master said, "Let us look at how *haikai* is written. Sometimes Japanese script is used to soften writing in Chinese, while at other times Chinese characters are used in Japanese poems. These practices result in language that is neither bad nor cheap. There are even those who write about human emotions, searching out wisdom in every nook and cranny of life—thus does Saikaku plumb the depths of the lower side of human existence. You too, my students, should find ways to write so that your writing will flow smoothly even when you use Chinese characters, and yet will remain sympathetic when you write about the mundane."[55]

And according to another disciple, Hattori Tohō (1657–1730), Bashō's understanding of these oppositions appears every bit as dialectical as Zeami's term *kyakurai* in his view that "the highest understanding of 'heart' in poetry is the return to the ordinary":

> Bashō taught that "to make oneself aware of the truth that elegance resides in the ordinary [*zoku*] is to return to the *haikai* spirit in the here and now." What he meant by "elegance residing in the ordinary" is that thought that is informed by the external manifestations [*iro*] of objects will be naturally incorporated into one's verse without being labored. Labored verse results from the fact that things that

---

[54] Ōta, *Bashō to To Ho*, 85, gives one illustration of Bashō's debt to Chinese poetry in a close analysis of the *haibun* essay "Words on Transplanting a Plantain Tree" (*NKBT*, 46:201–02).

[55] *Kyoraisho, NKBT*, 66:355.

appear in the mind are not elegant. This is what he meant by the mundane [zoku] quality of a mind that does not strive toward the truth that resides in the ordinary.[56]

The mid-Edo view of reality was founded on a conception of reality as emotion tempered, and thus given formal status, by what Chikamatsu called the restraint, and what Bashō saw as the leaven, of narrative description. This is an understanding of the relation of *ninjō* and *giri* that differs from the usual, and one we can see nowhere better illustrated than in Bashō's complex invocation of Hiraizumi in what seems the most "fictionalized" of language, framed by the remarkably "common" or "factual" scenes that surround it, mud flats and ill treatment on the one hand, "horse pishing by the pillow" on the other.[57]

In short, the Edo concept of *giri-ninjō* has as much to do with the formal structuring of Edo aesthetics in the currency of contemporary philosophy as it does with the sentimental theatrics of the dramatic dilemma. If, as I have argued, the violent abstraction of Sesshū's *Winter Landscape* can be said to represent the shattered medieval aesthetic vision, it had not yet produced a new one. Were we to seek a visual analogue of the structure of Genroku aesthetics, we could find no better example than Ogata Kōrin's pair of screen-paintings called *Red and White Plum Blossoms* (*Kōhakubai*, Atami Art Museum, Shizuoka Prefecture; fig. 9): with its absolutely native central motif of a meandering stream in pure abstracted swirls, framed by two very assimilated plum trees painted in a decorative "Chinese" style adapted from Kanō-school stylization, this painting seems to embody in one scene Chikamatsu's demand for the tension between emotion and restraint that informs all of Genroku aesthetics. The two compositional elements exist in perfect harmony, life balanced by form, movement by stillness, abstraction by concreteness, fluidity by angularity.

The reinterpretation in aesthetic terms of the essentially sociopolitical constructs of Neo-Confucianism during the first part of the mid-Edo period about 1700 parallels the earlier interpretation of Buddhist constructs in the critical and aesthetic theory of the medieval period about 1400. This tendency in the Japanese interpretation of Chinese institutions, as I have argued, can be seen as having been conditioned by the long history of the interpretation of meaning as something structured of ineffable native "content" given expression in alien "form." Thus, what in medieval aesthetics was discussed in terms of the Buddhist metaphysical polarity of Void (= sky) / Phenomenon (= color), or *kū/shiki*, appears in the discourse of the Edo period as Emptiness (= fiction) / Fullness (= truth), or *kyo/jitsu*. As poets and artists as well as thinkers, the medieval Zen monks were inclined by their training and vocation to emphasize Void over Color, and so tended in their ink-painting and poetry to

[56] *Sanzōshi, ibid.,* 398.
[57] Corman and Kamaike, *Back Roads,* 75.

9. *Red and White Plum Trees*, by Ogata Kōrin, pair of two-fold screens (MOA Museum of Art, Shizuoka). From Masao Ishizawa et al., eds., *The Heritage of Japanese Art* (Tokyo and New York, 1981), pp. 168–69, pl. 128.

10. *Lovers Embracing*, by Hishikawa Moronobu, circa 1680s (Yamamoto Kiyō Collection). From Shibui Kiyoshi et al., eds., *Ukiyoe* (Tokyo, 1969), p. 9, pl. 1.

reduce the colorful world of illusion to a severely monochromatic vision of reality. Edo artists and writers, by contrast, seem to have seized almost instinctively on the element of "Color," and most often reinterpreted the word in its most common Edo meaning of a hedonistic preoccupation with "sex" (*iro*). To this inner native element of content, to which they ascribed the realistic status of the human emotions, they opposed the external "Chinese" formal element of abstract "principle," interpreted not only as "duty" in the social sense required of the dramatic dilemma but, more importantly, in the aesthetic sense of that which was necessary to "restrain" and thus give form to emotive content. Genroku aesthetics further distinguished between these as "low" (*zoku*) as opposed to "elevated" (*ga*), and took its stand firmly in the human world of the base and the mundane, and so by extension in the realm of the passions as opposed to the social norms that restrained them. This analysis helps to account for the sudden rise of the genre of erotic art (*shunga*) during the seventeenth century. The almost perfect balance of form and content, of line and passion, in even so subdued a work as Moronobu's *Lovers Embracing* (fig. 10) reveals in a way that later *shunga* does not the concern in this period for the representation of every facet of human emotional life within the context of restraining form.

The course of the development of erotic art after the first decade of the eighteenth century, in the direction of a freeing of the passions from all restraint (even to the point of the distasteful and the grotesque), is a clue to the course taken by post-Genroku thought in general as it continued to intensify what were still complementary oppositions into conflicting opposites.

Already even before the end of the Genroku era in 1703, we can find the new elements of philosophical discourse introduced by Itō Jinsai plunged into what seems in retrospect the inevitable crisis that would require their still further synthesis. That crisis is embodied most clearly in the incident of the "forty-seven rōnin [masterless samurai] of Akō" on the fourteenth day of the twelfth month of 1702 that so caught the public imagination. In this well-known incident, upon which the drama Chūshingura was based, can be seen the classic statement of the widespread social perception of the giri-ninjō dilemma: in satisfaction of the demands of the passions, the samurai involved were required to avenge the murder of their lord; but in satisfaction of restraining social principles, those same samurai were put to death for transgressing a legal code that forbade their just vendetta. For his part, Ogyū Sorai (1666–1728), perhaps the most important philosophical thinker of his time, saw these conflicting obligations as defining separate realms of "private" (shi, 私) passion as opposed and subordinate to the demands of "public" (kō, 公) duty. Maruyama Masao has made the point that Sorai's distinction between the private and public realms, and the dilemma that it entails, is a sign of a "modern" in contrast to a "premodern" age, no doubt on the grounds that a premodern system of thought leaves no room at all for considerations of "private" claims.[58] While as a public figure in an age of increasing social and economic crisis Sorai was naturally interested in the maintenance of public order, his philosophical thought is still based on an abiding interest in the individual and his relationship to society, and especially on the need to reconcile, as in the case of the "righteous samurai of Akō," the respective legitimate claims of the individual and those of society at large.

In his analysis of the Sorai school of thought, Maruyama cites as its fundamental characteristics especially a positivist methodology in philological studies and the development of a historical consciousness.[59] He further distinguishes

[58] Maruyama Masao, Studies in the Intellectual History of Tokugawa Japan (Princeton: Princeton University Press, 1974), 102ff. This controversial work, which originally appeared as three separate articles published in Japan between 1940 and 1944, continues to provide a starting point for scholarly discussion of the intellectual concerns of the period. For one critical evaluation of Maruyama's work, see David A. Dilworth, "Jitsugaku as Ontological Conception: Continuities and Discontinuities in Early- and Mid-Tokugawa Thought," in de Bary and Bloom, Principle and Practicality, 496ff. Dilworth characterizes Maruyama's thought as "linear, . . . a kind of bunmei kaika thesis reminiscent of, if not indebted to, the progress assumptions of Fukuzawa Yukichi, Nishi Amane, and other 'civilization and enlightenment' figures of the first decade of the Meiji Era" (497). Dilworth argues instead that Japanese thought is "synchronistic," which seems to misrepresent both Maruyama in particular and Japanese thought in general.

[59] Maruyama, Studies, 76ff., 92ff., and 172.

from these public concerns others in the private sphere of Sorai's interests,
which include a determined "opposition to moral rigorism"— that is, to the
notion that literature must be subjected to ethical interpretation—and a concomitant "defense of the independence of literature" itself. The refusal to
interpret everything in Neo-Confucian terms as intended either to "reward
good" or to "punish evil" Sorai inherited from Jinsai, who may have been the
first to state that whatever else it may be good for, poetry was certainly *not* for
governing the state and therefore not susceptible to ethical interpretations—
except, as we have seen, insofar as it corresponded naturally to real human
emotions that informed it and so would naturally move the hearts of men by a
sort of sympathetic resonance. For this reason he was especially impressed with
the T'ang poet Tu Fu, not only because the Ming criticism that shaped his own
critical attitudes agreed in general that the High T'ang had been the golden age
of poetry and Tu Fu its paragon, but also because without attempting to
moralize, Tu Fu's poetry as Sorai saw it was informed by pure and sincerely felt
emotion used in the service of his country.[60] I have shown, however, that Jinsai
had claimed that poetry was essentially neutral with respect to its interpretation,
"good and evil jumbled together ... the good appearing all the better, and the
evil all the worse [by the contrast]";[61] and Sorai was even more explicit than
Jinsai about the nature of the separate claims of poetry and politics:

> *The Book of Odes* is not something that can regulate one's conduct or explain the
> principles of things, nor can it explain the way to govern the nation and the world.
> It consists only of the words the ancients used to give expression to happiness and
> sorrow. Because the words in it are well suited to the human emotions [informing
> it], we can indeed deduce from them the customs of the country at that time....
> Even though one can learn nothing of principles by studying the *Odes*, since the
> words are used skillfully they relate human emotions effectively and so naturally
> have the power to develop the heart and the reasoning faculties. What poetry can
> do from the point of view of principle is to transfer to our hearts matters pertaining
> to the customs of an age or of a state that we could not otherwise perceive. It thus
> naturally enables one's heart to experience the emotions of others; it enables those in
> high position to know about matters concerning those in low position; it enables
> men to understand the workings of women's minds, and the wise to understand the
> thinking of the foolish. Because they make skillful use of words, poets are able to
> make others understand a state of mind naturally without having to explain it, and
> are thus able to instruct and reprove.[62]

[60] *NKBT*, 94:184–85.
[61] Matsushita, *Shifū*, 330.
[62] *KNBT*, 94:169. The last sentence should be compared with Chikamatsu's statement, recorded
in *Naniwa Miyage*, about the superiority of making an audience feel sadness for themselves over
telling them how sad something is.

But Sorai went even further than this in what amounts to a direct attack upon the basis of Neo-Confucian moral interpretation:

> The significant error of the Sung Neo-Confucianists in their interpretation of the *Odes* is their insistence that the *Odes* were written in order to "reward good and punish evil" [*kanzen chōaku*]. This is their greatest mistake. If that is what their intention was, there are far better ways to achieve it than poetry. . . . There are many lascivious poems in the *Odes*. In his commentary Chu Hsi states that such poems were intended to "punish evil," but I think that they are more likely to incite people to evil instead. . . . In short, there is no difference between the *Odes* and later poetry, and we should regard the poems in the *Odes* simply as poetry.[63]

Jinsai had insisted on the mastery of a classical Chinese prose style, especially that of the *Analects (Lun Yü)* or *Mencius (Meng Tzu)*, as the only method of "clarifying one's Way." He wrote of poetry that "one may certainly write poetry, but there is no harm in not doing so."[64] Sorai, however, again went one step further in asserting that it was absolutely essential not only to study but to actually write poetry oneself:

> Later poetry and letters all follow from the *Odes*. The closer that people were to the *Odes* in time, the more easily they comprehended them. Thus one can benefit greatly from studying the state of mind [*kokoromochi*] of later poets as well. What the Sages said is recorded in books in the Chinese language. It is therefore difficult to understand the Way of the Sages unless one knows Chinese characters well.[65] The fact is that in order to understand Chinese characters, one must put oneself in the state of mind of the ancients when they wrote. It is therefore quite impossible to understand what they wrote [in the *Odes*] if one does not write poetry and prose oneself. Those who only study the classics cannot really master Chinese characters, and their reasoning will always be crude and unnatural.[66]

This very practical argument for the study of Chinese constitutes the backbone of Sorai's interest in philology—he wanted to know in as unmediated and accurate a way as possible what the ancients really said—and is part of the methodology of the contemporary positivism known as "practical learning" (*jitsugaku*).[67] It is this philological interest that led to the development of a new kind of historical consciousness that we first encounter embedded within the context of linguistics. In much the same way as Rousseau, Sorai understood that language evolved over time; and while like Rousseau he also confused the

[63] *NKBT*, 94:176. Cf. Maruyama, *Studies*, 176.
[64] *NKBT*, 97:183.
[65] Compare *NST*, 36:190–91.
[66] *NKBT*, 94:169.
[67] See William T. de Bary, "Sagehood as a Secular and Spiritual Ideal in Tokugawa Neo-Confucianism," in de Bary and Bloom, *Principle and Practicality*, 155.

functions of writing and speech, we may concede that changes in the written language are in some partial and complex way related to changes in the spoken:

> Characters are the language of China. The morphology [lit. "appearance of words," *kotoba no tachi*] of Japanese has changed over time, and so too has that of ancient Chinese. It was the Sung commentators that were responsible for the loss of the ancient language, but it can be discovered by studying the ancient texts.[68]

It would appear that Sorai was already having to anticipate the objections of advocates of the nascent school of National Learning (*Kokugaku*) to the effect that perhaps Japanese rather than Chinese texts reflected Japanese realities more accurately, for he continues:

> For Japanese scholars the writing of Chinese poetry and prose is especially important for these reasons. Although Japanese poetry may have much the same import as Chinese poetry, it somehow has a feminine air to it because it comes from a land without Sages.[69]

A country without Sages, a land of effeminate poetry—Sorai's role in the development of Japanese nativist thought can be sensed in this passage that pushes the methodology of Jinsai to the point where powerful reaction seems almost inevitable. To deny Japan in such provocative terms was bound sooner or later to invite its affirmation, and the accusation of "feminine airs" seems to be practically begging Kamo no Mabuchi (1686–1759) to discover "manliness" (*masuraoburi*) as the informing spirit of Japan's oldest poetry in the *Man'yōshū*.

It is on this ground, oddly enough, that the "public" and "private" meet in Sorai's philosophy. The necessity of ascertaining exactly what the Sages had said (by means of a positivist methodology based on philological inquiry) meant peeling away layers of interpretation deposited over the course of centuries (the development of a historical consciousness); this in turn required stripping from literature, especially from poetry, the accretions of Neo-Confucian moral interpretation to discover in it the "true emotions" that informed it so that one could establish an unmediated and direct connection with the ancient Way of the Sages.

When the problem is seen in this light, it seems little wonder that Motoori Norinaga should have essentially taken over Sorai's methodology wholesale, in the end needing only to throw out China itself as the last irrelevant issue. Sorai's methodology consisted in burning away the middle ground—the geographical distance between China and Japan, and the temporal distance between ancient and modern—in an attempt to draw them all together into a single unity. To do this he proceeded to eliminate not only Sung Neo-Confucian interlopers but

---

[68] *NKBT*, 94:173.
[69] *Ibid.*

contemporary Japanese ones as well. To know the classics only through the eyes of Chu Hsi or the Ch'eng brothers in China was bad enough; to know them only through the interpretations of Itō Jinsai or Yamazaki Ansai (1618–1682), Sorai said, was "to be like those Japanese Buddhists who know nothing of Shākyamuni and worship instead only such latter-day Japanese 'saints' as Hōnen and Shinran."[70]

In his discussion of poetry in terms of "human emotion" rather than of "rewarding good and punishing evil," Sorai further significantly polarized Jinsai's own innovative interpretation, seeing in poetry not something essentially neutral but rather a historical process in which authentic human emotion had come to be expressed in terms of a distorting prism of ethics that was fundamentally alien to it. As this interpretation developed over time in Japan, authentic emotion was increasingly identified as that which was native to Japan, the vital wellspring of the vibrant Genroku culture that could no longer be denied; and the distorting ethical system as literally alien, increasingly identified from all points of view, revisionist or nativist, as part of the detested orthodoxy of Chu Hsi Neo-Confucianism.

In his essay *On Distinguishing Terms* (*Benmei*, 1717), Sorai discussed the interpretation of the term *gi* (the first half of the technical term *giri*) precisely in terms of its use in the Neo-Confucian interpretation of poetry. In response to Chu Hsi's labeling the *Odes* a "treasury of *gi*," Sorai wrote:

> Ancient poetry is no different from that of today in that the words of both are primarily concerned with human emotion. What is there in it that could be called "*giri*"? It was the Neo-Confucians of later ages with their interpretation of the *Odes* as "rewarding good and punishing evil" who were responsible for misinterpreting poetry in this fashion.[71]

Sorai's rejection of Sung revisionism in favor of Ming fundamentalism was complete, down to his preferences in poetry and poetic theory. These preferences he made clear in a passage in which he distinguishes "injurious" from "profitable friends." Among the former he listed Chu Hsi and his school's commentaries on the Four Books and Five Classics, Chu Hsi's revisionist historical commentary (the *Kang-mu*) on Ssu-ma Kuang's *Tz'u-chih T'ung-chien*, and the Sung poets Su Tung-p'o and Huang T'ing-chien, favorites of the Muromachi Gozan monks, as well as the Sung poetry handbooks *San-t'i Shih* and *Ying-k'uei Lü-sui*, two works that we have seen were enormously influential in the development of early mid-Edo aesthetics. Instead, he advocated among the latter group China's earliest histories, the *Tso Chuan*, *Kuo Yü*, *Shih Chi*, and *Ch'ien Han Shu*, as well as the "old" (that is, the Han through the T'ang)

[70] *Ibid.*, 175.
[71] *NST*, 36:80.

commentaries on the classics, and in literature especially the Ming imitative and antiquarian "formalist" poets Li Meng-yang (1473–1529), Ho Ch'ing-ming (1483–1521), Li Yü-lin (P'an-lung, 1514–1570), and Wang Shih-chen (1526–1590), as well as the two handbooks of poetry influenced by this school, Li Yü-lin's *T'ang Shih Hsüan* and Kao Ping's (1350–1423) *T'ang-shih P'in-hui*.[72] The school known as the formalists (*ko-tiao*) combined Yen Yü's (1180–1235) ideas of orthodox lineage in *Ts'ang-lang Shih-hua* with its practical expression in Kao Ping's collection, emphasizing the poets of the High T'ang, especially Li Po and Tu Fu, and rejecting the poetry of the late T'ang and Sung periods.[73] This rather peculiar choice of a school often criticized for its slavish imitation of old styles points up the importance in Sorai's thought of the Chinese concept of a "return to antiquity" (*fu-ku*) as a radical technique, refuting contemporary fad and latter-day misconstruction in the interest of a more profound reinterpretation of the very sources of poetry as the basis for a coherent philosophy.

Sorai wrote of his nearly ruinous purchase of the works of Li Yü-lin and Wang Shih-chen from a book-dealer about 1704 when he was thirty-nine, a fortuitous event that can be credited with initiating his scholarly career in a somewhat indirect way:

> In my middle years I obtained the collections of Li Yü-lin and Wang Shih-chen, but they contained so many antique words that I could scarcely read them. I was therefore overcome with a passion for old books, and swore that nothing later than the end of the Former Han dynasty [A.D. 25–220] would ever offend my eyes again. As it turned out, this was exactly in accordance with Li Yü-lin's teachings. Over a period of years, beginning with the Six Classics, I worked my way through the Former Han, and when I finished I began all over again, reading these works over and over endlessly. After a long time I had mastered them to the point that it seemed as if their words came from my own mouth, and their words and ideas fit together so well that I no longer required commentaries. After this the writings of these two men were as sweet to me as candy.[74]

Sorai's unusual interest in modern spoken Chinese began not long after this purchase, initiated in the belief that even if it were not the same language spoken by the Chinese Sages of antiquity, still it was at least the real thing, and not "forgetting Shākyamuni and worshipping Hōnen and Shinran." He formed a Translation Society at his school in 1711 under the guidance of the Nagasaki interpreter Okajima Kanzan (d. 1727), and wrote proudly that he and his friends were able to carry on entirely in Chinese, "never making errors,

---

[72] *NKBT*, 94:172.

[73] See Richard Lynn, "Orthodoxy and Enlightenment: Wang Shih-chen's Theory of Poetry and Its Antecedents," in de Bary, ed., *The Unfolding of Neo-Confucianism*, 218; and Matsushita, *Shifū*, 847.

[74] *NST*, 36:537.

inverting words, or having to resort to a brush, even for the most ordinary banter."[75] He was proud of owning a set of texts of the Chinese classics that lacked any Japanese punctuation marks, and remarked with some pretension that he was unable to write without Chinese paper and brushes.[76]

Despite such minor affectations, Sorai's purpose was serious, and resulted in some serious thinking on the question of language as central to the interpretation of culture.[77] In the same year the Translation Society was founded, Sorai published his *Guide to Translation* (*Yakubun Sentei*, 1711), the preface to which contains views on language that clearly prefigure those of Motoori Norinaga discussed above in chapter one. In this preface, Sorai states his views on language and literary style, citing the works of Li Yü-lin in support. His conclusion is striking, not only because it reads so much like a mirror-image of Norinaga, but also for the reason he gives in contradicting Jinsai in favoring the "elegant" (*ga*) over the "common" (*zoku*) in literature:

> Ancient literary styles are terse and decorous [簡 に し て 文], modern styles prolix and vulgar [冗 に し て 俗]. Elegant styles are also terse and decorous, while common styles are prolix and vulgar. The Chinese language is terse and decorous, while the Japanese language is prolix and vulgar.[78]

At bottom, Sorai's distinction between ancient and modern rests upon the problem posed by grammatical particles and case inflections, which Japanese uses and Chinese lacks, as well as the problem of ornamental rhetoric, which as we have seen in chapter one Norinaga also considered a hallmark of what he saw as the "Chinese mentality" (*karagokoro*). Again like Rousseau, Sorai saw language as moving over time away from an elegant ancient simplicity toward a vulgar modern prolixity:

> Discovering that the two languages differ is like a Southerner's residing in the South and so not being aware of regional differences, as opposed to a Northerner's going

[75] *Ibid.*, 706.

[76] *Ibid.*, 325, also cited in Kate Wildman Nakai, "The Naturalization of Confucianism in Tokugawa Japan: The Problem of Sinocentrism," *Harvard Journal of Asiatic Studies* 40:1 (1980), 1,57–99, esp. 170. Nakai shows Arai Hakuseki (1657–1725) grumbling about people who, wanting to imitate Chinese pronunciation, "learn to mumble with bad accents a few phrases of the sort of Chinese spoken by the crews of the ships which come to Nagasaki" (171). In the same spirit, James Cahill remarks on the poor quality of the Chinese art this class of men purveyed to the Japanese *bunjin* painters (*Sasaki Hyakusen*, 17).

[77] For an interesting discussion of the centrality of language to philosophical discourse in this period, see H. D. Harootunian, "The Consciousness of Archaic Form in the New Realism of Kokugaku," in Tetsuo Najita and Irwin Scheiner, eds., *Japanese Thought in the Tokugawa Period, 1600–1868: Methods and Metaphors* (Chicago: University of Chicago Press, 1978), 63ff., esp. 64.

[78] Yoshikawa Kōjirō and Maruyama Masao, eds., *Ogyū Sorai Zenshū* (Tokyo: Mizusu Shobō, 1974), vol. 2, 14; cited in Samuel Hideo Yamashita, "Compasses and Carpenters' Squares: A Study of Itō Jinsai and Ogyū Sorai" (Ph.D. diss., University of Michigan, 1981), 167.

South and discovering that it is hot. By studying the Japanese practice of reversing Chinese word order and reading from bottom to top, one realizes that syntax, word order, and punctuation are different in Chinese and Japanese. . . . There is also the matter of particles. Japanese can read a Chinese sentence only after adding certain particles, and clearly we use many more particles than the Chinese. If there are no Japanese readings for the Chinese particles *yeh, i,* and *yen,* neither are there Chinese equivalents for certain Japanese particles. . . . If many Chinese words have the same Japanese readings, many Japanese words lack Chinese equivalents. . . . Although the same Japanese reading may be used for many Chinese words, a single Chinese word may have many Japanese readings.[79]

Sorai was apparently the first Japanese to understand that if Japanese readings of Chinese often revealed a faulty understanding of what was being read,[80] Sung Chinese commentaries also often seem to have misinterpreted their own culture's texts out of an even more willful ideological blindness. Yoshikawa Kōjirō has shown that Sorai perceived this as a "fracture" or "rupture" in the fabric of what ought by rights to have been a history of cultural continuity.[81]

Summarizing the development of Sorai's thought to this point, Maruyama observes how little was required for Norinaga to pluck the fruits of this very ripe tree for his own. Sorai may have denied Buddhism, but he still clung fast to a belief in the Chinese Sages, and retained China as the essential cornerstone of his faith in what was developing as a truly native understanding of reality:

How precarious! Remove this keystone, and the Way of the Sages, and with it the entire system, instantly crumbles. The Sages are the political rulers of ancient China. Why should a Way created by historically and geographically restricted [i.e., Chinese] personalities be thus revered and respected? The Sorai school inevitably led those with the capacity to think things out by stepping outside the shell of the Confucian mode of thought to this question.[82]

The attack on the Ancient Studies school by the proponents of National Studies certainly did not begin with Norinaga, who rejected Sorai's ideas and traced the origin of his school to Keichū (1640–1701) instead. Despite his denials, however, as Maruyama shows, Norinaga imbibed much of the Sorai school's methodology by his study with Hori Keizan (1688–1757), a relationship that echoes Mabuchi's friendship with Hattori Nankaku as representative of the "private" side of the mainstream of Sorai's school.[83]

Norinaga's appropriation of Sorai's thought can be grouped into three

[79] Yamashita, "Compasses," citing *Ogyū Sorai Zenshū,* vol. 2, 4–5.
[80] Cf. Kanda Kiichirō, "Washū Dangi," *Bungaku* 34 (July 1966), 81–87.
[81] *NST,* 36:650–51.
[82] Maruyama, *Studies,* 149.
[83] *Ibid.,* 146ff.

categories: (1) the development of a positivist philological methodology; (2) the evolution of a historical consciousness; and (3) an opposition to ethical determinism that is seen especially in their similar attitudes toward the function of literature.[84] Sorai had rejected the authority of fossilized Sung Neo-Confucian metaphysics, postulating a Way that manifested itself differently in different times and places. The idea that what revealed itself authentically in the writings and actions of the ancient Chinese Sages would naturally reveal itself differently but just as authentically in eighteenth-century Japan formed the core of the historical consciousness that permitted the final translation of *ninjō*, which Jinsai and Sorai both found to be the central element of the *Odes*, into *mono no aware* as this term appears in Norinaga's view of ancient Japanese literature.

The idea of the mutability of institutions over time was, as Maruyama shows, the weak point in the Ancient Studies school's armor that National Learning attacked first:[85] if there can be said to be a universal Way, revealed through individual men in particular times and places, then there is just as legitimately a particular and valid Japanese Way that is like but not the same as the Chinese. Norinaga borrowed Sorai's view of history as process, but rejected the view that it had to do either with a Chinese "Way" or with the alien individuals who revealed it. Instead, he located it in the continuity of the Japanese people and their own gods (*kami*). Sorai had demonstrated in his researches a significant rupture between the age of the Sages and the later Chinese who misinterpreted them, thereby forfeiting, as it were, the Mandate of Heaven. Norinaga insisted that, unlike the Chinese, the Japanese people had always sustained a direct genealogical relationship with their gods unbroken through the ages. The consequences of this I have already discussed in chapter one.

Much as in the early medieval period, early modern Japanese thought around 1600 also began with China almost eclipsing native concerns in aesthetic discourse. By the mid-Edo (that is, around 1700) adaptation and digestion of Chinese ideas had proceeded to the point where Chinese and Japanese concerns—which is to say the antithetical pressures of external form and internal passion—had arrived at a balance point. This period of balanced tension in the dialectical structure of meaning is, I think not coincidentally, the period of greatest cultural achievement. With the further passage of time, the constant necessity of having to cope with ideas that were increasingly alien to Japanese perceptions inevitably exacerbated polarization, the chrysalises of newly synthesized ideas, as it were, sloughing off the cumbersome and now unnecessary cocoons that had been so essential to their development but were no longer needed when they emerged as fully mature. By 1800, after more than one thousand years of considerable relevance, China had become, finally,

---

[84] *Ibid.*, 159ff., 163ff., and 165ff.
[85] *Ibid.*, 149.

entirely irrelevant to Japan and was discarded for good as an ongoing part of the Japanese structuring of meaning.

As I have noted in chapter one, Japan's successful emergence in a final period of synthesis with China set the stage for her dialectical encounter, already underway, with a West that was not to permit her the same breathing space in which new syntheses might develop gradually. One feels that Japan today is still in the period of dominating influence progressing toward increasingly less haphazard if still sometimes seemingly eccentric selection, that the balance point will soon be reached, perhaps by the end of the twentieth century, as Japan begins to play a more major role in world events consistent with her economic status. As this happens, it should come as no surprise to find the West as well becoming increasingly irrelevant to whatever new understanding of the structure of meaning is to evolve in Japan in the twenty-first century.[86]

[86] For a penetrating study of the modern dialectic of "Japanese spirit, Western learning" (*wakon-yōsai*) and its significance for modern Japanese culture and especially literature, see Hirakawa Sukehiro, *Wakon-Yōsai no Keifu* (Tokyo: Kawade Shobō, 1971).

Conclusion

In this study I have attempted in investigate the idea of a fundamental "fracture of meaning" in Japanese civilization through its development in aesthetic terms over the course of a thousand years. In every period and in every area touched by aesthetics—which is to say nearly everything, for aesthetics in its widest sense includes everything that is expressed—the structure of meaning has been polarized into antithetical but complementary terms: inner and ineffable native "content" on the one hand, exterior and alien "form" on the other. I have also proposed that these terms constitute the thesis and antithesis of a dialectical process, and that it is this dialectical process that originated in and continued to govern Japan's absorption of China throughout its literate history. Because it was concerned with the opposition of surface or "outside" to center or "inside," this dialectical process also defined the dimension of "depth" in cultural discourse. It is in this more difficult and abstract sense, then, rather than merely by seeking the historical record of immediate "influence" of one country upon another, that this study traces the "fracture of meaning" through Japanese cultural history.

As a corollary to this methodology, we must further understand that once this dialectic was initiated (and I have always emphasized that the question of origins per se has no place in this study), neither China nor even the *idea* of China was necessarily always involved in its operation. We do acknowledge certain periods of obvious and important Chinese influence in Japan, of course, as well as periods in which China seems almost inconsequential to what was happening there. And we regularly find an abiding concern with the interpretation of Chinese materials and ideas even in periods where no suggestion of direct influence at all is to be be found. But because I am concerned here with a dialectical process, the question of influence has always been subordinated to that of interpretation, so that this study becomes more than anything else a hermeneutics of Japanese culture, a study of the ways in which the Japanese interpretation of themselves and their culture evolved over time.

I have tried to demonstrate that the impetus toward this dialectically structured conception of meaning can be seen (although it obviously does not originate) in Japan's "first" extant written text, the *Kojiki*, and is related to the most basic dilemma of expression as it is revealed in that text: the fact that the primal native Japanese matter of myth and genealogy could only be recorded in alien Chinese form. Writing in Chinese, known in Japan well before the *Kojiki* was first set down, was already regarded as an entirely alien business. At what can be called the level of referentiality, the *Kojiki* contains myth, legend, lineage, and country-building; at the level of self-referentiality, however, its very appearance speaks clearly of the obviously traumatic schism of language that happens to any culture in the transition from orality to literacy. But unlike other literate cultures, Japan was not permitted the opportunity to make this transition, already traumatic enough in itself, either by developing her own script or by means of the sort of borrowed alphabetic script whose alien presence is reduced to the minimally intrusive level of the phoneme. We do not need to agree with Motoori Norinaga's personal animus toward the event, but we can agree with his observation that this transition involved not only the imposition of writing upon speech but the imposition as well of an alien mode of thought, at once powerfully acculturating and uncongenial, upon native Japanese patterns of thought and expression. If Norinaga did not go far enough in his argument, it was only because it was impossible in his time to do so: had he been able to go one step further, he might have understood that the opposing terms of his argument were dialectical in nature, and not seen China and Japan merely as antagonistic and China as ultimately and fatally anathema to Japan.

To talk of the "dilemma" or the "trauma" posed by writing is, of course, to use the modern critical language of Derrida and Barthes to say what Norinaga was feeling. Any discomfort that Ō no Yasumaro himself may have felt in having to record speech in writing, while clearly expressed, is considerably more attenuated, scarcely more than a murmur of demurral that there may be some problems for anyone reading his text that necessarily reflect those he faced.

The "problem" of China as it is referred to Japan, continually faced and resolved throughout the history of Japanese thought, presents itself in radically different guise in different ages. By the twelfth century, writing itself, while still full of fascinating cultural problems, was no longer a problematic matter in the sense that its very commission was felt to be alien—at least this is true for women, who were not constrained as were men to write in Chinese. In *Genji Monogatari*, as I have shown in chapter two, China is less an actual geographical entity than it is a part of the process of cultural self-definition, the archetypal background against which native Japanese patterns of thought and action were felt to attain greatest significance.

If Japan's early experiments with Chinese writing reveal a sense of antagonism, even something of the almost ethical incompatability that Norinaga felt, later texts often emphasize instead this element of mutuality. Although China may have been perceived as past its peak of cultural greatness, even perhaps decidedly inferior by contrast to a periodically burgeoning sense of native vitality, China continues throughout the medieval period to provide the glittering stage setting that serves as the heightening backdrop for purely native developments in thought and the arts. But the shift in emphasis away from an occasionally more tangible China is clear. After centuries of little official contact, the Heian courtiers were prepared to find in Po Chü-i the very ideal of the court poet; to Fujiwara Teika, he was the ideal of the cultivated man who not only sang more sweetly but also felt more deeply. Later poets, however, were more inclined to take their view of the Chinese poet's cultivation and depth from Teika, rather than from Po himself.

In investigating the currents of thought that often seem to have swirled in contradictory directions in Teika's age, I have paid a great deal more attention to China as part of the context of that age than is usually thought appropriate. That the court poetry of the late twelfth and early thirteenth centuries continued that of the tenth and eleventh in important ways is, of course, undeniable; but it is also important that it differed in ways that are perhaps even more significant. The emphasis of Tsurayuki's preface to the *Kokinshū* on the dialectical balance of content and form, of "heart" and "words," seems already (or again, depending upon one's point of view) in the early tenth century to reflect the problem of an essential orality that had necessarily to be subordinated to literacy. This same sense of the antagonism of speech and writing in a society by now both highly oral and complexly literate is reinforced by the Japanese adoption of the Zen hostility to "words" that, while in some sense necessary, will always ultimately betray meaning, often portrayed in koans as a baffling silence.

Thus we find that by 1300 the wakan dialectic had become enormously complicated, involving the opposition of contrasting elements that defined one another, as well as the production of a synthesis that was always to become the thesis of yet further dialectical opposition. I have tried to examine this dialectic at each of its many levels to show, for example, how it figured in native Japanese literary theory and practice as well as the ways that it governed Japan's adaptation of Chinese ideas, especially at the start of the Kamakura and Edo periods, but equally important in the development of the medieval arts between these points.

I should like to return here in concluding to the problems entailed in the transition from orality to literacy. That literacy should have been felt, more or less strongly in different periods, to be antagonistic to a sense of what was properly native speaks, I think, of a powerful sense of suppressed orality. One recent attempt to uncover the profound dilemma that the traumatic imposition of literacy exerted upon an already highly developed oral culture can be seen in Masao Miyoshi's exploration in *Accomplices of Silence* of what he has called the element of "silence" in the development of modern Japanese fiction. In his references to "an element native to the core and as such utterly intransigent and unreconstructible" (x), "the still present belief in a communal storytelling persona" (xi), the "obscurity of the self" (xii), and "the divergence between the spoken and the written language" (xiii), Miyoshi is clearly heading in the direction of establishing for Japanese culture a fundamental and superordinate orality to which formal literate representation is profoundly alien. He finally skirts the issue, however, to arrive instead at his conclusion of a "typical Japanese dislike of the verbal" (xv), a conclusion that has been criticized, properly I think, as running counter to all evidence.

I think that what we find is, rather, a profound discomfort with *literacy* and its consequences for a people that, while highly and successfully involved with it, have from the beginning regarded it as an alien intrusion upon the native domain of oral expression. "Silence" can thus be seen rather as the sign of the dilemma, the *aporia*, of a powerfully frustrated orality in the face of the necessity of literate expression, and is made to substitute for writing whenever it threatens the privileged role of oral communication. If we try to imagine the reaction of a modern *rakugo* or *manzai* comic storyteller forced to deliver his lively monologue with brush and ink, I think we can get some idea of just how powerfully frustrating writing can be to orality, and how a turning inward to silence might be the result.

This view can also help account for the intense Japanese concern for the intrinsic value of the superficial—that is, the surface—aspects of writing as a signifier fractured from its signification, the fascination with pattern and effect, seen for example in the almost incredible elaborations of script and its setting against various sorts of backgrounds (figs. 2, 3, 4). At the same time that Buddhism was being used to provide a philosophical rationale for tacking writing down firmly to the expression of deeper concerns, the writing on the elaborate sutra scrolls of the Heian and Kamakura periods seems at every moment ready to fly off into self-referentiality—to offer itself, that is, rather than what it was ostensibly intended to represent, for our aesthetic involvement (fig. 3). These scrolls provide an illustration of the often-noted fact that religious and aesthetic expression in Japan have never been separate matters.[1] Nor philosophic discourse, as I have shown in chapter seven.

In every Japanese cultural form, orality seems likewise always about to break free from the fetters of an alien and confining literacy, only to be caught up and trapped once again within this recurring dilemma of expression. Even in dramatic forms in which orality naturally dominates, it is carefully set into the context of literacy: the *jōruri* chanter begins with a ritual obeisance to his otherwise disregarded and unnecessary text, his recitation first unwrapped from and later rewrapped into its constraining box of literacy. There is no oral art whose orality has not been thus subordinated at least superficially to literacy.

---

[1] See Joseph M. Kitagawa, *Religion in Japanese History* (New York: Columbia University Press, 1966); and William LaFleur, *The Karma of Words: Buddhism and the Literary Arts in Medieval Japan* (Berkeley: University of California Press, 1983).

The recitations of the blind *biwa-hōshi* have been preserved in texts for transmission, the blind no longer taught to sing as they once were, but to massage instead, the tradition of aliterate orality turned to one of illiterate dexterity, stereotyped in the popular contemporary movie and television figure of the blind swordsman and masseur Zatōichi whose blindness in the context of his impassioned heroism is stirring, but in that of his more restrained social calling merely pathetic.

Having traced this dialectical "fracture of meaning" through its expression in the Heian and subsequent aristocratic poetic of "heart/words," the medieval Zen-centered "Void/Color," and the early modern philosophical and dramatic "emotion/restraint," I will end by noting that it persists still today in the pervasive and uniquely Japanese concern for inner content as *honne*, or "true intention," and outer form as *tatemae*, or "appearance." *Honne* is literally ineffable and formless precisely because it is what one cannot say or do: it is the deepest motivation, never to be itself revealed, that underlies all action. What is revealed, assumes form, is *tatemae*, which both refers to itself as form and also hints at the content that underlies and informs it. This reflects the principle, as observed by Roland Barthes in chapter one, that the center is felt to lack an existence of itself but instead is constantly defined by reference to its peripheral context. The propriety of *tatemae* also embraces the principle of *tate*, or verticality, the hierarchical subordination that establishes meaning among individual elements that constitute a subgroup, or of subgroups that make up still larger units. "Proper" relations are vertical ones, and within the group all horizontal relations as among equals are referred to this dominant vertical principle. This referral of meaning simultaneously to the center and to the periphery establishes a communal and corporate (社) identity that can be seen both as prompted by and as defining that which is alien and does not belong. This study is therefore also concerned in the broadest sense with the theory and practice of the historical formation of the Japanese corporate body; of how it was defined, or rather how it defined itself, in contrast to the alien presence of China; and how that model of self-definition continued to function through the ages to structure meaning in Japan.

BIBLIOGRAPHY

Akamatsu Toshihide and Philip Yampolsky. "Muromachi Zen and the Gozan System." In Hall and Toyoda, *Japan in the Muromachi Age*, 322–29.

Akira Toshio. "The Songs of the Dead: Poetry, Drama, and Ancient Death Rituals of Japan." *Journal of Asian Studies* 61 : 3 (May 1982), 485–509.

Andō Tsuguo. *Fujiwara Teika (Nihon Shijinsen*, vol. 11). Tokyo: Chikuma Shobō, 1979.

Araki Kengo. "Confucianism and Buddhism in the Late Ming." In de Bary, ed., *The Unfolding of Neo-Confucianism*, 39–66.

Aston, W. G., trans. *Nihongi: Chronicles of Japan from Earliest Times to 697*, 2 vols. London: Allen and Unwin, 1956.

Barthes, Roland. *The Empire of Signs (L'Empire des Signes*, 1970; trans. Richard Howard). New York: Hill and Wang, 1982.

Beasley, W. G., and E. G. Pulleyblank, eds. *Historians of China and Japan.* London: Oxford University Press, 1961.

Bitō Masahide. *Nihon Bunka to Chūgoku (Chūgoku Bunka Sōsho*, vol. 10). Tokyo: Taishūkan, 1968.

Brazell, Karen, and Monica Bethe. *Nō As Performance: An Analysis of the Kuse Scene of Yamamba.* Ithaca: Cornell University East Asia Papers No. 16, 1978.

Burch, Nöel. *To the Distant Observer: Form and Meaning in the Japanese Cinema.* London: Scholar Press, 1979.

Bussho Kankōkai, ed. *Dai Nippon Bukkyō Zensho*, 100 vols. Tokyo: Nippon Bukkyō Zensho Kankōkai, 1956. Reprinted Tokyo: Suzuki Gakujutsu Zaidan, 1972.

Cahill, James. *Sakaki Hyakusen and Early Nanga Painting.* Berkeley: Institute of East Asian Studies Japanese Research Monograph, 1983.

Chaves, Jonathan. *Mei Yao-ch'en and the Development of Early Sung Poetry.* New York: Columbia University Press, 1976.

Chu, Yu-kuang. "The Chinese Language." In Meskill, ed., *Introduction to Chinese Civilization*, 599–664.

Collcutt, Martin. *Five Mountains: The Rinzai Zen Monastic Institution in Medieval Japan.* Cambridge: Harvard University Press, 1981.

Corman, Cid, and Kamaike Susumu. *Back Roads to Far Towns: Bashō's Oku-no-Hosomichi.* New York: Grossman, 1968.

Curtius, Ernst Robert. *European Literature and the Latin Middle Ages.* New York: Harper Bollingen Library, 1963.

de Bary, William T. "Sagehood as a Secular and Spiritual Ideal in Tokugawa Neo-Confucianism." In de Bary and Bloom, eds., *Principle and Practicality*, 127–88.

————, ed. *The Unfolding of Neo-Confucianism*. New York: Columbia University Press, 1975.

————, and Irene Bloom, eds. *Principle and Practicality: Essays on Neo-Confucianism and Practical Learning*. New York: Columbia University Press, 1979.

Derrida, Jacques. *Of Grammatology* (*De la Grammatologie*, 1967; trans. Gayatri Chakravorti Spivak). Baltimore: Johns Hopkins University Press, 1976.

————. *Writing and Difference* (*L'Ecriture et la Différance*, 1967; trans. Alan Bass). Chicago: University of Chicago Press, 1978.

Dilworth, David A. "*Jitsugaku* as Ontological Conception: Continuities and Discontinuities in Early- and Mid-Tokugawa Thought." In de Bary and Bloom, eds., *Principle and Practicality*, 471–514.

Elison, George, and Bardwell L. Smith, eds. *Warlords, Artists and Commoners: Japan in the Sixteenth Century*. Honolulu: University of Hawaii Press, 1981.

Eoyang, Eugene. "The Wang Chao-chün Legend: Configurations of the Classic." *Chinese Literature: Essays, Articles, and Reviews* 4:1 (January 1982), 3–22.

Erh-Ch'eng Ch'üan-shu, ed. *Ssu-pu Ts'ung-k'an*.

Erh-shih-wu Shih. Hong Kong: Wen-hsüeh Yen-chiu She, 1959.

Fairbanks, John K., Edwin O. Reischauer, and Albert O. Craig. *East Asia*. New York: Houghton-Mifflin, 1973.

Feifel, Eugene. "The biography of Po Chü-i." *Monumenta Serica* 17 (1958), 255–311.

Fujiwara Kintō. *Wakan Rōeishū*. In Kawaguchi Hisao, ed., *Wakan Rōeishū* (*NKBT*, vol. 73). Tokyo: Iwanami Shoten, 1973.

Fujiwara Shunzei. *Korai Fūteishō*. In Ariyoshi Tamotsu et al., eds., *Karonshū* (*NKBZ*, vol. 50). Tokyo: Shogakkan, 1979.

Fujiwara Teika. *Maigetsushō*. In Hisamatsu, ed., *Karonshū* (*NKBT*, vol. 65); and Fujihira Haruo, ed., *Karonshū* (*NKBZ*, vol. 50). Tokyo: Shogakkan, 1975.

————. *Meigetsuki*. In Sekimoto, ed., *Meigetsuki*.

Furuta Shōkin. *Furuta Shōkin Chosakusho*. Tokyo: Kōdansha, 1981.

Go-Toba-in. *Go-Toba-in On-kuden*. In Hisamatsu, ed., *Karonshū* (*NKBT*, vol. 65).

Gotō Tanji and Kamada Kisaburō, eds. *Taiheiki* (*NKBT*, vols. 32–36). Tokyo: Iwanami Shoten, 1960.

Haga Kōshirō. *Chūsei Zenrin no Gakumon Oyobi Bungaku ni Kansuru Kenkyū*. Tokyo: Nippon Gakujutsu Shinkōkai, 1956.

————. *Higashiyama Bunka*. Tokyo: Hanawa Shobō, 1962.

Hall, John W., and Toyoda Takeshi, eds. *Japan in the Muromachi Age*. Berkeley:

University of California Press, 1977.

Hanawa Hokiichi. *Gunsho Ruijū*, 29 vols., including *Zokuhen* and *Zoku Gunsho Ruijū*, 82 vols. Tokyo: Zoku Gunsho Ruijū Kangeikai, 1922–1933, reprinted 1977.

Harootunian, H. D. "The Consciousness of Archaic Form in the New Realism of Kokugaku." In Najita and Scheiner, eds., *Japanese Thought in the Tokugawa Period, 1600 to 1800*, 63–104.

———. "The Functions of China in Tokugawa Thought." In Akira Iriye, ed., *The Chinese and the Japanese: Essays in Political and Cultural Interactions*, 9–36. Princeton: Princeton University Press, 1980.

Hashimoto Fumio et al., eds. *Karonshū* (*NKBZ*, vol. 50). Tokyo: Shogakkan, 1975.

Hawkes, Terence. *Structuralism and Semiotics*. Berkeley: University of California Press, 1977.

Hayashiya Tatsusaburō, ed. *Kodai Chūsei Geijutsuron* (*NST*, vol. 23). Tokyo: Iwanami Shoten, 1973.

Hirakawa Sukehiro. *Wakon Yōsai no Keifu*. Tokyo: Kawade Shobō, 1971.

Hirota, Dennis. "Heart's Mastery: *Kokoro no Fumi*, The Letter of Murata Shukō to his Disciple Choin." *Chanoyu Quarterly* 22 (1979), 7–24.

Hisamatsu Sen'ichi, ed. *Karonshū* (*NKBT*, vol. 65). Tokyo: Iwanami Shoten, 1961.

———, ed. *Man'yōshū Kōza*, 5 vols. Tokyo: Yūseidō, 1973.

Ienaga Saburō et al., eds. *Kinsei Shisōka Bunshū* (*NKBT*, vol. 97). Tokyo: Iwanami Shoten, 1966.

Ijichi Tetsuo. "Zeami to Nijō Yoshimoto to Renga to Sarugaku." In Nihon Bungaku Shiryō Kankōkai, ed., *Yōkyoku, Kyōgen*, 28–32.

Ise Monogatari. In Fukui Teisukc ct al., eds., *Taketori Monogatari, Ise Monogatari, Yamato Monogatari, Heichū Monogatari* (*NKBZ*, vol. 8). Tokyo: Shogakkan, 1972.

Ishida Yoshisada. *Shinkokin Sekai to Chūsei Bungaku*. Komazawa: Komazawa Tosho, 1972.

Itō Haku. "Man'yōjin to Kotodama." In Hisamatsu, ed., *Man'yōshū Kōza*, vol. 3 (*Gengo to Hyōgen*), 46–63.

Itō Shō. *Rinkō Chōsho*. Kyoto: Kyōto Sōgo Shiryōkan edition, dated 1838.

Kageki Hideo. *Gozan Shishi no Kenkyū*. Tokyo: Kazama Shobō, 1977.

———. *Kunchū Kūge Nichiyō Kufū Ryakushū*. Kyoto: Shibunkaku, 1982.

Kamei Takashi. "*Kojiki* wa Yomeru ka." In Takeda, ed., *Kojiki Taisei*, vol. 3, 97–154.

Kamo no Chōmei. *Mumyōshō*. In Hisamatsu, ed., *Karonshū* (*NKBT*, vol. 65).

Kanda Hideo et al., eds. *Hōjōki, Tsurezuregusa, Shōbōgenzō Zuimonki, Tan'ishō* (*NKBZ*, vol. 27). Tokyo: Shogakkan, 1971.

Kanda Kiichirō. "Washū Dangi." *Bungaku* 34 (July 1966), 81–87.

Kaneko Hikojirō. *Heian Jidai Bungaku to Hakushi Monjū*. Tokyo: Baifūkan, 1943. Reprinted Kamakura: Geirinsha, 1977, 3 vols.

Kaneko Kinjirō. *Tsukubashū no Kenkyū*. Tokyo: Kazama Shobō, 1965.

Katō, Hilda. "The *Mumyōshō* of Kamo no Chōmei and Its Significance in Japanese Literature." *Monumenta Nipponica* 22 : 3–4 (October 1968), 321–425.

Katō Shūichi. *A History of Japanese Literature*, vol. 1 (*The First Thousand Years*). Tokyo and New York: Kodansha International, 1982.

Kawabata Yasunari. *A Thousand Cranes* (*Senbazuru*, 1955; trans. Edward Seidensticker). New York: Knopf, 1958.

Kawaguchi Hisao. *Heianchō no Kanbungaku*. Tokyo: Yoshikawa Kōbundō, 1981.

———. "Wagakuni ni okeru Daiga Bungaku no Tenkai." In Yamagishi, ed., *Nihon Kanbungakushi Ronkō*, 201ff.

Keene, Donald. *The Battles of Coxinga*. London: Taylor's Foreign Press, 1951.

———. "Literature." In Tiedemann, ed., *Introduction to Japanese Civilization*, 375–422.

———. *World Within Walls* (*WWW*). New York: Grove Press, 1976.

Kidō Saizō. *Renga Ronshū* (*NKBT*, vol. 66). Tokyo: Iwanami Shoten, 1961.

———. *Rengashi Ronkō*, 2 vols. Tokyo: Meiji Shoin, 1973.

Kiparsky, Paul, and J. F. Staal. "Syntactic and Semantic Relations in Pānini." *Foundations of Language* 5 (1969), 83–117.

Kitagawa, Joseph M. *Religion in Japanese History*. New York: Columbia University Press, 1966.

Kobayashi Yoshinori. "The *Kun* Readings of the *Kojiki*." *Acta Asiatica* 46 (1984), 62–84.

Kojima Noriyuki. *Jōdai Nihon Bungaku to Chūgoku Bungaku*, 3 vols. Tokyo: Hanawa Shobō, 1962.

———. "*Kojiki* no Bunshō." In Takeda, ed., *Kojiki Taisei*, vol. 3, 207–251.

Kokan Shiren. *Saihoku Shiwa*. In Uemura, ed., *Gozan Bungaku Zenshū*, vol. 1, 228–41.

Komiya Toyotaka, ed. *Kōhon Bashō Zenshū*, 10 vols. Tokyo: Kadokawa Shoten, 1959–1969.

Konishi Jin'ichi. "Shunzei no Yūgenfū to Shikan." *Bungaku* 20 : 2 (February 1952), 108–16.

———. "Hie to Yase." *Bungaku Gogaku* 10 (November 1957), 12–29.

———. "Yoshimoto to Sōdai Shiron." *Gobun* 14 (1968), 1–9.

———. *Zeami* (*Nihon no Shisō*, vol. 8). Tokyo: Chikuma Shobō, 1970.

Kōno Tama. *Utsuho Monogatari Denbon no Kenkyū*. Tokyo: Iwanami Shoten, 1973.

Kurano Kenji, ed. *Kojiki* (*NKBT*, vol. 1). Tokyo: Iwanami Shoten, 1962.

Kuriyama Riichi. "Bashō Hairon no Kōzō." In Nihon Bungaku Kenkyū Shiryō Kankōkai, ed., *Bashō*, vol. 2, 228–46.

————. *Haikaishi*. Tokyo: Hanawa Shobō, 1966.

Kuroita Katsumi, ed. *Shintei Zōho Kokushi Taikei*. Tokyo: Yoshikawa Kōbunkan, 1933.

LaFleur, William. *The Karma of Words: Buddhism and the Literary Arts in Medieval Japan*. Berkeley: University of California Press, 1983.

Lattimore, Owen. *Inner-Asian Frontiers of China*. Boston: Beacon Press, 1962.

Lynn, Richard. "Orthodoxy and Enlightenment: Wang Shih-chen's Theory of Poetry and Its Antecedents." In de Bary, ed., *The Unfolding of Neo-Confucianism*, 217–70.

Makita Tairyō. "Zekkai Chūshin to Minsō to no Kōshō." *Zengaku Kenkyū* 57 (1970), 167ff.

Maruyama Masao. *Studies in the Intellectual History of Tokugawa Japan* (trans. Mikiso Hane). Princeton: Princeton University Press, 1974.

Matsumoto, Shigeru. *Motoori Norinaga*. Cambridge: Harvard University Press, 1970.

Matsuo Bashō. *Oku no Hosomichi*. In Sugiura et al., eds., *Bashō Bunshū* (*NKBT*, vol. 46).

Matsushita Tadashi. *Edo Jidai no Shifū Shiron*. Tokyo: Meiji Shoin, 1972.

McCullough, Helen C., trans. *Tales of Ise*. Stanford: Stanford University Press, 1968.

Meskill, John, ed. *An Introduction to Chinese Civilization*. New York: Columbia University Press, 1973.

Miller, Roy Andrew. *Japanese and the Other Altaic Languages*. Chicago: University of Chicago Press, 1971.

————. *The Japanese Language*. Chicago: University of Chicago Press, 1967.

————. "The 'Spirit' of the Japanese Language." *Journal of Japanese Studies* 3:2 (Summer 1977), 251–98.

Minamoto Shunrai. *Shunrai Zuinō*. In Hashimoto et al., eds., *Karonshū* (*NKBZ*, vol. 50).

Minemura Fumito. *Shinkokin Wakashū* (*NKBZ*, vol. 26). Tokyo: Shogakkan, 1974.

Miner, Earl. *An Introduction to Japanese Court Poetry*. Stanford: Stanford University Press, 1979.

————, and Robert H. Brower. *Japanese Court Poetry*. Stanford: Stanford University Press, 1962.

Mishima Yukio. *Runaway Horses* (*Honba*, 1969; trans. Michael Gallagher). New York: Knopf, 1973.

Miyoshi, Masao. *Accomplices of Silence: The Modern Japanese Novel*. Berkeley: University of California Press, 1975.

Mizuta Norihisa and Rai Tsutomu, eds. *Nihon Kagaku* (*Chūgoku Bunka Sōsho*, vol. 8). Tokyo: Taishūkan, 1968.

Morisue Akira. "Tōgen Zuisen no *Shikishō* ni Miru Zeami." In Nihon Bungaku Kenkyū Shiryō Kankōkai, ed., *Yōkyoku, Kyōgen*, 44ff.

Morrell, Robert E. "The Buddhist Poetry in the *Goshūishū*." *Monumenta Nipponica* 28:1 (Spring 1973), 87–138.

Morris, Ivan. *The Nobility of Failure: Tragic Heroes in the History of Japan*. New York: Meridian, 1975.

Mujū Ichien. *Shasekishū*. In Watanabe Tsunaya, ed., *Shasekishū* (*NKBT*, vol. 85). Tokyo: Iwanami Shoten, 1973.

Murasaki Shikibu. *Genji Monogatari*. In Abe Akio et al., eds, *Genji Monogatari* (*NKBZ*, vols. 12–17). Tokyo: Shogakkan, 1970.

———. *Genji Monogatari*. In Yamagishi Tokuhei, ed., *Genji Monogatari* (*NKBT*, vols. 5–10). Tokyo: Iwanami Shoten, 1959.

———. *The Tale of Genji* (*Genji Monogatari*; trans. Edward Seidensticker). New York: Knopf, 1976.

Murayama Shichirō and Roy Andrew Miller. "The Inariyama Tumulus Sword Inscription." *Journal of Japanese Studies* 5:2 (Summer 1979), 405–38.

Musō Soseki. *Muchū Mondō*. In Karaki Junzō, ed., *Zenka Gorokushū* (*Nihon no Shisō*, vol. 10). Tokyo: Chikuma Shobō, 1969.

Nagashima Fukutarō. *Ōnin no Ran*. Tokyo: Shibundō, 1965.

Nagazumi Yasuaki and Shimada Isao, eds. *Kokon Chomonjū* (*NKBT*, vol. 84). Tokyo: Iwanami Shoten, 1966.

Najita, Tetsuo, and Irwin Scheiner, eds. *Japanese Thought in the Tokugawa Period, 1600–1868: Methods and Metaphors*. Chicago: University of Chicago Press, 1978.

Nakada Norio. *Nihon no Kanji* (*Nihongo no Sekai*, ed. Ōno Susumu, vol. 4). Tokyo: Chūō Kōronsha, 1982.

Nakai, Kate Wildman. "The Naturalization of Confucianism in Tokugawa Japan: The Problem of Sinocentrism." *Harvard Journal of Asiatic Studies* 40:1 (Spring 1980), 157–99.

Nakamura Yukihiko. *Bashō no Hon*, vol. 1 (*Sakka no Kiban*). Tokyo: Kadokawa, 1970.

———, ed. *Kinsei Bungaku Ronshū* (*NKBT*, vol. 94). Tokyo: Iwanami Shoten, 1973.

———. *Kinsei Bungei Shichōkō*. Tokyo: Iwanami Shoten, 1977.

———. "'Kyōjitsu Hiniku Ron' no Saikentō." In Nihon Bungaku Shiryō Kankōkai, ed., *Chikamatsu*, 64–74. See also Nakamura, *Kinsei Bungei Shichōkō*, 128–55.

Nakane, Chie. *Japanese Society* (*Tate Shakai no Ningen Kankei*, 1967). Berkeley: University of California Press, 1970.

Needham, Joseph. *Science and Civilization in China*, vol. 1 (Introductory Orientations). Cambridge: Cambridge University Press, 1954.

Nihon Bungaku Kenkyū Shiryō Kankōkai, ed. *Bashō*, 2 vols. Tokyo: Yūseidō, 1977.

————. *Chikamatsu*. Tokyo: Yūseidō, 1976.

————. *Shinkokin Wakashū*. Tokyo: Yūseidō, 1980.

————. *Yōkyoku, Kyōgen*. Tokyo: Yūseidō, 1981.

Nijō Yoshimoto. *Tsukuba Mondō*. In Kidō, ed., *Renga Ronshū* (*NKBT*, vol. 66).

Nishitani Keiji, ed. *Kōza Zen*, 8 vols. Tokyo: Chikuma Shobō, 1968.

Nose Asaji. "*Oi no Susami* (Sōgi Renga Ronsho) Hyōshaku." In Nose Asaji Chosakushū Henshū Iinkai, ed., *Nose Asaji Chosakushū*, vol. 7, 395ff.

————. *Renku to Renga*. Tokyo: Kaname Shobō, 1950.

————. *Yūgenron*. In Nose Asaji Chosakushū Henshū Iinkai, ed., *Nose Asaji Chosakushū*, vol. 2.

Nose Asaji Chosakushū Henshū Iinkai, ed. *Nose Asaji Chosakushū*, 8 vols. Kyoto: Shibunkaku, 1981.

Ō no Yasumaro, comp. *Kojiki*. In Kurano Kenji and Takeda Yūkichi, eds., *Kojiki* (*NKBT*, vol. 1). Tokyo: Iwanami Shoten, 1962.

Ogisu Jundō. *Nihon Chūsei Zenshūshi no Kenkyū*. Tokyo: Mokujisha, 1965.

Omote Akira, ed. *Nōgaku Ronshū* (*NKBZ*, vol. 51). Tokyo: Shogakkan, 1973.

Ōno Kitarō. "Gozan Shisō no Renku." In *Hattori Sensei Koki Shukugen Kinen Ronbun*, 195–202. Tokyo: Hōzanbō, 1943.

Ōno Susumu. *Nihongo no Seiritsu* (*Nihongo no Sekai*, vol. 1). Tokyo: Chūō Kōronsha, 1980.

Ōno Susumu and Okubo Tadashi, eds. *Motoori Norinaga Zenshū* (*MNZ*). Tokyo: Chikuma Shobō, 1968–1977.

Ōta Seikyū. *Bashō to To Ho*. Tokyo: Hōsei Daigaku Shuppankai, 1971.

————. *Nihon Kagaku to Chūgoku Shigaku*. Tokyo: Shimizu Kōbundō, 1968.

Ou-yang Hsiu. *Ou-yang Wen-chung Kung Chi*, ed. Ssu-pu Ts'ung-k'an.

Philippi, Donald L., translator and annotator. *Kojiki*. Princeton: Princeton University Press, 1965.

Po Chü-i. *Po Hsiang-shan Shih-chi*. Taiwan: Shih-chieh Shu-chü, 1969.

Pollack, David. "Kyōshi: Japanese 'Wild Poetry.'" *Journal of Asian Studies* 38:3 (May 1979), 499–517.

————. "Linked-Verse Poetry in China: A Study of Associative Linking in *Lien-chü* Poetry with Emphasis on the Poems of Han Yü and His Circle." Ph.D. dissertation, University of California at Berkeley, 1976.

————. *Zen Poems of the Five Mountains*. Chico: Scholars Press, 1985.

Prusek, Jaroslav. "History and Epic in China and the West: A Study in Differences in Conception of the Human Story." *Diogenes* 42 (1963), 20–43.

Reischauer, Edwin O, trans. *Ennin's Diary: The Record of a Pilgrimage in Search of the Law*. New York: Ronald Press, 1955.

Robinson, G. W. "Early Japanese Chronicles: The Six National Histories." In Beasley and Pulleyblank, eds., *Historians of China and Japan*, 213–28.

Rosenfield, John M., and Edwin H. Cranston. *The Courtly Tradition in Japanese*

Art and Literature. Cambridge: Fogg Museum of Art, Harvard University, 1973.

Sansom, Sir George. *A History of Japan to* 1334. Stanford: Stanford University Press, 1958.

Sasaki Nobutsuna. *Nihon Kagaku Taikei*, 4 vols. Tokyo: Kayama Shobō, 1956.

Sei Shōnagon. *Makura no Sōshi*. In Matsuo Satoshi, ed., *Makura no Sōshi* (*NKBZ*, vol. 11). Tokyo: Shogakkan, 1974.

———. *Makura no Sōshi* (*The Pillow Book of Sei Shōnagon*; translated and annotated by Ivan Morris). Baltimore: Penguin Books, 1974.

Seigan Shōtetsu. *Shōtetsu Monogatari*. In Hisamatsu, ed., *Karonshū* (*NKBT*, vol. 65).

Sekimoto Yukio, ed. *Meigetsuki*. Tokyo: Kokusho Kankōkai, 1970.

Shibatani, Masayoshi. "Grammatical Relations and Surface Cases." *Language* 53:4 (1977), 798–809.

Shimonaka Kunihiko, ed. *Moji no Meguriai* (*Nihongo no Rekishi*, vol. 2). Tokyo: Heibonsha, 1963.

———, ed. *Shodō Zenshū*. Tokyo: Heibonsha, 1957.

Shinkei. *Nagusamegusa*. In Hayashiya, ed., *Kodai Chūsei Geijutsuron* (*NST*, vol. 23).

———. *Sasamegoto*. In Kidō, ed., *Renga Ronshū* (*NKBT*, vol. 66).

Shinma Shin'ichi, ed. *Ryōjin Hishō* (*NKBZ*, vol. 25). Tokyo: Shogakkan, 1976.

Su Tung-p'o. *Su Tung-p'o Chi*, Shanghai: Basic Sinological Series, 1940.

Sugiura Seiichi et al., eds. *Bashō Bunshū* (*NKBT*, vol. 46). Tokyo: Iwanami Shoten, 1961.

Takakusu Junjirō and Watanabe Kaigyoku, eds. *Taishō Shinshū Daizōkyō* (*T*). Tokyo: Daizō Shuppan K. K., 1924–1932.

Takeda Yūkichi. *Kojiki Taisei*, 3 vols. Tokyo: Heibonsha, 1957.

Tamagami Takuya. *Genji Monogatari Hyōshaku*, 14 vols. Tokyo: Kadokawa Shoten, 1964.

Tamamura Takeji. *Gozan Bungaku Shinshū* (*GBSS*), 7 vols. Tokyo: Tokyo Daigaku Shuppankai, 1971.

———. *Gozan Shisō* (*Nihon no Zen Goroku*, vol. 8). Tokyo: Kōdansha, 1978.

———. *Musō Kokushi*. Kyoto: Sara Shobō, 1977.

———. *Nihon Zenshūshi Henshū*, 3 vols. Kyoto: Shibunkaku, 1981.

Tanaka Ichimatsu. *Japanese Ink Painting: Shubun to Sesshu* (*Suibokuga: Shūbun kara Sesshū e*, 1972; trans. Bruce Darling). Tokyo: Weatherhill/Shibundō, 1974.

Tiedemann, Arthur E., ed. *An Introduction to Japanese Civilization*. New York: Columbia University Press, 1974.

Tsuji Zennosuke, ed. *Kūge Nichiyō Kufū Ryakushū*. Tokyo: Taiyōsha, 1938.

———. *Nihon Bukkyōshi*, 8 vols. Tokyo: Iwanami Shoten, 1960–1961, revised edition.

Tsukamoto Tarō et al., eds. *Nihon Shoki* (*NKBT*, vol. 67). Tokyo: Iwanami Shoten, 1974.

Tsunoda, Ryūsaku, and L. Carrington Goodrich. *Japan in the Chinese Dynastic Histories*. Pasadena: Perkins Asiatic Monograph Series, 1951.

Ueda, Makoto. *Matsuo Bashō*. New York: Twayne, 1970.

Uemura Kankō, ed. *Nihon Gozan Bungaku Zenshū* (*GBZS*), 5 vols. Tokyo: Gozan Bungaku Zenshū Kankōkai, 1936. Reprinted Kyoto: Shibunkaku, 1979.

Varley, H. Paul, and George Elison. "The Culture of Tea: From Its Origins to Sen no Rikyū." In Elison and Smith, eds., *Warlords, Artists and Commoners*, 187–222.

Wei Ch'ing-chih, comp. *Shih-jen Yü-hsieh*, ed. Yang Chia-lo. Taipei: Shih-chieh Shu-chü, 1971.

Weigl, Gail Capitol. "The Reception of Chinese Painting Models in Muromachi Japan." *Monumenta Nipponica* 35:3 (Autumn 1980), 257–72.

Wittfogel, Karl. *Oriental Despotism*. New Haven: Yale University Press, 1957.

Wright, Arthur F. "The Chinese Language and Foreign Ideas." In Wright, ed., *Studies in Chinese Thought*. Chicago: University of Chicago Press, 1967.

Yamagishi Tokuhei, ed. *Nihon Kanbungakushi Ronkō*. Tokyo: Iwanami Shoten, 1974.

Yamashita, Samuel Hideo. "Compasses and Carpenters' Squares: A Study of Itō Jinsai and Ogyū Sorai." Ph.D. dissertation, University of Michigan, 1981.

———. "The Early Life and Thought of Itō Jinsai." *Harvard Journal of Asiatic Studies* 43:2 (December 1983), 453–80.

Yampolski, Philip. *The Platform Sutra of the Sixth Patriarch*. New York: Columbia University Press, 1967.

Yanagida Seizan. *Chūgoku Zenshūshi*. In Nishitani, ed., *Kōza Zen*, vol. 3.

———. *Eisai* (*NST*, vol. 16). Tokyo: Iwanami Shoten, 1972.

Yasuda Ayao. *Fujiwara Teika Kenkyū*. Tokyo: Shibundō, 1967.

Yasuraoka Kōsaku. *Chūseiteki Bungaku no Tankyū*. Toyko: Yūseidō, 1971.

Yokoyama Iseo. "Sō Shiron ni Miru 'Heitan no Tai' ni Tsuite." *Kanbun Gakkai Kaihō* 20 (1961), 33ff.

Yoshida Kenkō. *Tsurezuregusa*. In Kanda et al., eds., *Hōjōki, Tsurezuregusa* (*NKBZ*, vol. 27).

Yoshikawa Kōjirō. *Sōshi Gaisetsu* (*Nihon Shijinsen*, vol. 11). Tokyo: Iwanami Shoten, 1971.

———. "Toshi Shōshō." In *Yoshikawa Kōjirō Zenshū*, vol. 22, 62ff. Tokyo: Chikuma Shobō, 1975.

———, and Maruyama Masao, eds. *Ogyū Sorai Zenshū*. Tokyo: Mizusu Shobō, 1974.

———, Maruyama Masao, et al., eds. *Ogyū Sorai* (*NST*, vol. 36). Tokyo:

Iwanami Shoten, 1973.

————, and Shimizu Shigeru, eds. *Itō Jinsai, Itō Tōgai* (*NST*, vol. 33). Tokyo: Iwanami Shoten, 1971.

Yūasa Kiyoshi. *Shinkei no Kenkyū*. Tokyo: Kazama Shobō, 1977.

Zeami Motokiyo. *Fūshikaden*, *Shikadō*, *Kadenshō*, *Shūgyoku Tokka*, *Kakyō*, *Kyūi*, *Sarugaku Dangi*. In Nishio Minoru, ed., *Nōgaku Ronshū* (*NKBT*, vol. 65). Tokyo: Iwanami Shoten, 1961.

Zoku Gunsho Ruijū. Tokyo: Zoku Gunsho Ruijū Kangeikai, 1926. See Hanawa, ed., *Gunsho Ruijū*.

INDEX

LIBRARY OF CONGRESS CATALOGING-IN-PUBLICATION DATA

Pollack, David.
   The fracture of meaning.

   Bibliography: p.   Includes index.
   1. Japan—Civilization. 2. Japan—Civilization—Chinese influences. I. Title.
DS821.P59 1986   952   85-43305
ISBN 0-691-06678-7